Towards a System of European Criminal Justice

With the developing landscape of a European criminal justice sphere comes an increasing imperative for scholars and practitioners to gain some insight into the diversity that exists in the criminal justice systems of European Union Member States.

This book explores the mutual admissibility of evidence, a facet of EU criminal justice that is proving difficult to realise. While the Lisbon Treaty places the issue of mutual admissibility of evidence squarely on the agenda, the EU instruments to date have not succeeded in achieving this goal. Andrea Ryan argues that part of the reason for this failure is that while the mutual recognition instruments have focused on the issue of gathering evidence and safeguarding suspects' rights, they have not addressed how evidence is to be presented and contested at trial.

Drawing upon case studies from Ireland, France and Italy, and adopting a legal cultural perspective enriched by the author's observations of criminal trials, the book presents a detailed analysis of the developments to date in EU criminal justice and evidence law. By examining evidence practices the book asks whether the inquisitorial and accusatorial traditions within the EU systems are too irreconcilable to achieve a system of mutual admissibility of evidence.

The book will be of great interest and use to academics and practitioners with an interest in European and comparative criminal justice, criminal procedure, human rights and socio-legal studies.

Andrea Ryan is Director of the Centre for Criminal Justice at the University of Limerick, Ireland.

Routledge Research in EU law

Available titles in this series include:

Centralized Enforcement, Legitimacy and Good Governance in the EU
Melanie Smith

EU External Relations and Systems of Governance
The CFSP, Euro-mediterranean partnership and migration
Paul James Cardwell

The European Constitution, Welfare States and Democracy
The four freedoms vs. national administrative discretion
Christoffer C. Eriksen

EU External Relations Law and the European Neighbourhood Policy
A paradigm for coherence
Bart Van Vooren

The Evolving EU Counter-terrorism Legal Framework
Maria O'Neill

The Early Warning System for the Principle of Subsidiarity
Constitutional theory and empirical reality
Philipp Kiiver

European Perspectives on Environmental Law and Governance
Suzanne Kingston

The Tangled Complexity of the EU Constitutional Process
The frustrating knot of Europe
Giuseppe Martinico

Criminal Law and Policy in the European Union
Samuli Miettinen

Local Government in Europe
The 'fourth level' in the EU multi-layered system of governance
Carlo Panara and Michael R. Varney

The Legitimacy of the European Union through Legal Rationality
Free movement of third country nationals
Richard Ball

New Governance and the European Strategy for Employment
Samantha Velluti

Human Rights and Minority Rights in the European Union
Kirsten Shoraka

Turkey's Accession to the European Union
The politics of exclusion?
Edel Hughes

Forthcoming titles in this series include:

The Legal Order of the European Union
The institutional role of the European court of justice
Timothy Moorhead

Kadi on Trial
A multifaceted analysis of the Kadi judgment
Matej Avbelj, Filippo Fontanelli and Giuseppe Martinico

The Governance of the European Union and the Internal-External Nexus
Paul James Cardwell

Towards a System of European Criminal Justice
The problem of admissibility of evidence
Andrea Ryan

Towards a System of European Criminal Justice

The problem of admissibility of evidence

Andrea Ryan

Routledge
Taylor & Francis Group
LONDON AND NEW YORK

First published 2014
by Routledge
2 Park Square, Milton Park, Abingdon, Oxfordshire OX14 4RN

and by Routledge
711 Third Avenue, New York, NY 10017

First issued in paperback 2016

Routledge is an imprint of the Taylor & Francis Group, an informa business

British Library Cataloguing in Publication Data
A catalogue record for this book is available from the British Library

Library of Congress Cataloging-in-Publication Data
Ryan, Andrea, author.
Towards a system of European criminal justice : the problem of admissibility of evidence / Andrea Ryan.
pages cm. – (Routledge research in EU law)
Includes bibliographical references and index.
ISBN 978-1-138-78077-4 (hbk) – ISBN 978-1-315-77003-1 (ebk)
1. Admissible evidence–Italy. 2. Admissible evidence–France.
3. Admissible evidence–Ireland. 4. Admissible evidence–European Union countries. I. Title.
KJC9604.R93 2014
345.4'062–dc23
2013049205

ISBN 13: 978-1-138-68646-5 (pbk)
ISBN 13: 978-1-138-78077-4 (hbk)

Typeset in Baskerville
by Cenveo Publisher Services

Contents

Acknowledgments xii
Table of cases xiii
Table of legislation xix
Table of official publications xxxii

1 Introduction **1**

1.1 General background 1
1.2 Perceptions of difference and convergence 5
1.2.1 Perceptions of difference 5
1.2.2 Perceptions of truth 7
1.2.3 Perceptions of convergence 9
1.3 Structure of the book 11

2 Aspiration to mutual admissibility of evidence in the European Union **14**

2.1 Introduction 14

Part I
2.2 The development of cooperation in criminal matters on the basis of 'mutual recognition' 16
2.2.1 From mutual legal assistance to mutual recognition 16

Part II
2.3 Gathering and transfer of evidence 23
2.3.1 The European Evidence Warrant and the European Investigation Order 24
2.3.2 Admissibility of evidence 26
2.3.3 Exchange of information regarding previous convictions 28
2.3.4 Hearsay evidence 28

Part III
2.4 Developing safeguards for suspects and defendants 31
2.4.1 Safeguards contained in the evidence-gathering instruments 31

2.4.2 Promoting 'mutual trust' – development of minimum procedural safeguards 32
2.4.3 Latest developments in providing common procedural rights 35
2.5 Conclusion 46

3 Theoretical approaches to the comparison of procedural systems 49

3.1 Introduction 49

Part I
3.2 The development of criminal procedural systems and approaches to proof – a historical perspective 50
3.2.1 Criminal procedure up to the thirteenth century in France and England: accusatory type procedure in common 51
3.2.2 Beginnings of divergence – the thirteenth to the seventeenth centuries 53
3.2.3 Pre-eighteenth-century approaches to proof 57
3.2.4 Eighteenth- and nineteenth-century England – development of adversarial trial and the establishment of the law of evidence 59
3.2.5 Eighteenth- and nineteenth-century France – development of the principle of free proof and trial by jury 61
3.2.6 Divergence of procedure in England and France 64

Part II
3.3 Comparative approaches through use of models of criminal procedure 65
3.3.1 Accusatorial and inquisitorial models 65
3.3.2 Adversarial and non-adversarial procedure 70
3.3.3 Approaches to proof in adversary and non-adversary procedure 72
3.3.4 Hierarchical and coordinate models of authority 74
3.3.5 The analytical value of the models 76
3.3.6 Lost in translation: *procédure contradictoire* and adversarial procedure 77
3.4 Conclusion 80

4 Gathering, receiving and contesting evidence in Ireland 82

4.1 Introduction 82

Part I
4.2 Gathering evidence in the pre-trial phase 83
4.2.1 Organisational structure of the pre-trial phase 83
4.2.2 Means of evidence-gathering during investigation 85
4.2.3 Search and seizure 85

4.2.4 Surveillance 86
4.2.5 Obtaining evidence from witnesses 87
4.2.6 Obtaining evidence from the suspect during detention in police custody 87

Part II
4.3 Rules of evidence 97
4.3.1 Unlawfully obtained evidence 97
4.3.2 Fruit of the poisoned tree – causative link 99
4.3.3 Confession evidence 108
4.3.4 Potentially unreliable evidence – hearsay evidence 109
4.3.5 Potentially prejudicial evidence – evidence of bad character 111

Part III
4.4 Receiving, presenting and challenging evidence 113
4.4.1 The presumption of innocence 114
4.4.2 The trial setting 114
4.4.3 The course of the trial 115
4.5 Conclusion 129

5 Gathering, receiving and contesting evidence in France 133

5.1 Introduction 133

Part I
5.2 Gathering evidence in the pre-trial phase 135
5.2.1 Organisational structure of the pre-trial phase 135
5.2.2 *Enquête préliminaire* procedure; *instruction* procedure 137
5.2.3 Means of gathering evidence 138

Part II
5.3 Approach to evidence law in France 155
5.3.1 Principle of *loyauté* with respect to gathering evidence – illegally obtained evidence 155
5.3.2 Nullity system 157

Part III
5.4 Receiving, presenting and challenging evidence 159
5.4.1 The trial setting 160
5.4.2 Parties to proceedings 161
5.4.3 Jury selection 161
5.4.4 Witnesses 162
5.4.5 Course of the trial 162
5.5 Verdict 178
5.5.1 Reasons for decision 179
5.6 Role of president of the court at trial 181
5.7 Conclusion 182

6 Gathering, receiving and contesting evidence in Italy 187

6.1 Introduction 187

Part I

6.2 Gathering evidence in the pre-trial phase 189
6.2.1 Organisational structure of the pre-trial phase 189
6.2.2 Means of evidence-gathering during investigation 190
6.2.3 Search and seizure 191
6.2.4 Intercept evidence 192
6.2.5 Obtaining evidence from the suspect 193

Part II

6.3 Rules of evidence 201
6.3.1 Unlawfully obtained evidence – nullity system 202
6.3.2 Hearsay evidence 208
6.3.3 Statements of the accused 210
6.3.4 Documentary evidence 211
6.3.5 Character evidence 212

Part III

6.4 Receiving, presenting and challenging evidence 213
6.4.1 The trial setting 213
6.4.2 The course of the trial 214
6.4.3 Presentation of evidence 217
6.4.4 Witnesses 219
6.4.5 Examining and cross-examining witnesses 220
6.4.6 Questioning by the trial judge 222
6.4.7 Evidence from the accused 223
6.4.8 Power of trial judge to seek further evidence 224
6.4.9 Use of evidence from the prosecutor's file through the 'readings' system 230
6.5 Evaluation of evidence and judgment 230
6.5.1 Search for truth 232
6.6 Conclusion 233
6.6.1 Adversarial trial? 235

7 Prospects for realising a mutual admissibility system in light of the differences revealed 238

7.1 Introduction 238

Part I

7.2 Differences 238
7.2.1 Theoretical considerations 238
7.2.2 Differences in pre-trial investigation procedure 239

7.2.3 Differences in right of access to a lawyer afforded to suspects 240
7.2.4 Differences in approach to rules of evidence 241
7.2.5 Differences in evidence procedure within trial structure 242

Part II

7.3 Synthesis 245
7.3.1 Adversarial and *contradictoire* types of procedure 245
7.3.2 Prospects for a principle of mutual admissibility of evidence 247

Bibliography 250
Index 257

Acknowledgments

This book originates from my PhD thesis and my thanks first and foremost go to my supervisor, Professor John Jackson, for his excellent guidance throughout. It has been a privilege to work with him. I am also very grateful to Professor John Spencer and Dr Tom Mohr for their vigorous examination, and to the anonymous reviewers for their encouragement and helpful comments.

I am very grateful to Professor Michele Caianiello, Professor Elisabetta Grande and Dr Teresa Magno for all their assistance in arranging my court observations and meetings with practitioners in Italy, and to Professor Thierry Garé and Professor Catherine Ginestet for their likewise assistance in France. I thank also all the practitioners in Ireland, France and Italy who were so generous with their time and their insights, and the court tipstaff in each of the jurisdictions for their ever-friendly assistance in accommodating me at the court hearings.

This work could not have been completed without the constant invaluable support of my family, most especially Ken, and Andrew and Ian.

This book is dedicated to the memory of my father who instilled in me a love of languages and, despite his best efforts, a curiosity in law.

Table of cases

European Court of Human Rights

Adamkiewicz v Poland no. 54729/00 (ECtHR 2/3/2010) 46
Al-Khawaja and Tahery v United Kingdom [GC] 26766/05 and 22228/06 ECHR 2011 3, 4, 20, 29, 30, 77, 81, 110
Brusco v France 1466/07 (ECtHR 14/10/2010) 46, 134, 144
Dayanan v Turquie 7377/03 (ECtHR 13/10/2009) 44, 46, 94, 144
Edwards v United Kingdom 16/12/1992 Series A 247-B 38
Faure v France 19421/04 (ECtHR 15/1/2009) 133
Funke v France 25/2/1993 Series A 256-A 133
Gäfgen v Germany [GC] 22978/05 ECHR 2010 3, 20
Jasper v United Kingdom [GC] 27052/95 (ECtHR 16/2/2000) 38
Krasniki v Czech Republic 51277/99 (ECtHR 28/2/2006) 30
Letellier v France, 26/6/1991 Series A 207 133
Lucà v Italy 33354/96 ECHR 2001-II 29
Medvedyev v France [GC] 3394/03 ECHR 2010 136, 150
Menet v France 39553/02 (ECtHR 14/6/2005) 152
Moulin v France 37104/06 (ECtHR 23/11/2010) 136, 150
Öcalan v Turkey [GC] 46221/99 ECHR 2005-IV 46
P.S. v Germany 33900/96 (ECtHR 20/12/2001) 30
Padalov v Bulgaria 54784/00 (ECtHR 10/8/2006) 37
Panovits v Cyprus 4268/04 (ECtHR 11/12/2008) 37, 41, 94
Papon v France 54210/00 ECHR 2002-VII 179
Pishchalnikov v Russia 7025/04 (ECtHR 24/9/2009) 105
Salduz v Turkey [GC] 36391/02 ECHR 2008 35, 40, 41, 42, 44, 45, 46, 90, 91, 92, 94, 144
Şaman v Turkey 35292/05 (ECtHR 5/4/2011) 105
Sartory v France 40589/07 (ECtHR 24/9/2009) 133
Selmouni v France [GC] 25803/94 ECHR 1999-V 133
Talat Tunc v Turkey 32432/96 (ECtHR 27/3/2007) 105
Taxquet v Belgium [GC] 926/05 ECHR 2010 3, 128, 179
Tomasi v France 27/8/1992 Series A 241-A 133
Unterpertinger v Austria 24/11/1986 Series A 110 30

Ireland

Bunreacht na hÉireann (Irish Constitution)

Article 38.1	110, 114
Article 38.3	113
Article 40.4.1	88, 110
Article 40.5	85
AD [2012] IESC 30	102
Balfe [1998] 4 IR 50 (CCA)	107
Barry v Waldron (unreported HC 23 May 1996)	93
Breathnach (1981) 2 Frewen 43	108
Buck [2002] 2 ILRM 454 (SC)	91, 100, 105
Byrne v Grey [1988] IR 31	86
Cash [2007] IEHC 108	82, 99, 103, 106
Connell [1995] 1 IR 244	96
Connolly [2003] 2 IR 1	96
Cooney [1998] 1 ILRM 321	89
Creed [2009] IECCA 95	92, 104
Cullen v Clarke [1963] IR 368	109
Cummins [1972] IR 312	95
Cunningham [2012] IECCA 64	86
Damache v DPP [2012] IESC 11	86
Darcy (unreported CCA 29 July 1997)	96
Edgeworth [2001] 2 IR 131 (SC)	107
Farrell [1978] IR 13	93, 96, 108
Finnegan (unreported CCA 15 July 1997)	90
Foley [1995] 1 IR 267	114, 118
Gormley [2009] IECCA 22	92
Hanley [2010] IECCA 101	111
Healy [1990] 2 IR 73 (SC)	89, 90, 99, 102
Heaney v Ireland [1997] 1 ILRM 35	94
Hoey [1988] ILRM 666	108
Holland (unreported CCA 15 June 1998)	96
Kenny [1990] 2IR 110 (SC)	98, 99, 104, 106, 107
Lacy [2005] IECCA 70 [2005] 2 IR 241	117
Lavery v MC Carrickmacross GS [1999] 2 IR 390	93
M (a minor) v MC Coolock GS [2013] IEHC 251	93, 94
McCann [1998] 4 I.R 397	95, 108
McCrea [2009] IEHC 39 [2010] IESC 60	102, 103
McGlynn [1967] IR 232	119
McGowan [1979] IR 45	119
McGrail [1990] 2 IR 38	113, 124
McKeever (unreported CCA 16 July 1992)	96
McNeill [2007] IECCA 95	112
Madden [1977] IR 336	90, 98

Mallon [2011] IECCA 29 107
Minister for Posts and Telegraphs v Campbell [1966] IR 69 118
Murphy [1947] IR 236 108
Murphy [2005] IECCA 1 96
Murphy [2005] IECCA 52 96
Murphy [2013] IECCA 1 111
O'Brien [1965] IR 142 (SC) 97, 98, 99, 105, 107
O'Brien v DPP [2005] IESC 29, [2005] IR 206 92, 102, 105
O'Connor (Cork Circuit Court) 6–17 July 2011 115
O'Leary v Attorney General [1991] ILRM 454 (SC) 114
PA [2008] IECCA 21 96
Pringle, McCann & O'Shea [1981] 2 Frewen 57 90, 108
Rattigan v DPP [2008] IESC 34 96
Richards, Smolen, Da Silva Roy, Miller & Noel (Cork Circuit Court) 10–28 February 1997 115
Rock v Ireland & AG [1997] IR 484 94
Ryan [2011] IECCA 6 101, 106
Shaw [1982] IR 1 29 88, 98
Simple Imports Ltd v Revenue Commissioners [2000] TITR 141 86
Spratt [1995] 2 ILRM 117 90, 102
Sullivan v Robinson [1954] IR 161 108
Taylor [1974] 1 IR 97 111
Walsh v O'Buaccalla [1991] 1 IR 56 102, 103
Ward (unreported SCC 27 October 1998) 108
White [2011] IECCA 78 103
Yu Jie [2005] IECCA 95 93

France

Declaration of the Rights of Man and of the Citizen 1789 66
Article 9 175

La Constitution du 1958 (French Constitution)

Article 64 135
Article 65 135
Article 66 143, 147, 155

Cases of the **Cour de Cassation** *(French Supreme Court)*

Available at: http://www.courdecassation.fr/publications_cour_26/bulletin_arrets_chambre_criminelle_2712/
Crim. 6 April 1993 *JCP* 1993 II.22144 156
Crim. 30 March 1999, *Bull Crim.* no. 59 155

Crim. 26 February 2003, *Bull Crim.* no. 56 154
Crim. 13 October 2004, *Bull Crim.* no. 243 156
Crim. 13 December 2006, *Bull Crim.* no. 312 141
Ass. Plén 15 April 2011, *Bull Crim.* no. 10-30.316 144
Crim. 31 May 2011, *Bull Crim.* no. 10-30.313 144, 158
Crim. 31 May 2011, *Bull Crim.* no. 10-88.809 144

Cases of the Conseil Constitutionnel *(Constitutional Council)*

Available at: http://www.conseil-constitutionnel.fr/conseil-constitutionnel/francais/les-decisions/les-decisions.95486.html
Conseil constitutionnel Décision no. 2010-14/22 QPC July 30th 2010 143, 144
Conseil constitutionnel Décision no. 2011–191/194/195/196/197 QPC 18 November 2011 140, 145

Italy

Costituzione della Repubblica Italiana *(Italian Constitution)*

Article 13 194, 205
Article 14 191
Article 15 191
Article 27 213
Article 109 189
Article 111 209, 213

Cases of Corte Suprema di Cassazione *(Italian Supreme Court)*

Cass. pen. 31 January 1992, no. 24 208
Cass. pen. 3 June 1992, no. 254 208
Cass. pen. 3 June 1992, no. 255 208
Cass. pen. 21 November 1992, no. 11227 224
Cass. pen. 7 April 1993, no. 16256 195
Cass. pen. 9 July 1993, no. 6861 203, 205
Cass. pen. 27 October 1993, no. 3115 201
Cass. pen. 27 December 1995, no. 2793 203
Cass. pen. 16 May 1996, no. 5021 203, 205
Cass. pen. 5 September 1996, no. 8314 231
Cass. pen. 12 March 1997, no. 2389 211
Cass. pen. 26 June 1997, no. 6282 221

Cass. pen. 24 July 1997, no. 2005 210
Cass. pen. 10 September 1997, no. 84 192
Cass. pen. 9 June 1998, no. 1671 192
Cass. pen. 3 July 1998, no. 7844 211
Cass. pen. 25 May 2000, no. 4587 192
Cass. pen. 23 November 2000, no. 1208 224
Cass. pen. 9 August 2001, no. 31085 225
Cass. pen. 17 June 2002, no. 00000 (ud.16 May 2002) 221
Cass. pen. 16 April 2003, no. 18103 194
Cass. pen. 17 September 2003, no. 35656 212
Cass. pen. 11 November 2003, no. 43063 195
Cass. pen. 18 February 2004, no. 6842 206
Cass. pen. 11 March 2004, no. 11526 230
Cass. pen. 16 February 2006, no. 6221 210
Cass. pen. 18 December 2006, no. 41281 225
Cass. pen. 29 March 2007, no. 12874 212
Cass. pen. 19 June 2007, no. 23887 203
Cass. pen. 8 October 2007, no. 36941 195
Cass. pen. 5 February 2008, no. 5636 210
Cass. pen. 13 February 2008, no. 6743 197
Cass. pen. 6 October 2008, no. 38076 210
Cass. pen. 7 October 2008, no. 38221 220
Cass. pen. 15 October 2008, no. 38894 209
Cass. pen. 31 October 2008, no. 40973 204
Cass. pen. 3 November 2008, no. 41040 211
Cass. pen. 9 December 2008, no. 45496 210
Cass. pen. 12 December 2008, no. 46040 197
Cass. pen. 13 January 2009, no. 1150 196
Cass. pen. 26 March 2013, no. 20288 215

Corte di assise

Knox & Sollecito no. 8/2008, *Corte di assise di Perugia* 5 December 2009, *Corte di assise di appello di Perugia* 3 October 2011, *Corte di assise di appello di Firenze* 30 January 2014 208, 215, 231

England & Wales

Ambrose v HM Advocate [2011] UKSC 43 47
Baldry (1852) 2 Den 430 108
Ibrahim v R [1914] AC 599 108
Lambe (1791) 2 Leach 552 108
Patel v Comptroller of Customs [1965] AC 356 211
R (Ullah) v Special Adjudicator [2004] UKHL 26 [2004] 2 AC 323 47

R (Al-Skeini and others) v Secretary of State for Defence [2007] UKHL 26 47

Scotland

Cadder v HM Advocate [2010] UKSC 43; 2010 1 WLR 2601 247

Table of legislation

Treaties

Treaty Establishing the European Coal and Steel Community [1951] 261 UNTS 140 14
Treaty of the European Economic Community (TEEC) 1957 (Treaty of Rome) [1957] 298 UNTS 11 (renamed TEC by TEU) 14
Treaty on European Union [TEU] (Maastricht Treaty) [1992] OJ C 191/1 Art. 31 TEU 14, 34
Treaty of Amsterdam amending the Treaty on European Union, the Treaties Establishing the European Communities and Certain Related Acts [1997] OJ C 340/1 14
Consolidated versions of the Treaty on European Union and the Treaty on the Functioning of the European Union and the Charter of Fundamental Rights of the European Union [2010] OJ C 83 30.3 (Lisbon Treaty TFEU) Art. 82(2) TFEU 14, 20
Protocol 21 of the Lisbon Treaty 31, 39

Council of Europe Conventions

European Convention for the Protection of Human Rights and Fundamental Freedoms 1950 (European Convention on Human Rights, as amended) (ECHR) 2
Art. 5(2) 37
Art. 6 34, 40, 41, 45, 79, 114, 144, 154, 179
Art. 6(1) 37, 41, 90, 152
Art. 6(3)(a) 37
Art. 6(3)(b) 37
Art. 6(3)(d) 77, 78, 110
European Convention on Mutual Assistance in Criminal Matters 1959 16
Art. 3 16
Art. 3, as supplemented by Art. 8, 2001 Protocol 16
Art. 4, as supplemented by 2001 Protocol 16
Art. 7 17

Second Additional Protocol to the European Convention on Mutual Assistance in Criminal Matters, 2001 17
Art. 3, 2001 Protocol 17
Art. 5, 2001 Protocol 17
Art. 18, 2001 Protocol 17
Art. 19, 2001 Protocol 17
European Convention on the International Validity of Criminal Judgments 1970 28
Art. 56 28

EU Conventions

Convention on Mutual Assistance in Criminal Matters between Member States of the European Union [2000] OJ C 197/1 17
Art. 4 26
Art. 4(1) 18
Art. 18 18
Art. 19 18
Convention on Mutual Assistance in Criminal Matters between Member States of the European Union, Explanatory Report [2000] OJ C379/7 17
Protocol to Convention [2001] OJ C 326/1 17

EU Legislation

Council Framework Decision of 13 June 2002 on the European arrest warrant and the surrender procedures between Member States [2002] OJ L 190/1 43
Council Framework Decision on the execution in the European Union of orders freezing property or evidence [2003] OJ L 196/45 23
Council Decision 2005/876/JHA of 21 November 2005 on the exchange of information extracted from the criminal record [2005] OJ L 322/33 28
Council Framework Decision 2008/675/JHA of 24 July 2008 on taking account of convictions in the Member States of the European Union in the course of new criminal proceedings [2008] OJ L 220/32 28
Council Framework Decision 2008/978/JHA of 18 December 2008 on the European evidence warrant for the purpose of obtaining objects, documents and data for use in proceedings in criminal matters [2008] OJ L 350/72 15
Recital 14 27
Recital 27 31
Art. 1(3) 31
Art. 2(c) 25

Art. 2(d) 25
Art. 7 31
Art. 11 25
Art. 12 25
Art. 15(2) 25
Art. 17(1)(a) 26
Art. 18(2) 32

Council Framework Decision 2009/315/JHA of 26 February 2009 on the organisation and content of the exchange of information extracted from the criminal record between Member States [2009] OJ L 93/23 28

Council Decision on the establishment of the European Criminal Records Information System (ECRIS) in application of Article 11 of Framework Decision 2009/315/JHA [2009] OJ L 93/33 28

Directive of the European Parliament and of the Council on the right to interpretation and translation in criminal proceedings [2010] OJ L 280/1 36
Art. 3 36

Directive 2012/13/EU of the European Parliament and of the Council of 22 May 2012 on the right to information in criminal proceedings [2012] OJ L 142/1 36
Recital 36 37
Art. 7 39
Art. 7(4) 39
Art. 8 37

Directive 2013/48 of the European Parliament and of the Council on the right of access to a lawyer in criminal proceedings and on the right to communicate upon arrest [2013] OJ L 294/1 43
Recital 10 45
Recital 23 44
Recital 25 46
Recital 39 46
Recital 50 44
Art. 2(1) 44
Art. 2(2) 44
Art. 2(4) 44
Art. 3 44
Art. 3(3)(b) 44, 46
Art. 3(3)(c) 44
Art. 3(6) 46
Art. 4 44
Art. 4(2) 45
Art. 5 46
Art. 6 46
Art. 8(c) 46

Art. 8(2) 46
Art. 9 46
Art. 12 43

EU Proposed Directives and Regulations

Initiative of the Kingdom of Belgium, the Republic of Bulgaria, the Republic of Estonia, the Kingdom of Spain, the Republic of Austria, the Republic of Slovenia and the Kingdom of Sweden for a Directive of the European Parliament and of the Council regarding the European Investigation Order in criminal matters, 29/4/2010 Inter-institutional File: 2010/0817 (COD) 9145/10
Recital 17 15
Art. 1(3) 26, 31
Art. 2 26, 31
Art. 5(a) 25
Art. 8 31
Art. 8(2) 25
Art. 9 25
Art. 11 25
Art. 12 25
Art. 13 31
Art. 21 28
Art. 21(6)(c) 32
Art. 21(6)(e) 32
Commission, Proposal for a Directive on the right of access to a lawyer in criminal proceedings and on the right to communicate upon arrest COM (2011) 326 final 3, 39
Recital 10 45
Recital 17 41
Art. 4(2) 45
Art. 10 41
Art. 13 3, 21, 41
Commission, Proposal for a Council Regulation on the establishment of the European Public Prosecutor's Office, Brussels 17. 7. 2013 COM (2013) S34 27
Recital 32 27
Art. 30 27

Ireland

Criminal Evidence Act 1992 109
s. 5 109
s. 16(1)(b) 87
Criminal Justice Act 1984 89

s. 4 89
s. 4(8) 89
s. 4(8A) 89
s. 4(8B) 89
s. 5 90
s. 5A 91
s. 6 89
s. 6A 89
s. 7(3) 89
s. 10 89
s. 15 94
s. 16 94
s. 18 94
s. 19 94
s. 19A 95
s. 20 113
Criminal Justice Act 1999 110
s. 9 110
s. 17 89
Criminal Justice Act 2006 86
s. 6 86
s. 14 89
s. 16 110, 111, 127
s. 16(3) 111
s. 17 87
s. 19 87
Criminal Justice Act 2007 89, 94
s. 28 94
s. 29 94
s. 30 94, 95
s. 48 89
s. 50 89
s. 50(3)(g)(i) & (ii) 89
s. 57 109
Criminal Justice Act 2011 89
s. 7(c) 89
s. 9 90, 91, 95
Criminal Justice (Amendment) Act 2009 89
s. 24 89
Criminal Justice (Drug Trafficking) Act 1996 86, 115
s. 2 89
s. 2(2) 89
s. 2(3) 89
s. 8 86
Criminal Justice (Evidence) Act 1924 112

s. 1(b) 127
s. 1(f)(i) 112
s. 1(f)(ii) 124
Criminal Justice (Forensic Evidence) Act 1990 89
s. 1(1) 89
s. 1(4) 89
s. 3 89
Criminal Justice (Miscellaneous Provisions) Act 1997 89
s. 10 86
Criminal Justice (Search Warrants) Act 2012 86
Criminal Justice (Surveillance) Act 2009 86, 109
s. 4 109
s. 7 86, 87
s. 7(10) 87
s. 8 87
s. 14 87
Criminal Justice (Theft and Fraud) Offences Act 2001 85
Criminal Law Act 1997 88
s. 6(1) 85
Criminal Procedure Act 1865 111
ss. 3, 4 & 5 111
Criminal Procedure Act 1967 110
s. 4F 110
s. 4G 110
Criminal Procedure Act 2010 112
s. 33 112
s. 34 113
European Convention on Human Rights Act 2003 114
s. 4 114
Gaming and Lotteries Act 1956 85
Juries Act 1976 115
Misuse of Drugs Act 1977 85
Offences Against the State Act 1939 94
s. 30 94
Offences Against the State (Amendment) Act 1972 94
s. 2 94
Offences against the State (Amendment) Act 1998 89
s. 5 94
s. 10 89
Prosecutions of Offences Act 1974 84
Road Traffic Act 1994 103
s. 13(2) 103
Road Traffic Act 2002 103
s. 23 103

Bills

Criminal Law (Admissibility of Evidence) Bill 2008 106

Statutory Instruments

Criminal Justice Act 1984 (Electronic Recording of Interviews) Regulations 1997, SI 74/1997 88, 96
Criminal Justice (Forensic Evidence) Act 1990 Regulations 1992, SI 130/1992 88
Criminal Justice Act 1984 (Treatment of Persons in Custody in Garda Síochána Stations) Regulations 1987, SI 119/1987 88, 96
Art. 12 96
Art. 12(6) 100
Art. 12(10) 96
Offences Against the State Acts, 1939–1972 (Special Criminal Court Rules) 1975, SI 234/1975 128
Offences Against the State Acts, 1939–1998 (Special Criminal Court Rules) 2001, SI 536/2001 128

France

French Constitution, Codes and Laws available on: <http://www.legifrance.gouv.fr/>

Laws

Ordinance of 1539 54, 149
Ordinance of 1670 54, 62, 66
Law of October 1789 61
Law of 16–29 September 1791 61
Law of 5 March 1932 64
Law of 25 November 1941 64
Loi n° 93-2 du 4 janvier 1993 portant réforme de la procédure pénale 182
Loi n° 2000-516 du 15 juin 2000 renforçant la protection de la présomption d'innocence et les droits des victimes 133, 141, 147, 162
Loi n° 2003-239 du 18 mars 2003 pour la sécurité intérieure 141
Loi n° 2004-204 du 9 mars 2004 portant adaptation de la justice aux évolutions de la criminalité 147
Loi n° 2006-64 du 23 janvier 2006 relative à la lutte contre le terrorisme et portant dispositions diverses relatives à la sécurité et aux contrôles frontaliers 137
Loi n° 2007-291 du 5 mars 2007 tendant à renforcer l'équilibre de la procédure pénale 133, 146, 150

Loi organique n° 2009-1523 du 10 décembre 2009 relative à l'application de l'article 61-1 de la Constitution 134
Loi n° 2011-392 du 14 avril 2011 relative à la garde à vue 133, 137, 142, 144, 145
Circular Crim-00-13/F1 4th décembre 2000 140, 141, 149
Code des Délits et Peines 1795 63
Code of Criminal Examination 1808 63
Art. 342 63

Articles from Code du procédure pénale

Preliminary article (*Article préliminaire*) 175
Art. 2 161
Art. 7 149
Art. 8 149
Art. 12 137
Art. D 16 165
Art. 31 136, 161
Art. 40.1 136
Art. 40.2 136
Art. 51 151
Art. 53 138
Art. 54 138
Art. 55.1 138, 149
Art. 56 139
Art. 56.1 139
Art. 56.2 139
Art. 56.3 139
Art. 57 139
Art. 59 139
Art. 60.1 139
Art. 62 140
Art. 63 140
Art. 63.1 141
Art. 63.3 141
Art. 63.4.1 145
Art. 64 141
Art. 64.1 146
Art. 68 141
Art. 75.1 149
Art. 76 139
Art. 77 140
Art. 77.1 149
Art. 77.1.1 139
Art. 77.2 149

Art. 78	140
Art. 80.1	151
Art. 81.1	166
Art. 82	154
Art. 85	151
Art. 95	149
Art. 113.2	151
Art. 116	152
Art. 116.1	152
Art. 117	152
Art. 120	153
Art. 137	161
Art. 138	161
Art. 144	147
Art. 145.2	148
Art. 149	159
Art. 152	153
Art. 170	157
Art. 171	157
Art. 172	157
Art. 173	159
Art. 174	157
Art. 199	148
Art. 257	162
Art. 262	162
Art. 266	162
Art. 269	162
Art. 289	162
Art. 304	162
Art. 311	178
Art. 317	161
Art. 325	162
Art. 328	167
Art. 335	169
Art. 340	178
Art. 353	178
Art. 393	143
Art. 397	143
Art. 427	172
Art. 429	172
Art. 706.29	142
Art. 706. 89	139
Art. 706.96	140
Art. 802	157, 159

Italy

Italian Constitution, Codes and Laws accessible on: <http://www.altalex.com/>

Legge (Laws)

Law No. 287 10 April 1951, 26 *Gazz. Uff.* no. 102 7 May 1951, *Riordinamento dei giudizi di assise* 213

Codice Penale

Art. 270 *bis* 216
Art. 368 208
Art. 606 191
Art. 608 191
Art. 609 191
Art. 617 *bis* 191

Codice di Procedura Penale

Art. 5 196, 213
Art. 6 196
Art. 34 201
Art. 55 189
Art. 60 200
Art. 62 210
Art. 64 198
Art. 65 200
Art. 97 195
Art. 103 192
Art. 103.5 212
Art. 103.6 211
Art. 104.3 196
Art. 104.4 195
Art. 141 *bis* 197
Art. 146 214
Art. 149 217
Art. 177 202
Art. 178 202
Art. 179 203
Art. 181 203, 218
Art. 183 203
Art. 185 203
Art. 185.4 203

Art. 187	220
Art. 188	191
Art. 190	218
Art. 191	204, 206, 218
Art. 192	231
Art. 192.2	231
Art. 194	220
Art. 194.7	209
Art. 195	209
Art. 195.3	209
Art. 195.4	209
Art. 196	220
Art. 198	220
Art. 200	202
Art. 211	199
Art. 213	199
Art. 218	225
Art. 219	225
Art. 221	225
Art. 225	225
Art. 234	211
Art. 235	211
Art. 240	211
Art. 244	191
Art. 245	191
Art. 247	191
Art. 249	192, 195
Art. 250	195
Art. 253	192
Art. 253.2	192
Art. 266	192
Art. 267	193
Art. 268.7	193
Art. 271	212
Art. 271.2	212
Art. 273	194
Art. 274	194
Art. 291	194
Art. 299	201
Art. 303	196
Art. 333	190
Art. 348	189
Art. 350	196
Art. 350.6	196
Art. 350.7	197, 211

Art. 353	193
Art. 354.2	206
Art. 362	193
Art. 364	197
Art. 364.4	197
Art. 364.5	197
Art. 364.7	197
Art. 369 *bis*	194
Art. 370	197
Art. 375	193
Art. 380	193
Art. 381	193
Art. 382	193
Art. 383	193
Art. 384	193
Art. 386	194
Art. 388	197
Art. 390	195
Art. 391	194
Art. 391 *ter*	198
Art. 392	199
Art. 392(e)	221
Art. 404	199
Art. 407	199
Art. 416	200
Art. 420	200
Art. 420 *quinquies*	200
Art. 421	200
Art. 421 *bis*	200
Art. 431	201
Art. 438	216
Art. 477	214
Art. 492	217
Art. 493	218
Art. 495	218
Art. 495.4	218
Art. 499.2	220
Art. 499.6	220
Art. 500.1	210
Art. 500.3	210
Art. 500.4	209
Art. 503.3	197
Art. 507	224, 226, 228
Art. 512	230
Art. 513	230

Art. 513.1 211
Art. 515 230
Art. 526.1 *bis* 209
Art. 533 229
Art. 544 232
Art. 593 196
Art. 606 196
Art. 628 196

England and Wales

Assize of Clarendon 1166 52
1 & 2 Phil & Mary c. 13 1554 55
Criminal Justice Act 2003 109, 113
Criminal Procedure and Investigations Act 1996 113

Statutory Instruments

Criminal Justice and Public Order Act 1994 Code C (April 1995)
para. 10(4) 95

Table of official publications

Council of Europe documents

Council of Europe, Opinion of the Secretariat on the Commission's Proposal for a Directive of the European Parliament and of the Council on the right to access to a lawyer in criminal proceedings and on the right to communicate upon arrest, Council of Europe: Strasbourg, 9 November 2011 41

European Council documents

Tampere, European Council, 15–16 October 1999, Presidency Conclusions 2, 16, 18
European Council, Programme of measures to implement the principle of mutual recognition of decisions in criminal matters [2001] OJ C 12/10 19, 20, 32
European Council, The Hague Programme [2005] OJ C 198/1 20
European Council, Resolution of the Council on a Roadmap for strengthening procedural rights of suspected or accused persons in criminal proceedings of 30 November [2009] OJ C 295/1 35
European Council, The Stockholm Programme – an open and secure Europe serving and protecting citizens [2010] OJ C 115/1 19, 35, 247

European Commission documents

Commission, Green Paper on the Criminal law protection of financial interests and the establishment of a European Public Prosecutor COM (2001) 715 22
Commission, Green Paper on certain procedural safeguards for suspects and defendants in criminal proceedings throughout the European Union Com (2003) 75 33
Commission, Proposal for a Council Framework Decision of 14th November 2003 on the European Evidence Warrant for obtaining objects, documents and data for use in proceedings in criminal matters COM (2003) 688 final 15

Commission, Proposal for a Framework Decision on certain procedural rights in criminal proceedings throughout the European Union COM (2004) 328 final 33
Commission, Assessment of the Tampere programme and future orientations (Communication) Com (2004) 4002 final 20
Commission, Green Paper on the presumption of innocence, COM (2006) 174 final 33
Commission, Green Paper on Obtaining Evidence in Criminal Matters from One Member State to Another and Securing Its Admissibility, COM (2009) 624 final 15, 22
Commission, Proposal for a Directive on the right to information in criminal proceedings COM (2010) 392 final 37
Commission, Impact Assessment accompanying the Proposal for a Directive on the right to information in criminal proceedings, 20 July 2010 SEC (2010) 907 32
Commission, Proposal for a Directive on the right of access to a lawyer in criminal proceedings and on the right to communicate upon arrest COM (2011) 326 final 3, 21
Commission, Impact assessment accompanying the Proposal for a Directive on the right of access to a lawyer, 8 June 2011 SEC (2011) 686 final 34

EU inter-institutional documents

European Parliament Report on the Proposal for a Council framework decision on certain procedural rights in criminal proceedings throughout the European Union, A6-0064/2005 40
Proposal for a Council Framework Decision on certain procedural rights in criminal proceedings throughout the European Union, 19 May 2006, 9600/06 DROIPEN 36 (Austrian Presidency) 34
Proposal for a Council Framework Decision on certain procedural rights, 27 September 2006, 13116/06 DROIPEN 60 (Finnish Presidency) 34
Proposal for a Council Framework Decision on certain procedural rights, 22 December 2006, 16874/06 DROIPEN 76 (German Presidency) 34
Initiative of the Kingdom of Belgium *et al.*, European Investigation Order, Explanatory Memorandum, 3 June 2010, Interinstitutional File: 2010/0817 (COD) 9288/10 ADD 1 15, 24
Initiative of the Kingdom of Belgium *et al.*, European Investigation Order Detailed Statement, 23 June 2010, Interinstitutional File: 2010/0817 (COD) 9288/10 ADD 2 27
Proposal for a Directive on the right of access to a lawyer, Note from Presidency to Delegations – Follow-up of the WP meeting on 26 July and CATS on 6 September, 9 September 2011, Interinstitutional File: 2011/0154 (COD) 13360/11 42

Proposal for a Directive on the right of access to a lawyer, Note by Belgium, France Ireland the Netherlands, UK to Council of European Union, 22 September 2011, Interinstitutional File: 2011/0154 (COD) 14495/11 43, 45

Proposal for a Directive on the right of access to a lawyer, Orientation debate, Note from Presidency to Coreper/Council, 14 October 2011, Interinstitutional File: 2011/0154 (COD) 15533/11 42

Proposal for a Directive on the right of access to a lawyer, Consultative forum of prosecutors general and directors of public prosecutors of Member States of EU Progress Report of 6 December 2011, Note from General Secretariat to Delegations, 30 January 2012, Interinstitutional File: 2011/0154 (COD) 5894/12 42

Proposal for a Directive on the right of access to a lawyer, Responses to questionnaire, Note from General Secretariat to Working Party on Substantive Criminal Law, 2 February 2012, Interinstitutional File: 2011/0154 (COD) 5897/12 44

Initiative of the Kingdom of Belgium *et al.*, European Investigation Order, Note from Presidency to Delegations, 29 February 2012, Interinstitutional File: 2010/0817 (COD) 7014/12 25

Proposal for a Directive on the right of access to a lawyer, Note from Belgian Delegation to Working Party on Substantive Criminal Law, 13 March 2012, Interinstitutional File: 2011/0154 (COD) 7593/12 45

Initiative of the Kingdom of Belgium *et al.*, European Investigation Order: 'Frequently Asked Questions', Note from ten member states to delegations, 4/4/2012, Interinstitutional File: 2010/0817 (COD) 8182/12 25

Proposal for a Directive on access to a lawyer, Note from Presidency to Coreper 31/5/2013, Interinstitutional File: 2011/0154 (COD) 10190/13 35

Ireland

Balance in the Criminal Law Review Group Final Report 2007, Chairman Gerard Hogan; available at: <http://www.justice.ie/en/JELR/Pages/Balance_in_criminal_law_report> 82, 93, 112, 113, 123

Report of the Committee to Recommend Certain Safeguards for Persons in Custody, Chairman Justice Barra O'Briain (Prl 7158 1978) 92

Report of the Working Group on the Jurisdiction of the Courts: the Criminal Jurisdiction of the Courts (PN 237 2003); available at: <http://www.courts.ie> 123

Law Reform Commission *Consultation Paper on Hearsay in Civil and Criminal Cases* (LRC CP 60 2010) 109

Director of Public Prosecutions *Report on Prosecution Policy on the Giving of Reasons for Decisions* (2008) <http://www.dppireland.ie> 84

France

Rapport du groupe de travail chargé de tirer les enseignements du traitement judiciaire de l'affaire dite 'd'Outreau', chaired by Jean Viout, February 2005; available at: http://www.ladocumentationfrancaise.fr/rapports-publics 133, 149

Rapport du Comite de réflexion sur la justice pénal, chaired by Philippe Léger, September 2009; available at: <http://www.ladocumentationfrancaise.fr/rapports-publics> 134, 142, 147, 148, 150, 174, 179, 180, 181, 182, 186

Avant-Projet du Future Code de Procédure Pénal (March 2010); available at: <http://www.ladocumentationfrancaise.fr/rapports-publics> 138

England and Wales

Select Committee on European Union, *The Hague Programme: A Five Year Agenda for EU Justice and Home Affairs, Report with Evidence* (HL 2004-05, 84) 31

1 Introduction

1.1 General background

It has long been acknowledged that common law jurisdictions differ in their method of investigation, trial and approach to proof of criminal offences from their civil law counterparts. In Europe the common law system is followed in the jurisdictions of Ireland and Britain while the majority of countries in continental Europe follow a civil law model.[1] The common law system is generally associated with an accusatorial/adversarial procedural tradition, while the civil law system is associated with an inquisitorial tradition. In relation to proof, the common law systems adhere to a distinct 'Law of Evidence', a discrete discipline developed in the nineteenth century in the treatises of jurists who isolated the study of evidence from the study of procedure and substantive law.[2] Evidentiary rules, most pertinently the hearsay rule, propensity rules and rules regarding unlawfully obtained evidence, are essentially common law constructs that embrace an exclusionary principle. Laws relating to evidence in continental systems are more commonly contained within the general codes of criminal procedure rather than as a discrete discipline, and while also placing limitations on some types of proof

1. Cyprus and Malta operate mixed common law and civil law systems, see J. Jackson and N. Kovalev, 'Lay Adjudication and Human Rights in Europe' (2006) 13 *Columbia J. European Law* 83, 85. For a detailed account of the historical evolution of criminal procedures of common law and civil law systems see: A. Esmein, *History of Continental Criminal Procedure with Special Reference to France* (Little, Brown 1913); S. Landsman, 'The Rise of the Contentious Spirit: Adversary Procedure in Eighteenth Century England' (1989–90) 75 (3) *Cornell L. Rev.* 497; J. Langbein, *The Origins of Adversary Criminal Trial* (Oxford University Press 2003); J. Langbein, *Torture and the Law of Proof: Europe and England in the Ancien Régime* (first published 1977, University of Chicago Press 2006); F. Quintard-Morenas, 'The Presumption of Innocence in the French and Anglo-American Legal Traditions' (2010) 58 (1) *Am. J. Comp. L.* 107; R. Fraher, 'Conviction According to Conscience: The Medieval Jurists' Debate Concerning Judicial Discretion and the Law of Proof' (1989) 7 (1) *Law & Hist. Rev.* 23; R. Groot, 'The Jury of Presentment before 1215' (1982) 26 (1) *American J. Legal Hist.* 1.
2. For an overview of the various treatises on evidence see W. Twining, *Rethinking Evidence* (2nd edn) (Cambridge University Press 2006) Ch. 3.

that may be produced, since the close of the eighteenth century these systems have eschewed a rigid system of 'legal proof' and embraced a system of 'free proof'.

In response to the problem of trans-European crime faced by all Member States of the EU, the past decade has seen a developing body of law in the field of EU criminal justice relating to both substantive criminal law and criminal procedure, and while we cannot yet speak of a fully developed EU criminal justice system, it certainly exists in fledgling form. Criminal justice is typically a sovereign matter for each national system. As such, the development of a common justice system is faced with the challenge of finding solutions that do not radically alter individual systems; any solution must try to accommodate the different approaches of national systems so as not to impinge too greatly on their sovereign patch.

In recognition of the differences between jurisdictions, a principle of 'mutual recognition' has been adopted in an effort to achieve a common approach to dealing with the problem of trans-European crime whereby decisions taken in one Member State are to be accepted as valid in any other Member State so that they may be acted on, regardless of whether that decision would have been arrived at in a different way or would have reached a different outcome in a national context.[3] The mutual recognition principle is also dependent on the acceptance by all Member States of common minimum standards of procedural rights for suspects and accused persons. Fundamental to the mutual recognition principle is the idea that it proceeds from a basis of tolerance of diversity of legal systems.

Far-reaching reforms have occurred over the past decades within jurisdictions stemming from the two traditions, to no small degree as a result of the interpretations by the European Court of Human Rights (ECtHR) of the European Convention on Human Rights (ECHR) to which all Member States must conform. It has been suggested that the jurisprudence of the ECtHR may be bringing about a convergence or 'realignment' of the two traditions.[4] The greatest obstacle to achieving meaningful convergence appears to be in the area of proof. The ECtHR has time and again insisted that its primary concern is to assess whether the criminal proceedings overall

3. The principle was born in Tampere, 15–16 October 1999, Presidency Conclusions <http://www.europarl.europa.eu/summits/tam_en.htm>.

4. J. Jackson, 'The Effect of Human Rights on Criminal Evidentiary Processes: Towards Convergence, Divergence or Realignment?' (2005) 68 (5) *MLR* 737; Roberts suggests there is a visible increase of adversarial trial features: P. Roberts, 'Faces of Justice Adrift', in J. Jackson, M. Langer and P. Tillers (eds), *Crime, Procedure and Evidence in a Comparative and International Context: Essays in Honour of Prof. Mirjan Damaška* (Hart 2008) 326; Weigend suggests the ECHR has brought about an 'advance of adversarial elements' across the procedural traditions at the expense of some inquisitorial features but also notes a convergence of the two traditions in other respects: T. Weigend, 'Should We Search for Truth, and Who Should Do It?' (2010–11) 36 (2) *NCJ Int'l L. & Com. Reg.* 389, 405.

have been fair,[5] and considers that it has no role in deciding whether evidence should or should not be admissible; rather, the proper forum for deciding that issue is the national court in accordance with national law.[6]

There has been an ongoing effort to achieve a position of mutual admissibility of evidence across the EU, but so far there has been little progress in realising the aspiration. The Lisbon Treaty requires minimum rules to be established by the Council and Parliament regarding 'mutual admissibility of evidence between Member States'. 'Mutual admissibility of evidence' is not defined. On the basis of references to mutual admissibility found in various Commission documents, the definition offered here is that the principle of mutual admissibility of evidence that is being aspired to embraces the objective that 'evidence lawfully gathered by one Member State's authorities should be admissible before the courts of other Member States', and that it should embrace all types of evidence: real evidence, forensic evidence, documentary evidence and statements, including statements of suspects made to authorities.

The negative response by Member States to the attempt by the Commission to establish a EU-wide rule on inadmissibility of evidence where statements of suspects are taken in the absence of a lawyer[7] serves to highlight that the area of proof is one that accentuates the sharpest divergence between the two procedural traditions, embracing as it does complex layers of values reflecting legal cultural preference which inform the procedural practices. There is a perception that the continental systems place a priority on seeking truth while the common law systems are primarily committed to the value of fairness in the process, even where it has the effect of losing some truth along the way.

The starting hypothesis of this work is that the most acute difference between the criminal justice systems of the common law and those of the civil law lies in their approach to proof, in terms of the collection of, receiving of, presentation of and opportunity to challenge evidence, differences that arise as a result of diversity in procedural arrangements, the evidence rules themselves and different conceptions of 'admissibility', 'inadmissibility' and 'exclusionary' rules of evidence. This difference between jurisdictions of the Member States makes the development of a EU-wide mutual admissibility system a problematic proposition.

Taking as a starting point the idea that a mutual admissibility design involves three facets: the gathering of evidence; the rights of suspects; and

5. Most recently stated in *Taxquet v Belgium* [GC] 926/05 ECHR 2010, 84; *Al-Khawaja and Tahery v United Kingdom* [GC] 26766/05 and 22228/06 ECHR 2011, 118; see also *Gäfgen v Germany* [GC] 22978/05 ECHR 2010.
6. *Al-Khawaja and Tahery* (note 5).
7. Commission, Proposal for a Directive on the right of access to a lawyer in criminal proceedings and on the right to communicate upon arrest (Brussels, 8/6/2011 COM (2011) 326, Article 13.

the receiving, presentation and challenge of evidence, three broad questions correspondingly arise:

1. Is there a difference between the systems in the way that they gather evidence? If so, do such differences militate against a convergence of evidence law on that score?
2. Is there a difference between the systems in the rights that are afforded to suspects during the evidence-gathering process? Have such differences now been reconciled by the jurisprudence of the ECtHR making convergence towards mutual admissibility a realistic proposition as far as that aspect is concerned?
3. Is there a difference between the systems in their approach to the reception, presentation and provision of opportunity to challenge evidence? Is it the case that the ECtHR has resolved any differences that might have existed historically in this regard by requiring that all evidence be presented 'with the view to adversarial argument'[8] and have thus brought about a convergence of trial practice across Member States in so far as they should follow an 'adversarial' format? Or is it an incorrect assumption to make that 'adversarial argument' is equivalent to *un débat contradictoire*, the terms used in the official translated versions of the ECtHR cases, and a further fallacy to take from this translation any impression that the concepts of adversarial trial and *un procédure contradictoire* are one and the same?

Do the differences posed by these two procedural arrangements relating to inadmissibility of evidence present the greatest obstacle for achieving convergence? Is this an irreconcilable difference, because of the fact that one procedure takes an exclusionary position of concealing the evidence from the ultimate fact-finders while the other generally reveals all the evidence and simply directs the fact-finder not to use it? Is it irreconcilable because the latter procedural practice accords a higher priority to truth and is the expression of a divergence of view between continental and common law legal cultures on the prominence that truth-seeking should hold in the criminal process?

Is the aspiration for a EU-wide mutual admissibility system therefore caught between two stools in that a design that would contain an exclusionary orientation would be intolerable to the continental legal culture while a system designed in such a way that would reveal inadmissible evidence to the fact-finders would be intolerable to the common law culture?

8. *Al-Khawaja and Tahery* (note 5) 118.

1.2 Perceptions of difference and convergence

1.2.1 Perceptions of difference

Some commentators have downplayed differences between the criminal procedural systems of common law and civil law jurisdictions. Goldstein and Marcus have argued that one of the key perceived differences between the two traditions, judicial supervision of pre-trial investigations, in reality is a 'myth'; they suggested that in practice, officials in the European systems left the task of investigation of offences to the police and were no more likely to leave their offices than their American counterparts.[9] This argument was later rebuked when it was suggested that the 'Americanized account' of the European systems 'misinterpreted the most important characteristics of the procedures they intended to describe';[10] it was argued that they had failed to take account of the different roles and professional standing of the 'judicial' officials in the continental systems as compared with those in the American system and undertook their examination of the European systems from the presupposition that these differences were irrelevant.[11] In short, the importance of legal culture had been overlooked.[12]

Chase has argued that cultural differences present formidable barriers to the transplantation of practices from other systems.[13] Since culture is a multifaceted concept, a definition that will be adopted here is that advanced by Hofstede: 'Culture is to a human collectivity what personality is to an individual.' In this sense, personality is 'the interactive aggregate of characteristics that influence the individual's response to the environment', therefore culture may be defined as 'the interactive aggregate of common characteristics that influence a human group's response to its environment'.[14] Culture is

9. A. Goldstein, and M. Marcus, 'The Myth of Judicial Supervision in Three "Inquisitorial" Systems: France, Italy and Germany' (1977) 87 (2) *Yale LJ* 240.
10. J. Langbein and L. Weinreb, 'Continental Criminal Procedure: "Myth" and Reality' (1978) 87 (8) *Yale LJ* 1549.
11. Ibid., 1558; see later response to Langbein and Weinreb criticisms in A. Goldstein and M. Marcus, 'Comment on Continental Criminal Procedure' (1978) 87 (8) *Yale LJ* 1570; another key difference examined by Langbein is the mixed adjudicating panels of judges and lay assessors in the German system: J. Langbein, 'Mixed Court and Jury Court: Could the Continental Alternative Fill the American Need?' 1981 (1) *Am. B. Found Res. J.* 195.
12. On the importance of culture in shaping legal institutions, see J. Jackson, 'Playing the Culture Card in Resisting Cross-Jurisdictional Transplants: A Comment on Legal Processes and National Culture' (1997) 5 *Cardozo J. Int'l & Comp. L.* 51; for a discussion of how different legal cultures approach the function of prosecuting see J. Jackson, 'The Effect of Legal Culture and Proof in Decisions to Prosecute' (2004) 3 *Law Probability and Risk* 109; for discussion of an emerging European identity (and therefore a new culture) see M. Hildebrandt, 'European Criminal Law and European Identity' (2007) 1 *Crim. Law and Philos.* 57.
13. O. Chase, 'Legal Processes and National Culture' (1997) 5 *Cardozo J. Int'l & Comp L.* 1.
14. G. Hofstede, *Culture's Consequences: Comparing Values, Behaviors, Institutions and Organizations Across Nations* (2nd edn) (Sage 2001) 10; see also P. Legrand: 'Culture ... is about collective

manifested through values, symbols and rituals.[15] Applying this to 'legal culture', it embraces 'ideas and attitudes which are specifically legal in content – ideas about courts, justice' and legal actors and actions in general.[16]

In a number of empirical studies of French investigation procedure, Hodgson has examined the roles of the legal actors in the process. She has concluded that judicial supervision of investigations by judges is a rarity and where it does occur it is more in the nature of verification of investigations already carried out rather than a fresh inquiry; the bulk of cases, although purportedly supervised by a prosecutor, are essentially police investigations rubber stamped by the prosecutor.[17] She and other commentators have concluded that defence lawyers in France are effectively 'outsiders' in the process, simply tolerated for their instrumental role of legitimising the pre-trial investigation.[18]

The difference in legal culture surrounding the trial process in France has also been noted: Munday has analysed the differences between the jury in France and the common law variant, concluding that both types of jury system 'encounter a constellation of problems in accommodating a significant lay element within the administration of criminal justice';[19] Field has highlighted the approach to character evidence in France as compared with the common law, noting that the French criminal trial proceeds from the basis *on juge l'homme, pas les faits* and concluding that the difference may be related to a different view of the purpose of the criminal trial.[20]

mental programmes ... that have formed ... as a function of the community to which we belong' ('European Legal Systems Are Not Converging' (1996) 45 (1) *Int'l & Comp. L. Q.* 52, 56).

15. *Culture's Consequences* (note 14) 10.
16. L. Friedman, 'Law, Lawyers, and Popular Culture' (1988–9) 98 (8) *Yale LJ* 1577. A further definition of legal culture is 'a specific way in which values, practices and concepts are integrated into the operation of legal institutions and the interpretation of legal texts': J. Bell, 'English Law and French Law – Not So Different?' (1995) 48 (2) *CLP* 63.
17. J. Hodgson, *French Criminal Justice: A Comparative Account of the Investigation and Prosecution of Crime in France* (Hart 2005).
18. J. Hodgson, 'Constructing the Pre-trial Role of the Defence in French Criminal Procedure: an Adversarial Outsider in an Inquisitorial Process?' (2000) 6 (1) *Int'l J. Evidence & Proof* 1; see also J. Hodgson, 'Suspects, Defendants and Victims in the French Criminal Process: The Context of Recent Reforms' (2002) 51 *Int'l & Comp. L. Q.* 781; S. Field and A. West, 'Dialogue and the Inquisitorial Tradition: French Defence Lawyers in the Pre-trial Criminal Process' (2003) 14 (3) *Crim. L. Forum* 261; see also A. West, 'Reform of French Criminal Justice' (2000) 150 *NLJ* 1542, 1630 and 1667 (three-part article); for an overview of French criminal procedure see V. Dervieux, 'The French System', in M. Delmas-Marty and J. Spencer (eds), *European Criminal Procedures* (first published 2002, Cambridge University Press 2005).
19. R. Munday 'What Do the French Think of Their Jury' (1995) 15 *Legal Studies* 65, 85; see also R. Munday, 'Jury Trial, Continental Style' (1993) 13 *Legal Studies* 204.
20. S. Field, 'State, Citizen, and Character in French Criminal Process' (2006) 33 (4) *Journal of Law and Society* 522, 536; see also J. Hodgson, 'Conceptions of the Trial in Inquisitorial and Adversarial Procedure', in A. Duff, L. Farmer, S. Marshall and V. Tadros, *The Trial on Trial Volume Two: Judgment and Calling to Account* (2006 Hart), 232.

Two useful observational studies have been undertaken of the entire trial procedure:[21] Lerner provides an interesting account of a trial of an American/French citizen in a French court, highlighting aspects of the trial procedure which appear so alien to an American eye, concluding that the differences in trial procedure 'were more striking than the similarities'.[22] McKillop provides an extensive account of a murder trial he observed of a French citizen in the *cour d'assises*; he found the trial itself to be extremely brief and concluded that the most important aspect of French criminal process is the pre-trial stage; that the investigative dossier forms a central part of the trial, indeed that the trial was really a review of the dossier rather than a fresh hearing and testing of the evidence.[23] Differences in approach to receiving evidence have been noted by Van Kessel who suggests that 'exclusionary rules in continental courts are more appropriately described as rules of decision than rules of exclusion – what evidence the fact-finder may use to support its decision, rather than what evidence may be presented to the fact-finder'.[24]

1.2.2 Perceptions of truth

Centrally connected with the idea of legal culture are questions about the role of truth in the process. Is the aim of the trial simply to discover the truth, or are other values, such as fair trial and integrity of the process, equally or indeed more important? It has been said that the ultimate aim of the trial is to ascertain the truth. However, 'it is not only the case that truth is needed to do justice, the court must do justice in finding the truth.'[25] It has been suggested by many commentators that a major point of difference between the common law system and the continental system is the lesser commitment by the former to discovering the truth behind an accusation.

While some suggest that the ultimate goal of the common law system is truth discovery,[26] it is more often suggested that the adversarial trial is more

21. An early example of an observational study is the work by the novelist Sybille Bedford who sat as an observer of trials in England, France, Germany, Austria and Switzerland in the late 1950s and published her account *The Faces of Justice* (first published 1961, Faber & Faber 2011).
22. R. Lerner, 'The Intersection of Two Systems: An American on Trial for an American Murder in the French *Cour d'assises*' (2001) (3) *U. Ill. L. Rev.* 791, 852.
23. B. McKillop, 'Anatomy of a French Murder Case' (1997) 45 *Am. J. Comp. L.* 527; McKillop also provides accounts of trials in the lower courts, 'Readings and Hearings in French Criminal Justice: Five Cases in the *Tribunal Correctionnel*' (1998) 46 (4) *Am. J. Comp. L.* 757.
24. G. Van Kessel, 'European Perspectives on the Accused as a Source of Testimonial Evidence' (1998) 100 (4) *W. Va. L. Rev.* 799, 831.
25. H. L. Ho, *A Philosophy of Evidence Law* (Oxford University Press 2008) 51.
26. Ibid., 52; see also M. Frankel, 'The Search for Truth: An Umpireal View' (1975) 123 *U. Pa. L. Rev.* 1031; M. King, 'Security, Scale, Form and Function: The Search for Truth and the Exclusion of Evidence in Adversarial and Inquisitorial Justice Systems' (2001–2) 12 *Int'l Legal Persp.* 185.

concerned that the parties fight the contest in accordance with the rules of the game rather than reaching a verdict that reflects the truth of the matter in dispute.[27] The importance of truth discovery has also been related to the underlying purposes of the criminal trial: a purpose of policy implementation will be more concerned that the truth is established so that policy may be realised, whereas a purpose of conflict resolution is merely concerned that the dispute is settled according to the satisfaction of the parties to the conflict.[28] In such a situation, the 'whole truth' does not emerge because unstipulated or undisclosed facts 'do not exist as far as the judge is concerned, who aims at establishing only that relative truth which is attainable within the limits set by the procedural acts of the parties'.[29] Furthermore, if the trial is concerned with conflict resolution, 'the judicial proceedings may be characterized less as a search for substantive truth than as a search for a definite winner'.[30]

Weigend suggests the adversarial system 'does not lead to the discovery of "true" truth but of an artificially generated set of facts euphemistically called "procedural truth"'.[31] It has also been suggested that 'any view that portrays truth as the, or even as an, aim of the criminal trial' is mistaken on the basis that 'the actual operations' of the common law criminal trial actually inhibit the search for truth.[32] Langbein has highlighted the unresolved 'theoretical challenge' facing the common law adversary trial of 'the truth-impairing tendencies of a procedure that remits to partisans the work of gathering and presenting the evidence upon which accurate adjudication depends'.[33] Spencer has also noted the truth-impairing nature of common law rules of evidence that, in his view, are 'considerably more exacting' than those of continental systems.[34]

Any discussion of truth in the process will depend on what is actually understood by the idea of truth. Packer has distinguished between 'legal truth' and 'factual truth'. While the capture of a person in the act of committing an offence may be sufficient to indicate factual guilt, it is not sufficient to establish legal guilt. The latter is established only where 'factual determinations are made in procedurally regular fashion' that respect the integrity of the process.[35] Weigend has identified two approaches to the question of truth, the 'correspondence' approach and the 'consensus' approach. Under the

27. M. Damaška, 'Evidentiary Barriers to Conviction and Two Models of Criminal Procedure' (1973) 121 *U. Pa. L. Rev.* 506.
28. M. Damaška, *Evidence Law Adrift* (Yale University Press 1997).
29. Ho (note 25) 62.
30. R. Summers, 'Formal Legal Truth and Substantive Truth in Judicial Fact-Finding – Their Justified Divergence in Some Particular Cases' (1999) 18 *Law and Philosophy* 497,506.
31. T. Weigend, 'Is the Criminal Process about Truth? A German Perspective' (2003) 26 *Harv. J. L. Pub. Pol'y* 157, 160.
32. A. Duff, L. Farmer, S. Marshall and V. Tadros, *The Trial on Trial Volume Three: Towards a Normative Theory of the Criminal Trial* (Hart 2007) 65.
33. J. Langbein, *The Origins of Adversary Criminal Trial* (Oxford University Press 2003) 8.
34. J. Spencer, 'Evidence', in Delmas-Marty and Spencer (note 18) 595.
35. H. Packer, 'Two Models of the Criminal Process' (1964–5) 113 (1) *U. Pa. L. Rev.* 1.

correspondence approach, 'a sentence is true if it corresponds with reality'. By contrast, the consensus approach does not assume 'that "true facts" exist a priori; truth, according to these theories, is what reasonable people agree upon after a complete and fair discourse'. Under the correspondence theory, he suggests that it is 'the result that legitimizes the process'. By contrast according to the consensus theory, 'the content of the rules that determine the process becomes more important than the outcome itself, and adherence to these rules acquires paramount importance for truth finding'.[36]

Grande contributes to this discussion by drawing a distinction between 'ontological truth' which reflects the belief that 'an objective reconstruction of reality is attainable' and which she associates with a non-adversarial process, and 'interpretative truth' which she associates with an adversarial system. The reasoning underlying 'interpretative truth' is that a neutral inquirer can in fact never be truly neutral as their hypotheses on the information available to them will inevitably be formed and moulded by unconscious bias. Therefore the more accurate means to seek the truth, according to the adversarial model, is through 'fair confrontation of two parties'. This results in a different notion of truth, which is 'a product of a contest between two interpretations of reality'.[37] This 'interpretative truth' is a 'second-best' truth, which materialises from the two parties' opposing views of reality, 'provided of course that fair rules are established and respected'. On this basis she argues that justice and fairness are 'inevitably strictly equated in the adversary model because only a fair contest can bring about just results'.[38]

Weigend has also suggested that there are different concepts of 'procedural truth', each traditionally associated with a different procedural system. He associates correspondence theory with inquisitorial procedural systems, and consensus theory with the adversarial process of common law countries. He suggests that neither model of trial, inquisitorial and adversarial, differ in their aim of finding the truth, but they do differ in terms of allocating responsibility for finding the truth. Nonetheless, he concludes 'there are strong indications for a convergence of the two models toward shared responsibility, with judges becoming more active in adversarial systems and parties obtaining greater participation rights in inquisitorial systems.'[39]

1.2.3 Perceptions of convergence

A burgeoning debate examines the idea that we are seeing an ongoing convergence of both traditions. The convergence debate centres on whether systems

36. Weigend (note 4) 395.
37. E. Grande, 'Dances of Criminal Justice: Thoughts on Systemic Differences and the Search for Truth', in Jackson *et al.*, *Essays … Damaška* (note 4).
38. Ibid., 148.
39. Weigend (note 4) 414.

are moving in a more inquisitorial or adversarial direction, a convergence that is driven by the demands arising from the developing 'Europeanisation' of criminal justice and the internationalisation of criminal procedures (through the International Criminal Court and international ad hoc tribunals).[40] Some commentators see a shift towards more adversarial methods, others noting a move towards practices more strongly associated with the inquisitorial tradition.[41] It has been suggested that what was once distinctively 'civil' or common law is now a blend of the two.[42] These shifts are put down to jurisdictions of both traditions seeking solutions to common problems, such as rising crime rates, organised crime at national and trans-national levels, drug trafficking and international terrorism. The convergence has also been related to the effect of decisions of the ECtHR on national jurisdictions. Jackson suggests that rather than seeing the effect of the jurisprudence of the ECtHR as being one of convergence, 'we may be witnessing a realignment of the two existing models of proof' which can accommodate 'diverse application in different institutional and cultural settings'.[43]

While the convergence debate adheres to the inquisitorial, accusatorial and adversarial taxonomies, it has been increasingly debated that there is no clear consensus on what these terms actually mean. As a result some have suggested that their usefulness as a theoretical basis for the analysis of systems is limited.[44] Nonetheless, these labels continue to feature prominently in comparative discourse and it has been suggested that their limitations as analytical tools ought not equate with their complete abandonment.[45]

40. J. Jackson and S. Summers, *The Internationalisation of Criminal Evidence: Beyond the Common Law and Civil Law Traditions* (Cambridge University Press 2012) 6.
41. B. Markesinis (ed.), *The Gradual Convergence: Foreign Ideas, Foreign Influences and English Law on the Eve of the 21st Century* (Clarendon Press 1994); Legrand (note 13); J. Merryman suggests the two systems 'are converging from different directions toward equivalent mixed systems of criminal procedure', in *The Civil Law Tradition: An Introduction to the Legal Systems of Western Europe and Latin America* (3rd edn) (Stanford University Press 2007) 126; D. Luban, J. O'Sullivan and D. Stewart note 'a clear trend towards harmonisation if not actual convergence', in *International and Transnational Criminal Law* (Aspen 2010) 136.
42. G. Reamey, 'Innovation or Renovation in Criminal Procedure: Is the World Moving Towards a New Model of Adjudicating?' (2010) 27 (3) *Ariz. J. Int'l & Comp. L.* 693.
43. Jackson (note 4) 740; see also P. Roberts and J. Hunter, *Criminal Evidence and Human Rights: Reimagining Common Law Procedural Traditions* (Hart 2012).
44. S. Field, 'Fair Trials and Procedural Tradition in Europe' (2009) 29 (2) *OJLS* 365, 386; J. Jackson, 'Taking Comparative Evidence Seriously', in P. Roberts and M. Redmayne (eds), *Innovations in Evidence and Proof: Integrating Theory, Research and Tteaching* (Hart 2007) 291; Jackson (note 4); S. Summers, *Fair Trials: The European Criminal Procedural Tradition and the European Court of Human Rights* (Hart 2007) 11; Jackson and Summers (note 40) Ch. 1.
45. Roberts (note 4) 299; D. Sklansky, 'Anti-Inquisitorialism' (2009) 122 (6) *Harv. L. Rev.* 1634, 1704.

1.3 Structure of the book

Various methods have been used to compare legal systems. One such method is to draw comparisons using a grid-like system advanced by Delmas-Marty.[46] Other methodologies have been taken that have been neatly referred to as a 'virtual comparative approach', a 'researching there approach' and a 'living there approach'.[47] At a more conceptual level, a much-used comparative approach is to compare systems by the use of a methodology of 'models'.

This book draws on aspects of each of these various approaches. The book does not take a normative approach in so far as it does not set out to explore what a common regime of evidence law ought to look like. Nor is it intended to suggest that one procedural approach is superior to the other; the purpose of the comparative study is to try to identify the possible obstacles to devising a singular system of evidence admissibility. It will take an analytical approach of how evidence law – in terms of the gathering, receiving and presentation of evidence – operates in each of the countries that will be used as the case studies for this book.

That said, it will not take a strictly taxonomic approach, but will offer instead a more nuanced view, by taking account not only of the laws and jurisprudence of each jurisdiction, but also of the way the law operates in practice and how the systems are influenced by their adherence to the ideal types identified through the models methodology. The approach will be a reflective one, informed by my observations gleaned from 'researching there/living there';[48] it uses a similar method to that of Lerner and McKillop of attending criminal trials and interviewing practitioners in the selected jurisdictions to gain a better understanding of the legal culture of each. That said, a common law perspective must inevitably tinge my observations on the civil law jurisdictions, since that is the legal culture in which I was raised and therefore my inescapable yardstick.[49]

Three jurisdictions within the European Union have been chosen as case studies for the purpose of examining how evidence is gathered at the pre-trial phase and how it may be received, presented and challenged at the trial stage.

46. M. Delmas-Marty, *Procédures Pénal d'Europe* (Paris 1995), cited by R. Vogler, *A World View of Criminal Justice* (Ashgate 2005) 4; in the *Corpus Juris* project and in Delmas-Marty and Spencer, *European Criminal Procedures* (note 18), 69, the authors devised an analysis grid that examined the 'actors' and their 'powers' engaged in the criminal process at the various stages in an effort to find a 'common grammar'.
47. P. Roberts, 'On Method: The Ascent of Comparative Criminal Justice' (2002) 22 (3) *OJLS* 539 (review article of D. Nelken (ed.), *Contrasting Criminal Justice: Getting from Here to There* (Ashgate 2000)).
48. While I cannot claim to have lived in either France or Italy to the extent of commentators such as Nelken, I have spent block periods in these countries over my lifetime.
49. Damaška, *Faces of Justice and State Authority* (Yale University Press 1986) 15, notes the difficulty of escaping one's legal culture: 'It is hard to be at once comfortable everywhere and at home anywhere.'

The three jurisdictions that form the basis for the comparative study are Ireland, France and Italy. I have selected France and Italy as the civil law examples. France has been selected because it is here that the classic 'inquisitorial' model became firmly rooted and it was from the French system that criminal procedures across continental Europe drew their inspiration. Italy has been selected because of its relatively recent major reform of criminal procedure, which, it has been suggested, moves it closer towards an adversarial model. Italy provides an example of a how a legal culture can prove resistant to change. Ireland has been selected as the common law example because it operates according to the classic adversarial model and of all the common law jurisdictions it has arguably the strictest exclusionary rules of evidence, principally because of its constitutional requirements. The book will explore through these case studies whether the systems originating from the two broad legal traditions are in fact too diverse and irreconcilable, such as to prevent any significant convergence in evidence law in the form of a mutual admissibility system.

It will not engage in intricacies of specific rules relating to particular types of evidence, nor does the book aim to analyse the merits or coherence of EU policy in criminal justice. The following chapter analyses the efforts to achieve a mutual admissibility system across the EU through examination of the various instruments proposed or adopted to date. It explores the development of cooperation in criminal matters on the basis of mutual recognition, the so-called 'cornerstone' of the EU criminal justice system. The second part examines evidence gathering instruments published to date, the European Evidence Warrant (EEW) and the more recent European Investigation Order (EIO), and their attempts to grapple with the elusive issue of admissibility of evidence. The third part turns to an analysis of the arduous efforts to establish common minimum procedural safeguards for suspects and defendants that have culminated most recently in the adoption of a Directive on the right to legal advice.

The book then moves on to an exploration of the fundamental differences between the Member State jurisdictions of common law and civil law traditions. This begins in Chapter 3 with an exploration of the theoretical approaches taken in comparative research. It first presents an outline of the historical development of criminal procedures and approaches to proof in Europe, thus setting a basis for understanding the conceptual dichotomies that will then be discussed and relied on throughout the book: the accusatorial/inquisitorial dichotomy and the adversarial/non-adversarial dichotomy. The chapter will close with a discussion of the idea that the concept of adversarial procedure has been 'lost in translation' and that the discussion would benefit from the inclusion of an additional typology that provides a closer fit for the continental systems, a *procédure contradictoire.*

The three jurisdictions will each be examined in turn in the subsequent three chapters, beginning with the jurisdiction of Ireland and followed by those of France and Italy respectively. Each chapter will broadly follow the same structural format, beginning first with an examination of the roles and powers of those involved in the investigation of offences to show the institutional arrangements for investigations and the powers available for the gathering of evidence in the pre-trial stage, followed by an overview of the laws relating to the principle evidence-gathering practices. The second part of Chapter 4 turns to an analysis of three mainstays of common law evidence law: the exclusionary rules relating to unlawfully obtained evidence, hearsay evidence and character evidence, as they function in the Irish context, followed by an analysis in the third part of the presentation of evidence during the trial stage and the way in which the exclusionary rules operate at trial. These common law constructs will each be examined in turn in the French and Italian settings followed by a discussion of how evidence is presented at trial and the way in which evidence rules function in these jurisdictions (Chapters 5 and 6).

The concluding chapter will draw together the comparisons made of the three jurisdictions, synthesising the differences revealed through the case studies and then assessing potential obstacles for achieving mutual admissibility of evidence in the EU.

2 Aspiration to mutual admissibility of evidence in the European Union

2.1 Introduction

In 1946 Sir Winston Churchill suggested that the remedy for Europe wracked by two world wars was 'to re-create the European Family, or as much of it as we can, and to provide it with a structure under which it can dwell in peace, safety and freedom. We must build a kind of United States of Europe'.[1]

Since the close of the Second World War, Europe has embarked on a path to guard against a repeat of the power struggles between European nations by uniting them through conventions and treaties to safeguard common interests and values. The first body to be established was the Council of Europe that set about establishing (*inter alia*) common European standards of human rights. The early European Economic Community (EEC) treaties did not impinge upon criminal justice matters, generally regarded as the sovereign preserve of individual Member States.[2] European unity was advanced in 1992 by the creation of a European Union by the Treaty on European Union (TEU),[3] giving the Union competence in criminal matters, and this was developed and refined by the most recently adopted treaty, the Lisbon Treaty.[4]

The culmination of all these treaties has brought about the creation of a European Union (the EU) that guarantees freedom of movement for all citizens, their goods, services and capital across all Member States of the EU, in an 'area of freedom, security and justice'.[5] As people move freely, so also

1. Speech by Sir Winston Churchill (Parliamentary Assembly, Council of Europe, Zurich, 19 September 1946).
2. Treaty establishing the European Coal and Steel Community [1951] 261 UNTS 140; Treaty of the European Economic Community (TEEC) 1957 (Treaty of Rome) [1957] 298 UNTS 11 (renamed TEC by TEU – see below note 3).
3. Treaty on European Union (TEU) (Maastricht Treaty) [1992] OJ C 191/1.
4. The Lisbon Treaty consists of the original EC Treaty, now know as the Treaty on the Functioning of Europe (TFEU) and the Treaty on European Union (TEU); see Consolidated versions of the TEU, TFEU and the Charter of Fundamental Rights of the European Union [2010] OJ C 83 30.3.
5. This concept was created by the Treaty of Amsterdam, amending the Maastricht Treaty: Treaty of Amsterdam [1997] OJ C 340/1; for analysis of this terminology see M. Fletcher, R. Lööf and B. Gilmore, *EU Criminal Law and Justice* (Edward Elgar 2008).

does criminal activity. The growth in transnational crime has presented the EU with a key challenge: how to successfully prosecute an offence in one Member State for which the evidence necessary to secure a conviction needs to be obtained from another Member State, in a context where the Member States have different laws and procedures regulating the collection of evidence and different rules relating to the admissibility of evidence at trial.

To date, the movement of evidence from one State to another has been conducted through a system of mutual legal assistance. In the past decade the EU has attempted to replace the mutual assistance regime by a new method, one based on the principle of mutual recognition.

The gathering of evidence and the safeguarding of suspects' rights are two sides of the same coin in so far as the gathering of evidence must be conducted in a manner that respects the rights of suspects. Despite the fact that the ECHR already protects the rights of suspects, a number of Directives have been adopted that aim to ensure common minimum standards being applied across the EU. Obtaining agreement on these Directives was a tortuous process, in part due to the pre-Lisbon legislative procedure that required Member State unanimity for adoption of criminal justice measures, but also at a more fundamental level, as a result of the coexistence of different legal traditions within the EU. This coexistence poses the most acute challenge where the issue of admissibility of evidence obtained in breach of suspects' rights is concerned.

The first part of this chapter will examine the concept of mutual recognition and its relationship to the concept of mutual trust. It will then turn to an analysis of the aspiration of the mutual recognition project that a common standard of mutual admissibility of evidence be achieved, and the efforts of the Commission towards realising this ambition. Part II will outline the first instrument adopted for obtaining evidence on the basis of mutual recognition, the European Evidence Warrant (EEW),[6] together with the more recent Proposal for an evidence-gathering instrument, the European Information Order (EIO), currently under negotiation,[7] and analyse the approach of these instruments to the issue of admissibility of evidence. The final part of

6. Council Framework Decision 2008/978/JHA 18/12/2008 on the European evidence warrant for the purpose of obtaining objects, documents and data for use in proceedings in criminal matters [2008] OJ L 350/72; first proposed by the Commission in 2003, Commission, Proposal for a Council Framework Decision of 14/11/2003 on the European Evidence Warrant for obtaining objects, documents and data for use in proceedings in criminal matters, COM (2003) 688 final; the (much amended) Proposal was eventually adopted in 2008.

7. Initiative of the Kingdom of Belgium, the Republic of Bulgaria, the Republic of Estonia, the Kingdom of Spain, the Republic of Austria, the Republic of Slovenia and the Kingdom of Sweden for a Directive of the European Parliament and of the Council regarding the European Investigation Order in criminal matters, Brussels 29/4/2010, Interinstitutional File: 2010/0817 (COD) 9145/10; Explanatory Memorandum 3/6/2010, Interinstitutional File: 2010/0817 (COD) 9288/10 ADD 1; the Proposal followed on from the Green Paper on Obtaining Evidence in Criminal Matters from One Member State to Another and Securing its Admissibility, COM (2009) 624 final.

the chapter will then discuss the various Directives for achieving minimum procedural safeguards across the EU that have developed piecemeal over the last decade, and the attempt by the Commission to firmly establish a common rule of inadmissibility of evidence where the specific safeguard of a suspect's right of access to a lawyer is breached.

PART I

2.2 The development of cooperation in criminal matters on the basis of 'mutual recognition'

2.2.1 From mutual legal assistance to mutual recognition

(a) Mutual legal assistance

The European Council, meeting in Tampere in 1999, set an agenda to bring to fruition a common area of freedom, security and justice. One of the conclusions reached at Tampere was that 'enhanced mutual recognition of judicial decisions and judgments and the necessary approximation of legislation would facilitate co-operation between authorities and the judicial protection of individual rights'.[8] Cooperation between authorities in obtaining evidence was by no means a new phenomenon, but it had always been rooted in a principle of mutual assistance as part of the remit of the Council of Europe.

The legal framework for mutual assistance for obtaining evidence is the Council of Europe Convention on Mutual Assistance in Criminal Matters 1959 (the 1959 Convention) and subsequent protocols of 1978 and 2001. Under the 1959 Convention, State parties undertake to afford each other the 'widest measure of mutual legal assistance'; however, the request for assistance is executed in a manner provided by domestic law.[9] The requesting State in seeking the procuring of evidence may nonetheless specify formalities or procedures which are necessary under its law and the requested State should comply with the request even if the formality or procedure is unfamiliar, provided it is not contrary to its fundamental principles of law.[10] The requesting State may ask for its own officials to be present when executing requests and the requested State should not refuse where it would make the execution 'more responsive to the needs of the requesting party'.[11] The 1959

8. Tampere European Council, 15–16 October 1999, Presidency Conclusions, para. 33, available at <http://www.europarl.europa.eu/summits/tam_en.htm>.
9. Council of Europe Convention on Mutual Assistance in Criminal Matters 1959, Article 3.
10. Article 3, 1959 Convention, as supplemented by Article 8, 2001 Protocol.
11. Article 4, 1959 Convention, as supplemented by 2001 Protocol.

Convention makes provisions for the summonsing of witnesses and experts in the requested State to appear in the requesting State,[12] and makes provisions for persons in custody, subject to that person's consent, to be temporarily transferred to the territory where the hearing is to take place.[13]

The 2001 Protocol to the 1959 Convention makes provisions for mutual assistance through hearings by videoconference of witnesses and experts, and in certain cases of suspects or accused persons. In all of these cases the witnesses or suspect/accused enjoy the right not to testify. The Convention also provides for the carrying out of controlled deliveries[14] and covert investigations (investigations by officers covertly or under false identification), the decision to comply with a request for the latter being taken by the requested party 'with due regard to its national law and procedures'.[15] Requests for mutual assistance may be refused on grounds that the request is prejudicial to sovereignty, security, *ordre public* or other essential interests of the requested country, or where reservations have been entered into by the State making execution of requests dependent on double criminality (i.e. that the act is an offence under both requesting and requested State) or on consistency with its law generally.[16]

The 1959 Convention and Protocols were considered an inefficient means of obtaining evidence due to the cumbersome procedures involved, in that the norm was for requests to be sent via diplomatic channels rather than directly between judicial authorities. It was also considered ineffective because of the degree of latitude for refusal left to State parties.

The 1959 Convention was supplemented by an EU measure, the 2000 Convention on Mutual Assistance in Criminal Matters between Member States of the European Union, which attempted to improve mutual assistance procedures by providing that requests be made directly between judicial authorities rather than through political authorities, and by narrowing the scope for refusing to comply with a request for assistance.[17] In addition, it supplements the 1959 Convention and Protocols by making provision for

12. Article 7, 1959 Convention.
13. Article 3, 2001 Protocol, substituting Article 11, 1959 Convention.
14. Article 18, 2001 Protocol; controlled deliveries are mainly used in investigations related to offences of illicit trafficking.
15. Article 19, 2001 Protocol to 1959 Convention.
16. Article 5, 2001 Protocol to 1959 Convention; Ireland made a Declaration that requests were dependent on double criminality being satisfied. See generally J. Hamilton, 'Mutual Assistance in Criminal Matters in Ireland and the Proposed European Evidence Warrant (2005) *ERA Forum*, Special Issue on European Evidence Warrant, 53.
17. [2000] OJ C 197/1; Protocol to Convention, primarily relating to assistance in relation to information on bank accounts: [2001] OJ C 326/1. The Convention entered into force in August 2006. Being supplemental to the 1959 Convention means that the Convention cannot, of itself, be used as the only basis for a request for mutual assistance (see Explanatory Report [2000] OJ C379/7).

requests between Member States to conduct investigations by means of interception of telecommunications.[18]

The request for assistance may be made by the competent authority in the requesting State to the competent authority in the requested State, and as such includes a judicial authority or whichever authority has been deemed competent by the Member States in their adoption of the Convention. It provides that the collection of evidence by the requested Member State 'shall comply with the formalities and procedures expressly indicated by the requesting Member State' and that there is an obligation to comply with a request for mutual legal assistance unless to do so would conflict with 'fundamental principles of domestic law'.[19] This latter provision clearly leaves room for refusal by States of requests for assistance in addition to the possibilities for refusal under the 1959 Convention, and it is primarily this broad scope for refusal of requests under all these mutual assistance instruments that has generated the impetus for the creation of a new system of judicial cooperation.

(b) Mutual recognition

At Tampere, the European Council pressed for the achievement of 'better compatibility and more convergence between the legal systems of Member States'.[20] It has been suggested that an approach to this objective requiring the harmonisation of laws, in the sense of creating uniform substantive laws, would be impossible because of the wide disparity in legal systems of the Member States, and in addition on the basis that it risks encroachment of the sovereignty principle.[21] Therefore, in preference to the harmonisation route, it was agreed that the principle of mutual recognition 'should become the cornerstone of judicial co-operation' within the European Union.[22]

Mutual recognition has been defined as 'the agreement to accept decisions taken in one Member State as valid in any other Member State and to act on them accordingly, regardless of whether that decision might have been taken in a different way or would even have had a different outcome in a national context'. This has an advantage over harmonisation in that it is based on 'tolerance of diversity on the basis of mutual confidence and trust in each other's legal systems, as opposed to insistence of uniformity for its own sake'.[23]

The concept of mutual recognition greatly reduces the possibilities for refusal of requests that are available under the regime of mutual assistance – it

18. Articles 18 and 19, 2000 Convention on Mutual Assistance.
19. Ibid., Article 4(1).
20. Presidency Conclusions, Tampere (see note 8) 5.
21. *Statewatch News Online*, June 2000; see also C. Brants, 'Procedural Safeguards in the European Union: Too Little, Too Late?', in J. Vervaele (ed.), *European Evidence Warrant: Transnational Judicial Inquiries in the EU* (Intersentia 2005).
22. Presidency Conclusions, Tampere (see note 8) 33.
23. Brants, 'Procedural Safeguards in the European Union' (see note 21) 106.

is based on the assumption that Member States meet the human rights requirements set out in the European Convention on Human Rights.[24]

The 'necessary approximation' of laws was considered a key element to facilitate judicial cooperation when the mutual recognition principle was first proposed in Tampere[25] and this is now given treaty status, as is the principle of mutual recognition, in the Lisbon Treaty. The concept of 'approximation' involves a process whereby diverse legal orders maintain individuality but adapt to form a coherent whole in order to accommodate a particular objective. It requires agreement on identical or similar definitions of certain criminal offences and procedural rules.

Approximation is nowhere defined in the various EU instruments; indeed it has been noted that the terms 'harmonisation' and 'approximation' are not always used consistently – in some instances the former term is used even though the latter is more correct and that which is now required under the Lisbon Treaty. Harmonisation has been defined as 'the convergence of the legal practice of the various legal systems based upon a common standard' in contrast to approximation which 'allows Member States more discretion in the choice of the means with which to comply with their Union obligations'.[26]

In 2001 the Council adopted a 'Programme of measures to implement the principle of mutual recognition of decisions in criminal matters' thus paving the way for a new era of cooperation in criminal justice across the EU.[27] Mutual recognition has been described as 'the motor of European integration in criminal matters'.[28] While mutual assistance and mutual recognition are essentially directed to a common purpose – a Member State assisting another in relation to criminal proceedings in that other's territory – they are nonetheless fundamentally different. As one commentator has described it:

> In MLA the basis is a polite request: 'State B, please would you take this step for us? – if you can, and when you can', whereas with mutual recognition the basis is an order 'State B, we require you to execute this order for us.' With MLA, State B has in principle an open-ended discretion to refuse, and an equally wide discretion as to how, in any given case, it will carry out the task that State A wants done. With MR, by contrast, State B is in principle obliged to carry out the order, and furthermore, it may be required to carry it out in the manner that State A wants it done.[29]

24. S. Alegre and M. Leaf, 'Mutual Recognition in European Judicial Cooperation: A Step Too Far Too Soon? Case Study: The European Arrest Warrant' (2004) 10 (2) *European Law Journal* 200, 201.
25. Reiterated in the Stockholm Programme – see section 2.4.3 below.
26. A. Klip, *European Criminal Law: An Integrative Approach* (Intersentia 2009) 32.
27. [2001] OJ C 12/10.
28. V. Mitsilegas, *EU Criminal Law* (Hart 2009) 116.
29. J. Spencer, 'The Green Paper on obtaining evidence from one Member State to another and securing its admissibility: the reaction of one British lawyer'. Available at: <http://www.eucriminallaw.com/publications/>.

(c) Mutual admissibility of evidence

Approximation is set to be achieved not by requiring all Member States to adopt identical laws, but by requiring them to establish 'minimum rules' as a means of enhancing cooperation between Member States. Such rules shall take into account the differences between the legal traditions and systems of the Member States.[30] The idea of mutual admissibility of evidence has been an aspiration of the mutual recognition project from the outset. As will be discussed further below, the ECHR does not address the issue of admissibility of evidence gathered in breach of the Convention rights, and the ECtHR has shied away from stating that such evidence should be ruled inadmissible, consistently holding that 'the admissibility of evidence is a matter for regulation by national law and the national courts and that the Court's only concern is to examine whether the proceedings have been conducted fairly.'[31]

One of the stated aims of the Programme of Measures to implement the principle of mutual recognition is 'to ensure that evidence is admissible'.[32] The Commission later reaffirmed this where it noted that measures to ensure mutual trust between the national judicial authorities of Member States should cover 'the definition of fundamental guarantees' and 'the conditions for the admissibility of evidence'.[33]

The Lisbon Treaty has finally established a Treaty basis for a common approach to admissibility of evidence by requiring that minimum rules be established concerning the 'mutual admissibility of evidence', together with the rights of individuals in criminal procedure.[34] At the same time, however, these rules should take account of the differences between legal traditions. Implicit, arguably, is an assumption that the differences between the legal traditions are not so great as to be unable to accommodate a common approach to admissibility of evidence. It is also implicit that the terminology of 'admissibility' is one that is shared by all Member States; as will be seen in later chapters admissibility has different connotations in the jurisdictions examined in this work.

While the Lisbon Treaty lays down the broad legal basis for establishing a system of mutual admissibility of evidence, there remains the task of formulating the minimum rules to realise the provision. Since this process has commenced, the Commission have thrown down the gauntlet for a EU-wide rule on inadmissibility of evidence specifically where the right of access to a

30. Article 82(2), TFEU; the rules are to be established by means of directives adopted in accordance with the ordinary legislative procedure.
31. *Al-Khawaja and Tahery v The United Kingdom* [GC] 26766/05 and 22228/06, ECHR 2011; *Gäfgen v Germany* [GC] no. 22978/05, ECHR 2010.
32. [2001] OJ C 12/10.
33. Commission, 'Assessment of the Tampere programme and future orientations' (Communication) COM (2004) 4002 final, para. 2.8. This agenda was re-affirmed by the European Council Hague Programme [2005] OJ C 198/1, para. 3.3.1.
34. Article 82(2), TFEU.

lawyer has been breached.[35] The reactions of Member States have not been positive. This will be discussed in more detail below in the context of the discussion on the EU efforts to create a common procedural rights standard across the EU.[36]

The project of mutual admissibility has been an ongoing one, commenced long before the Lisbon Treaty. The aspiration to mutual admissibility of evidence was first mooted in the Corpus Juris project.[37] The aim of that project was to produce a set of guiding principles for the protection of the financial interests of the European Union.[38] The study took the form of a 'grid' system, an approach similarly adopted in subsequent Commission-funded studies of Member States' criminal procedure[39] that examined the 'actors' and their powers in an effort to find a 'common grammar'. The Corpus Juris study identified two types of 'legal grammar', an 'accusatory grammar, which assigns most of the powers to private parties' including the gathering of evidence, and an 'inquisitorial grammar', which assigns most of the powers to public actors', especially investigating magistrates.[40]

Based on the guiding principles of the ECHR that the authors suggest embody a 'hybrid "grammar" called *contradictoire*',[41] the substantive text of the Corpus Juris consisted of provisions relating to the criminal law, criminal procedure and the establishment of a European Public Prosecutor.[42] The provisions relating to the admissibility of evidence envisaged that 'the national law applicable to determine whether the evidence has been obtained legally or illegally must be the law of the country where the evidence was obtained'.

35. Commission Proposal for a Directive on the right of access to a lawyer in criminal proceedings and on the right to communicate upon arrest (Brussels, 8/6/2011 COM (2011) 326 final, Article 13).
36. See section 2.4 below.
37. M. Delmas-Marty and J. Vervaele (eds), *The Implementation of the Corpus Juris in the Member States*, Vol. IV (Intersentia 2001).
38. The project was funded by the European Commission 1997.
39. Examples include T. Spronken, *An EU-Wide Letter of Rights – Towards Best Practice* (Intersentia 2010); E. Cape, J. Hodgson, T. Prakken and T. Spronken, *Suspects in Europe – Procedural Rights at the Investigative Stage of the Criminal Process in the European Union* (Intersentia 2007); E. Cape, Z. Namoradze, R. Smith and T. Spronken, *Effective Criminal Defence in Europe* (Intersentia 2010); K. Ligeti (ed.), *Toward a Prosecutor for the European Union: A Comparative Analysis* (Hart 2013).
40. M. Delmas-Marty, 'Reflections on the "Hybridisation" of Criminal Procedure', in J. Jackson, M. Langer and P. Tillers (eds), *Crime, Procedure and Evidence in a Comparative and International Context – Essays in Honour of Prof. Mirjan Damaška* (Hart 2008) 253.
41. Ibid., 254; the principle of proceedings that are *contradictoire* as set out in the text of the *Corpus Juris* implies 'that the parties can have access to any evidence or observation presented to the judge (even where this is presented by a party to the proceedings or by an independent prosecutor), with a view to influencing and discussing the judge's decision' and the accused enjoys the rights of defence guaranteed by the ECHR.
42. The *Corpus Juris* draft was published in M. Delmas-Marty and J. Vervaele (eds), *The Implementation of the Corpus Juris in the Member States*, Vol. I (Intersentia 2000).

It went on to provide that where the evidence has been obtained legally, 'it should not be possible to oppose the use of this evidence because it was obtained in a way that would have been illegal in the country of use' provided that it has not been obtained in breach of rights enshrined in the ECHR.[43]

This sentiment was echoed in a subsequent Green Paper by the Commission that considered 'mutual admissibility' to be the most realistic solution to the difficulties posed by the different rules of evidence across Member States, rather than a unified code on admissibility of evidence and that 'evidence lawfully gathered by one Member State's authorities should be admissible before the courts of other Member States'.[44]

In 2009 the Commission published a Green Paper on Obtaining Evidence in Criminal Matters from One Member State to Another and Securing Its Admissibility.[45] The Commission highlighted that existing rules are geared towards 'ensuring' the admissibility of evidence, but that only involves creating 'the optimal conditions in the procuring of the evidence so as to be confident that the court in the requesting State will have no difficulty in admitting it at trial'.[46] 'Ensuring' that the evidence will be admitted is not the same as making admissibility mandatory, at least where its collection has followed all prescribed procedures. The Commission pointed out that the existing rules only approach the issue of admissibility of evidence in an indirect manner, as they do not set any common standards for gathering evidence. That poses a risk that the existing rules would only function effectively between Member States with similar national standards for gathering evidence. On this basis it was proposed to adopt common standards for gathering evidence in criminal matters.

Responses to the Green Paper were mixed and suggest that it is the difference between the two legal traditions of the EU Member States that poses the greatest obstacle to a common regime of evidence law. Of the jurisdictions that will be examined in this book, Ireland's response was that 'it is not possible or advisable to establish common criteria for admissibility of evidence because this, of necessity, varies between Member States according to the nature of the legal system in place'. It was suggested that more rigid rules for admissibility of evidence 'are appropriate in the context of the common law jury system, but may not be appropriate in a "judge-heard case" as a judge would be presumably trained to exclude inappropriate evidence or inferences from his or her consideration'.[47]

43. Article 33, Draft text *Corpus Juris* (Draft agreed at Florence, meeting of rapporteurs). Available at <http://ec.europa.eu/anti_fraud/documents/fwk-green-papercorpus/corpus_juris_en.pdf>.
44. Commission, Green Paper on the criminal law protection of financial interests and the establishment of a European Public Prosecutor (COM (2001) 715).
45. COM (2009) 624.
46. Ibid.
47. Response of Government of Ireland; all responses available at: <http://ec.europa.eu/justice/news/consulting_public/news_consulting_0004_en.htm>.

France was broadly in favour of common standards for admissibility of evidence but with the caveat that 'the person under investigation should have the right to demand that evidence obtained in violation of these rules not be used against him' and that the Commission should be 'mindful of the differences between criminal proceedings in Member States' in devising any common admissibility standard. Italy was also in favour but only if such common standards were to include a number of specific safeguards, most pertinently that a concept of a 'European defence lawyer' be devised who would represent persons subject to an evidence-gathering procedure, and that a form of judicial supervision should be available to screen evidence and exclude any that was gathered illegally or in breach of the standards.[48] A demand for safeguards was also a common theme reflected in the responses of NGOs, and the UK Parliament was 'cautious about the case for introducing common standards for the collection of evidence because of the difference between the common and civil law systems in the EU'.[49]

PART II

2.3 Gathering and transfer of evidence

Instruments for cooperation in the field of evidence law have developed piecemeal. The first instrument to be adopted was for the freezing of evidence to prevent its destruction or disposal, but the transfer is processed in accordance with the rules applicable to MLA.[50] In the Commission's view, this Framework Decision was too limited in that it explicitly provides that where coercive measures are necessary, they must be taken in accordance with national procedural rules, therefore if the national rules do not permit a search to be carried out in order to seize the evidence the cooperation envisaged by the Framework Decision may be ineffective. Furthermore, the processing of the subsequent transfer in accordance with MLA procedures results

48. Centro Studi di Diritto Penale Europeo, *Risposte al Libro Verde sulla ricerca delle prove in materia penale tra Stati Membri e sulla garanzia della loro ammissibilità.* Available at: <http://ec.europa.eu/justice/news/consulting_public/0004/civil_society/insubria_university_ii_it.pdf)>.
49. The UK Parliamentary Under-Secretary of State was 'cautious about the case for introducing common standards for the collection of evidence because of the difference between the common and civil law systems in the EU'. European Scrutiny Committee House of Commons, 5th Report, Session 2009–10, p. 11, available at: <http://www.publications.parliament.uk/pa/cm200910/cmselect/cmeuleg/5-v/5v.pdf>; response of Council of Bars and Law Societies of Europe (CCBE), available at: <http://ec.europa.eu/justice/news/consulting_public/0004/civil_society/ccbe_en.pdf>. See also responses by Fair Trials International and of Amnesty International calling for safeguards to underpin any evidence-gathering instrument.
50. Council Framework Decision on the execution in the European Union of orders freezing property or evidence [2003] OJ L 196/45.

in 'a substantial difference' between the rules applicable to the freezing of evidence and to the subsequent transfer.[51]

2.3.1 The European Evidence Warrant and the European Investigation Order

The Commission's Proposal for the European Evidence Warrant aimed to address these shortcomings by developing an instrument to cover the obtaining and subsequent transfer of evidence on the basis of a purely mutual recognition procedure. After a lengthy legislative process lasting six years, it was finally adopted having undergone significant changes since it was first proposed.[52] The European Evidence Warrant (EEW) is limited in scope, extending only to securing objects, documents or data specified in the warrant, and does not cover statements of suspects or witnesses, forensic samples or interception of communications unless these materials are already in the hands of the authorities before the issue of the warrant.[53] Any request for evidence falling into these categories continues therefore to be governed by MLA principles.

The thinking of the Commission in limiting the scope of the Evidence Warrant so as to exclude initiating interviews of suspects and taking statements of other witnesses was that this type of evidence gathering requires 'special consideration'. In that context the Commission considered it preferable to delay including interviews and statements within the scope of the EEW until an instrument on procedural rights for suspects and defendants had been finalised and further research on other aspects of taking evidence from suspects, defendants, victims and witnesses undertaken.[54]

Because of the limited scope of the EEW, it is now in a sort of no man's legislative land: it has been adopted though only implemented by some Member States, and has been overtaken and repealed by a new instrument, the European Investigation Order (EIO), that remains at the negotiation stage.[55] The limited scope of the EEW has led many to conclude that the coexistence of the EEW in its present limited format alongside the MLA regime is unsatisfactory. The reasoning underpinning the EIO was that 'the numerous instruments have created a fragmented approach making the task of the judicial authorities even more burdensome, which is exactly the opposite of what mutual recognition is supposed to achieve.'[56] The EIO is therefore intended

51. Commission, EEW Proposal (see note 6).
52. For detailed consideration of the provisions as they stood at 2006 see A. Ryan, 'The European Evidence Warrant: The Emergence of a European Law of Evidence?' (2006) 16 (4) *ICLJ* 8.
53. Article 4.
54. See discussion on procedural rights in section 2.4 below.
55. EIO (see note 7).
56. EIO, Explanatory Memorandum, 3/6/2010, Interinstitutional File: 2010/0817 (COD) 9288/10 ADD 1.

to replace all the MLA arrangements for gathering evidence, and though initially restricted regarding some investigative measures now covers all types of investigative activities and as such allows for all types of evidentiary material to be obtained.[57]

Given the legislative limbo, both the instruments will be discussed in tandem since some common provisions exist between them, but the greater focus will be on the EIO since this is the instrument that is more likely to survive. The EEW and the EIO provide for warrants to be issued for any criminal proceedings by a 'judicial authority'[58] and to be automatically executed within strict time limits[59] by the executing authority unless one of the limited grounds of refusal apply.[60] It is obligatory for the executing authority to comply with formalities and procedures expressly indicated by the issuing authority provided they are not contrary to the 'fundamental principles' of the law of the executing State. The idea behind this provision is to reduce obstacles to the admissibility of the evidence at trial.[61]

While the EIO does not list the specific investigative measures that may be requested, some particular measures of a sensitive nature are expressly referred to. Provisions facilitating the transfer of a person in custody in the executing State to the issuing State (or indeed vice versa) are specifically included so as to emphasise that the reason for the transfer is for the purpose of carrying out an investigative measure. The consent of the person to be transferred must be obtained, and if not then the execution may be refused; this differs from the provision on transfer of persons in custody under the EU Convention on mutual assistance, which requires the consent of the person

57. EIO, 'Frequently Asked Questions', Note from ten member states to delegations, 4/4/2012, Interinstitutional File: 2010/0817 (COD) 8182/12; a general approach was reached in December 2011 except for some recitals: Note from Presidency to Delegations, 29/2/2012, Interinstitutional File: 2010/0817 (COD) 7014/12.
58. Article 2(c), EEW; Article 2, EIO; both instruments require a validation procedure through which the Member States which designated police authorities as issuing authorities may be required by the executing State to have the order validated by a judicial authority of the status of a judge, prosecutor, court or investigating magistrate.
59. Article 15(2), EEW; Article 11, EIO: a decision on recognition or execution must be made within 30 days (unless urgent, in which case the decision must be taken without delay) after receipt and the executing authority must transfer the items immediately, with an outer limit of 90 days (Article 12, EIO).
60. Article 2(d), EEW defines the executing authority as 'an authority with competence under the national law'; Article 11, EEW requires the executing authority to recognise the warrant 'without any further formality being required and shall forthwith take the necessary measures for its execution in the same way as the objects, documents or data would be obtained by an authority of the executing State'.
61. Article 12, EEW; Article 8(2), EIO; Article 9, EIO provides that in limited cases the executing authority may have recourse to an investigative measure other than that provided for in the order. Article 8, EIO creates an obligation for the executing State to accept the presence of a competent authority of the issuing State during the execution of measures unless it would be contrary to the fundamental principles of law of the executing State.

only where it is required to be obtained under the national law of the requested State concerned. The EIO also provides a ground for refusal where the transfer is liable to prolong the detention of the person concerned. An EIO may also be issued for the purpose of hearing a suspected or accused person within the executing State by videoconference arrangements, but this may be refused if the person does not consent or the execution would be contrary to the fundamental principles of the law of the executing State.

There is a general provision in the EIO stating that the 'Directive shall not have the effect of modifying the obligation to respect the fundamental rights and legal principles as enshrined in Article 6 of the Treaty on European Union',[62] and this is reinforced in a Recital which provides for refusal to execute where there are reasons to believe that the EIO has been issued for the purpose of prosecuting or punishing a person on account of, *inter alia*, racial or ethnic origin, religion or political opinions, or that the person's position may be prejudiced for any of these reasons.[63]

2.3.2 Admissibility of evidence

The aspiration that evidence gathered under an EEW should be admissible provided it has been lawfully gathered was included in the original Commission Proposal, which noted that the instrument was intended to facilitate the admissibility of evidence obtained from another Member State.[64] It envisaged that admissibility would be facilitated by the inclusion of procedural safeguards to protect fundamental rights; by clarifying the principle that the requested State must provide assistance in accordance with the formalities and procedures expressly indicated by the requesting State to the maximum extent possible,[65] and that an EEW should be only issued when the issuing authority is satisfied that it would be possible to obtain the objects, documents or data in similar circumstances if they were on the territory of its own Member State. It was considered that the obligation placed upon the executing authority to inform the issuing authority immediately if the former believes the warrant was executed contrary to its national law should provide reassurance that the evidence was lawfully obtained, thereby further facilitating admissibility.[66]

The only specific reference to admissibility of evidence in the EEW as finally adopted appears in a Recital which provides that it should be possible for the issuing authority to ask the executing State to follow formalities and

62. Article 1(3), EIO.
63. Recital 17, EIO; an identical Recital appears in the EEW.
64. Commission, EEW Proposal (see note 6), Explanatory Memorandum to Proposal.
65. This principle is set out in Article 4 of the Convention on Mutual Assistance in Criminal Matters between Member States of the European Union [2000] OJ C 197/1.
66. Article 17(1)(a), EEW, Original Proposal.

procedures indicated by the issuing authority which might 'assist in making the evidence sought admissible'.[67]

The issue of admissibility of evidence has become somewhat the 'elephant in the room' in the EIO. There is no mention of admissibility anywhere in the proposed directive despite it having been discussed in the supporting statement to the Proposal. That document identifies the general objective of the Proposal as one 'to improve the search for truth in criminal proceedings' on the basis that 'the need to improve the search for truth in criminal proceedings is constantly challenging the efficiency and the quality of the criminal justice systems' and that the search for truth 'is an important element to strengthen the trust of the citizen in their national system and in the EU framework'.[68] It is noteworthy in this context that the initiators of the Proposal are all Member States of the civil law legal systems; the importance of truth in the process appears to be forefront, rather than admissibility of evidence or fair procedures. Perhaps the emphasis would have been different if the Proposal had emanated from predominantly common law jurisdictions?

This general objective of improving the search for truth contains the more specific objectives of 'ensuring the admissibility of evidence' and 'maintaining a high level of protection of fundamental rights, especially procedural rights'. It is noted that collecting evidence in another State 'raises specific challenges in this regard as the rules for admissibility and collection of evidence are often different' across the Member States. The only proposed solution to ensuring admissibility is that the authorities from the issuing State would be present during the execution of the measure. While this features as a provision in the proposed directive, its objective of ensuring admissibility is not mentioned.

The most recent proposal from the Commission on the establishment of the European Public Prosecutor's Office (EPPO) again grapples with the question of admissibility of evidence. The approach taken is a presumption of admissibility, and the trial court would be unable to rule the evidence inadmissible on the ground that procedures for gathering the evidence differ from its national law, provided it respects the fairness of the procedure and the suspect's rights of defence. The Regulation goes on to provide that once the evidence is admitted, the national court retains its competence to 'assess freely' the evidence presented.[69] This distinction between admissibility and assessment of evidence will be explored in later chapters.

67. Recital 14, Framework Decision, EEW.

68. EIO, Detailed Statement, 23 June 2010, Interinstitutional File: 2010/0817 (COD) 9288/10 ADD 2, 21.

69. Proposal for a Council Regulation on the establishment of the European Public Prosecutor's Office, Brussels, 17/7/2013, COM (2013) 534, Recital 32 and Article 30. Ireland and the UK are set not to opt in to this Regulation; see the discussion of presumed admissibility of evidence in G. Vermeulen, *Free Gathering and Movement of Evidence in Criminal Matters in the EU* (Maklu 2012) 44.

2.3.3 Exchange of information regarding previous convictions

As originally proposed, the EEW was to be used to obtain copies of criminal records, but this was subsequently deleted and is similarly not contained in the EIO. Four separate instruments now contain provisions for the transfer and subsequent use of criminal records.[70] One of these instruments is designed to determine the conditions under which, in the course of criminal proceedings against a person, previous convictions handed down against that person for different facts in other Member States are taken into account. It aims at enabling consequences to be attached to a previous conviction handed down in one Member State in the course of new criminal proceedings in another Member State 'to the extent that such consequences are attached to previous national convictions under the law of that other Member State'.[71]

As will be seen in the later chapters, the manner in which previous convictions are treated at *trial* (as opposed to in sentencing deliberations) differ considerably as between the jurisdictions of Ireland, France and Italy. The triers of fact in both France and Italy will have full knowledge of the defendant's criminal past whereas in Ireland this material would be inadmissible; the triers of fact are normally shielded from this information so as not to prejudice their verdict.

2.3.4 Hearsay evidence

Under the EIO, statements may be received directly from witnesses through audio-visual transmission or videoconferencing. In such situations, if a witness refuses to give evidence 'or does not testify to the truth' the national law of the Member State where the witness is being heard applies in the same way as it would apply in national proceedings.[72] Whether not testifying to the truth is the same thing as a recanting witness – where a witness does not stand

70. Council Decision 2005/876/JHA 21/11/2005 on the exchange of information extracted from the criminal record [2005] OJ L 322/33; Council Framework Decision 2009/315/JHA 26/2/2009 on the organisation and content of the exchange of information extracted from the criminal record between Member States [2009] OJ L 93/23; Council Framework Decision 2008/675/JHA 24/7/2008 on taking account of convictions in the Member States of the European Union in the course of new criminal proceedings [2008] OJ L 220/32; this Framework Decision replaces Article 56 of the Council of Europe European Convention of 28 May 1970 on the International Validity of Criminal Judgments, concerning the taking into consideration of criminal judgments, as between the Member States parties to that Convention; Council Decision on the establishment of the European Criminal Records Information System (ECRIS) in application of Article 11 of Framework Decision 2009/315/JHA [2009] OJ L 93/33.
71. Council Framework Decision 2008/675/JHA of 24 July 2008 on taking account of convictions in the Member States of the European Union in the course of new criminal proceedings [2008] OJ L 220/32.
72. Article 21, EIO.

over an earlier statement made to authorities – is unclear. Other evidence could result from an EIO which could be classified as hearsay, certainly from a common law perspective, such as may result from the collection of objects, documents, data and any evidence already in the hands of the authorities, so it could include witness statements obtained other than through the video-conferencing procedure. A more detailed discussion of how these types of evidence may constitute hearsay at trial will be examined in later chapters. For now it is sufficient to point out that there is no standard admissibility provision in relation to hearsay contained in the EIO, other than an attempt to avoid hearsay testimony by ensuring that witnesses may be heard through the technological media.

A standard has been set recently by the ECtHR that does address the issue of the absent witness and therefore could meet the issue posed by allowing the collection of evidence, more specifically witness statements already in the hands of the authorities. The difficulty with the situation where the witness is absent is that the court or jury has no opportunity to assess the overall credibility of the witness by observation of the general demeanour of the witness in providing their testimony and answering questions in cross-examination. In *Al-Khawaja and Tahery v UK* the ECtHR held:

> Article 6.3(d) enshrines the principle that, before an accused can be convicted, all evidence against him must normally be produced in his presence at a public hearing with a view to adversarial argument.[73] Exceptions to this principle are possible but must not infringe the rights of the defence, which, as a rule, require that the accused should be given an adequate and proper opportunity to challenge and question a witness against him, either when that witness makes his statement or at a later stage of proceedings.[74]

The court noted that 'hearsay remains a problematic source of evidence which requires special caution because of the general inability to test the reliability of hearsay statements'.[75] The majority in *Al-Khawaja and Tahery* held that where:

> A conviction is based solely or to a decisive degree on depositions that have been made by a person whom the accused has had no opportunity to examine or to have examined, whether during the investigation or at the trial, the rights of the defence may be restricted to an extent that is incompatible with the guarantees provided by Article 6 (the so-called 'sole or decisive rule').[76]

73. As worded in the official translation in French *en vue d'un débat contradictoire.*
74. *Al-Khawaja and Tahery* (see note 31) 118, referring to the principle as set out in *Lucà v Italy* 33354/96, ECHR 2001-II.
75. Ibid., partly dissenting and partly concurring opinion of Judges Sajo and Karakas.
76. *Al-Khawaja and Tahery* (see note 31) 19.

The court took the opportunity to clarify its earlier jurisprudence by explaining what is meant by the 'sole or decisive rule', more particularly the meaning of 'decisive', stating that it 'should be narrowly understood as indicating evidence of such significance or importance as is likely to be determinative of the outcome of the case'.[77] The Court went on to explain that the 'sole and decisive rule' is predicated on the principle that the greater the importance of the evidence, the greater the potential unfairness to the defendant in allowing the witness to remain anonymous or to be absent from the trial and the greater the need for safeguards to ensure that the evidence is demonstrably reliable or that its reliability can properly be tested and assessed. Nonetheless, it was not advocating that an automatic breach of Article 6.1 would always arise where a hearsay statement that is the sole or decisive evidence against a defendant is admitted in evidence. The failure of a witness to give testimony arising from fear of reprisal from the accused and consequent admission of that witness's prior statement would not breach Article 6.1 on the basis that 'to allow the defendant to benefit from the fear he has engendered in witnesses would be incompatible with the rights of victims and witnesses'.[78] However, 'the Court must subject the proceedings to the most searching scrutiny'.[79] In addition, 'the specificities of the particular legal system concerned and, in particular its rules of evidence' must be taken into account.[80]

Given the absence of any provision in the EIO in relation to an approach to hearsay evidence, the ECtHR jurisprudence provides the only guidance. Again, it should be noted that the EIO emanates from a bloc of Member States that adhere to the civil law tradition so it is perhaps unsurprising that hearsay would not feature, since the civil law jurisdictions traditionally do not embrace strict hearsay rules. Nonetheless, it is ironic that this latest decision from the ECtHR involves a common law jurisdiction that has traditionally strongly guarded against the use of hearsay and the court specifically noted that 'the present cases have arisen precisely because the legal system in England and Wales has abandoned the strict common law rule against hearsay evidence'.[81]

Since the EIO has originated post-Lisbon, the possibility of opting in to the directive arises for those States which made ratification of the Lisbon Treaty contingent on the inclusion of a protocol to the effect that they could elect to opt in to any legislative proposals in the area of judicial cooperation.[82]

77. Ibid., 131; the rule was first stated in *Unterpertinger v Austria* 24/11/1986 Series A no. 110; *P.S. v Germany* 33900/96 (ECtHR 20/12/2001) and *Krasniki v Czech Republic* no. 51277/99 (ECtHR 28/2/2006).
78. *Al-Khawaja and Tahery* (see note 31) 123.
79. Ibid., 147.
80. Ibid., 146.
81. Ibid., 130.
82. Ireland, the United Kingdom and Denmark.

The UK decided to participate in the EIO by using the opt-in option provided for in Protocol 21 to the Lisbon Treaty. Ireland initially decided to opt in,[83] but later decided not to opt in, noting that the EIO 'reflects the civil law system of the sponsoring States and presents problems for common law States'. Nonetheless Ireland continues to participate in the negotiations and hopes to opt in provided 'Irish concerns can be adequately addressed'.[84]

PART III

2.4 Developing safeguards for suspects and defendants

2.4.1 Safeguards contained in the evidence-gathering instruments

A criticism that has been levied at the EU mutual recognition programme is that it has 'focused primarily on enforcement measures at the expense of human rights and civil liberties'.[85] A specific list of safeguards for the execution of an EEW was included in the original Commission Proposal, but it was later thought preferable to subsume the specific rights listed into a general human rights clause obliging Member States to respect fundamental rights in their use of the EEW,[86] and to permit Member States to refuse execution of a warrant where there are reasons to believe it is being pursued on account of a person's gender, race, religion, ethnic origin, political opinions, etc.[87] The EIO contains identical provisions.[88] In both instruments, the warrant may only be issued where it is necessary and proportionate for the purpose of the proceedings.[89]

Substantive reasons for issuing the EIO, repeating a provision in the EEW, may not be challenged in the executing State.[90] While the fact that a warrant may be issued only where it is necessary and proportionate, its value as a safeguard is questionable. Since it is for the issuing State to decide that the issue of

83. 3081st Council meeting, Justice and Home Affairs, Luxembourg, 11–12 April 2011, Press Release.
84. 3096th Council meeting, Justice and Home Affairs, Luxembourg, 9 and 10 June 2011, Press release. There is some confusion as to whether the EEW would continue to apply to any Member States who do not opt into the new instrument: D. Sayers, *The European Investigation Order: Travelling without a 'Roadmap'*, CEPS Paper in Liberty and Security in Europe, June 2011; A. Hinarejos, J. Spencer and S. Peers, *Opting Out of EU Criminal Law: What Is Actually Involved?*, CELS Working Paper, New Series, No.1.
85. House of Lords Select Committee on European Union, *The Hague Programme: A Five Year Agenda for EU Justice and Home Affairs, Report with Evidence* (HL 2004–05, 84).
86. Article 1(3), EEW.
87. Recital 27, EEW.
88. Article 1(3), EIO and Recital 17.
89. Article 7, EEW; Article 5(a), EIO.
90. Article 13, EIO.

a warrant is necessary and proportionate, and the reasons for issuing a warrant may be challenged only in the issuing State, it is beyond the brief of the executing authority to inquire into whether the warrant is necessary and proportionate.[91] Furthermore, providing a right to challenge the reasons for issuing the warrant is quite different from providing a right to challenge how the evidence-gathering process was conducted so as to argue that it should be inadmissible.

In the EIO, specific safeguards are contained in the provision for video-conference hearings which include that the person must be informed prior to the hearing of their rights under the law of the issuing State, and a 'competent authority' of the executing State must be present during the hearing, who must ensure that the fundamental principles of the law of the executing State are not infringed. The hearing is, however, conducted 'directly by, or under the direction of, the competent authority of the issuing State in accordance with its own laws'.[92] The person may claim the right not to testify where such right exists under the law of either the executing State or issuing State, and must be informed of that right.[93]

2.4.2 Promoting 'mutual trust' – development of minimum procedural safeguards

Clearly, the safeguards contained in the evidence-gathering instruments are minimal and contain no specific procedural safeguards for suspects and defendants. It has come to be understood that mutual recognition can only function effectively if there is mutual trust between the Member States that their respective systems will meet the requirements for protection of the rights of their nationals.

In everyday relationships, trust is achieved through a process of coming to know one another. It would be a huge imposition to have each Member State know precisely the details of the legal systems of all the jurisdictions throughout the European Union, so the approach to achieving mutual trust is to adopt a position where all Member States can know and trust the other by the fact that all States adhere to a common standard, a set of minimum rules in the area of specific procedural rights for suspects.[94] In the words of the Commission: 'This trust depends on adherence to sufficiently high fair trial standards and the availability of effective defence rights across the EU. Where this trust is found to be wanting, mutual recognition will not work.'[95] Achieving this has been a slow and arduous process, as yet not fully realised.

91. Article 18(2), EEW.
92. Article 21(6)(c), EIO.
93. Article 21(6)(e), EIO.
94. Common minimum standards were first demanded in the Programme of Measures to Implement the Principle of Mutual Recognition in Criminal Matters [2001] OJ C 12/10.
95. Commission, Impact assessment accompanying the Proposal for a directive on the right to information in criminal proceedings, Brussels, 20/7/2010, SEC (2010) 907, 10.

The process of developing common standards was initiated in 2003 by the publication of a Green Paper by the Commission on procedural safeguards for suspects and defendants.[96] While accepting that common standards exist under the ECHR to which all Member States are signatories, it was considered that Member States operated divergent practices that hindered mutual trust, therefore action at the EU level was justified 'to promote a "European best practice" aimed at facilitating and rendering more efficient and visible the practical operation of these rights'.[97]

Five 'basic rights' were identified as being so fundamental to a right to a fair trial that they should be given priority and these were contained in a Proposal for a Framework Decision on procedural rights in criminal proceedings.[98] The proposed Framework Decision had a dual aim: to improve levels of compliance of Member States with their ECHR obligations and to promote confidence in Member States in the criminal justice systems of each Member State. The Commission's stated intention was not to duplicate the provisions of the ECHR but to 'promote compliance at a consistent standard ... by orchestrating agreement between the Member States on a Union wide approach to a "fair trial"'.[99]

The Proposal set out 'common minimum standards' in five key areas: (a) access to legal advice, both before the trial and at trial; (b) access to free interpretation and translation; (c) ensuring that persons who are incapable of understanding or following proceedings receive appropriate attention; (d) the right to communicate; (e) notification of rights through the provision to all suspects of a written 'Letter of Rights'. Other rights, such as the right to silence, were not included as it was considered that it would be difficult to get agreement on the Framework Decision if they were to be included in the 'first step' stage.[100] The scope of the procedural rights extended to 'all proceedings taking place within the European Union aiming to establish the guilt or innocence of a person suspected of having committed a criminal offence'.[101] It therefore applied not just to criminal proceedings with a cross-border dimension but also to purely domestic proceedings.

While the rights proposed by the Framework Decision appeared laudable, nonetheless as the Proposal evolved, it met with increasing opposition from various Member States. There followed protracted discussions, redrafts and

96. Commission, Green Paper on certain procedural safeguards for suspects and defendants in criminal proceedings throughout the European Union, COM (2003) 75.
97. Ibid., 1.7.
98. Proposal for a Framework Decision on certain procedural rights in criminal proceedings throughout the European Union, COM (2004) 328.
99. Ibid., 3.
100. The right to silence and rights in relation to fairness in the gathering and handling of evidence were later the subject of a Commission Green Paper on the presumption of innocence, COM (2006) 174.
101. Article 1, Proposal on procedural rights (see note 98).

more redrafts. Two fundamental objections to the Proposal dominated the negotiations: one related to grounding the legal basis in Article 31(c), TEU because its remit encompassed domestic cases with no cross-border dimension; the other concerned the possibility of confusion and conflict with the ECHR.[102] Despite a number of compromise proposals submitted by various Member State groupings,[103] eventually the original Proposal was abandoned.[104]

As the legislative process then stood, being a Third Pillar instrument the Proposal required unanimity in order to be adopted. The Lisbon Treaty now provides for adoption of (most) criminal justice measures through a majority vote. This change in legislative procedure, together with a change in the 'wider legal landscape',[105] most notably more precise rulings from the ECtHR on the particular right of access to a lawyer, spurred on further initiatives from the Commission for the creation of common procedural rights and, within this, a common approach to admissibility (or rather inadmissibility) where certain procedural rights are breached.

The Commission argued for the desirability of common procedural standards being adopted at EU level despite the fact that rights are already safeguarded by the ECHR. While the Commission accepted that Article 6, ECHR, in particular the rights of defence, have been interpreted by the ECtHR in a way that 'has progressively extended the concrete rights an individual may derive from them', it considered that some particular issues remain unclear, in particular the consequences of a violation of the right of access to a lawyer.[106] Other arguments from the insufficiency of the ECHR perspective are that the system of protection granted by the ECtHR is *ex post* only, and the delay involved in reaching final resolution of ECtHR cases results in a remedy being achieved many years after the violation occurred; in addition, the expense involved may act as a barrier to complainants whose rights were violated. This would be resolved by an EU directive because it would be applicable in the domestic courts and would take primacy over conflicting domestic provisions. Questions of violations could be referred to the ECJ for preliminary rulings during the course of national proceedings rather than having to take the long road to the ECtHR after exhaustion of domestic remedies.

102. States raising this objection were: the United Kingdom, Ireland, the Czech Republic, Malta, Slovakia and Cyprus.
103. Draft compromise Proposals were drawn up by the Austrian Presidency, 19/05/2006, 9600/06 DROIPEN 36; Finnish Presidency, 27/09/06 13116/06 DROIPEN 60; German Presidency, 22/12/06 16874/06 DROIPEN 76.
104. Press release, 2807th Council meeting, JHA, Luxembourg, 12–13 June 2007.
105. J. Hodgson, 'Safeguarding Suspects' Rights in Europe: A Comparative Perspective' (2011) 14 *New Criminal Law Review* 612.
106. Commission, Impact assessment accompanying the Proposal for a Directive on the right of access to a lawyer in criminal proceedings and on the right to communicate upon arrest, 8 June 2011, SEC (2011) 686, 18.

The Commission also argued that developing rights at national level based on the case law of the ECtHR 'at best promotes piecemeal and ad hoc pressure to reform national practice' and pointed to the inconsistency of interpretation of ECtHR decisions between the Member States. The Commission highlights as an example of this the groundbreaking decision of the ECtHR in *Salduz*,[107] which 'demonstrates the inherent limits of the dialectics ECHR/Member States'.[108] In short, being party to the ECHR 'in itself does not always provide a sufficient degree of trust in the criminal justice systems of other Member States'.[109]

The argument is therefore made that EU-wide procedures would give added value to the protection available under the ECHR, provide consistency in their interpretation and ensure compliance with fair trial rights.

2.4.3 Latest developments in providing common procedural rights

The European Council created a new impetus for the development of a common approach to procedural rights for suspects and defendants in 2010. In the Stockholm Programme,[110] the European Council reiterated the importance of mutual trust stating 'the Union should continue to enhance mutual trust in the legal systems of the Member States by establishing minimum rights as necessary for the development of the principle of mutual recognition'.[111] It considered that 'a certain level of approximation of laws is necessary to foster a common understanding of issues among judges and prosecutors'[112] and adopted an earlier Resolution of the Council on a Roadmap for strengthening procedural rights of suspected or accused persons in criminal proceedings.[113]

In that Resolution, the Council invited the Commission to submit Proposals in relation to five of the six measures listed in the Roadmap.[114] The five measures are:

- Measure A: Translation and Interpretation
- Measure B: Information on Rights and Information about the Charges

107. *Salduz v Turkey* [GC] no. 36391/02 ECHR 2008, paras 53–55).
108. Impact assessment (see note 106), 20.
109. Recital 6 'compromise text' proposal access to a lawyer, Note from Presidency to Coreper, Brussels, 31 May 2013, Interinstitutional File: 2011/0154 (COD) 10190/13.
110. European Council, The Stockholm Programme – an open and secure Europe serving and protecting citizens [2010] OJ C 115/1.
111. Ibid., 12.
112. Ibid., 14.
113. European Council Resolution of 30 November [2009] OJ C 295/1.
114. The Roadmap is a non-exhaustive list of measures – the European Council suggested the Commission should also examine other measures to promote better cooperation, for example the presumption of innocence.

- Measure C: Legal Aid and Legal Advice
- Measure D: Communication with Relatives, Employers and Consular Authorities
- Measure E: Special Safeguards for Vulnerable Persons

(a) Translation and interpretation

The first of these measures, considered to be the easiest to achieve, has now been adopted.[115] The Directive provides suspects and accused persons with the right to an interpreter as soon as they have been made aware that they are suspected of having committed a criminal offence, and the right continues through to the final disposal of the case, including any appeals. In addition, suspected or accused persons are to be provided with a written translation of all documents 'which are essential to ensure that they are able to exercise their right of defence and to safeguard the fairness of the proceedings'.[116]

(b) Right to information about rights

The second measure on the Roadmap, the right to information in criminal proceedings, has also been adopted.[117] The Directive addresses two sets of rights to information: information about procedural rights and information about the charges. Mindful of the objections to the earlier 2004 Proposal on procedural rights which were raised about a potential clash with the ECHR, the Commission has been very anxious to underline that the Directive is no more than a clear statement of those rights found under the ECHR and its associated jurisprudence, especially under Article 6 of the Convention. By making the rights more explicit, it is hoped that the overall result will create better compliance with the fair trial rights provided by the ECHR. The benefit would also lie in the fact that remedies to breaches would be available to a person early on in the proceedings, rather than have breaches remedied after remedies in domestic courts have been exhausted followed finally by an appeal to the ECtHR.[118]

The Directive creates the right to information about rights at the EU level, so as to make more explicit those rights such as they exist under the ECHR

115. Directive 2010/64/EU of the European Parliament and of the Council on the right to interpretation and translation in criminal proceedings [2010] OJ L 280/1; deadline for transposition: 27/10/2013; Ireland and UK have opted to apply the Directive.
116. Article 3; the costs of interpretation and translation are to be met by the Member States concerned.
117. Directive 2012/13/EU of the European Parliament and of the Council on the right to information in criminal proceedings [2012] OJ L 142/1; deadline for transposition: 2/6/2014; Ireland announced its wish to participate in the Directive (3034th Council meeting, Justice and Home Affairs, Luxembourg, 7–8 October 2010, Press Release).
118. Impact assessment (see note 106) 19.

and following the case law of the ECtHR. Article 5(2) of the ECHR provides: 'Everyone who is arrested shall be informed promptly, in a language which he understands, of the reasons for his arrest and of any charge against him' and Article 6(3) of the ECHR provides:

> Everyone charged with a criminal offence has the following minimum rights:
> (a) to be informed promptly, in a language which he understands and in detail, of the nature and cause of the accusation against him;
> (b) to have adequate time and facilities for the preparation of his defence.

While the ECHR does not explicitly mention the right to information about rights, the Commission considered that the proposed Directive did not create any entirely new rights and that the means of informing suspects of their rights envisaged under the Proposal through a Letter of Rights reflected current ECHR minimum standards of fair trial rights.[119] The Directive does not lay down any sanction where a suspect has not been informed of his rights by the authorities. As originally proposed, Member States were required to provide an effective remedy, leaving it to each Member State to decide on the consequences of a breach of the right according to their own rules of criminal procedure.[120]

Under the Directive as adopted it now provides that:[121]

> Suspects or accused persons or their lawyers have the right to challenge, in accordance with procedures in national law, the possible failure or refusal of the competent authorities to provide information in accordance with this Directive.[122]

The rights would be activated from the time that a person is made aware that he is suspected or accused of having committed a criminal offence and apply to both domestic and cross-border criminal cases. Member State authorities

119. Commission Proposal for a Directive on the right to information in criminal proceedings, COM (2010) 392. The Commission relies on case law in relation to the issue of providing information about legal aid and the right to legal assistance citing: *Padalov v Bulgaria* 54784/00 (ECtHR 10/8/2006); *Talat Tunc v Turkey* 32432/96 (ECtHR 27/3/2007); *Panovits v Cyprus* 4268/04 (ECtHR 11/12/2008).
120. Article 8, Commission Proposal for a Directive on the right to information in criminal proceedings (note 119).
121. Directive 2012/13/EU of the European Parliament and of the Council of 22/5/2012 on the right to information in criminal proceedings [2012] OJ L 142/1.
122. Ibid., Article 8; it is also provided in Recital 36 'That right does not entail the obligation for Member States to provide for a specific appeal procedure, a separate mechanism, or a complaint procedure in which such failure or refusal may be challenged'.

would be required to inform suspects of the following rights, as they apply under national law:

1. the right of access to a lawyer, and any entitlements to free legal advice;
2. the right to be informed of the accusation;
3. the right to interpretation and translation;
4. the right to remain silent.

As originally proposed, it did not include the right to silence since on the basis of research studies which had informed the creation of the Proposal, the right to silence is a qualified right in some Member States.[123] The arrested person should be given the information 'promptly' by means of a Letter of Rights, which must also contain information about the following rights as they apply under national law:

1. the right of access to the materials of the case;
2. the right to have consular authorities and one person informed;
3. the right of access to urgent medical assistance; and
4. the maximum number of hours or days suspects or accused persons may be deprived of liberty before being brought before a judicial authority.

As originally proposed, the right to information about the charge was to be further effected by giving the accused and his legal advisers access to the 'case-file'. The jurisprudence of the ECtHR requires that all material evidence for or against the accused be disclosed so as not to give the prosecution an unfair advantage over the defence when it comes to the trial. This is required under the *equality of arms* principle.[124] The Directive makes the right to disclosure more specific. The original version envisaged access to the case-file being given to suspects or their lawyers where the investigation of the crime has concluded. There was no definition of the 'case-file' in the Proposal and it was recognised that the term was subject to different interpretation by different Member States.[125] Indeed, it was noted by the Council that 'one of

123. The Commission has funded a number of studies into criminal procedural rights and draws heavily from that of T. Sproken and G. Vermeulen, *EU Procedural Rights in Criminal Proceedings* (Intersentia 2009); E. Cape, J. Hodgson, T. Prakken and T. Sproken, *Suspects in Europe* (Intersentia 2007); E. Cape, Z. Namoradze *et al.*, *Effective Criminal Defence in Europe* (Intersentia 2010); T. Spronken, *An EU-Wide Letter of Rights – Towards Best Practice* (Intersentia 2010).

124. *Edwards v United Kingdom* 16 December 1992, Series A, no. 247; *Jasper v United Kingdom* [GC] 27052/95 (ECtHR 16/2/2000).

125. Caroline Morgan (member of Judicial Cooperation in Criminal Matters Unit, European Commission): 'The Draft Directive on the Right to Information in Criminal Proceedings', paper given at ERA Conference, *Guaranteeing Procedural Safeguards in the EU – A First Step Taken*, Trier, 18–19 November 2010.

the main difficulties in devising a Directive on the right to information lies in taking account of the various legal systems, especially the differences between civil law and common law countries'.[126]

The adopted version now refers to a right of access to 'materials of the case' and requires Member States to make available to the arrested person or his lawyer:

> documents related to the specific case in the possession of the competent authorities which are essential to challenging effectively, in accordance with national law, the lawfulness of the arrest or detention …

and to ensure that:

> access is granted at least to all material evidence in the possession of the competent authorities, whether for or against suspects or accused persons, to those persons or their lawyers in order to safeguard the fairness of the proceedings and to prepare the defence.[127]

The Directive would give courts the power to refuse access to certain documents and evidence in the file where the life or fundamental rights of another person may be at risk, where it might prejudice ongoing investigations or where there are national security implications.[128]

(c) Right to legal advice

Two further measures on the Roadmap, the right to legal advice and the right to communicate with relatives, employers and consular authorities, were included in a proposed Directive from the Commission.[129] For the first time, the Commission threw down the gauntlet for a EU-wide rule on the exclusion of evidence obtained in breach of the provisions for access to a lawyer. The Proposal, in its original draft, provided that Member States must provide an effective remedy where a person's right of access to a lawyer has been breached, and that remedy 'shall have the effect of placing the suspect or

126. 3043rd Council meeting, Justice and Home Affairs, Brussels, 8 and 9 November 2010, Press release.
127. Directive 2012/13/EU of the European Parliament and of the Council on the right to information in criminal proceedings [2012] OJ L 142/1, Article 7.
128. Ibid., Article 7(4).
129. Proposal access to a lawyer (see note 35); see also Impact assessment (see note 106); the UK and Ireland will not use their 'opt-in' (in application of Article 3 of Protocol 21 to the Lisbon Treaty), but will constructively participate in the work on the draft directive with a view to being able to accept the measure once it has been adopted (in application of Article 4 of the Protocol): Press release 3111th Council meeting, Justice and Home Affairs, Brussels, 22–23 September 2011, Press release 14464/11.

accused person in the same position in which he would have found himself had the breach not occurred'. The Proposal then specifically provided that statements obtained in breach of the right of access to a lawyer, even in a case where there has been a permitted derogation from the right, 'may not be used at any stage of the procedure as evidence against him, unless the use of such evidence would not prejudice the rights of the defence'.[130]

The Commission justified this rule in the following terms:

> Only in three Member States (Spain, Italy, Portugal), it is not allowed to use as evidence in court statements made by a suspect in the absence of his lawyer. The lack of a prohibition to use such evidence in court is conducive to lengthy litigation (and possible appeals to the ECtHR), which in turn affects the credibility of the justice system and is liable to generate mistrust in judicial authorities from other Member States.[131]

This clause is similar to an amendment to the original 2003 Commission Proposal on procedural rights by the European Parliament that proposed the inclusion of a provision to the effect that failure to comply with the obligation to provide legal advice 'shall invalidate all subsequent acts and those dependant on them throughout the criminal proceedings'; that amendment, however, was not carried.[132]

The Commission found support for the proposition of inadmissibility of the statements by reference to recent ECtHR jurisprudence. It noted that ECtHR case-law has so far not touched on the precise consequences of a violation of the right of access to a lawyer other than to systematically hold that 'it is up to the national authorities to undo the adverse consequences of any such violation, by placing the person in the same position he would have found himself had the violation not occurred'.[133] Although the ECtHR has consistently stated that admissibility is a matter for the national courts, nonetheless the Commission suggested that recent judgments have added further clarity to the consequences that may result for breach of the right of access to a lawyer. In *Salduz v Turkey* the ECtHR held that there had been a violation of Article 6 of the ECHR where a suspect was denied legal assistance while in police custody and made a confession that he claimed at trial was made under duress. The court stated:

130. Article 13, Proposal, access to a lawyer (see note 35).
131. Impact assessment (see note 106).
132. Amendments proposed in the European Parliament Report on the Proposal for a Council framework decision on certain procedural rights in criminal proceedings throughout the European Union A6-0064/2005, 8; the view of the Committee on Legal Affairs was that any infringement of the minimum rights contained in the Proposal should result in invalidation of procedural acts: Ibid. 31.
133. Impact assessment (see note 106) 18.

> The rights of the defence will in principle be irretrievably prejudiced when incriminating statements made during police interrogation without access to a lawyer are used for a conviction.[134]

In *Panovits v Cyprus*, the ECtHR found that the lack of assistance during the applicant's interrogation breached his right to a fair trial guaranteed by Article 6 of the ECHR. It also held that there had been a violation of Article 6(1) due to the use of the applicant's confession in his trial.[135]

The Commission was supported in the idea of an exclusionary rule by the Council of Europe. The opinion from the Secretariat of the Council suggested the rule be strengthened by providing better clarity.[136] The rule in the Proposal appeared in two articles. One of these referred to the situation where a witness becomes a suspect during the course of questioning by authorities, providing that in such a situation the person should be given access to a lawyer and 'Member States shall ensure that any statement made by such person before he is made aware that he is a suspect or an accused person may not be used against him'.[137] The other article under the heading of 'remedies' provided that all Member States should ensure an effective remedy where the right of access is breached and stated:

> The remedy shall have the effect of placing the suspect or accused person in the same position in which he would have found himself had the breach not occurred. Member States shall ensure that statements made by the suspect or accused person or evidence obtained in breach of his right to a lawyer or in cases where a derogation to this right was authorised in accordance with Article 8, may not be used at any stage of the procedure as evidence against him, unless the use of such evidence would not prejudice the rights of the defence.[138]

The rule was also stated in a Recital which provided that authorised derogations from the right 'should not prejudice the right to a fair trial and in particular should never lead to statements made by the suspect or accused person in the absence of his lawyer to be used to secure his conviction'.[139]

The Opinion of the Secretariat of the Council suggested that the first provision 'seems to duly reflect' the decision in *Salduz*. It suggested the Recital should be clarified and strengthened by the inclusion of a prohibition on use of statements not just in derogation situations but also where the rights of

134. *Salduz* (see note 107) 53–5.
135. *Panovits v Cyprus* 4268/04 (ECtHR 11/12/2008) 69–77.
136. Opinion of the Secretariat on the Commission's Proposal, Council of Europe: Strasbourg, 9/11/2011.
137. Article 10, Proposal access to a lawyer (see note 35).
138. Ibid., Article 13.
139. Ibid., Recital 17.

access have been breached. It also suggested that the inclusion of the final phrase: 'unless the use of such evidence would not prejudice the rights of the defence', was circular and should be omitted. Citing the statement in *Salduz* that the 'rights of the defence will in principle be irretrievably prejudiced when incriminating statements made during police interrogation without access to a lawyer are used for a conviction', the Opinion reasoned:

> If there is in principle an irrefutable presumption that the use of evidence will prejudice the right of access to a lawyer, it is difficult to apply a provision which prohibits the use of such evidence unless defence rights are not prejudiced.

The opinion also cautioned against repeated reference to national law since it 'may affect the effectiveness of these instruments as regards the harmonisation of the legal systems of EU Member States and, ultimately, the consistency of the rules with the ECHR standards as implemented in Member States'.

The response of Member States to the prohibition on the use of statements obtained in breach of the right of access was, by contrast with the Council of Europe, in quite the opposite direction and it was noted that the provision was considered to be 'very problematic'.[140] As the Proposal has moved through the legislative negotiations it has become clear that Member States believe that judges should be free to decide the question of the value to be given to statements obtained in breach of the right of access to a lawyer rather than the blanket rule set out in the Proposal.[141]

It was also considered that the provision is too broad in that the Proposal comprises not just statements but also 'material evidence' such as might result from a search and seizure. On that basis concern has been expressed that 'extending the scope of the evidence ban to material evidence might undermine the efficacy of the criminal proceedings', and the preferred approach was to leave it to the national courts to decide which material could be used as evidence on the basis that 'the ECtHR always looks at a case as a "whole" to verify compliance with the ECHR, including the way in which evidence is obtained'.[142]

140. Note from Presidency to Delegations – Follow-up of the WP meeting on 26 July and CATS on 6 September, Brussels, 9/9/2011, Interinstitutional File: 2011/0154 (COD) 13360/11.
141. It is unclear from the document which Member States held this view; none are specifically mentioned: Proposal for a Directive on the right of access to a lawyer – Orientation debate, Note from Presidency to Coreper/Council, 14/10/2011, Interinstitutional File: 2011/0154 (COD) 15533/11; allowing the judge to decide the issue is also the view of prosecutors in Europe: Consultative forum of prosecutors general and directors of public prosecutors of Member States of EU Progress Report of 6/12/2011, Note from General Secretariat to Delegations, Brussels, 30/1/2012, Interinstitutional File: 2011/0154 (COD) 5894/12.
142. Note from Presidency to Delegations – Follow-up of the WP meeting on 26 July and CATS on 6 September, Brussels, 9/9/2011, Interinstitutional File: 2011/0154 (COD) 13360/11.

A group of Member States indicated that they had 'serious reservations' about the Commission's approach on the basis that it would present substantial difficulties for the effective conduct of criminal proceedings by their investigating, prosecuting and judicial authorities', noting that the Commission's Proposal 'does not take into account the differences which exist between different systems and between different types and stages of proceedings'.[143] This group, which included Ireland and France, came from both sides of the common law civil law divide. The financial and human resources required to implement the provision were cited as reasons to amend the draft; it was also considered that the Commission Proposal was too ambitious, and that it went unnecessarily beyond the ECHR as interpreted in the jurisprudence of the ECtHR.

The Directive has finally been adopted, reflecting a 'compromise text' agreed at the final trilogue. This contains a much watered-down provision to address the remedy for breach of the right of access to a lawyer.[144] The article simply provides:

1. Member States shall ensure that a suspects or accused persons in criminal proceedings as well as requested persons in European Arrest Warrant proceedings have an effective remedy under national law in instances where their rights under this Directive have been breached.
2. Without prejudice to national rules and systems on the admissibility of evidence, Member States shall ensure that, in criminal proceedings, in the assessment of statements made by a suspect or accused person or of evidence obtained in breach of his right to a lawyer or in cases where a derogation to this right was authorised in accordance with Art. 3(6), the rights of the defence and the fairness of the proceedings are respected.[145]

The closest the Directive comes to reaching a common admissibility rule is through the reminder to Member States contained in a Recital of the ECtHR principle that 'the rights of the defence will in principle be irretrievably prejudiced when incriminating statements made during police interrogation without access to a lawyer are used for a conviction', the sub-text being that such statements should be inadmissible as evidence. However, the Recital then goes on to state that the assessment of such statements should be 'without prejudice to national rules or systems regarding admissibility of evidence, and should not prevent Member States from maintaining a system whereby

143. Proposal for a Directive on the right of access to a lawyer, Note by Belgium, France, Ireland, the Netherlands and the UK to Council of European Union 22/9/2011, Interinstitutional File: 2011/0154 (COD) 14495/11.

144. Directive of the European Parliament and of the Council on the right of access to a lawyer in criminal proceedings and on the right to communicate upon arrest [2013] OJ L 294/1, deadline for transposition: 27/11/2016.

145. Ibid., Article 12.

all existing evidence can be adduced before a court or a judge, without there being any separate or prior assessment as to admissibility of such evidence'.[146]

(d) Scope of the right to legal advice

The Directive applies as soon as a person is made aware by the authorities that he is suspected or accused of committing an offence and this is regardless of whether he is deprived of liberty.[147] The Directive, like all other measures on the Roadmap, extends to both domestic and cross-border cases.[148] During the negotiations on the Commission Proposal, the Presidency dispatched a questionnaire to all Member States in an effort to amend provisions so that account could be taken of the differences in procedures regarding access to a lawyer.[149]

The Directive sets out in detail what the right of access would consist of: access must be granted 'without undue delay' and must be granted before being interviewed by the authorities.[150] It is left to Member States to determine the investigative acts that a person has the right for his lawyer to attend, but if the legal system includes procedures of identity parades, confrontations or experimental reconstructions of the scene of crime, and involve the suspect's participation, the suspect 'shall as a minimum have the right for his lawyer to attend'.[151] Member States may make 'practical arrangements' regarding the duration and frequency of meetings by the suspect or accused with a lawyer but these arrangements must not be so limited as to prejudice the 'effective exercise and essence' of the suspect or accused person's right to meet with a lawyer.[152]

The Directive is groundbreaking in so far as it embraces the right of the suspect or accused to have a lawyer present during any questioning.[153] The Commission in its original Proposal derived support for this position from recent ECtHR case law, in particular *Salduz* and the later case of *Dayanan*.[154]

146. Ibid., Recital 50.
147. Ibid., Article 2(1).
148. The Directive also specifically extends protection to persons subject to an EAW: Article 2(2); the Directive applies to minor offences in cases where a person is deprived of their liberty: Article 2(4).
149. See responses in Note from General Secretariat to Working Party on Substantive Criminal Law 2/2/2012, Interinstitutional File: 2011/0154 (COD) 5897/12.
150. Directive Access to lawyer (see note 144), Article 3; authorities include police or other law enforcement or judicial authorities.
151. Ibid., Article 3(3)(c)
152. Ibid., Recital 23; all forms of communication between the suspect or accused person and the lawyer must be confidential (Article 4).
153. Ibid., Article 3(3)(b).
154. *Dayanan v Turquie* no. 7377/03 (ECtHR 13/10/2009); at para. 32 the Court stated 'an accused person is entitled, as soon as he or she is taken into custody, to be assisted by a lawyer, and *not only while being questioned*' (emphasis added).

It therefore offers some clarity to *Salduz* and the subsequent line of decisions of the ECtHR, which has been subject to differing interpretation by some Member States.[155] It was held in *Salduz* that Article 6 of the ECHR 'requires that, as a rule, access to a lawyer should be provided as from the first interrogation of a suspect by the police'.

There is some ambiguity in that statement, in so far as it is not absolutely clear whether 'as from the first interrogation' embraces a requirement of the actual presence of a lawyer during the interrogations, or whether it extends simply to providing suspects with a right to consult with a lawyer from that period of time onwards, meaning that interrogations could be *interrupted* to allow for such access. As will be seen in later chapters, Ireland has not interpreted *Salduz* to require the presence of a lawyer during questioning while France by contrast has changed its procedures to specifically provide for the presence of a lawyer during the interrogation process. The Directive therefore provides absolute clarity for this aspect of access to a lawyer.

As originally drafted, the Proposal was specific in the role that a lawyer would play during interrogations, in that the lawyer 'would have the right to ask questions, seek clarification and make statements'.[156] This provision was strongly objected to by Belgium, who expressed its concern that the provision as worded would have the effect of changing the fundamentals of its criminal procedure that is 'characterised by an inquisitorial system'. It failed to take account of the other procedural guarantees of fairness contained in their system, specifically the role of an impartial investigating judge who must investigate *à charge et à décharge* (both for and against the suspect), and the obligation on the investigating judge and the public prosecutor to ensure fairness in the gathering of evidence.[157]

As a result of these and earlier objections,[158] the provision has been weakened in the Directive. The Member States should ensure that the suspect or accused has the right for a lawyer to 'participate effectively when he is questioned', but then goes on to provide that such participation 'shall be in

155. By way of examples, England already provides for the presence of a lawyer during questioning; Scotland has followed the same route as France, which has amended the law to provide for the presence of the lawyer during questioning; Italy already requires a lawyer to be present for police questioning, but not for questioning by a prosecutor and has made no amendments in this regard; Ireland provides for questioning to be postponed until the arrival of the lawyer, or at least for a reasonable period, but does not permit the presence of a lawyer during police questioning, under s. 9 of the Criminal Justice Act 2011, but the section is not yet in force. This section will not be commenced until regulations are in place to set out the details of how this new regime of access to a lawyer will operate.

156. Article 4(2) and Recital 10, Proposal access to a lawyer (see note 35).

157. Note from Belgian Delegation to Working Party on Substantive Criminal Law 13/3/2012, Interinstitutional File: 2011/0154 (COD) 7593/12.

158. Earlier objections along similar lines were stated in the Note by Belgium, France, Ireland, the Netherlands and the UK to Council of European Union, Interinstitutional File: 2011/0154 (COD) 14495/11.

accordance with procedures in national law'.[159] A Recital provides that national law may regulate the participation of the lawyer during questioning, provided that such rules do not prejudice the 'effective exercise and essence of the right', and the Recital somewhat vaguely suggests that such rules would provide that a lawyer may 'ask questions, request clarification and make statements' during questioning.[160]

The Directive does not go so far as to make access to a lawyer obligatory, but provides that the right may not be waived unless the suspect clearly understands the extent of the right and the consequences of waiving it, and waives the right voluntarily and unequivocally.[161] The Directive follows the ECtHR jurisprudence that the right of access to a lawyer is not absolute by including the possibility for temporary derogation from the right in exceptional circumstances, subject to necessity and to procedural safeguards.[162] Systematic derogation on the basis of type or seriousness of offence is not expressly prohibited, but derogation may not be based exclusively on those grounds.[163] Situations foreseen as justifying temporary derogations include: 'when there is a need, in cases of urgency, to avert serious adverse consequences for the life, liberty or physical integrity of a person, or to prevent substantial jeopardy to criminal proceedings'.[164]

The Directive would also require that any derogation must be authorised by a reasoned decision of 'a judicial authority, or by another competent authority on condition that the decision can be subject to judicial review'.[165] The police would therefore not be precluded from taking a decision to derogate from the right. A similar derogation clause applies to the right of suspects or accused persons to have 'at least one person' informed that they have been detained and to the right to communicate with that person.[166]

2.5 Conclusion

This chapter has examined the development of the mutual recognition project of the EU and has highlighted the difficulties encountered in reaching agreement, most especially in the area of mutual admissibility of evidence and adherence to common minimum standards of procedural rights. The change

159. Article 3(3)(b) Directive (see note 144).
160. Ibid., Recital 25.
161. Ibid., Article 9; this follows ECtHR jurisprudence, *Talat Tunc v Turkey* 32432/96 (ECtHR 27/3/2007); *S aman v Turkey* 35292/05 (ECtHR 5/4/2011) 32.
162. Article 3(6), Recital 39; *Salduz* (see note 106) 53–55; *Öcalan v Turkey* [GC] no. 46221/99 ECHR 2005-IV; *Adamkiewicz v Poland* 54729/00 (ECtHR 2/3/2010) 84; *Dayanan v Turquie* 7377/03 (ECtHR 13/10/2009) 32; *Brusco v France* 1466/07 (ECtHR 14/10/2010).
163. Article 8(c) Directive (see note 144).
164. Ibid., Article 3(6).
165. Ibid., Article 8(2).
166. Ibid., Articles 5 and 6.

brought about to the legislative procedure of the EU by the Lisbon Treaty, together with the opt-in mechanisms for the common law countries of Ireland and the UK would appear to have somewhat accelerated the pace at which the instruments are being negotiated.

However, while the mutual recognition principle attempts to tolerate the diversity of legal systems, there is a resistance by Member States to aspects that are seen by some as changing the fundamentals of their criminal procedure, as the objections of Belgium to specific provisions of the proposed Directive on access to a lawyer have demonstrated. This would suggest that the difficulties facing the mutual recognition project stem not only from the broad differences that arise as between the common law and civil law countries, but also from countries within the civil law tradition being unwilling to tolerate any radical change to their system. It should also be remembered that the mutual recognition project, in contrast to the MLA regime, impinges upon the traditional sovereignty enjoyed by Member States in criminal justice matters, and this, along with resource implications (financial and human) of the Directives, was undoubtedly a factor contributing to the slow progress of the mutual recognition instruments.[167]

Should the EIO Proposed Directive be adopted, it will allow for all types of evidence to be gathered in one Member State for use in proceedings in another Member State. The instrument, however, is solely directed at creating a regime for evidence gathering and transfer, and makes no attempt to address the vital issue of admissibility. Nor does it address the problem of the use of hearsay evidence at trial. This is justified on the basis that it is only concerned with evidence gathering and transfer, and not with the subsequent use of the evidence at trial.

It has been suggested that the 'duty of national courts is to keep pace with the Strasbourg jurisprudence as it evolves over time: no more, but certainly no less'.[168] It has also been remarked that the sentence could as well have ended: 'no less, but certainly no more'.[169] Given the varying adherence to ECHR standards by Member States it is perhaps plausible to say that adherence to the Strasbourg jurisprudence is a case of 'more or less but not quite', and as such, a clear regime of common standards of procedural rights that would be provided by the EU instruments outlined in this chapter is laudable. Nonetheless, the procedural safeguards have been weakened as negotiations on the various Proposals have progressed. The ambition to establish a meaningful common standard for access to a lawyer has been thwarted – and by extension, so also

167. For a thoughtful account of the tension between a supranational order and state sovereignty see A. Arnull *et al.* (eds), *A Constitutional Order of States? Essays in EU Law in Honour of Alan Dashwood* (Hart 2011); see also Mitsilegas (see note 28) and Hinarejos *et al.* (see note 84) 165.

168. Lord Kerr in *Ambrose v HM Advocate* [2011] UKSC 43, citing Lord Bingham in *R (Ullah) v Special Adjudicator* [2004] UKHL 26.

169. Per Lord Brown in *R (Al-Skeini and others) v Secretary of State for Defence* [2007] UKHL 26.

a meaningful common standard of admissibility of statements – given that it is left to national procedures to regulate the level of participation a lawyer may enjoy during interviews by authorities.

While the Lisbon Treaty puts the issue of mutual admissibility of evidence squarely on the agenda, it is clear that the EU instruments adopted to date have so far not succeeded in achieving this goal. The one attempt by the Commission to set down an EU-wide inadmissibility rule regarding statements made in the absence of a lawyer was met with strong resistance, a resistance that appears to stem from the make-up of the EU of legal systems originating from the two broad inquisitorial and accusatorial traditions.

Part of the reason for the failure perhaps lies in the fact that the mutual recognition instruments adopted to date have broached only two sides of the triangle that is involved in evidence law: the instruments have been directed at the aspect of gathering evidence and the aspect of safeguarding the suspect's rights when gathering the evidence, but have left untouched the issue of how the evidence is presented and contested. It is chiefly in that aspect of criminal procedure that the whole question of admissibility comes to the fore. That aspect therefore needs to be addressed if an aspiration to mutual admissibility is to be realised.

However, it may be that it is precisely that aspect which poses the greatest obstacle to mutual admissibility since it is here that a vital difference arises between the systems. This difference emerges from the practice in some jurisdictions of a procedure operating in accordance with a principle of *contradictoire* and others (principally the common law jurisdictions) following a procedure that is 'adversarial'. The idea of 'admissibility' has different connotations in each of these contexts, and it is here that a clear contrast emerges between the distinctive nature of exclusionary rules in the common law setting that are designed to shield the fact-finders from certain information as opposed to rules which are more common in continental systems that prohibit the use of evidence, but that do not at the same time necessarily prohibit its presentation to the fact-finders. This factor does not appear to have been taken into account in the Commission Proposal for the EPPO.

The three facets of evidence law: gathering evidence, rights of suspects in its gathering, and the reception, presentation, contesting and associated rules of admissibility of evidence, will be addressed in the following chapters in an attempt to identify the extent of diversity in evidence law between legal systems through case studies of criminal procedural systems in Ireland, France and Italy. But first, it is necessary to gain an insight into the development and theoretical underpinnings of the procedural systems examined in this work and their approaches to proof.

3 Theoretical approaches to the comparison of procedural systems

3.1 Introduction

Various approaches may be used for comparing systems of criminal procedure and proof. Since one argument against the possibility of a unified system arises from a cultural perspective, that the legal culture of the common law and civil law jurisdictions is fundamentally different, it is useful to see how the systems of the European Continent and the British Isles have developed over time. One approach is therefore to examine the systems from a historical standpoint. An understanding of the historical evolution of the common law and civil law systems is useful for identifying trends and practices that have featured in the past and to identify the various points of commonality or divergence that have occurred over the centuries.

Another comparative approach that has been advocated by commentators is to explain criminal justice systems by the use of a methodology of 'models'. The models that have been advanced generally follow the Weberian concept of 'ideal types'.[1] As such, it is accepted that systems do not absolutely adhere to the ideal types, but it has been considered that they are nonetheless useful 'to liberate us from the tyranny of details, so that we can discern the overall distinguishing attributes of complex phenomena'.[2] They are useful 'provided it is clearly understood that constructing ideal-typical models should be a starting point, rather than the ultimate destination, of comparative legal analysis'.[3]

The traditional and dominant mode of analysis that has been relied upon in comparative literature, at least as a starting point for inquiry, is the 'inquisitorial' 'accusatorial' dichotomy. Somewhat confusingly, commentators have a tendency to conflate accusatorial with a model of adversarial trial process,

1. Weber's 'ideal type' 'is not a *description* of reality but it aims to give unambiguous means of expression to such a description': M. Weber, 'Objectivity in Social Science', in H. Finch and E. Shils (trans and eds), *The Methodology of the Social Sciences* (Free Press 1949).
2. M. Damaška, 'Structures of Authority and Comparative Criminal Procedure' (1974–5) 84 *Yale LJ* 480, 482.
3. P. Roberts, 'Faces of Justice Adrift?', in J. Jackson, M. Langer and P. Tillers (eds), *Crime, Procedure and Evidence in a Comparative and International Context: Essays in Honour of Prof. Mirjan Damaška* (Hart 2008) 325.

and often use the terms accusatorial and adversarial interchangeably. Damaška has juxtaposed adversarial proceedings with non-adversarial proceedings, which to some extent assists in clarifying the accusatorial adversarial conflation.[4] Another approach advanced in an attempt to break away from the traditional modes of analysis has been to relate the differences between systems to differences in the conception of the organisation of judicial authority between the European continental and the Anglo American world.[5] Damaška suggests that two models of authority may be contrasted which he names the 'hierarchical' and the 'coordinate', that in turn adhere to hierarchical and coordinate models of criminal process.[6]

The first part of this chapter will present an outline of the history of criminal procedure and approaches to proof as it developed since Roman times. Space does not permit a detailed analysis of any given period; the purpose here is simply to highlight that the differences between the systems are to some extent rooted in the different designs of criminal procedure adopted across the continent of Europe, most particularly in France, on the one hand, and in the British Isles on the other, from the thirteenth century onwards. It will also serve to demonstrate that the two criminal justice systems have always been in a constant state of flux, and that there have been varying degrees of cross-fertilisation. It will also provide the basis to an understanding of the accusatorial inquisitorial dichotomy that will be discussed in the second part of this chapter. The more current theoretical dichotomy, the adversarial and non-adversarial type procedure, will be examined and Damaška's hierarchical and coordinate models will be outlined.

The chapter will close with a consideration of the usefulness of the models as a theoretical basis for this work. I will suggest that the idea of adversarial procedure has been 'lost in translation' and that the discussion would benefit from an additional typology, the idea of a *procédure contradictoire.*

PART I

3.2 The development of criminal procedural systems and approaches to proof – a historical perspective

Modern procedures of criminal justice can be found to have emerged from procedures that were practised by two dominating powers in Europe, first that of the Roman Empire which extended across much of the European

4. M. Damaška, 'Evidentiary "Barriers" to Conviction and Two Models of Criminal Procedure: A Comparative Study' (1973) 121 *U. Pa. L. Rev.* 506, 562; M. Damaška, *Evidence Law Adrift* (Yale University Press 1997).
5. Damaška, 'Structures' (note 2).
6. See, generally, M. Damaška, *Faces of Justice and State Authority: A Comparative Approach to the Legal Process* (Yale University Press 1986).

continent surviving intact up to the fifth century, at which point the second dominant power took hold on the continent, that of the Germanic peoples. The Roman tradition persisted on the continent of Western Europe through the redevelopment of the Roman law in the twelfth century by Italian Glossators who, incorporating some aspects of the procedures of the church-promulgated Canon Law, created a 'jus commune' throughout continental Europe, often referred to as the 'civil law'.[7] Roman law had a lesser influence on the system that took hold in England that was broadly put in place by the Anglo-Saxon peoples following a Germanic tradition which developed from the twelfth century into the system referred to as the 'common law'.

It has been suggested that the criminal procedure during the period of Republican Rome[8] was accusatory in nature.[9] A criminal prosecution could proceed only on the basis of a formal accusation by an accuser who had to produce evidence to prove his case at an oral and public forum before a popular jury. The accused benefited from a presumption of innocence – indeed this concept has been found to exist even in pre-Roman law in the criminal procedure of Babylon.[10] A practice of cross-examination by an advocate for the accused has been identified and the role of the judge appears to have been relatively passive.[11]

With the coming of the Roman Empire, the procedure incorporated a more systemised method of instituting proceedings on the basis of investigations by officials appointed by the Emperor and while retaining public trial, there was more reliance on the written testimony of witnesses. The popular jury of the Republic disappeared and the presiding judge took an active part in examining the witnesses and the accused. It was in this period also that a law of evidence began to emerge, binding the accuser to certain rules of evidence.[12]

3.2.1 Criminal procedure up to the thirteenth century in France and England: accusatory type procedure in common

The criminal procedure in the feudal courts of France was essentially conceived as an accusatory procedure in that it was a contest between two private

7. A. Padoa-Schioppa, 'A Sketch of Legal History', in J. Lena and U. Mattei, *Introduction to Italian Law* (Kluwer 2002) 4.
8. For a timeline see C. Scarre, *The Penguin Historical Atlas of Ancient Rome* (Penguin 1995) 8–11.
9. See, generally, J. Strachan-Davidson, *Problems of the Roman Criminal Law*, Vols 1 and 2 (Rothman 1991); A. Esmein, *History of Continental Criminal Procedure with Special Reference to France* (Little, Brown 1913) Ch. II.
10. F. Quintard-Morenas, 'The Presumption of Innocence in the French and Anglo-American Legal Traditions' (2010) 58 (1) *Am. J. Comp. L.* 107.
11. Strachan-Davidson (note 9) 113–15.
12. C. Morrison, 'Some Features of the Roman and the English Law of Evidence' (1958–9) 33 (3) *Tul. L. Rev.* 577.

parties, the accuser and the accused. The accusation was made orally in a precise form, and the accused was obliged to refute the accusation through denial of every aspect of the complaint. The accuser had three means of proof open to him: proof by witnesses, proofs by judicial duel or proofs by ordeal.

In the case of proof by witnesses, two eyewitnesses were required and their testimony was given under oath, orally and in public. The judicial duel was a physical combat between the two private parties, the winner being considered to have justice on his side.[13] The ordeal, practised across Europe from at least the ninth century[14] up to the early thirteenth century, was in effect an appeal to God for judgment. The ordeal was preceded by an accusation before a local popular court which came to a decision as to whether the accusation was well founded. If such was the case, the accused could purge himself through the ordeal, the most common being ordeal by fire, ordeal by water and ordeal by poison.[15] This method of trial was finally prohibited by the Church in 1215 in a decree of the Fourth Lateran Council.

In the same period in England, criminal procedure was that established by the Germanic settlers who had brought their tradition of accusatory trial and popular justice, which was retained and augmented by the Normans following their settlement in England.[16] By the time of Henry II[17] there were two means of bringing a person to trial: through appeal, which was an accusation by a private party proved by means of ordeal or duel; or through the inquest procedure, an institution borrowed from the Frankish kings of the Carlovingian period.[18]

Under the procedure of inquest, the means of proof was the 'verdict of the country'.[19] The Assize of Clarendon extended the inquest, formerly confined to land disputes, to criminal matters by the use of an accusing jury,[20] thus creating a form of public prosecution.[21] This 'jury' consisted of twelve men chosen by the sheriff from the neighbourhood, but unlike the modern form of jury, they were chosen for their means of knowledge of the alleged offence. As soon as they were chosen, they were expected to make their own inquiries, in effect gathering the evidence against the suspect, and have been described as

13. 'Judicial' in that it was judicially sanctioned.
14. J. B. Thayer, *A Preliminary Treatise on Evidence at the Common Law* (Little, Brown 1898) 35, note 1.
15. F. Maitland and F. Montague, J. Colby (ed.), *A Sketch of English Legal History* (Lawbook Exchange 1915) 48–50.
16. Thayer (note 14) Ch. 1.
17. Reigned 1154–89.
18. Circa 800.
19. J. Proffatt, *A Treatise on Trial by Jury including Questions of Law and Fact* (Whitney 1877) 40.
20. Thayer (note 14) 69.
21. M. Kerr, 'Angevin Reform of the Appeal of Felony' (1995) 13 (2) *Law & Hist. Rev.* 351.

'neither exactly accusers, nor exactly witnesses; they are to give voice to common repute'.[22]

Given that the jurors were in some sense also witnesses, the justices[23] could interrogate them as to their means of knowledge, and question them separately where there was reason to believe that they may conceal the truth by reason of personal motives.[24] If the jurors swore under oath that a person was suspected of a crime, that was sufficient to put the person on trial. This process was known as the 'indictment'. This indicting jury also gave the final verdict in the case.[25] It has been suggested that when the ordeals were abolished by the Fourth Lateran Council, trial by jury provided a ready-made replacement.[26]

3.2.2 Beginnings of divergence – the thirteenth to the seventeenth centuries

(a) The growth of an inquisitorial tradition in France

By the thirteenth century a new procedure began to emerge in France, a procedure influenced by the Canon Law of the ecclesiastic courts, which had in turn drawn inspiration from earlier secular institutions.[27] Under Canon Law, this was known as *processus per inquisitionem* – procedure by inquisition. This procedure was developed further throughout the fourteenth and fifteenth centuries in France. Having being made aware of the crime two procedures were open to the judge: to proceed either by 'ordinary procedure' or by 'extraordinary procedure'.[28] The ordinary procedure was the method used where there had been a formal accusation by a private party but the accused asked the court to take over the case so that it proceeded through 'inquest by the country'. The entire proceeding was held in public; the accused was allowed to defend the accusation and to call witnesses. The use of torture, as a means of proof, was forbidden under the ordinary procedure.

The 'extraordinary' procedure was quite the opposite. Secrecy was central and torture was its principle means of proof. Under the 'extraordinary' procedure, the accused had no knowledge of the charges nor had sight of depositions of witnesses. While the information stage of the procedure and the torture stage were conducted in secrecy, the accused was still entitled to a public hearing in order to plead his defence before sentence, which was also

22. F. Pollock and F. Maitland, *The History of English Law before the Time of Edward I* (Cambridge University Press 1895) Bk 2, 642.
23. Many of the justices were ecclesiastics conversant with Roman law. See Proffatt (note 19) 33.
24. Ibid., 44.
25. See Pollock and Maitland (note 22) Bk 2, 626–7.
26. Thayer (note 14) 69.
27. Ibid., 78.
28. See, generally, Esmein (note 9) 121ff.

held in public. It was not long before the extraordinary procedure came to be used in all cases, whether those of accusation or those in which the accused had submitted to the inquest. The prohibition on torture in the ordinary procedure coupled with the strict system of 'legal proofs' is considered to have brought this about.[29]

An Ordinance passed in 1539 marked the beginning of a purely inquisitorial procedure in France. The criminal examination was to be initiated by the king's or lord's procurator who would petition the judge to conduct an examination. It was then the judge's responsibility to search for evidence and to compile the evidence in a written record. This record was then sent to the tribunal who would pass judgment, having first interrogated the accused. The entire proceeding was in private. No documents were made available to the accused. He was given no opportunity for summoning witnesses and had no right to the advice of counsel.

The first codification of laws was achieved through the Ordinance of 1670. This Ordinance, building on that of 1539, firmly established an inquisitorial procedure in France. The principle was laid down that there would be only one true accuser, the king's or lord's procurator; the role of the injured party was merely to ask for damages. The principle of secrecy of the proceedings, established by the 1539 Ordinance, was to be strictly followed and the depositions of witnesses were to be written in the presence of an examining judge. The accused could be summoned or arrested, and interrogated, under oath, by the examining judge. No counsel was permitted for the assistance of the accused if the offence was sanctioned by capital punishment; for other offences, the accused could consult with counsel after the interrogations at the judge's discretion. It was considered that the judge 'defends the accused at the same time that he prosecutes him'.[30]

The examining judge could decide whether the action was to proceed under the ordinary procedure or extraordinary procedure. Where the extraordinary procedure was employed, the accused was made aware of the charges against him only after the witnesses were reheard by the judge and had confirmed their depositions, and it was at the discretion of the examining judge to permit him to confront the witnesses. At the close of the examination, all of which was reduced to writing, the papers were first passed on to the king's procurator who could seek motions for the penalty to be passed, for torture to be applied or for further proof, without any reasons being included for these motions. The papers along with the motions, if any, were then passed on to the reporting judge, who gave his opinion to the 'assembled bench' consisting of three judges, or graduates in law.[31] Before passing judgment the accused was interrogated by the assembled judges, and if they

29. Ibid., 132.
30. Ibid., 229.
31. Ibid., 232, 237.

were not satisfied with the proofs in the case, they could order that the accused be tortured, or, where there was doubt as to the guilt of the accused which arose from the record of the interrogations or confrontation, the judges could take further proof by hearing witnesses named by the accused.

What emerges from this discussion is that concepts of an examining investigative judge, secrecy of proceedings with an emphasis on written depositions, active participation by judges in examining the accused and witnesses, together with the idea of judges seeking further proof of their own motion, have been embedded in the French legal culture for almost five centuries.

(b) England: variations on an inquisitorial theme

Prosecutions in England continued to be brought by private accusers up to the mid-sixteenth century at which point a system of preliminary examination was first established. This procedure, conducted by the justices of the peace, according to Stephen cast the justice of the peace into 'the part of a public prosecutor'.[32] His role was to examine the accused through questioning, and to conduct the examination of witnesses. The latter was done in the absence of the accused and their recorded depositions were not shown to him.[33] While the practice of the self-informing jury had continued up to the sixteenth century,[34] and along with it little room for any evidence law, this new preliminary examination made way for a different dynamic in criminal trials.[35] The preliminary examination had created a pre-trial stage, with the evidence collected at that stage being forwarded on to the court of trial.

By the mid-sixteenth century the jury had ceased to be self-informing and depended on witnesses to provide the information upon which they could reach their verdict. This allowed for an increased role for the trial judge and for the development of the practice of the judge directing the jury. This paved the way for the distinction between law and fact, and for the division of functions between the judge and jury to decide on the law and the fact respectively.[36]

Trials in this period have been referred to as 'altercation trials', or by Langbein as 'accused speaks' trials. Stephen describes trials of this period in the following terms: the prisoner was imprisoned before trial, examined before trial in secret and the examination noted down; he had no notice of

32. J. Stephen, *A History of the Criminal Law of England*, Vol. 1 (Macmillan 1883) 190–221.
33. 1 & 2 Phil. & Mary c. 13 (1554).
34. See, generally, on the developments of jury trial: Pollock and Maitland (note 22) 649; Thayer (note 14) 83; Proffatt (note 19); M. Macnair, 'Vicinage and the Antecedents of the Jury' (1999) 17 (3) *Law & Hist. Rev.* 537; B. Shapiro, 'To a Moral Certainty: Theories of Knowledge and Anglo-American Juries 1600–1850' (1986–7) 38 (1) *Hastings LJ* 155.
35. See, generally, J. Langbein, 'The Historical Foundations of the Law of Evidence: A View from the Ryder Sources' (1996) 96 (5) *Columbia L. Rev.* 1168, 1171.
36. See discussion on this point in A. Duff, L. Farmer, S. Marshall and V. Tadros, *The Trial on Trial Volume Three: Towards a Normative Theory of the Criminal Trial* (Hart 2007) 36.

the evidence against him, no counsel at any stage and was compelled to answer the case made against him at the trial; he had no opportunity to call witnesses for his defence and was not always confronted face to face with witnesses against him; no rules of evidence governed the trial and a confession by an accomplice was considered 'specially cogent evidence'.[37] The trial was directed by the judge, who examined witnesses 'acting as both examiner and cross-examiner' working from the indictment and from the depositions taken in the preliminary examination.[38] Stephen notes that trials during the reigns of the Tudors and the Stuarts[39] were quite similar to trials in Europe as regards the element of secrecy involved although he suggests 'it never thoroughly adopted torture, which was practically an essential part of that system' nor, except in cases of treason and perjury, did it require two witnesses.[40] Langbein suggests that there were few rules of evidence during this period but identifies evidence of torture being fairly common practice, especially during the reign of Elizabeth I, for a wide range of offences.[41]

The documented trials of the later Stuart period indicate an absence of any rules of evidence, for example hearsay evidence was received without objection. Furthermore, in the 'accused speaks' type trial, there was no place for a privilege against self-incrimination. As Langbein puts it, 'for almost all criminal defendants, defending meant responding in person to the details of the accusation', therefore 'the defendant's refusal to respond to the incriminating evidence against him would have been suicidal'.[42] It also appears that during this period, though still not allowed the benefit of counsel, the accused was allowed to cross-examine the witnesses against him. There is no indication of an accused enjoying a presumption of innocence at trial. Indeed it has been suggested it was out of kilter with the practice that a person was returned for trial by the indictment of the grand jury, which was worded to the effect that the person had already been found guilty.[43]

Reforms were introduced after the Revolution of 1688 by the 1696 Treason Trials Act to remedy what was perceived to be a dysfunctional system.[44] The reforms, limited to treason trials, provided that before the trial the accused be given a copy of the indictment, a list of the witnesses and of the jury, and was

37. Stephen (note 32) 350.
38. J. Langbein, *The Origins of Adversary Criminal Trial* (Oxford University Press 2003) 15.
39. The reign of the Tudors spanned 1485 to 1603; that of the Stuarts lasted from 1603 to 1649 and following the Restoration after the period of the Long Parliament, from 1660 to 1714.
40. Stephen (note 32) 426.
41. See, generally, J. Langbein, *Torture and the Law of Proof: Europe and England in the Ancien Régime* (first published 1977, University of Chicago Press 2006) 94ff.; Elizabeth I reigned from 1558 to 1603.
42. J. Langbein, 'The Historical Origins of the Privilege Against Self-Incrimination at Common Law' (1993–4) 92 (5) *Michigan L. Rev.* 1047, 1048.
43. Stephen (note 32) 397.
44. Langbein, *Origins* (note 37) 69.

to have recourse to counsel. Witnesses for the accused, who had previously been confined to giving un-sworn testimony and therefore afforded little weight, were permitted to give evidence under oath. It was also settled by the Act that treason required proof from two witnesses.[45]

Although the Act did not extend to 'ordinary' trials, Langbein marks this as 'a turning point' in the history of Anglo-American criminal procedure. In his view, 'adversary criminal trial traces to the 1696 Act'.[46] The reason he considers it pivotal is because of the introduction of counsel for the accused.

The system in England therefore was initially not altogether dissimilar to that pertaining in France, involving an examination by a judicial figure before trial with the accused being kept largely in the dark, and active judicial involvement during the trial. However, the jury system was all the while developing side by side with this procedure and with it, the ideas of oral presentation of evidence through a process of examination and cross-examination at a public trial. There is therefore less emphasis on written depositions. At the same point that France began to wholly embrace an inquisitorial approach, England began to go on a different trajectory that embraced the gradual acceptance of the practice of providing an accused with more information in the proceedings and providing an accused with a better ability to defend himself through recourse to counsel.

3.2.3 Pre-eighteenth-century approaches to proof

(a) France: the system of 'legal proofs'

Garraud, in his exposition of the history of the continental system of evidence, outlines two principal systems of proof: the system of legal proofs and the system of moral proofs. The system of legal proofs set up standard criteria for establishing guilt: if the requisite quality and quantity of proofs were present then the judge had no discretion but to convict. The system of legal proofs had emerged during the last years of the Roman Empire and had become firmly established in France by the 1500s. Under the system of legal proofs, four means of proof existed: confession, proof by witnesses, documentary proof and conjecture (presumptions).[47] A certain level of proof had to be reached in order to convict, and anything short of that necessarily resulted in acquittal. Only a 'complete proof' was sufficient for a capital conviction, although most crimes at that time were capital offences.

In order to establish guilt it first had to be proved that the crime had in fact occurred by proving the material traces of the offence – the *corpus delicti* – for example, by exhibiting the corpse or through reports by experts who had

45. See Stephen (note 32) 336.
46. Langbein, *Origins* (note 37) 68.
47. The work of Professor Garraud appears as an appendix to Esmein (note 9).

personally examined the corpse or wound or other material traces. Where the crime was such as to contain no possibility of material traces such as in a case of slander, the requirement of actual proof of the *corpus delicti* was dispensed with. Having established proof that the crime had in fact been committed, the second stage was dedicated to establishing proof of guilt of the perpetrator.

Evidence to prove guilt was classified according to its strength. There were three classes of proofs: complete proofs, proximate presumptions and remote presumptions. Proof by witnesses was considered the best form of proof, but to be acceptable as proof, two unimpeachable eyewitnesses had to testify to the same fact and had to give the same testimony at three separate hearings – the interrogation, confirmation and confrontation, and the depositions had to be identical in each. If these conditions were satisfied their testimony constituted a complete proof and conviction was then mandatory. These witnesses could not be hearsay witnesses even where they had received a confession from the accused. Witnesses also had to be competent, and could be objected to on grounds of age, weakness of intellect or personal interest.[48] Where all the conditions were satisfied, the evidence of two eyewitnesses constituted a complete proof sufficient for conviction.

Written proof could amount to a complete proof if it was precise as to the facts of the crime and authentic. Written proof was generally relied upon only in those cases where the establishment of the crime was possible only through production of a document, for example in a case of conspiracy.

Presumptions, what we would today refer to as circumstantial evidence, could constitute a complete proof provided they were based on established facts: the example given to illustrate this is where eyewitnesses testify to having seen the accused leave a place with a bloodied sword in his hand, and the body of the deceased is later found in the same place having suffered a wound inflicted by a sword.[49]

Proximate presumptions, often referred to as half proofs, were insufficient for a capital conviction. A proximate presumption could arise where there was testimony from just one witness, and the presence of a proximate presumption was sufficient to permit the judge to order the administration of torture. When added to a confession obtained through torture, a proximate presumption then constituted a complete proof. Confessions on their own were never accepted as a complete proof. The system of legal proofs, where the evidence of two eyewitnesses was absent (which was not unusual), in effect forced the judges to obtain a confession from the accused through administration of torture. Although intended as a safeguard for the accused,

48. Esmein (note 9) 260.
49. Esmein (note 9) 624, note 3, citing Muyart de Vouglans.

this system, referred to by Garraud as 'the tyranny of the proof', 'led fatally to the use of torture'.[50]

Overall, the system of legal proofs was a rigid one, and contained elements that are familiar to English evidence rules, rules relating to corroboration and a rule against hearsay witnesses.

(b) Approach to proof in England

Based on the treatise of Gilbert, evidence law as it existed in England in the early 1700s appears not too dissimilar to the system of legal proofs in France. Gilbert's guiding principle is referred to by commentators as 'the best evidence rule'[51] and his work has been interpreted as giving preference to documentary proof over oral testimony in open court.[52] With regard to oral evidence, under Gilbert's scheme certain categories of witnesses were incompetent to testify, such as those with an interest in the case, those lacking in integrity and those lacking in discernment (in which he includes children and lunatics). This was due to the centrality of the oath in the procedure: it was the oath which gave credibility to the testimony rather than the actual credibility of the witnesses themselves.[53] Gilbert approached the law of proof by giving proof a mathematical value. Each piece of proof had a value, and a total value could be calculated by adding together all the proof presented in the case to reach the measure of 'full proof' required for conviction.[54]

3.2.4 Eighteenth- and nineteenth-century England – development of adversarial trial and the establishment of the law of evidence

Up to the 1730s trials in England continued to be judge dominated.[55] From that period onwards there appears to be a decrease in the practice of questioning by the trial judge and an increase in the involvement of counsel, whether for the prosecutor, the defence or both. In this period also, more instances of objections to hearsay testimony, referred to as 'no evidence', have been identified by legal historians.[56] With the increase in the use of

50. F. Garraud, 'History of the Continental System of Evidence' (Appendix B in Esmein (note 9) 626).
51. W. Twining, *Rethinking Evidence* (2nd edn) (Cambridge University Press 2006) 37; see also W. Twining, *Theories of Evidence: Bentham and Wigmore* (Stanford University Press 1985).
52. S. Landsman, 'From Gilbert to Bentham: The Reconceptualization of Evidence Theory' (1989–90) 36 *Wayne L. Rev.* 1149, 1154; T. Gallanis, 'The Rise of Modern Evidence Law' (1998–9) 84 (3) *Iowa L. Rev.* 449, 509.
53. Landsman (note 52) 1155.
54. Ibid., 1158.
55. J. Langbein 'The Criminal Trial Before Lawyers' (1977–8) 45 (2) *U. Chi. L. Rev.* 263, 315.
56. S. Landsman, 'The Rise of the Contentious Spirit: Adversary Procedure in Eighteenth Century England' (1989–90) 75 (3) *Cornell L. Rev.* 496, 568; see also J. Beattie, 'Scales of

counsel, the practice of cross-examining witnesses gradually became established. By the mid-1700s Landsman identifies not just a practice, but also a right of cross-examination. Although the role of the defence lawyer was limited at least until 1836, in that they were permitted to examine witnesses and address any matters of law but were not permitted to put forward a defence case, defence lawyers used the mechanism of cross-examination as a means of circumventing these restrictions. Defence counsel could in this way 'present his theory of the case, refute an opponent's claims, develop favourable proof, and discredit opposing witnesses'.[57]

By 1770 there is more evidence of 'adversarial contests'.[58] Trial judges became less involved in directly questioning the witnesses and took on the mantle of the 'passive umpire' guarding the integrity of the process.[59] Landsman concludes from his analysis of one of the trials of this period that counsel in a trial had substantial power over the operation of the courtroom through the manipulation of the rules of evidence.[60] Langbein suggests 'the true historical function of the law of evidence may not have been so much jury control as lawyer control'.[61]

By the early 1800s, adversary procedure predominated. Orally presented evidence came to be given greater importance over written evidence.[62] The practice of excluding certain categories of witnesses also began to change towards a more inclusionary approach with an emphasis placed on the credibility of witnesses rather than exclusion for want of competence.

Both Langbein and Landsman have linked the growth of the law of evidence with the emergence of the adversary type trial. The adversarial trial provided the locus for the practice of the law of evidence that had been developed in the earlier treatises. In the adversarial trial setting, the law of evidence became, as Langbein puts it, a 'bonanza for the lawyers'.[63] Lawyers had a tool for manipulating their way through the trial so as to have control over the information that was to be presented to the triers of fact. This

Justice: Defense Counsel and the English Criminal Trial in the Eighteenth and Nineteenth Centuries' (1991) 9 (2) *Law & Hist. Rev.* 221.

57. Landsman (note 56) 535; Evans highlights the importance of cross-examination, favouring the testing of evidence by 'judicious advocates' and hearsay evidence is identified by Phillips as problematic because of the absence of opportunity to cross-examine, W. Evans, 'Of the Law of Evidence' in Pothier, *Treatise on Obligations*, Appendix no. XVI, Vol. 2 (Robert Small 1826); Phillips' *Treatise on the Law of Evidence* was first published in 1814 and updated eight times up to 1843: see Twining, *Rethinking Evidence* (note 51) 49.
58. Blackstone, *Commentaries* (first published Clarendon Press 1765–9; Hein 1992) represented the court system as an adversarial process: Book 4, Ch. 27 353.
59. Landsman (note 56) 522.
60. Ibid., 523.
61. Langbein (note 55) 306.
62. Landsman (note 56) discussing the works of Peake, Evans and Phillips.
63. Langbein, *Origins* (note 38) 251.

brought with it an exclusionary principle that in turn created truth-impairing tendencies within the modern common law criminal trial.

3.2.5 Eighteenth- and nineteenth-century France – development of the principle of free proof and trial by jury

By the mid-1700s in France the philosophical movement of the Enlightenment, guided by principles of reason and humanity, began to attack the secret and repressive criminal procedure and the theory of legal proofs. The French procedure was contrasted with the trial procedure in England and commended for its virtues of public trial and judgment by peers.[64] Inspired by the writers of the Enlightenment, a new spirit of liberalism had taken root and public opinion sought an end to the repressive inquisitorial procedure, at least to the secrecy aspects and to the limitations on defence. The Cahiers of 1789 contained a demand by the people of France for an end to the secrecy of proceedings, for the abolition of the requirement for an oath by the accused, for the accused to be represented by counsel, for the ability for the accused to provide proof of his innocence, for freedom from punishment for witnesses who changed their testimony at the confrontation and for determination of the facts by a jury.[65]

Many of these demands were achieved in the early years of the French Revolution.[66] Broad principles were first set out in the Declaration of the Rights of Man and Citizen drawn up by the National Assembly in 1789; this established (*inter alia*) the principle that all men were to be considered innocent until proven guilty.[67] Two reforming pieces of legislation were passed, the first making the proceedings public and allowing the accused the benefit of counsel.[68] The publicity of proceedings was confined to the period after a charge had been made, so the denunciation was still to be made in secret to a judge. Once the writ to proceed with the prosecution was issued, the remainder of the examination – be it of the accused or of witnesses – was held in public.

The accused was assisted by a lawyer of his own choosing at the first interrogation, in which no oath by the accused was required; if the accused did

64. 'In France the Criminal Code seems framed purposely for the destruction of the people: in England it is their safeguard': Voltaire, *Prix de la justice et de l'humanité*, xxiii, 101 (1777), cited by Esmein (note 9) 361.
65. The Cahiers were the written instructions of constituencies given to their representatives elected to the assembly of the States-General in relation to matters likely to be the subject of legislative reform. See Esmein (note 9) 397, note 6.
66. The time frame of the Revolution is 1789–99; see A. Wills, *Crime and Punishment in Revolutionary Paris* (Greenwood Press 1981).
67. Ibid., 28–45.
68. The first was a provisional law, October 1789, later completed by Law of 16–29 September 1791.

not appoint a lawyer, the judge would choose one on his behalf. Immediately after the interrogation, all the documents obtained during the proceedings were given to the accused and to his counsel. Any additions to the case file from that point onwards were made in public, so any further depositions from witnesses were given in the presence of the accused who could question them afterwards. The extraordinary procedure of the 1670 Ordinance was retained but, crucially, the practice of torture as a means of obtaining proof was abolished. At the judgment stage of the proceedings the accused was present only for his interrogation but could be represented by counsel who could lodge defence pleas.

The second piece of legislation was more ambitious. It repealed the Ordinance of 1670 and was strongly inspired by English procedure as a model for a new procedure of criminal justice. It established that a justice of the peace would be in charge of the first stage of the investigation, to hear witnesses and to draw up reports. It also created a jury procedure, a system comprising a 'grand jury' and a 'petit jury'. The grand jury – made up of eight citizens and a 'director of the jury' – would decide on whether an accusation should proceed. The most active figure in the grand jury appears to have been the 'director of the jury' who was a permanent magistrate to whom the reports of the justice of the peace were sent and who had power to question the accused and any further witnesses. The proceedings before the grand jury were held in private, and they came to their decision to proceed with an accusation on the basis of written reports and the statements of witnesses, but the latter had to be heard orally.

Where the accusation proceeded, the case went before a tribunal comprised of three judges and a president and twelve jurors (the 'petit jury'). The judges were to decide on punishment while it was for the jury to decide on questions of fact. As described by Esmein, the hearing in the tribunal was 'an oral and public, and very simple, procedure'.[69] The centrality of the idea of orality of proceedings was underscored by the requirement that the evidence of witnesses was to be given orally – the jury was not given any written depositions but supplied only with the written indictment. They were to give their decision by answering the issues put to them in writing, by a simple 'yes' or 'no'.[70]

The system of legal proofs contained in the old Ordinance of 1670 was repealed and replaced by a system of moral proof. This was essentially a system of free proof: there was no longer a pre-set quantum of proof required in order to convict. It appealed instead to the conscience of the jury: the new system did not require that the jury should account for the 'means by which they are convinced'. Instead:

> It enjoins them to interrogate themselves in silence and meditation, and to seek in the sincerity of their conscience for the impression made upon

69. Esmein (note 9) 415.
70. See ibid., 417.

> their reason by the proofs brought against the accused and his pleas in defence. The law ... only asks them this one question, comprising the whole measure of their duties: are you thoroughly convinced?[71]

That is not to say that the judge or jury were permitted to reach a decision based solely on their intuition. Their decision was to be based on rational inference from the evidence presented, but in doing so they were free from 'the strict hierarchical principles and restrictions on their assessment of the weight of the evidence'.[72] This system of free proof continues to be the basis for evidence law in France today.

The 1791 Law also reduced any role for a public prosecutor. The prosecutor retained supervision over police but had no role in decisions to proceed or not with prosecutions. This position was revisited in the middle period of the Revolution in the Code of Brumaire that revived a role for the public prosecutor and also made provision for the taking of evidence in writing.[73] This paved the way for a return to a written pre-trial procedure that had fallen by the wayside in the early Revolutionary laws, reinstituted at the close of the Revolution in 1801.[74]

It was not until 1808 that criminal procedure in France was finally settled with the adoption of Napoleon's Code of Criminal Examination, which became the template of criminal procedure for most nations in Europe at least down to the end of the Second World War. The Code of 1808 established that the function of public prosecutor and examining judge should remain separate.[75] The preliminary examination was to be a secret and written procedure, affording the accused no knowledge of the charges or of any prior acts that had already been conducted. The accused was to be interrogated in secret without the aid of defence counsel – in short, many of the reforms adopted during the time of the Revolution, which had been to the advantage of the accused, were undone. At the end of the preliminary examination, the documents were sent forward for arraignment, and then on to the *Chambre d'accusation* where the charges would be framed. Between the preliminary examination and the trial, the accused was furnished with all the documents of the preliminary examination. The accused would then be interrogated again by the president of the *cour d'assises* and provided the opportunity to have his complaints heard. The trial became a fully public affair; the accused was considered to be on an equal footing with the prosecution and given the

71. Article 342, Code of Criminal Examination, cited in Esmein (note 9) 516.
72. J. Jackson and S. Summers, *The Internationalisation of Criminal Evidence: Beyond the Common Law and Civil Law Traditions* (Cambridge University Press 2012) 69.
73. The *Code des Délits et Peines* 1795.
74. See, generally, Esmein (note 9) 426ff.; see also the account in R. Vogler, *A World View of Criminal Justice* (Ashgate 2005) Ch. 3.
75. Esmein (note 9) 502.

right to the assistance of a lawyer, the right to produce witnesses and the right of the final address to the court.

The Code also retained the jury, which had been adopted by the Law of 1791. The model for jury trial had been transplanted from England, although not without objectors. It was considered to be incompatible with the written procedure; jurors were thought to be inexperienced and ignorant, and the method of selection too indiscriminate.[76] Despite opposition, the trial jury was retained; however, the grand jury was abolished. At the end of the trial, in order to reach their verdict, the jury would receive all the documents from the preliminary examination and any interrogations of the accused, but would not receive the statements of witnesses. The jury were to decide by majority verdict on the basis of the system of moral proofs; the jury reached their verdict alone, following a summing up of the case by the trial judge.

Gradually the use of the jury in all trials was reduced, facilitated by the introduction of the *Tribunal Correctionnelle* which was presided over by three judges sitting without a jury to hear less serious offences; by 1890 a large number of serious offences had been reclassified through the process of 'correctionalisation', thus limiting the use of the jury to deciding only cases of serious offences heard in the *cour d'assises*.[77] While the Napoleonic Code retained the jury in the original format first established by the Revolutionary laws, whereby the jury reached their verdict unassisted by the judge, over the course of the following century the practice of a mixed bench developed. By 1932 the judge and jury decided together on the issue of sentence,[78] and the current practice in France of judge and jury retiring together to consider the verdict and sentence was established in 1941.[79]

3.2.6 Divergence of procedure in England and France

The eighteenth and nineteenth centuries may be considered a period where the divergence between the procedure in France and that in England becomes most pronounced. In England the focal point of criminal procedure became the trial itself, dominated by lawyers for both prosecution and defence and the role of the judge moved from active examiner to a more passive umpire. In this period the law of evidence became fully fledged and worked for the protection of the accused. Around the same period that England was developing the modern foundations for a strongly regulated approach to proof, France began to move away from its rigid system of legal proof culminating after the Revolution in the establishment of the system of

76. See ibid., 473.
77. Vogler (note 74) 239.
78. Law 5 March 1932.
79. Law 25 November 1941.

free proof. Like England, the accused was assisted by a lawyer at the trial, one that was similarly public, oral and included a jury. However, France continued to place a strong emphasis on a secret preliminary investigation, the findings of which were a considerable informational source at the subsequent trial.

Each system during this period gave much greater recognition to the accused as a human subject deserving of protective rights. It has even been suggested that these developments in the nineteenth century marked not divergence but convergence of systems through the emergence of a distinct 'European criminal procedural tradition'.[80] Nonetheless, while there were a number of converging practices during this period, on the face of it at least, there was also a strong divergence, most notably in the area of the approach to proof.

PART II

3.3 Comparative approaches through use of models of criminal procedure

3.3.1 Accusatorial and inquisitorial models

The dominant mode for comparison of Anglo-American criminal procedure with its continental European counterpart is by juxtaposing them as accusatorial and inquisitorial models. These historically based constructs have been examined above in terms of their evolution. They will now be discussed more specifically in terms of their usage by comparativists as analytical tools. Broadly speaking, the accusatorial model is generally associated with Anglo-American procedure and the inquisitorial model with European continental procedure.

The accusatorial type of procedure is associated with the idea that an accusation is made by an accuser, the accused person is presumed innocent until proven guilty, and the accuser bears the burden of proving his accusation.[81] The accused is not required to help him to do so and therefore may not be made to contribute in alleviating that burden by testifying himself. Accusatorial procedure denotes also a public trial where evidence is presented orally. The role of the court is principally one of facilitating the parties to the dispute and as described by Goldstein, the accusatorial model is therefore 'reactive'.[82]

The accusatorial procedure is contrasted with the inquisitorial model which is described as proactive:[83] it is the state rather than the private accuser who is charged with assembling the case against the accused, and under

80. S. Summers, *Fair Trials: the European Criminal Procedural Tradition and the European Court of Human Rights* (Hart 2007) 21.
81. J. Jackson and S. Doran, *Judge Without Jury: Diplock Trials in the Adversary System* (Clarendon 1995) 57.
82. A. Goldstein, 'Reflections on Two Models: Inquisitorial Themes in American Criminal Procedure' (1973–4) 26 (5) *Stan. L. Rev.* 1009, 1017.
83. Ibid., 1018.

the classic inquisitorial model, this task lies with members of the judiciary who are given the powers of deciding on the course of the investigation and with examining the witnesses at trial.[84] Inquisitorial systems are characterised by secrecy of proceedings, reliance on written material contained in an investigative dossier and control over proceedings by the trial judge, where the trial is the culmination of a lengthy pre-trial investigation conducted by the investigating judge.[85]

The classic inquisitorial procedure is associated, especially by Anglo-American commentators, with the practice of extracting evidence from the accused through torture. There is thus 'an aura of dread and mistrust surrounding the adjective inquisitorial'.[86] In addition to describing the inquisitorial system as one that relies on torture for obtaining evidence, it has been noted there are also some Anglo-American commentators who hold the 'extraordinary misconception' that inquisitorial systems proceed from a point of presumption of guilt in contrast to the presumption of innocence enjoyed under the accusatorial procedure.[87] While this appears be true of the classic inquisitorial system as it stood from the time of the Ordinance of 1670 up to the French Revolution, primarily because the practice of torture to obtain confessions jars with any principle of presuming the accused to be innocent, it is not true of the system that replaced the pure inquisitorial system in the nineteenth century when the presumption of innocence was stated in the clearest of terms as being a fundamental principle of the French system.[88] Indeed, Quintard-Morenas traces the presumption as a constant thread prior to the Ordinance of 1670, apparent throughout Roman and medieval times.[89]

Some commentators have also linked the accusatorial and inquisitorial models with two further models that were advanced as a means of analysis of the competing values *within* any system: the 'crime control model' and 'the due process model' developed by Packer.[90] These models are two polarities that do not necessarily correspond with 'real-life' procedures, but provide a useful axis upon which to measure where on the scale of these polarities a criminal procedure is tending. Goldstein,[91] Langbein and Weinreb,[92]

84. See M. King, 'Security, Scale, Form and Function: The Search for Truth and the Exclusion of Evidence in Adversarial and Inquisitorial Justice Systems' (2001–2) 12 *Int'l Legal Persp.* 185, 194ff.
85. See, generally, for descriptions of inquisitorial procedure: Damaška, 'Barriers' (note 4) 506; M. Delmas-Marty and J. Spencer (eds), *European Criminal Procedures* (first published 2002, Cambridge University Press 2005); Vogler, (note 74) 129.
86. Damaška, 'Barriers' (note 4) 558.
87. Noted by Spencer (note 85) 22; see also Damaška, 'Barriers' (note 4) 569.
88. Declaration of the Rights of Man and Citizen 1789.
89. Quintard-Morenas (note 10) 110ff.
90. H. Packer, 'Two Models of the Criminal Process' (1964–5) 113 (1) *U. Pa. L. Rev.* 1, 5.
91. Goldstein (note 82).
92. J. Langbein and L. Weinreb, 'Continental Criminal Procedure: "Myth" and Reality' (1978) 87 (8) *Yale LJ* 1549.

Griffiths[93] and later, Frase,[94] increasingly associated the concept 'inquisitorial' with the crime control model and 'accusatorial' with the due process model. Images of 'contest' are employed to characterise the accusatorial model in which the judge acts as umpire of proceedings.[95] Rules of evidence are strongly associated with this type of proceedings, and as a result of their adherence to rules of evidence the proceedings are depicted as an 'obstacle course'. This accusatorial model is set in contradistinction to the inquisitorial model by these commentators who associate it with images of 'assembly-line' efficiency linking it with Packer's crime control model.[96]

These and other commentators often use the term 'accusatorial' side by side with 'adversarial' or even use the two terms interchangeably. This creates confusion since it conflates two concepts that are not necessarily the same, though there are significant overlapping features. The terms adversarial and accusatorial therefore need some clarification. It has been suggested by Goldstein that 'adversarial' refers to a *method* of resolving the disputed facts whereas 'accusatorial' has a broader meaning which in Goldstein's view is a 'classic procedural model', one that 'assigns great social value to keeping the state out of disputes' and one that affords the accused a presumption of innocence until the accuser has produced sufficient evidence of guilt to justify conviction.[97]

For Goldstein, the accusatorial model encompasses an adversary trial procedure and is a more overarching concept in that it includes at its heart a presumption of innocence. An accusatorial model is reactive, responding to accusations made by private parties. Since modern-day procedures are now instigated more often by state officials rather than private complainants, Goldstein suggests that an 'accusatorial model closely resembles the system of private prosecution which long dominated English criminal justice', and suggests that 'American criminal procedure has become much less accusatorial in theory'.[98] Nonetheless he does not consider the accusatorial model as simply a historical relic, because in his view the adversarial method itself does not necessarily embrace the mainstay of accusatorial process, the idea of the presumption of innocence.

Vogler stresses that the terms adversarial and accusatorial are not interchangeable and suggests their conflation by commentators to be an 'accusatorial fallacy'. He suggests that adversarial refers to the dominant mode of trial of the modern Anglo-American world while the term accusatorial refers

93. J. Griffiths, 'Ideology in Criminal Procedure or a Third Model of the Criminal Process' (1969–70) 79 (3) *Yale LJ* 359.
94. R. Frase, 'Comparative Criminal Justice as a Guide to American Law Reform: How Do the French Do It, How Can We Find Out, and Why Should We Care?' (1990) 78 (3) *Cal. L. Rev.* 539.
95. Langbein and Weinreb (note 92); Frase (note 94); Griffiths (note 93).
96. The phrases 'assembly line' and 'obstacle course' are used by Packer (note 90) 13.
97. Goldstein (note 82) 1017.
98. Ibid., 1018.

to the pre-eighteenth-century tradition.[99] In this context, Vogler links the presumption of innocence with adversarial trial as a feature of post-eighteenth-century English criminal procedure rather than with an 'ancient accusatorial tradition'. As already noted, however, the presumption of innocence is considered by others to have featured throughout history long before the adversarial procedure became established.[100]

It has been suggested that European scholars refer to their system as an accusatorial procedure, both as a means of describing the trial stage and as a means of distinguishing it from the classic inquisitorial procedure with which continental systems have long been associated.[101] As described by one French commentator, 'accusatory procedure is one that is oral, *contradictoire* and public as opposed to an inquisitorial procedure which is written secret and *non contradictoire*'.[102] Damaška notes that the term accusatorial is used by European scholars to denote that the accused has the right to be present during procedural stages and has the right to challenge the proof laid against him. It does not, however, imply:

> Partisan presentation of evidence and partisan zeal, even though the defendant is present and active in court. Rather it assumes a detached non-partisan examination of evidence in which the judge will play the dominant role.[103]

He also notes that accusatorial, in this sense, 'is better known in Latin countries under the label of "*procédure contradictoire*" ("*il contraddittorio*")'.[104]

Illuminati defines an accusatorial system as one that requires evidence to be produced in a public trial where it may be tested by cross-examination. This he contrasts to an inquisitorial process where the decision to convict or acquit is grounded on evidence gathered unilaterally and secretly during the preliminary investigation by the magistrate in charge.[105] He and other Italian commentators sometimes refer to their system as an accusatorial one and sometimes describe it as adversarial. Illuminati suggests that 'although it takes inspiration from the rules of the accusatorial system, the Italian criminal process moves considerably away from the Anglo-American model of the adversary system', highlighting the active role of the judge in the Italian trial.[106]

99. Vogler (note 74) 129.
100. See Quintard-Morenas (note 10) 110ff.
101. Damaška and 'Barriers' (note 4) 555ff.; see also C. Ambroise-Casterot, *La Procédure Pénale* (Gualino 2009) 4, 292; F. Fourment, *Procédure Pénale* (Paradigme 2009); G. Illuminati, 'The Accusatorial Process from the Italian Point of View' (2010) 35 *NCJ Int'l L. & Com. Reg.* 297.
102. Fourment (note 101) 10; the term *contradictoire* will be discussed in section 3.3.6 below.
103. Damaška, 'Barriers' (note 4) 561.
104. Ibid., 561, note 127.
105. Illuminati (note 101) 309.
106. Ibid., 316.

However, in an earlier article, Illuminati suggests the Italian system was 'inspired by the Anglo-American adversarial system'.[107] Grande refers to the Italian system as an attempted imitation of an adversarial model.[108] Other Italian commentators use the term adversarial and accusatorial interchangeably.[109]

French commentators describe their modern-day system not as accusatorial or inquisitorial but as a mixed system, one that combines inquisitorial and accusatorial features.[110] Damaška suggests that 'from the common law perspective, however, it is possible that both inquisitorial and mixed procedures appear as two branches of a common parent stem, that of non-adversary proceedings'.[111]

The initial investigation is pursued along inquisitorial lines. Institution of the investigation is normally by a public prosecutor; in classic form, evidence is gathered by an investigating judge, who compiles a file for the trial judge and the trial then is conducted along accusatorial lines: the trial is conducted in public; the defence is allowed to contest the charges against him during the trial, and to this end, will have been given full access to the investigative file at the close of the investigation; evidence gathered during the investigation is presented orally at trial in the presence of the defendant and the prosecution; the prosecution has the burden of proving guilt; the trial judge may question the witnesses and the defendant and may seek further evidence where he sees fit to do so. The role of the trial judge is that of an active 'inquisitor' who both seeks evidence and adjudicates on guilt, and sentencing follows as part of the single procedure.

Of all the analytical labels, accusatorial is perhaps the most complex because of the different ways in which the term is used by commentators. It has been seen that some commentators use the term interchangeably with the term 'adversarial' to describe a model of criminal procedure, and it has been seen that a number of European scholars refer to their current system

107. G. Illuminati, 'The Frustrated Turn to Adversarial Procedure in Italy (Italian Code of 1988)' 2005 4 *Wash. U. Glob. Stud. L. Rev.* 567, 571.
108. E. Grande, 'Italian Criminal Justice: Borrowing and Resistance' (2000) 48 (2) *Am. J. Comp. L.* 227, 232; see also L. Marafioti, 'Italian Criminal Procedure: A System Caught Between Two Traditions', in *Essays Damaška*, J. Jackson *et al.* (note 3), 91.
109. M. Panzavolta, 'Reforms and Counter Reforms in the Italian Struggle for an Accusatorial Criminal Law System' (2004–5) 30 (3) *NCJ Int'l L. & Com. Reg.* 577; Panzavolta uses both terms in his writing; W. Pizzi and M. Montagna, 'The Battle to Establish an Adversarial Trial System in Italy' (2003–4) 25 (2) *Mich. J. Int'l L.* 429, refer interchangeably to adversarial and accusatorial; W. Pizzi and L. Marafioti, 'The New Italian Code of Criminal Procedure: the Difficulties of Building an Adversarial Trial System on a Civil Law Foundation' (1992) 17 (1) *Yale J. Int'l L.* 1, refer to an adversarial system; E Amodio, 'The Accusatorial System Lost and Regained: Reforming Criminal Procedure in Italy' (2004) 52 *Am. J. Comp. L.* 489, refers to accusatorial but later (495) to 'the adversarial model'.
110. For example, Fourment, *Procédure Pénale* (note 101) 10; Ambroise-Casterot, *La Procédure Pénale* (note 101) 44; see also Damaška, 'Barriers' (note 4) 558.
111. Damaška, 'Barriers' (note 4) 559.

as accusatorial; others use it to differentiate between different systems of procedure in a historical context, principally as a counterpoint to inquisitorial procedure, with the accusatorial procedure predating adversarial procedure,[112] while another approach has been to view 'accusatorial' as a broad procedural model in a historical context that in modern times has subsumed adversarial procedure as the method of trial.[113]

3.3.2 Adversarial and non-adversarial procedure

Given the confusion surrounding the term 'accusatorial', a somewhat clearer theoretical basis for examining the differences between the common law and civil law systems is to look at how each system measures against a polarity of adversarial and non-adversarial procedure. England is considered to be the birthplace of the adversarial trial,[114] and as such the components of adversarial trial are usually illustrated from the perspective of common law norms and opposed to non-adversarial trial as is considered to have been the practice, at least historically, in continental Europe during the same period.[115]

Adversarialism 'is based on the premise that all people, including persons accused of criminal offences, enjoy rights and the freedom to express their legitimate independent perspectives'.[116] An adversarial process is characterised by the fact that responsibility for the investigation, as well as selection and presentation of the evidence, lies with the two parties to the case: the accuser and the accused.[117] The accuser (the prosecutor) will select what evidence is to be heard, but the accused also may conduct their own investigations, present their own witnesses, including if it is considered appropriate the defendant himself. The presentation of the case by the parties is through a tightly controlled system of examination of witnesses by the prosecutor who in theory is supposed to be non-partisan.

The defence may cross-examine the witness, but keeping within the bounds of what has been related during examination by the prosecution. Witnesses give testimony in response to the line of questions put to them and therefore do not narrate events in the same manner that would be usual for accounts of events that would appear in normal social intercourse. The judge does not question the witnesses but sees only that each side, prosecution and defence, 'abide by the rules of the contest', and is called on to rule out certain evidence that may lead the amateur jurors to reason inappropriately by giving it too

112. Vogler (note 74) 129.
113. Goldstein (note 82) 1017.
114. Langbein, *Origins* (note 38).
115. That is not to say that some form of adversarial trial was unknown on the continent, see Strachan-Davidson (note 9) Vol. 2, 125.
116. Vogler (note 74) 129.
117. See J. Hodgson, 'The Future of Adversarial Criminal Justice in 21st Century Britain' (2010) 35 *NCJ Int'l L. & Com. Reg.* 319.

much weight or where evidence should not be put before them that has been tainted by the manner of its collection. Each side are in a position of theoretical equality. The defendant may not be forced to give evidence; it is considered that to do so affects the equality of the parties, as it would give the advantage to the prosecution.[118]

The role of the judge in an adversarial trial is one of a neutral passive arbitrator, often referred to by commentators as an 'umpire' in a setting where the trial is seen as a contest. A cogent description of the adversarial versus non-adversarial procedure is that given by Damaška who suggests adversarial proceedings are 'structured as a dispute between two sides in a position of theoretical equality before a court which must decide the outcome of the contest'.[119] The aim of the proceedings is conflict resolution and 'the essence of the adversary system is that each side is accorded a participation in the decision that is reached, a participation that takes the form of presenting proofs and arguments'.[120]

In a pure form, the judge in the adversarial process is 'essentially passive'.[121] He has no role in selecting or examining witnesses, and where the witness is being questioned, has limited powers of intervention. To intervene, it is generally thought, weakens the position of impartiality of the judge. That is not to say that the judge has no part to play in the trial. In the classic common law adversarial trial the case is presented to a jury, a panel of lay citizens, who have no legal training. The judge therefore controls what is put before them and instructs them on what is legally required of them. At the close of the cases of the parties, he sums up the case for the jury and instructs them on the standard of proof that must be reached in order to convict the accused, that is proof beyond a reasonable doubt.

The jury decides alone, with no other assistance from the judge save for clarifications that may be sought in open court in the presence of the parties. Having reached a verdict, the jury gives no account to any other of the trial participants or indeed to the general public of how they came to their decision in the case.[122] The parties control the evidence, they decide what evidence to put forward, what to agree on and whether to object to the evidence of the other side, and it is only when such an objection is raised by either party that the judge takes an active role in coming to a decision as to whether the evidence should be put before the jury or not.

Damaška suggests that jury trial and oral testimony are not essential to an adversary model but that nonetheless the ideological underpinning of adversarial process, stemming from Lockean liberal values of distrust of the state

118. Damaška, 'Barriers' (note 4) 563.
119. Ibid.
120. Damaška, 'Barriers' (note 4) 570.
121. Damaška, *Evidence Law Adrift* (note 4) 74.
122. Ibid.

and freedom from restraint, may make these features a matter of choice.[123] Jackson and Doran suggest that while the arbiters in adversarial process may be lay or professional judges, provided that the arbiters are impartial and independent of the parties, the amateur jury 'may reinforce the image of the criminal process as contest because the jury is truly an outside arbiter and cannot be tinged with any taint of bias in favour of one side or the other'.[124]

In contrast to the adversary procedure, the ideology of non-adversary procedure is one of 'collectivist values and benevolent paternalism'. The proceedings are by way of an official inquiry where the judge and not the parties is the lead player in drawing out the evidence in the case. The protagonists are expected to contribute to the inquiry and the aim of the process is to discover the truth of the allegation. The emphasis is therefore on examining all available evidence, including the testimony of the accused. It is primarily the judge who questions the witnesses and the accused, the latter being compelled to answer, it is the judge who decides which evidence should be considered, and it is also for the judge to decide if further evidence should be brought to the trial. At the close of the trial, it is the judge who decides on the outcome, with or without the assistance of a jury. There are not two sides to a case, but a 'unilateral inquiry'.[125]

3.3.3 Approaches to proof in adversary and non-adversary procedure

Common to all systems is a requirement that the allegation made against an individual, whether by the state or by private accusation, be proved to a sufficient standard so as to justify imposing sanctions 'for then conscience permits us to inflict punishment according to knowledge, but not before'.[126] Differences do arise in the approach to proof across the common law–civil law divide.[127] In contrast to a non-adversary procedure, rules of evidence are strongly associated with adversarial procedure and are said to be 'considerably more exacting' than any that pertain in continental systems.[128]

Damaška has identified a unique fact-finding style in common law adversary proceedings and suggests it rests upon three 'institutional pillars': the 'bifurcated organization of the trial court', the 'temporal concentration of proceedings' and the 'prominent role of the parties'.[129] He argues that each

123. Damaška, 'Barriers' (note 4) 565.
124. Jackson and Doran (note 81) 59.
125. Damaška, 'Barriers' (note 4) 564–5.
126. Quintard-Morenas (note 10) 112.
127. That is not to say that civil law systems have one uniform system shared across the countries of continental Europe: see J. Nijboer, 'Common Law Tradition in Evidence Scholarship Observed from a Continental Perspective' (1993) 41 (2) *Am. J. Comp. L.* 299.
128. Spencer (note 85) 595.
129. Damaška, *Evidence Law Adrift* (note 4) 4.

of these pillars has a consequence for the way in which evidence is received in the court. Firstly, the division of labour between two parts, one lay and one professional, introduces the need for evidence law.[130] Because the jury is an amateur adjudicating body, the information going before them needs to be screened, so as to keep back from them particular information which may have a unwanted effect on their reasoning. There is an anxiety about the abilities of the jury to undertake their task of adjudicating impartially and fully understanding the issues. It has been said that 'jurors are rarely brilliant and rarely stupid, but they are treated as both at once'.[131]

At the same time, Damaška suggests that some rules do not depend on the lay attributes of decision-makers. For example, the justification for evidence rules that rests on the 'need to compensate for the alleged and emotional frailties of amateurs cast in the role of occasional judges' is weakened by the fact that for certain types of evidence which is held back from the jury on this reasoning, it would have to be shown that a professional body of decision-makers would not misevaluate it in the same manner. Why, he asks, is a professional judge better equipped than jurors to cope with hearsay?[132] As for character evidence, he suggests it is 'human cognitive imperfections' rather than whether a decision-maker is lay or professional that explains the justification for the rule. The more forceful rationale, he suggests, for evidentiary rules being required by reason of the jury is the fact that the verdict of the jury is given simply as a pronouncement of 'guilty' or 'not guilty', without any justification for how the verdict was reached. This inscrutability, he suggests, explains why the Anglo-American system focuses on the submission of evidence to the fact-finder and thus 'shores up' the legitimacy of the verdict.[133]

The second pillar supporting evidentiary arrangements in common law systems is the idea of 'day in court' proceedings: the idea that a trial is a single event rather than a series of hearings. This pillar offers greatest support for the hearsay rules: where the proceedings are a continuous event, the party affected by the hearsay evidence has no opportunity to seek out the original declarant to subject the testimony to cross examination, by contrast with the ability of a continental court to summon the declarant and hear them at 'the next procedural instalment'.[134] Nor do temporally compressed proceedings tolerate new evidence or evidence which has been preserved in records: the only evidence available for deciding is that which is made available on the day; there is therefore no space provided for a judge to seek out further evidence to reach a more accurate decision.

130. He also suggests that division of the tribunal equally could consist of two professional parts and have the same effect.
131. W. Urbom, 'Toward Better Treatment of Jurors by Judges' (1982) 61 (3) *Nebraska L. Rev.* 409, 425.
132. Damaška, *Evidence Law Adrift* (note 4) 28.
133. Ibid., 46.
134. Ibid., 65.

The third pillar supporting evidence law, he suggests, is the adversary system itself – by which he means a system of adjudication in which procedural action is controlled by the parties and the adjudicator remains essentially passive. This implies that the litigants are entrusted with seeking evidentiary material, preparing it for use at trial and presenting it at trial.[135] Because the adversary style is a contest type, and because the overarching purpose of the criminal process under adversary proceedings is dispute resolution, rules must be created to control the fact-finding process. Given that evidence of each side is partisan by nature, it must be subject to rigorous testing by the opposing party. Evidence is associated with each side to the dispute and each side can insist on the application of the rules where they, rather than the judge, deem necessary.

Having set out the foundational structure for common law evidence, Damaška goes on to argue that changes in the adversarial landscape have had the effect of creating a subsidence of the institutional pillars causing evidence law as a consequence to be set 'adrift' as it loses its supporting rationale. Allen and Alexakis dispute Damaška's conclusion that the rules of evidence have become any less important as a result of the decline in the use of the jury in the trial or the growth of plea bargaining, maintaining that the rules of evidence serve additional purposes and not simply the regulation of jury trial.[136] They suggest that Damaška's findings about the actual erosion of the three pillars is simply not true and that the analysis lacks any empirical foundation. Jackson and Summers suggest that the growing prominence of an individual rights tradition would appear to lend support to a system of evidentiary rules.[137]

3.3.4 Hierarchical and coordinate models of authority

Damaška has developed an alternative analytical framework to argue that the differences in procedural arrangements for the investigation and trial of offences may be related to the differences in the conception of the proper organisation of judicial authority between the European continental and the Anglo-American world.[138] He develops two models of authority: the hierarchical and the coordinate.

The hierarchical model of authority is one of a classic bureaucracy through which professional officials administer authority according to pre-set technical norms; the hierarchy consists of a pyramid structure whereby responsibility is delegated to those at the base and their activity is subject to review by those

135. Ibid., 74.
136. R. Allen and G. Alexakis, 'Utility and Truth in the Scholarship of Mirjan Damaška', in *Essays Damaška*, Jackson *et al.* (note 3) 338.
137. Jackson and Summers (note 72) 50–6.
138. Damaška, 'Structures' (note 2).

placed further up the pyramid. In criminal justice terms, the police occupy positions at the base of the pyramid while the prosecutor and judiciary occupy positions further up the hierarchical ladder. The requirement for review places an emphasis on documentation of activities. The model places a premium on certainty of decision-making. This requires the development of uniform policies, which in turn hinges on the centralisation of authority.[139] By contrast, in the coordinate model, authority is distributed horizontally across 'roughly equal lay officials'.[140] These lay officials are not bound to perform their functions in accordance with technical criteria but are instead informed by common sense and prevailing community norms.[141]

These different authority structures adopt distinct procedural styles: the hierarchical process and the coordinate process respectively. Damaška links the former with the legal process of the continental European tradition, while the latter reflects the legal process in the English tradition.[142] In the hierarchical process the case is developed through phases, starting with the investigation and passing along through the hierarchy to the top; a decision is not final until those at the upper end of the hierarchical pyramid have conclusively reviewed it. In the coordinate process the case is worked through as a single process with the information gathered in the investigatory stage being presented in oral form to decision-makers who make a decision that is presumptively final. There is thus an emphasis on oral rather than written testimony.

Under the hierarchical model the state is conceived as activist and the purpose of the criminal process is to implement state policy. A judicial structure dedicated to implementing state policy does not promote the idea of a case being structured by the wishes of the parties.[143] Nor does it depend on parties to instigate proceedings; the activist state may institute proceedings whenever it sees its interests under threat.[144] Personal rights are subordinate to the rights of the state in the implementation of its policy. Proceedings can incorporate parties in the presentation of the case but parties are viewed as an informational source rather than shapers of the procedure.[145] The role of the judge is one of implementing state policy; he must strive towards finding the right result in the case, is fully aware of all aspects of the case file and is not required to be impartial.[146]

The coordinate model conceives of the state as reactive with the purpose of criminal process being one dedicated to conflict-solving, resolving the dispute to the satisfaction of the parties concerned without reference to any requirements

139. Ibid., 485; Damaška, *Faces of Justice* (note 6) 18ff.
140. *Faces of Justice* (note 6) 25.
141. Ibid., 28.
142. Ibid., 47.
143. Ibid., 149.
144. Ibid., 84.
145. Ibid., 155ff.
146. Ibid., 168.

of state policy. The 'procedural edifice' is the idea of a contest between the two sides to the conflict, which is resolved by an impartial adjudicator who does not intervene other than to ensure 'fair disputation of incidental controversies'.[147]

3.3.5 The analytical value of the models

It is accepted by many commentators that while the models described above may not accurately describe either system, they are nonetheless useful as analytical tools. It is suggested that there is no clear agreement as to what components fit or are essential to the accusatorial, adversarial and inquisitorial models, and this has the result that 'locating particular systems along the spectrum of procedural types will always be controversial'.[148] Field suggests that 'there are cautious and careful ways in which the distinction between "inquisitorial" and "adversarial" traditions can inform and enrich analysis'.[149]

Others consider the dichotomy to be limited or even outdated. Jackson for example is somewhat sceptical of their continued usage arguing that the jurisprudence of the ECtHR 'has been steadily developing a new model of proof that is better characterised as 'participatory' than as 'adversarial' or 'inquisitorial'.[150] Summers suggests that the terms lack descriptive purpose and argues that the terms limit debate from a normative perspective and have fostered 'a type of legal nationalism'.[151] Jackson and Summers have suggested that the common law and civil law share in common two traditions within the 'criminal evidentiary domain', the 'rationalist tradition' and the 'individual rights tradition', which have enabled a common set of evidentiary principles to be developed across the common law/civil law divide. While acknowledging that the accusatorial inquisitorial dichotomy can be useful in encapsulating cultural differences, they have argued that 'an undue emphasis on legal cultural traditions has obscured the influence that shared epistemological, moral and political traditions' can have on the common law and civil law systems.[152]

The value of the adversarial/non-adversarial dichotomy is useful as an analytical tool, but clarification is needed as to what is embraced by these terms; one point of confusion is that commentators tend to associate adversarial procedure with an accusatorial process, while non-adversarial is linked to the inquisitorial process. Also there is not a clear agreement by commentators as to what are essential components of each procedure. For example, is procedural control by the trial judge anathema to adversarial procedure? Is a jury essential

147. Ibid., 79.
148. J. Jackson, 'Taking Comparative Evidence Seriously', in P. Roberts and M. Redmayne (eds), *Innovations in Evidence and Proof: Integrating Theory, Research and Teaching* (Hart 2007) 291.
149. S. Field, 'Fair Trials and Procedural Tradition in Europe' (2009) 29 (2) *OJLS* 365, 386.
150. J. Jackson, 'The Effect of Human Rights on Criminal Evidentiary Processes: Towards Convergence, Divergence or Realignment?' (2005) 68 (5) *MLR* 737.
151. Summers (note 80) 11; see also Field (note 149).
152. Jackson and Summers (note 72) 14.

for adversarial procedure? Roberts suggests that 'exposing the limitations of the adversarial-inquisitorial dichotomy as an analytical device should not automatically be equated with advocating its complete abandonment'.[153]

Not everyone agrees with Damaška's thesis on the crumbling of the support structure for common law evidence as a result of the decline of adversarial trial process.[154] It has been suggested that if anything, adversarial type procedures are on the rise and spreading into the traditionally inquisitorial systems.[155] Roberts also points to a visible increase of adversarial trial features rather than a decline, citing in support the procedures of the International Criminal Court, the ad hoc international criminal tribunals and the effect of the ECHR.[156]

3.3.6 Lost in translation: procédure contradictoire and adversarial procedure

This perception of an increase in adversarial procedures arises as a result of consideration of the jurisprudence of the ECtHR which has consistently stated that Article 6(3)(d) of the ECHR establishes the principle that, before an accused can be convicted, 'all evidence against him must normally be produced in his presence at a public hearing with a view to adversarial argument'.[157] It is interesting in this regard to compare the statement of the principle by the ECtHR as it appears in the French language and the English language official versions.[158] The French version is stated as follows:

> La jurisprudence de la Cour en ce qui concerne les droits de la défense dans le contexte de l'équité du procès s'articule autour de quatre propositions. Premièrement, ces droits découlent des principes de l'égalité des armes et du *caractère contradictoire de la procédure* ... En principe, l'article 6 3 (d) exige, afin de garantir le caractère contradictoire des débats, que les témoignages soient faits dans le cadre d'une audience publique et en présence de l'accusé. (*emphasis added*)

In the English version it reads:

> This Court's case-law supports four propositions concerning the rights of the defence in the context of a fair trial. Firstly, those rights are premised

153. Roberts (note 3) 299.
154. L. Friedman, 'Anchors and Flotsam: Is Evidence Law "Adrift"?' (1998) 107 (6) *Yale LJ* 1921; L. Kirkpatrick, 'Evidence Law in the Next Millennium' (1997–8) 49 (2) *Hastings LJ* 363; J. Jackson, 'Adrift but Still Clinging to the Wreckage' (1997–8) 49 (2) *Hastings LJ* 377.
155. Allen and Alexakis (note 136) 346.
156. Roberts (note 3) 326.
157. *Al-Khawaja and Tahery v The United Kingdom* ECHR 2011, 118.
158. The statements are taken from the joint partly dissenting and partly concurring opinions of Judges Sajo and Karakas in *Al-Khawaja and Tahery v UK*.

> on the principles of equality of arms and *adversarial proceedings* ... In principle, Article 6 3 (d) demands that witness statements be made at a public hearing in the presence of the accused with a view to adversarial argument. (*emphasis added*)

This raises a question as to whether there has been something of a loss in translation or indeed a leap in translation regarding the terminology used. Can it be said that 'le caractère contradictoire de la procédure' is precisely the same as 'adversarial proceedings'? Furthermore, is 'adversarial proceedings' one and the same with adversarial trial? The principle of proceedings being *contradictoire* as defined in the *Corpus Juris* implies 'that the parties can have access to any evidence or observation presented to the judge (even where this is presented by a party to the proceedings or by an independent prosecutor), with a view to influencing and discussing the judge's decision' and the accused enjoys the rights of defence guaranteed by the ECHR.[159]

As defined by a French commentator:

> *Contradictoire* embraces the right to know the case against one and to be given the possibility to defend oneself, that is, to oppose the arguments presented. Each party has the fundamental right to freely contest the proof of the other party.[160]

Following Damaška's analysis that evidence law is grounded *inter alia* on an adversarial system, a type of system that he considers to be in decline, one would expect to find that the less adversarial a system becomes, there would be a lesser place or indeed no place for a law of evidence. On the other hand, one would expect that if traditionally inquisitorial European systems increasingly adhere to adversarial procedures in order to keep in line with ECHR requirements, a law of evidence, associated as it is with adversary trial, would be seen to grow in these newly adversarial systems. If this were to be the case, then it ought to make a common admissibility of evidence regime unproblematic.[161]

159. *Corpus Juris* (Draft agreed at Florence, meeting of rapporteurs available at: <http://ec.europa.eu/anti_fraud/documents/fwk-green-paper-corpus/corpus_juris_en.pdf>; the *Corpus Juris* is discussed in section 2.2.1(c); see also M. Delmas-Marty, 'Reflections on the "Hybridisation" of Criminal Procedure', in *Essays Damaška*, J. Jackson *et al.* (note 3) 254 suggesting that *contradictoire* (in the context of the *Corpus Juris*) 'is a new conception, particularly with regard to evidence, which combines a written file (from the inquisitorial model) with strict exclusionary rules of evidence (from the accusatory model)'.
160. Ambroise-Casterot (note 101) 298.
161. Demleitner suggests 'expanding human rights protections in the Council of Europe Member States, particularly in criminal cases, may ultimately endorse the development of a flexible evidentiary system that includes exclusionary rules and possibly even a lay fact-finding body'. N. Demleitner, 'More Than "Just" Evidence' (1999) 47 (3) *Am. J. Comp. L.* 515.

But is it the case that it is simply a fallacy to translate 'un procédure contradictoire' into 'adversarial procedure' and thereby to expect that a trial will be the same in both settings?[162] I would argue that it is and that they are separate and distinct concepts, albeit that both proceed from a common point of departure. Adversarial procedure from the common law perspective envisages bi-party presentation of evidence and bi-party challenge to that evidence through the process of cross-examination. Three crucial distinctive elements are that, firstly, the principal procedural event is the trial itself rather than a pre-trial hearing; secondly, challenge to objected evidence (for example illegally obtained evidence) is normally made out of the hearing of the triers of fact so that if the objection is carried the triers of fact are unaware of the existence of such evidence; and thirdly, the presentation and challenging of evidence is done *to* the judge (and to the jury where the evidence is not excluded); the judge does not participate in the adversarial argument procedure.

Un procédure contradictoire is quite different. It shares the common baseline in that it requires that the opportunity must be given to challenge the evidence, be it to the general credibility of the evidence or to the unlawful nature of the evidence, but the procedural format for such challenge remains distinct. Firstly, it does not require that a challenge to objected evidence be made out of earshot of the triers of fact; all information, even unlawfully obtained information, may be brought before them provided the chance is given to object to it. Nor does it require the rigidity of the common law examination and cross-examination structure by the parties; it allows the trial judge to draw out the evidence through his questioning (or even to seek further evidence), provided that he gives the opportunity to the parties concerned to then contest that evidence with contradictory arguments. Crucially, it is not a trial-centred activity; the principle of *un procédure contradictoire* is satisfied even where the counter-argument occurs at the pre-trial stage rather than during the trial itself.

The translation of *contradictoire* directly into 'adversarial' may be a convenient translation in so far as it succeeds in conveying to common law and civil law systems alike that the Article 6 right to a fair trial provision requires that an opportunity is given to challenge the evidence, but it is a translation that masks the differences between the two concepts, and leads to the fallacy that the influence of the ECHR has brought about some convergence between the systems.

162. Spencer (note 85) 45 has noted that *le droit à une procédure contradictoire* is usually translated as 'an adversarial trial' that he considers is 'an uncomfortable translation, which wrongly suggests that a "fair trial" in the Strasbourg sense means undiluted doses of the kind of adversarial procedure that operates in England and the rest of the Anglo-American legal world'.

3.4 Conclusion

This chapter has highlighted various theoretical approaches that may be drawn on for comparative study of criminal procedural systems. The historical approach is useful to highlight how practices became embedded in the legal cultures over the centuries, and how systems have undergone degrees of cross-fertilisation and degrees of divergence, most notably in the area of the approach to proof.

I would argue that the inquisitorial/accusatorial dichotomy is not past its 'sell-by date' as an analytical tool. While the terms may indeed not accurately describe any system today, and indeed if they are to be seen as ideal types in the Weberian sense there should be no requirement that they would reflect real-life practices, they nonetheless retain value as a means of identifying tendencies within modern criminal justice systems, be they of inquisitorial or accusatorial origin. The theoretical base of the accusatorial and inquisitorial dichotomy has explanatory power, even if it is limited to providing an understanding of the historical influence of traditional procedures on procedures of today.[163] The accusatorial/inquisitorial dichotomy provides some measure by which to evaluate the reforms that have occurred in each of the systems. In addition, given that many European scholars describe their system as 'accusatorial', albeit somewhat confusingly, that term cannot be simply abandoned.

Like the accusatorial and inquisitorial models, the hierarchical and coordinate models are ideal types which do not necessarily reflect current procedures in either continental Europe or the Anglo-American jurisdictions, but despite criticisms of their shortcomings[164] they provide a useful base for analysis of the differing procedures across the jurisdictions. The conceptual notion of a criminal process dedicated to implementation of state policy opposed to one concerned with conflict-solving is very pertinent when considering the idea of a pan-European system of criminal justice. If adversarial process is aligned to conflict resolution, how can systems adhering to such a model be reconciled with a process envisaged by the new criminal justice measures that are most certainly directed at implementing European-wide policy? As institutional structures differ across the common law/civil law divide the ideas of judicial authority structures suggested by Damaška are especially pertinent.

The dichotomies highlighted through the models of accusatorial/inquisitorial, hierarchical/coordinate are useful to measure the positioning of the current procedures and to measure whether the cultural preferences of the opposing systems are too diverse to allow for a unified system of evidence law. However, while the adversarial/non-adversarial models as explained by

163. Damaška suggests the differences today are not significantly related to their historical past: Damaška, 'Barriers' (note 4) 560; Vogler (note 74) 129 argues that it is wrong to see the accusatorial and inquisitorial systems in terms of an 'evolutionary process' which is in his view a 'developmental fallacy'.

164. Vogler (note 74) 10 suggests Damaška's 'state typology is naïve in the extreme'.

Damaška are valuable as an analytical tool, I believe that a further classification could be usefully added: procedure that is *contradictoire*. As already noted, this term has been aligned to an idea of accusatorial procedure,[165] but given the confusion surrounding the term 'accusatorial', it is perhaps better viewed as a distinct method and set as a counterpoint to the adversarial method.

Adversarial conjures up images of battle: two opponents attempting to strike the other down, by means of striking out their evidence, so that as the case proceeds the opponent has less armoury with which to do battle. Non-adversarial as described by Damaška does not easily accommodate an idea of opponents, but places the judge at the helm; nor does it accommodate any idea of opponents striking out each other's evidence but rather places the emphasis on examining all available evidence.

Contradictoire by contrast does not conjure up a battle image but rather an image of rational debate: the idea of the proofs being contradicted by arguments of all participants putting a different 'spin' to the proof by offering a counter theory. It does not place the judge alone in the position of steering the course but provides him with co-pilots who may go off in diverse directions, with the ultimate reconciliation of arguments left to the judge who must remain impartial throughout. Nor does it require that the contradictory arguments occur only at a trial provided that opportunity is available at some point in the proceedings.[166] The *contradictoire* procedure is not averse to striking out evidence, so that, similar to the adversarial procedure, not every piece of the evidence will always be available to use in reaching a verdict of guilt or innocence. However, even though not available for use to reach a verdict, the evidence will still be revealed to the triers of fact through the challenge, a challenge that is made publicly before them. This is in contrast to the type of challenge made in the adversarial setting that conceals the objected evidence from the triers of fact while the argument against admitting it is made, and excludes it completely from their knowledge if the argument is successful.

The additional classification of *contradictoire* provides a perspective that is perhaps more reflective of modern-day continental practice and is therefore apposite as a counterpoint to the idea of adversarial procedure, to test the proposition that criminal procedures across the common law/civil law divide have become more adversarial as a result of the ECtHR jurisprudence that holds that an essential component of a fair trial encapsulates the right of the parties to challenge evidence in a public hearing. It will be used in the following chapters to highlight how each system is tied into their different procedural setting and it is that procedural setting that may militate against any possibility of achieving a unified system of evidence across the divide.

165. Damaška, 'Barriers' (note 4) 561, note 127; text to note 104 above.

166. It was stated in *Al-Khawaja* (note 157) 'in the absence of confrontation at trial, examination at the pre-trial stage may suffice' (opinions of Judges Sajo and Karakas).

4 Gathering, receiving and contesting evidence in Ireland

4.1 Introduction

This chapter will examine the process of evidence-gathering following the commission of a crime and its subsequent presentation and admissibility at trial in Ireland. There is a considerable amount of legislation governing the pre-trial investigative stage, much of which has been recently reformed, in some measure as a result of trial outcomes and also resulting from the recommendations following a recent review of criminal procedure by the Balance in the Criminal Law Review Group.[1] The reforms have also arisen in response to the jurisprudence of the European Court of Human Rights relating to the fair trial provisions of article 6 of the ECHR.

The first part of the chapter will detail the law relating to the gathering of evidence by the police, examining the principle evidence-gathering practices of search and seizure; surveillance; the taking of statements and samples from suspects, and the taking statements from witnesses. The second part of the chapter will turn to a discussion of the consequences for the use at trial of evidence that has been unlawfully gathered during the pre-trial and the rules governing its admissibility at trial. An extensive jurisprudence has developed an exclusionary rule in Ireland relating to unlawfully obtained evidence; indeed Ireland's exclusionary regime has been considered to be one of the strictest in the common law world.[2] Two other principal types of evidence will also be discussed that are subject to rules of admissibility at trial although primarily unrelated to the process of pre-trial evidence-gathering as such hearsay evidence and evidence of character. Legislation has recently reformed important aspects of the rule against hearsay. The rules relating to evidence of character have so far not been reformed in Ireland.

The third part of this chapter provides an analysis of how evidence law plays out during the trial process itself. It is during the trial that the rules of evidence come to life. The way in which evidence is presented at trial, and

1. *Balance in the Criminal Law Review Group Final Report* 2007, online at <http://www.inis.gov.ie/en/JELR/BalanceRpt.pdf/Files/BalanceRpt.pdf>.
2. Charlton J, *People (DPP) v Cash* [2007] IEHC 108, 58.

the interaction and roles of the players in the courtroom is as important to an understanding of the law of evidence as are the substantive rules themselves. To demonstrate the rules of evidence in action, I will draw on my observations of trials I attended at circuit court level.[3] I will principally draw on a trial for a robbery offence that I attended in 2011. This will provide an example of a fairly typical trial in Ireland in which much the same types of evidence arise as would equally arise in trials in France and Italy today, given the same technologies that are commonplace in each system, such as evidence from security cameras (CCTV), mobile phone and Internet data, and forensic samples, in addition to witness testimony.

I will also draw on trials I observed in an Irish circuit court over a decade ago, so as to gauge whether any differences in the trial process have been made by the reforms enacted since then.[4] In particular, I will refer to a drug-trafficking case I observed in 1997. Using these as examples, and drawing also on interviews I conducted with judges and lawyers, I will demonstrate the roles and interaction of the players in the trial process, looking at the manner in which witnesses are examined, the role of the judge, the decisions regarding presentation of evidence to the jury throughout the trial, the role of the jury, the evidence they hear and the manner of their decision-making.[5] This chapter will serve as a point of departure for comparison with the structural format of the trial process in France and Italy.

PART I

4.2 Gathering evidence in the pre-trial phase

4.2.1 Organisational structure of the pre-trial phase

Irish law operates under the common law system and follows an adversarial model of trial process. In addition to the common law[6] and legislation, Irish criminal law and procedure is governed by a written Constitution that includes the protection of liberty, privacy rights and the right to a fair trial. These rights will each have a bearing on the manner in which evidence is collected at the

3. The circuit court hears all indictable offences except for murder, rape and aggravated sexual assault.
4. Trials observed during 1997–2001.
5. I attended the robbery trial in June 2011 and conducted interviews with two judges who preside over the criminal sittings of the circuit court. I also had informal discussions with the prosecution and defence lawyers in that trial. All interviews were conducted on an anonymous basis. I had no sight of the book of evidence in the robbery trial but in the drug-trafficking case in February 1997 I was provided with access.
6. The common law refers to the law as built up historically by judicial decisions in response to the cases that came before the courts.

investigative stage of the process: the right to liberty will obviously be affected by an arrest; the right to privacy will come into play by the collection of evidence through search and seizure and through surveillance, and the right to a fair trial will depend on the manner in which all types of evidence, including statements and forensic samples, are taken from the suspect during the detention in police custody following an arrest. Ireland has also incorporated the ECHR into its domestic law through the European Convention on Human Rights Act 2003, an Act that requires the courts to interpret and apply any statutory provisions in a manner compatible with the State's obligations under the Convention and to take 'judicial notice' of the jurisprudence of the ECtHR.

Where a crime is suspected or reported it is the function of the Garda Síochána (the Irish police force) to initiate the investigation. The investigative function of the police is independent of the Director of Public Prosecutions (the DPP), nor are the police subject to direction or supervision by the judiciary.[7] The Garda Síochána has therefore full responsibility for the direction of the criminal investigation.[8]

The Office of the DPP is fully independent.[9] The DPP makes the decision whether to prosecute in any indictable offence, and in this enjoys full discretion. If the evidence is weak or unreliable the DPP may decide not to proceed with a prosecution but whatever the decision reached, the DPP is not obliged by law to give reasons to the public or to any affected parties.[10] The overall direction of the case after the decision to prosecute rests with the DPP, in so far as it is the DPP who will select the evidence from the general pool of information supplied to him by the police that is to be included in the book of evidence compiled by the DPP's office.

The role of the judiciary at the investigative stage is limited and can by no means be described as a supervisory one. Judges have no function in the investigation of offences other than issuing arrest/search/ surveillance warrants where required, determining whether the detention of arrested suspects may be lawfully extended, hearing bail applications and taking evidence by deposition where appropriate.[11] The role of the defence lawyer, the solicitor, is a limited but vital one in the investigative stage.[12]

7. See by contrast sections 5.2.3 and 6.2.5 below.
8. The Garda also prosecute in minor offences in the District Court.
9. The Office of the DPP was established by Prosecutions of Offences Act 1974.
10. See Office of the DPP, *Report on Prosecution Policy on the Giving of Reasons for Decisions* (2008) <http://www.dppireland.ie>.
11. I observed cases in the District Court over a period of two years 1998–2000; applications to extend police detentions were generally dealt with in a perfunctory manner without any probing into the reasons for seeking the extensions.
12. In Ireland, the legal profession is divided into solicitors and barristers; the former are directly in contact with the suspect and instruct the defence barrister who represents the accused at trial.

Criminal cases are conducted on behalf of the People, in the name of the DPP and are presented in court by barristers acting on behalf of the State.[13] These are private practitioners who do not belong, unlike the position of prosecutors in French and Italian systems, to the judiciary. All trial participants, the judges and prosecution and defence counsel, will have followed a career path as lawyers, working interchangeably as lawyers for the prosecution side or the defence side. Judges are appointed from this general pool of lawyers, usually quite late in their career, having sufficient experience in practice to qualify for the position.[14]

4.2.2 Means of evidence-gathering during investigation

The principal means of gathering evidence are through search and seizure, through surveillance of suspects and their premises, through obtaining statements of witnesses, and through arresting and questioning suspects and obtaining forensic samples from them. The manner in which evidence is collected at the pre-trial phase will have a direct bearing on the trial: if the evidence is gathered in breach of a person's legal or constitutional rights it may later be ruled inadmissible at trial.

4.2.3 Search and seizure

Irish law affords constitutional protection to citizens against arbitrary search, primarily in the case of their dwellings but also in relation to other premises.[15] Nonetheless, numerous statutes contain provision for entry and search. Arrest powers are accompanied by powers of search and entry.[16] The search power here rides on the back of the arrest warrant or on the back of the power to effect an arrest without a warrant; in other words, the Garda cannot simply enter the premises to search for evidence alone. Other statutes confer search powers that are not contingent on arrest, in the main specifically related to business premises.[17]

Those statutes that do extend a power of search to the dwelling will invariably require that a search warrant be first obtained.[18] The general principle

13. Cases for the most part commence in the District Court and proceed on to the Circuit or Central Criminal Court for trial before a judge and jury.
14. See, generally, Judicial Appointments Advisory Board, *Annual Report*, 2009 (available through the courts website <http://www.courts.ie>). The training, career path and appointment of the players in the process is very different from that of their counterparts in France and Italy.
15. Article 40.5.
16. Powers of arrest are provided for under s. 6(1), Criminal Law Act 1997.
17. Examples include the Misuse of Drugs Act 1977 and the Gaming and Lotteries Act 1956.
18. For example, Criminal Justice (Theft and Fraud) Offences Act 2001.

underlying these warrants is that they may be issued only by an 'independent person', a person unconnected with the investigation, and this principle may be departed from only in urgent situations.[19] The Gardaí may apply to a District Court judge for a search warrant for a broad spectrum of offences where they have reasonable cause to believe that items will be found.[20] Before granting a warrant, the judge must be satisfied that the suspicion that items would be found is reasonably held, and when a warrant is issued, it must be accurate and valid on its face.[21]

As will be seen below, the admissibility of evidence obtained on foot of a search warrant is contingent on the validity of the warrant, even where the probative value of the evidence is overwhelming. The question of admissibility of items as evidence is the decision of the judge at trial rather than during any pre-trial hearing.[22] There is no provision under Irish law that allows for the notification or presence of a lawyer during a search and searches may be conducted at any time, day or night.[23]

4.2.4 Surveillance

A new and far-reaching means of evidence-gathering lies in the measures introduced to allow for intercept evidence to be gathered. Citizens may now find that they have unbeknownst to themselves, been photographed, taped and listened to even in their own homes, by bugging devices placed there by organs of the State and by means of interception of their communication devices. The Criminal Justice (Surveillance) Act 2009 provides a statutory basis for the Gardaí to carry out surveillance.[24] Although introduced in the context of enabling the Gardaí to gather evidence against persons involved in 'gang crime', the act is all-embracing, extending the powers to cover all arrestable offences, whether involving individuals or groups. It is therefore in no way restricted to combating 'organised crime'. Surveillance may be initiated following authorisation by a judge who must consider all the circumstances, including its likely impact on the rights of any person, and must be satisfied that there are reasonable grounds for the application.[25] The judge may authorise surveillance devices to be placed in private dwellings and other premises unless the surveillance 'is likely to relate primarily' to privileged communications.

19. *Damache v DPP* [2012] IESC 11; see also *People (DPP) v Cunningham* [2012] IECCA 64; legislative provision for Superintendents to issue warrants include s. 8, Criminal Justice (Drug Trafficking) Act 1996; s. 7, Criminal Justice (Surveillance) Act 2009; Criminal Justice (Search Warrants) Act 2012.
20. Section 10, Criminal Justice (Miscellaneous Provisions) Act 1997 (as amended s. 6, Criminal Justice Act 2006).
21. *Simple Imports Ltd v Revenue Commissioners* [2000] TITR 141.
22. *Byrne v Grey* [1988] IR 31.
23. See sections 5.2.3(a) and 6.2.3 below.
24. Surveillance includes 'monitoring, observing, listening to or making a recording of' persons.
25. It must also be considered the least intrusive means available for obtaining the information.

While the norm is for application to be made to a judge, the Gardaí may initiate surveillance without prior authorisation from a judge in certain broadly defined circumstances, including where evidence is likely to be destroyed, lost or otherwise become unavailable or where the security of the State may be compromised.[26] Surveillance in these situations may not continue beyond 72 hours, after which time authorisation must be sought from a judge for its continuance.[27] The Act provides that any evidence obtained through surveillance or through the use of tracking devices[28] may be admissible as evidence.[29]

4.2.5 Obtaining evidence from witnesses

There are no special provisions for obtaining statements from witnesses. Where a crime is discovered, the Gardaí will appeal for witnesses to come forward and will take statements from those that do; there is no law in Ireland that compels witnesses to come forward. Statements are taken down in writing by the Gardaí and signed by the witness who has no right to assistance from a lawyer. Equally, no special procedure applies to taking statements from the victim of the offence, other than victims under 14 who may make their statement to a Garda or competent person by videotape.[30] A recent reform provides that where a witness makes a statement to the Garda, the witness may make a statutory declaration that the statement is true, or may give the statement under oath or affirmation administered by the Garda member.[31] The taking of the statement may also be recorded audio-visually; however, the Regulations envisaged by the Act to establish the procedure for this have not yet been published.[32]

4.2.6 Obtaining evidence from the suspect during detention in police custody

The police will attempt to gather evidence from the suspect following an arrest through questioning and by obtaining samples from the suspect. Prior to 1984, arrest was considered to be 'simply a process of ensuring the attendance

26. Section 7; the authorisation may be granted only where the officer is satisfied reasonable grounds exist for initiating the surveillance and circumstances of urgency exist.
27. Section 7(10).
28. These may be installed in vehicles and 'things' but not in dwellings and no warrant is required for their use: s. 8.
29. Section 14.
30. Section 16(1)(b), Criminal Evidence Act 1992.
31. Criminal Justice Act 2006, s. 17.
32. Ibid., s. 19; similar to the position with custody regulations and electronic recording, a failure to comply with provisions of the witness recording regulations shall not of itself render inadmissible in evidence anything said during the recording concerned (see section 4.3.1, note 95, below).

at court of the person so arrested' and was not permitted 'for the purpose of interrogation or the securing of evidence from that person'.[33] The Criminal Justice Act 1984 made detention for questioning following arrest the norm, thus creating a new source of challenge to the later admissibility at trial of the evidence gathered through questioning suspects.[34]

The detention period in police custody is the sole opportunity available for obtaining any evidence directly provided by the suspect in the form of statements or forensic samples regardless of whether he is remanded in custody or released on bail following the police detention. This, as will be seen in later chapters, is in sharp contrast to the availability of the suspect as a source of information in both France and Italy during the investigative stage of the process. In Ireland, the securing of any evidence from the suspect is confined to the forensic tests and interrogations undertaken by the police during the short window of the police custody stage. There is no culture of bringing the accused before a prosecutor or a judge to be further interrogated as the investigation advances, or of confronting the accused with witnesses or results of forensic tests.

Use of the suspect as an informational source is therefore very restricted, constrained by statutory time limits which of itself creates a pressurised environment for obtaining evidence, and by the concomitant danger of the temptation to take shortcuts. Since the collection of evidence from the suspect takes place in the relatively closed environment of the police station, various regulations have been put in place to provide safeguards for suspects in relation to questioning by police and to make the custody period more transparent.[35]

Detention in police custody must be preceded by a valid arrest,[36] otherwise everything that follows will be unlawful and evidence will have been obtained in breach of a suspect's constitutionally protected right to liberty.[37] The suspect must be brought to the police station without undue delay since it is only upon arrival at the station that the rights and safeguards of the suspect

33. Per Walsh J, *People v Shaw* [1982] IR 1 29. For the common law position see E. Ryan and P. Magee, *The Irish Criminal Process* (Mercier Press 1983); for discussion of case law following the passage of the 1984 Act see A. Ryan, 'Arrest and Detention: A Review of the Law' (2000) 10 *ICLJ* 2.
34. In addition to the common law powers of arrest, police officers were given statutory powers of arrest under some enactments, but with the exception of the Offences Against the State Act 1939, no provision existed for the detention of suspects following arrest for the purpose of questioning.
35. The principal regulations are: Criminal Justice Act 1984 (Treatment of Persons in Custody in Garda Síochána Stations) Regulations 1987 (SI 119/1987); Criminal Justice Act 1984 (Electronic Recording of Interviews) Regulations 1997 (SI 74/1997); Criminal Justice (Forensic Evidence) Act 1990 Regulations 1992 (SI 130/1992).
36. The Criminal Law Act 1997 gives Gardaí power to arrest anyone they have 'reasonable cause' to believe has committed an 'arrestable offence'.
37. Article 40.4.1: 'No citizen shall be deprived of his personal liberty save in accordance with law.'

are set in motion.[38] The norm for detention in police custody is 24 hours maximum, but a longer period is provided in the case of certain serious offences[39] and drug-trafficking offences, allowing a suspect to be held in police custody up to a maximum of seven days. However, within this timeframe, any period of detention going beyond 48 hours must be authorised by a judge of the District Court.[40]

In calculating the detention period, certain contingencies have the effect of 'stopping the clock', including the necessity of medical treatment in a hospital,[41] certified unfitness of a suspect to undergo questioning,[42] and the requirement to provide a suspect with rest where the person has been detained between midnight and eight in the morning.[43] Where a person appears before a court for the purpose of challenging the lawfulness of their detention, that period is also excluded from calculating the detention period.[44] During the detention period, forensic samples may be obtained from the suspect by the police pursuant to statutory and common law powers.[45] Non-intimate samples may be taken without the consent of the suspect.[46] Consent is required for taking intimate samples[47] but where consent is not given, adverse inferences may be drawn at trial.[48]

(a) Access to a solicitor while in police custody

It is by now well established that persons in custody have a constitutional right of access to a solicitor. The scope of this right is nonetheless unclear. In *DPP v Healy* the Supreme Court, in classifying the right as constitutional,

38. The detention provisions, ss. 4–10, Criminal Justice Act 1984, as amended by s. 9, Criminal Justice Act 2006, in conjunction with the Custody Regulations set out the legal basis for the administration of the detention powers.
39. The Criminal Justice Act 2007, s. 50 provides for seven days' maximum detention in cases of murder, false imprisonment and possession of firearms with intent to endanger life; s. 2, Criminal Justice (Drug Trafficking) Act 1996 provides up to seven days' detention; the Offences against the State (Amendment) Act 1998, s. 10 permits a maximum of 72 hours' detention.
40. Provisions for seeking authorisation from the judge are contained in: s. 50(3)(g)(i) and (ii), Criminal Justice Act 2007; s. 2(2) and (3), Criminal Justice (Drug Trafficking) Act 1996; s. 10, Offences Against the State (Amendment) Act 1998.
41. Section 4(8), Criminal Justice Act 1984.
42. Section 4(8B), inserted by s. 24, Criminal Justice (Amendment) Act 2009.
43. Section 7(c), Criminal Justice Act 2011; *People (DPP) v Cooney* [1998] 1 ILRM 321 (exclusion of rest period without consent rendered detention unlawful.
44. Section 4(8A), Criminal Justice Act 1984 (inserted by the Miscellaneous Provisions Act 1997).
45. These powers are contained in ss. 6 and 6A of the 1984 Act (as amended by s. 48, Criminal Justice Act 2007). These provisions apply also to the 1996 Drug Trafficking Act.
46. Section 1(1), Criminal Justice (Forensic Evidence) Act 1990, as amended by s. 14, Criminal Justice Act 2006.
47. Section 1(4), Criminal Justice (Forensic Evidence) Act 1990.
48. Section 3, Criminal Justice (Forensic Evidence) Act 1990, as substituted by s. 17, Criminal Justice Act 1999.

restricted its finding to the right of a person detained in custody to a solicitor where the person has requested one to attend or where one has been requested by a third party on the detainee's behalf.[49] Finlay CJ stressed that the court was not addressing the issue of the right to be informed of the right of access or 'any possible right' of a detained person to have a solicitor present during the police interview.[50] Nor did the court explicitly address the issue of whether the questioning of a detained person after he has requested a solicitor but before the solicitor arrives amounts to a breach of the detainee's right of access.

Healy is therefore authority only for the point that a person who has requested a legal adviser (or by third party) has a constitutional right of 'reasonable' access. This includes the right to be immediately told of the solicitor's arrival, to be afforded immediate access to the solicitor if requested[51] and access must be in private.[52] It has also been held that a refusal or postponement of access may not offend reasonable access if the detainee has already had prior consultations at an earlier stage of the detention.[53]

(b) Questioning prior to arrival of solicitor

The issue of questioning the suspect prior to the arrival of the solicitor has to some extent been clarified by recent legislation, a reform considered necessary in order to ensure Ireland's compliance with Article 6.1 of the ECHR, in light of recent jurisprudence of the ECtHR on the issue of access to legal advice. This new legislation appears to fall short of ECHR requirements. In *Salduz*, the ECtHR stated Article 6.1

> requires that, as a rule, access to a lawyer should be provided as from the first interrogation of a suspect by the police unless it is demonstrated in the light of the particular circumstances of each case that there are compelling reasons to restrict this right.[54]

This statement from the court is not itself completely unambiguous. The Criminal Justice Act 2011 in an attempt to follow this jurisprudence now prohibits questioning 'until such time as the person has had an opportunity to consult with a solicitor'; however, this is not as unequivocal as it would

49. [1990] 2 IR 73, Finlay CJ, 81.
50. Ibid., 78.
51. Healy [1990] 2 IR 73; see also on the issue of 'reasonable access' *People (DPP) v Madden* [1977] IR 336, 355; on the right to be informed of right of access see s. 5, Criminal Justice Act 1984; *DPP v Spratt* [1995] 2 ILRM 117.
52. *People (DPP) v Finnegan* (CCA 15 July 1997).
53. *People (DPP) v Pringle, McCann & O'Shea* [1981] 2 Frewen 57, 96.
54. *Salduz v Turkey* [GC] no. 36391/02 ECHR 2008, para. 55.

appear at first sight.[55] Section 9 goes on to provide that the period of time between the making of a request for a solicitor and the arrival of the solicitor shall be excluded from the overall reckoning of the permissible detention period. In other words, it has the effect of stopping the detention clock. The period that may be excluded shall not exceed six hours in the case of a person detained between the hours of midnight and 8 a.m. or three hours in all other cases. A certain ambiguity arises here by dint of the fact that the provision prohibiting questioning is immediately followed by the provision for excluding the waiting time from the overall detention period. This raises a question of whether the stop the clock provision means that questioning can commence after the three/six-hour period has elapsed or whether the Garda must still await the arrival of solicitor before commencing to question the suspect, even though waiting will have the effect of running down the detention period.

Section 9 also provides that questioning may proceed before consultation with a solicitor where a delay in questioning would involve the risk of interference or injury to other persons, loss or damage to property, destruction of or interference with evidence, the alerting of accomplices or the hindering of the recovery of property.[56] Such a saver would be in line with the 'compelling reasons' proviso referred to in *Salduz*.

Given the ambiguity surrounding the reform to the law, the earlier case law on this point may continue to be of relevance (once the provision comes into force) should disputes arise in the future relating to questioning commenced after the 'stop the clock' periods have elapsed. In *People (DPP) v Buck* the appellant had been arrested on suspicion of murder on a Sunday afternoon in summer at a time when there was a major sporting event going on in the area.[57] There were therefore difficulties in obtaining a solicitor and the appellant was questioned for three and a half hours by three different sets of Gardaí before receiving legal assistance. The appellant made an incriminating statement shortly after his first meeting with the solicitor. A point of law was referred to the Supreme Court that essentially involved two issues:

- whether an arrest in circumstances likely to pose difficulties in obtaining a solicitor amounts to a breach of the right of reasonable access;
- whether the questioning of a suspect between the time of making a request and arrival of a solicitor amounts to a breach of the right of reasonable access.

55. Section 9, Criminal Justice Act 2011, inserting s. 5A into Criminal Justice Act 1984; section not yet in force.
56. Ibid.
57. [2002] 2 ILRM 454; see: A. Ryan, 'Avoiding the Hard Question: *DPP v Buck* and the Constitutional Right of Access to Legal Advice' [2003] 25 *DULJ* 257.

Regarding the first issue, Keane CJ was satisfied that the trial judge was entitled to conclude on the evidence that there had been no breach of the appellant's right of access to a solicitor resulting from the Garda decision to effect the arrest on the Sunday. There was no obligation in the circumstances to defer the arrest to the Monday provided there was no *male fides* attempt to ensure he was without legal advice. On the issue of questioning after the request for a solicitor but before the arrival, Keane CJ stated 'it cannot be said that the constitutional right of access to a solicitor has necessarily been denied'.[58]

A subsequent decision of the Supreme Court by contrast found a breach of the right of access to a solicitor where the evidence showed that the Gardaí had chosen to contact a solicitor whose offices were a considerable distance from the Garda station. The court upheld the finding of the Court of Criminal Appeal that a breach of the appellant's rights arose because in selecting that solicitor the Gardaí must have known that a significant and unnecessary delay would ensue.[59] More recently, it has been suggested that behaviour on the part of the Gardaí amounting to 'colourable manoeuvres' having the effect of delaying or interfering with a person's right of access to legal advice would give rise to a breach of the constitutional right of reasonable access.[60]

Mere ineptitude on the part of an officer in attempting to contact a solicitor has been found not to breach the right of reasonable access. In *DPP v Creed*, the unsuccessful attempt of a Garda to contact a solicitor was found not to be a breach of the right, even though she had done no more than telephone the office number of the solicitor at a time clearly outside of office hours; she had made no attempt to secure an alternative contact number and had not informed the suspect of her failed attempts so as to allow him the opportunity of nominating an alternative solicitor.[61]

(c) Presence of a solicitor during questioning by police

As noted above, the '*Salduz* principle' is not without ambiguity. The interpretation of *Salduz* by some Member States has been that it requires that a lawyer be present with the suspect during the police interviews.[62] This issue of presence during questioning has been repeatedly raised in Ireland but to date has never been resolved. The most recent legislation discussed above similarly evaded the opportunity to do so. A number of committees have addressed the issue over the decades. In 1987, Justice Barra O'Briain recommended that a legal adviser should be present in the capacity of observer.[63] More recently,

58. [2002] 2 ILRM 454, 464.
59. *O'Brien v DPP* [2005] IR 206; [2005] IESC 29, McCracken J.
60. *DPP v Gormley* [2009] IECCA 22; judgment awaited from SC.
61. *DPP v Creed* [2009] IECCA 95; see section 4.3.2 below, text to note 123.
62. For example, France, Scotland and Malta.
63. *Report of the Committee to Recommend Certain Safeguards for Persons in Custody*, Prl 7158 (April 1978).

the minority in the *Report of the Committee to Review the Offences Against the State Acts 1939–1998 and Related Matters* recommended that a suspect should be entitled to the presence of a solicitor during the course of police interviews.[64] The majority were divided on the issue and made no recommendation, but conceded that in the context of the inference provisions of the Offences Against the State (Amendment) Act 1998, no inferences should be drawn from a suspect's silence unless the suspect has had 'an adequate opportunity' for consultation with a solicitor.[65]

The most recent committee, the Balance in the Criminal Law Review Group, did not make any recommendations on the issue per se, but referred to it in the context of reform to the law on the right to silence. The Review Group considered that if the law were to be changed so as to permit a general failure to answer questions while in police custody to amount to corroborative evidence of guilt, it would necessarily require permitting a suspect to have a solicitor present at all stages of the police interview. In their Final Report the Review Group were against any such change relating to the right to silence and consequently made no recommendations about presence of a solicitor during questioning.

The issue has also been raised in a number of cases and consistently rejected as forming an aspect of the right to reasonable access to a solicitor.[66] In *Lavery v MIC Carrickmacross Garda Station*, the question raised was whether the refusal to provide the solicitor with access to notes of police interviews rendered the detention unlawful.[67] Access to the interview notes was specifically sought because the inference provisions of the Offences Against the State (Amendment) Act 1998 were applicable. O'Flaherty J approached the issue from a balancing of rights perspective – the right of the suspect to reasonable access to a solicitor and the right of the Gardaí to interrogate a suspect.[68] He considered that it was going too far to require the Gardaí to give the solicitor a regular update and running account of the interviews concluding that: 'the solicitor is not entitled to be present at the interviews'.[69] While it has been suggested that this statement was *obiter*,[70] subsequent decisions of the Court of Criminal Appeal have reiterated that this represents the law in Ireland.[71]

64. Dublin (Stationery Office 2000).
65. Ibid., 181.
66. Examples include: *People (DPP) v Pringle, McCann O'Shea* (note 53); *People (Attorney General) v Farrell* [1978] IR 13.
67. *Lavery v Member in Charge, Carrickmacross Garda Station* [1999] 2 IR 390; see also *Barry v Waldron* (HC 23 May 1996).
68. See also *Pringle* (note 53).
69. [1999] 2 IR 390, 396.
70. D. Walsh, *Criminal Procedure* (Thomson Round Hall 2002) 274; see also *Report of the Committee to Review the Offences Against the State Acts 1939–1998 and Related Matters* 178ff. Online at: <http://www.justice.ie/en/JELR/Pages/Review_of_the_Offences_against_the_State_Acts>.
71. *DPP v Yu Jie* [2005] IE CCA 95; *M v MIC Coolock Gardaí Station* [2013] IEHC 251.

The Criminal Justice Act 2011 made no change to this position. The reform to provide for the postponing of questioning until the solicitor arrives was considered necessary because 'recent jurisprudence of the European Court of Human Rights emphasises the importance of detained persons having, as a rule, access to legal advice in advance of questioning'.[72] Clearly, the Irish legislature have interpreted the ECtHR jurisprudence simply to require consultation with a lawyer in advance of any questioning rather than the actual physical presence of the lawyer during the police interrogation. As the law currently stands, during the time the suspect is being questioned he has no on-the-spot assistance from the lawyer but could demand to see the lawyer again if needs be. Nonetheless, since the constitutional right of access embraces simply the entitlement to 'reasonable' access, in theory the police would not be breaching the constitutional rights of the suspect if access was refused in a situation where the suspect had already seen the lawyer on one or two occasions and then made repeated requests to consult with the lawyer.[73] The effect of a breach of the constitutional right of access to a lawyer on the admissibility of evidence obtained will be discussed below.[74]

(d) The suspect's right to silence during police questioning

The right to silence in Ireland has been firmly established as enjoying constitutional status; however, it is not an absolute right, and legislative encroachments to date have been upheld on the basis that they are proportionate to the aims they set out to achieve.[75] Early encroachments on the right to silence related to requirements to account for presence at or near a crime scene, objects in one's possession and marks on clothing or on the person.[76] A major encroachment occurred in relation to drug-trafficking offences that required a suspect to mention any fact to the questioning officers that he would later rely on in his defence.[77] The Criminal Justice Act 2007 has expanded the limitation of the right to silence in relation to all arrestable offences. The Act allows inferences to be drawn at trial from the failure of the accused to mention

72. See Dail debate, Wednesday, 18 May 2011 (available online at: http://www.oireachtas.ie/parliament/).
73. See above text to note 53.
74. See section 4.3.2 below. A recent decision of the High Court in a habeas corpus application has stated that neither *Salduz* nor *Panovits* 'go so far as to say that there is a right to have one's solicitor present at police interviews': *M v MIC Coolock Gardaí Station* [2013] IEHC 251, 27; *Dayanan v Turquie* no. 7377/03 (ECtHR 13/10/2009) was not opened to the Court.
75. *Heaney v Ireland* [1997] 1 ILRM 35 (SC); *Rock v Ireland & AG* [1997] IR 484 (SC).
76. Offences Against the State Acts 1939–98, s. 30; Offences Against the State (Amendment) Act 1972, s. 2; Criminal Justice Act 1984, ss. 15, 16, 18, 19 (as amended by ss. 28 and 29, Criminal Justice Act 2007).
77. See A. Ryan, 'The Criminal Justice (Drug Trafficking) Act 1996: Decline and Fall of the Right to Silence?' (1997) 7 (1) *ICLJ*, 22; an identical provision appears in s. 5, Offences Against the State (Amendment) Act 1998.

particular facts when questioned by the police.[78] Section 30 provides that in any proceedings where evidence is given that, either during questioning before being charged or upon being charged or informed that he/she might be prosecuted for the offence, the person

> failed to mention any fact relied on in his or her defence in those proceedings, being a fact which in the circumstances existing at the time clearly called for an explanation from him or her when so questioned, charged or informed, as the case may be, then, the court ... may draw such inferences from the failure as appear proper; and the failure may, on the basis of such inferences, be treated as, or as capable of amounting to, corroboration of any evidence in relation to which the failure is material.

No inferences may be drawn unless the accused was told in ordinary language what the effect of the failure to mention a fact might be. The most recent legislation, the Criminal Justice Act 2011, provides that inferences may not be drawn from failure to disclose any fact unless the failure occurred after the accused was informed of the right to consult a solicitor and given an opportunity for such consultation where requested.[79] Inferences may be drawn only where the questioning was recorded electronically, unless the person consented in writing to it not being so recorded. Despite the provisions allowing inferences to be drawn from the failure to mention certain facts, the caution in the Judges Rules (Rule 5) continues to be used.[80] As a result a suspect is told on the one hand that there is no requirement to speak and on the other that a failure to speak may result in inferences being drawn.[81]

(e) Regulation of questioning of suspects in custody

Although suspects do not currently benefit from the safeguard of the presence of a solicitor during questioning,[82] other safeguards are provided in an effort to counterbalance the coercive atmosphere of the custody environment. These are the provisions of the Custody Regulations, the Judges' Rules and the provisions for the electronic recording of interviews. The Judges' Rules relate to the cautioning of suspects and the taking of statements.[83] The Custody

78. Section 30 of the Act inserts a new s. 19A into the Criminal Justice Act 1984.
79. Section 19A of the Criminal Justice Act 1984 has been amended by s. 9 of the Criminal Justice Act 2011; section not yet in force.
80. Rule 5 caution: 'You are not obliged to say anything unless you wish to do so but what you do say may be put into writing and given in evidence.'
81. For England and Wales see Code C (April 1995), para. 10(4).
82. Although the presence of a solicitor has been questioned in its potential as an effective safeguard in England.
83. The Rules are set out in *People v Cummins* [1972] IR 312; Rule 7 provides where a person is making a statement to the police, he should not be cross-examined or questioned except for the purpose of removing ambiguities; see further *People (DPP) v McCann* [1998] 4 IR 397.

Regulations deal more generally with the procedures that must be followed when interviewing suspects in custody. The Judges' Rules are not rules of law but are 'intended for the guidance of persons taking statements' and 'will be departed from at peril'.[84] It has been held that a suspect is entitled to the protections provided by both.[85] The Custody Regulations require interviews to be conducted in a fair and humane manner, and regulate matters relating to the number of officers present during interviews, the duration of interviews and the taking of statements from the suspect.[86]

(f) Electronic recording of interviews

The 1984 Act made provision for the introduction of audio-visual recording of interviews of suspects in police custody; however, it was not until 13 years later that the Regulations were finally published. The Regulations create a mandatory regime for the electronic recording of interviews, but allow for an interview to proceed if the equipment is faulty, unavailable or where recording is 'not practicable'.[87] It is evident from the case law that initially there was a degree of reluctance by the Gardaí to record interviews with suspects as a matter of course.[88] In a number of cases the Court of Criminal Appeal was critical of the apparent reluctance to use the recording facilities, although the transcripts of interviews were not ruled inadmissible as evidence on that account.[89]

More recently, the issue as to whether the non-recording of interviews should lead to the exclusion of the interview evidence was addressed by the Supreme Court. Hardiman J was of the view that the admissibility of the interviews would be a matter for the trial judge, and Murray J preferred to leave the issue for decision in a future case.[90] Despite the provisions for the electronic recording of interviews, the requirement that the interviewing officer takes a written note of the interview as required under the Custody Regulations remains.[91] There is no obligation on the Gardaí to reduce everything that is said in the course of an interview to writing; however, they should note 'anything of consequence'.[92]

84. *Farrell* (note 66), 21.
85. *People (DPP) v Darcy* (CCA, 29 July 1997).
86. Article 12; *People (DPP) v Connell* [1995] 1 IR 244.
87. Electronic Recording Regulations (note 35).
88. *People (DPP) v Holland* (CCA, 15 June 1998).
89. Examples include: *DPP v Michael Murphy* [2005] IECCA 52; *DPP v Murphy* [2005] IECCA 1; *DPP v Connolly* [2003] 2 IR 1; *Rattigan v DPP* [2008] IESC 34.
90. *Rattigan v DPP* [2008] IESC 34; *DPP v PA* [2008] IECCA 21.
91. Article 12(10).
92. *People (DPP) v McKeever* (CCA, 16 July 992).

PART II

4.3 Rules of evidence

Being a common law jurisdiction, the rules of evidence in Ireland are by and large of an exclusionary nature, a feature that is often considered to be that which distinguishes the common law rules of evidence from their civil law counterparts. In the case of the former, the tendency is to withhold the information from the fact-finder altogether while the opposite is true of the civil law systems; the rules of the latter are generally more in the nature of rules that prohibit the use of the information for reaching a verdict, but the fact-finders are nonetheless generally made aware of the existence and content of such information.

The rules of evidence are invoked in Ireland during the currency of the trial. Where there is a dispute about the admissibility of any piece of evidence, the dispute is resolved during a process known as the *voir dire*, an application made to the trial judge in the absence of the jury. In gathering the evidence, the Garda officers need to bear in mind the rules of evidence since their methods for obtaining the evidence, be they real items obtained following a search or statements and confessions obtained from suspects in police custody, may be scrutinised at trial. The extensive law surrounding these issues will be discussed at this juncture. Two other stalwarts of evidence law unconnected to the manner of collection of evidence will then be outlined. These rules relate to the issue of reliability of evidence and the issue of potential prejudice certain evidence may arouse in the minds of the jury, the rule against hearsay and the rules relating to character evidence respectively.

4.3.1 Unlawfully obtained evidence

The manner in which evidence is collected at the pre-trial may have consequences for its subsequent admissibility at trial. If the evidence has been unlawfully obtained, the judge may use his discretion to exclude it, or will be obliged to exclude it, depending on the nature of unlawfulness. The starting point regarding the exclusionary rule for unlawfully obtained evidence is the Supreme Court decision in *People (AG) v O'Brien*[93] that has been gradually refined and extended in subsequent case law. The central issue in *O'Brien* concerned the admissibility of evidence obtained on foot of a search warrant that had misstated the address of the premises to be searched. The error had not been noticed by any of the parties concerned prior to the entry. The Supreme Court differentiated between evidence that is obtained illegally or improperly and evidence that is obtained in breach of a suspect's constitutional rights.

Kingsmill-Moore J approached the issue of illegally or improperly obtained evidence by balancing the competing interests: the public interest

93. [1965] IR 142 (SC).

that crime should be detected and punished on the one hand, and on the other 'that individuals should not be subjected to illegal or inquisitorial methods of investigation and that the State should not attempt to advance its ends by utilising the fruits of such methods'.[94] This balancing approach continues to prevail with regard to the admissibility of illegally or improperly obtained evidence. Admissibility is therefore always a matter for the discretion of the trial judge in such cases. A typical example of illegally obtained evidence would be evidence obtained during police custody involving a breach of the regulatory requirements.[95]

The position is much stricter where evidence has been obtained in breach of constitutional rights. *O'Brien* established that the courts *must* exclude evidence obtained 'as a result of a deliberate and conscious violation of the constitutional rights of the accused person where no extraordinary excusing circumstances exist'.[96] Examples offered in the judgment of 'extraordinary excusing circumstances' include: the need to rescue a victim in peril and the need to safeguard vital evidence from imminent destruction. Any evidence obtained in the absence of any excusing circumstances should be 'absolutely inadmissible'.[97]

It was implicit in the judgment that the phrase 'deliberate and conscious' did not include breaches resulting from inadvertence, and this interpretation continued to find favour in subsequent cases.[98] It was later considered that 'it is the violation of the person's constitutional rights, and not the particular act complained of, that has to be deliberate and conscious' in order to attract the exclusionary rule.[99] Furthermore, ignorance on the part of police officers of the fact that they were breaching constitutional rights would not save the evidence from the sanction of exclusion. Nor may the police decide in advance that they are entitled to breach a person's constitutional right because in their view the circumstances so warrant: the issue of whether evidence may be admitted despite a breach of constitutional rights is for the court of trial to decide having regard to whether in its view extraordinary excusing circumstances excuse the breach.[100]

The meaning of the phrase 'deliberate and conscious' was finally settled by the Supreme Court in *People (DPP) v Kenny* and this continues to be the authoritative decision regarding the exclusionary rule.[101] In *Kenny*, the Gardaí had found a quantity of heroin following a search of a private dwelling on

94. Ibid., 160.
95. Breach of Regulations does not 'of itself' make evidence obtained inadmissible: s. 7(3), Criminal Justice Act 1984.
96. *O'Brien* (note 93) 170.
97. Ibid.
98. *Madden* (note 51) 346; *Shaw* (note 33) 33.
99. *Shaw* (note 33) 56.
100. Ibid., 40.
101. *People (DPP) v Kenny* [1990] 2 IR 110.

foot of an invalid search warrant.[102] It was argued on behalf of the appellant that, irrespective of whether either of the police officers was aware that he was invading the constitutional rights of the accused and regardless of whether either of them could be described as being culpable or blameworthy, the evidence should have been ruled inadmissible on the basis that there was a conscious and deliberate breach of his constitutional rights. Finlay CJ focused on the nature of the particular act that has given rise to the breach of constitutional rights:

> I am satisfied that the correct principle is that evidence obtained by invasion of the constitutional personal rights of a citizen must be excluded unless a court is satisfied that either the act constituting the breach of constitutional rights was committed unintentionally or accidentally, or is satisfied that there are extraordinary excusing circumstances which justify the admission of the evidence in its (the court's) discretion.[103]

It is important to note that the reference to 'unintentionally or accidentally' is not related to an inadvertent breach of constitutional rights, such as entry to a premises without noticing a misstated address, but refers to the act itself; in other words, was the act of entry itself deliberate and conscious or was it accidental – accidental here having its ordinary meaning. Did the policeman fall over the threshold! This gave a very different slant to the meaning of deliberate and conscious to when the phrase was first used in *O'Brien* and recast the exclusionary rule in Ireland so as to make it the strictest in the common law world.[104]

4.3.2 Fruit of the poisoned tree – causative link

The exclusionary rule as expressed in *People (AG) v O'Brien* referred to evidence obtained *as a result* of a conscious and deliberate violation. In *People (DPP) v Healy* Finlay J stated:

> The vital issue which arises, therefore, if a breach of the right of access to a solicitor has occurred as a result of a conscious and deliberate act of a member of the Garda Siochana, is whether there is a causative link between that breach and the obtaining of an admission.[105]

There is little difficulty in finding a causative link in cases where the breach of a constitutional right is related to inviolability of the suspect's private

102. The Peace Commissioner, who had died before the case came to trial, had not inquired into the basis of the Garda's suspicion when issuing the warrant as required by law.
103. *Kenny* (note 101), 134; *People (DPP) v Healy* [1990] 2 IR 73, 89.
104. *DPP v Cash* [2007] IEHC 108, 66.
105. *Healy* (note 103) 81.

dwelling – where a Garda discovers real evidence on foot of an invalid search warrant that evidence has been procured as a result of the breach of the constitutional rights of the suspect and must be excluded, no matter how cogent. This is because the act of entry will always be a deliberate act (barring some accidental entry) and therefore a breach of constitutional rights, and no evidence would have been obtained but for that act of breach. The vital issue in such a case will be to decide if the warrant was in fact invalid.

The situation is somewhat more complex where the breach relates to failure to provide the suspect with access to legal advice when the suspect is in police custody. Where the suspect is refused access to legal advice this results in the detention becoming unlawful and therefore in breach of the constitutional right of liberty of the suspect. If a statement is taken from the suspect during this period of unlawful detention it will attract the strict exclusionary rule. However, once a suspect is given access to a lawyer, this will cure the earlier unlawful detention and the detention becomes lawful. Any statement taken during this lawful period remains admissible as evidence.

A restrictive approach to the causative link issue is evident in *Buck*.[106] The appellant had made an incriminating statement after having consulted with the solicitor. It was submitted that interrogating the appellant at a time when he was without advice from a solicitor was in breach, not only of his constitutional right of access to a solicitor, but also of the Custody Regulations. These provide that where an arrested person asks for a solicitor, he is not to be asked to make a written statement until a reasonable time for the attendance of a solicitor has elapsed.[107] Counsel for the appellant argued that the assertion by the Garda that he was simply questioning the appellant and not seeking a statement as such was 'disingenuous' and that the substance of the Regulation had not been observed. Counsel for the prosecution argued that what the Regulations envisage by a statement is 'a narrative by the person in detention which was reduced to writing by a Garda and signed by the person in detention' and therefore the responses to Garda questions would not fall under the type of written statement envisaged by the Regulation.[108]

The court adopted the latter meaning of the term 'statement' and found that since no written inculpatory statement had been made until after the consultation with the solicitor, no breach of the Regulation had occurred. Interpreting 'written statement' in such a formalistic way has negative implications for the way in which the causative link issue is approached, especially where a case involves an incriminating statement made during a time where a person is not in unlawful detention. To suggest that the earlier interviews with the police officers have no causative link to the statement taken after the suspect has received advice is to ignore the fact that a memo of the interview

106. *Buck* (note 57).
107. Regulation 12(6).
108. *Buck* (note 57) 462.

can be equally prejudicial to an accused as the formal statement. Indeed, it is not unusual to find answers made in response to Garda questioning and recorded in the memo of the interview to some extent re-emerging or reflected in a subsequent written statement.[109] Where the suspect has given answers to questions posed, the Gardaí may be in a stronger position to persuade the suspect to make a statement since they may, explicitly or implicitly, suggest to the suspect that its substance has already been recorded in the memo. Thus even where a statement is made after the suspect has received advice from a solicitor, which cures any earlier unlawful detention, it could be argued that there may still be a causative link because the statement may have had as its genesis the period where the suspect has been deprived access.

The issue of a causative link between a statement that was admitted at trial and those statements taken during a period of unlawful custody was examined in some depth in *DPP v Ryan*.[110] The argument before the Court of Criminal Appeal was that a statement made during the lawful period of custody should have been excluded at trial on the basis that there was a causative link between statements made during the earlier unlawful period and the statement made during the lawful period. It was argued that the latter statement was tainted as it had been obtained through reliance on information given by the accused during the earlier unlawful period. The court looked closely at the earlier statements to examine whether the information contained in the later statement was dependent on any information contained in the impugned statements and found on the facts that such was not the case.[111]

A related argument by the appellant was that there was a general causative link on the basis that the statement taken during the lawful period of detention was tainted by psychological effects of the earlier period of unlawful detention. The court rejected that argument in the following terms:

> In effect, this Court has been invited to conclude that there was such a causative link based upon 'human psychology' as it was put. The suggestion that such a link must exist is put forward as if it were a proposition so obvious that the Court should adopt it without any need for evidence, ... This Court does not consider that this follows at all in the circumstances of this case. Each case must depend upon its own facts. In some cases a causative link may exist; in others it may not.[112]

109. This occurred frequently in trials I attended during 1997–2000, and could be seen clearly in the statements and interview memos in the book of evidence of the drug-trafficking trial discussed in section 4.4.3(b) below.
110. *DPP v Ryan* [2011] IECCA 6.
111. Ibid., 14.
112. Ibid., 13; more recently the Supreme Court stated that '... part of a statement made or interview given during a period when the accused is in constitutionally unlawful custody must be excluded but that, prima facie, any part of the statement made or interview given during a period of lawful custody can be admitted. However, that latter statement is

In *O'Brien v DPP* McCracken J further clarified the position regarding the causative link as set out by Finlay J in *Healy* by stating that any implication arising from it that there may be circumstances in which statements taken at a time when an accused's constitutional rights were being breached could nevertheless be admissible if there was no causative link between the breach and the statement would be to misinterpret the position.[113] He explained that the causative link must be as between a statement made *after* the breach had ceased and the earlier unlawful detention period.

It used to be considered that even where a person was in unlawful detention due to denial of access to legal advice, evidence which the police are by statute empowered to take, such as breath samples or fingerprints, would be admissible since there would be no causative link between the breach of the constitutional right of access to a lawyer and the obtaining of the evidence. The view was taken that the evidence would have been obtained regardless of any advice that the suspect would have received from a lawyer as there is statutory power to obtain it.[114] The issue of whether a causative link is required to be shown in relation to these types of evidence before it could be ruled inadmissible was addressed recently by the High Court in *DPP v McCrea*,[115] which concluded from its reading of *O'Brien* that a causative link is not required in the sense that the concept was explained in an earlier case, *Walsh v O'Buachalla*.[116]

In that case relating to a drunk driving offence, it was argued that breath samples ought to have been excluded on the basis that they had been obtained following a refusal of access to a solicitor. Blayney J took the passage in *Healy* to mean that evidence obtained following a deliberate and conscious breach of a constitutional right must be excluded only where there is a causative link between the breach and the evidence sought to be excluded. Since the evidence at issue was a breath sample, one that the applicant was required to give by law and would commit an offence if he did not provide it, Blayney J questioned the utility of a solicitor in such a situation. In his view: 'No advice could have prevented the specimen being obtained and, accordingly, the applicant's not having had access to a solicitor in no way affected it's being obtained'.[117] He considered 'the evidence was obtained after the violation but not *as a result* of the violation'.[118]

subject to the caveat that, if it can be shown that there is a real risk of unfairness by admitting only part of a statement, then it may well be that the trial judge will have to exclude the entirety of the statement concerned': *DPP v AD* [2012] IESC para. 5.21.

113. [2005] IR 206; [2005] IESC 29.
114. *Walsh v O'Buaccalla* [1991] 1 IR 56 (HC); *DPP v Spratt* [1995] 2 ILRM 117 (CCA).
115. *DPP v McCrea* [2009] IEHC 39.
116. *Walsh v O'Buachalla* [1991] 1 IR 56 (HC).
117. Ibid., 60.
118. *Walsh v O'Buachalla* (note 116) (emphasis added).

In *McCrea* the High Court took a different approach. The charge in *McCrea* related to the offence of refusal to provide breath specimens as required under the Road Traffic Acts.[119] The Garda in question had refused to provide the applicant access to his solicitor because she had mistakenly believed that she could not make a second request of the applicant to carry out a toxicology test, in the event that she would have to interrupt the test to allow the consultation with the solicitor. She therefore told the applicant he would have to wait until she had completed the test. The court found that a deliberate refusal of access caused the detention to be unlawful. It reiterated that the deliberate act of refusal – and any subjective factors for doing the act are irrelevant to the consideration of whether an act is deliberate – results in the detention being unlawful. Therefore any evidence obtained during that time must be ruled inadmissible, and this holds equally whether the information is such that a person is required to give by law or otherwise.

The High Court found that *Walsh v O'Buachalla* no longer represents the law and that 'the appropriate question was not whether a lawyer *would* have made a difference but rather whether a lawyer *could* have made a difference'.[120] The court found that in such a case a person could benefit from advice, which would not necessarily simply be advice to comply, but could also include information regarding the consequences of a refusal.

The issue of access to legal advice in the context of taking forensic samples has arisen in a number of recent cases. In *DPP v White* the appellant had been convicted of murder.[121] The evidence linking the accused to the murder consisted of fingerprints on a bag containing the murder weapon found in the car used in the attack and DNA evidence also taken from the car that was found to match that of the appellant. It was argued at trial that the forensic samples he had given while in police custody ought not to be admitted in evidence on the basis that they had been unlawfully obtained in breach of the appellant's right of reasonable access to a solicitor. On arrival at the police station, the appellant had nominated a solicitor, the solicitor was called and a message was left on the latter's phone; at that point forensic samples were then taken from the appellant, with his consent.

The Court of Criminal Appeal found that the samples were admissible as evidence and did not accept that there was any requirement to wait for the solicitor before taking the sample, relying on the statement in *DPP v Cash* that a sample does not change.[122] Furthermore, the appellant had in any event consented to them being taken. The failure to await the solicitor's arrival therefore did not breach the right of reasonable access and the samples were taken during a period of lawful detention.

119. Section 13(2), Road Traffic Act 1994, amended by s. 23, Road Traffic Act 2002.
120. *McCrea* (note 115) 39.
121. [2011] IECCA 78.
122. [2007] IEHC 108.

What of the situation where the actions of a Garda in contacting the solicitor are inadequate? Would this amount to a deliberate and conscious breach of the suspect's right of 'reasonable access' thereby rendering samples taken during the period of unlawful detention inadmissible? The issue was recently discussed in *DPP v Creed* in which the admission of a hair sample was challenged by the appellant as having been obtained during a period when the appellant was in unlawful custody.[123] The circumstances of the case were that the appellant had requested a solicitor upon arrival at the Garda station following his arrest on a Saturday night on suspicion of robbery. The Garda attempted to contact the solicitor simply by phoning the office number of the solicitor even though it was obviously outside office hours. No attempt was made to find an alternative contact number, and furthermore the Garda did not inform the suspect about her failure to have made contact with the solicitor so as to enable the suspect to nominate another solicitor or to suggest a mobile number. The appellant had been questioned during that night and the following morning was asked by a different Garda for a sample; the appellant had consented to giving the sample at that point, and made no request of that particular Garda to obtain a solicitor before giving the sample.

The Court of Criminal Appeal did not find that the actions of the Garda in her attempts to contact a solicitor following the request by the appellant amounted to a 'conscious and deliberate breach' of his constitutional rights. The actions of the Garda, while considered by the court to show 'a lack of common sense and proper care', did not amount to a deliberate *refusal* as had happened in *McCrea*, and was consistent with *Kenny* that 'subjective factors like motive or personal knowledge are not relevant when considering whether infringement of a constitutional right is conscious and deliberate'.[124]

As for the failure to inform the suspect that she had been unsuccessful in contacting the solicitor and offering him the choice of nominating another, that was certainly a breach of the Custody Regulations – but such a breach does not render the detention unlawful. It calls for the trial judge to exercise his discretion to exclude the evidence as opposed to being required to exclude evidence, which would have been the case if a constitutional breach had been found. Since the trial judge had used his discretion to exclude the statements made while the suspect was without access to a lawyer, the Court of Criminal Appeal believed it unnecessary 'to consider too deeply what the precise status of the detention was'.

The court found that the decision of the trial judge to admit the DNA sample was not 'wrong in law'; the sample had been taken by a different Garda in the morning following the arrest, who had not been asked by the appellant whether the solicitor requested the previous night had been contacted, nor had the appellant requested a solicitor at the time he was asked for consent to the taking of the sample, and moreover he did give that consent.

123. [2009] IECCA 95.
124. Ibid.

The court concluded that since the sample could have been procured without consent, 'it would have been reasonable to assume that the applicant did not require a solicitor in connection with it. His request for a solicitor the previous evening was clearly related to the questioning which he was about to undergo'.[125]

Why it was not necessary to examine the issue of detention 'too deeply' is questionable. Given that the statements had been excluded by the trial judge using his discretion to do so because of the manner in which the Garda had responded to the request for the solicitor, together with the breach of the Custody Regulations (her failure to inform the appellant of her inability to contact the solicitor), perhaps the court believed that sufficient care had been taken by the trial judge to ensure that the appellant was not unfairly prejudiced. However, the decision would appear to take no account of the Supreme Court decision of *O'Brien* that any evidence, if obtained during an unlawful period of detention, must be excluded if the unlawful detention comes about by reason of a breach of the person's constitutional rights. Because the Court of Criminal Appeal did not consider the 'precise status' of the detention, it did not examine whether any period of the detention was unlawful. It has been seen in *Buck* that any evidence taken during an unlawful detention in breach of constitutional rights must be excluded, but any evidence taken after a unlawful detention ceases – such as where the person has been granted access to a solicitor – may be admitted. But to come to a decision in such a scenario, the beginning and ending of an unlawful detention must at least be identified.

Essentially the court appears to have decided that the appellant, by not making the request of the second Garda, had waived his right to a solicitor – as far as that procedural aspect went. This seems to suggest, if indeed the prior detention had been found to be unlawful, that an unlawful detention comes to an end by such a 'waiver'. Is a person considered to have waived a right simply because he has not repeated his request where the earlier request has not been fulfilled? In light of recent ECtHR jurisprudence on the issue of waiver of the right of access to a lawyer, the approach of the Court of Criminal Appeal would appear to fall short of the ECtHR requirement for a clear and unequivocal waiver.[126]

Perhaps the court's reticence to inquire into whether the detention was unlawful may be explained by the type of evidence in dispute – DNA evidence as opposed to statements. If that evidence had not been admitted, given that the statements had already been excluded, there would have been no evidence to connect the appellant to the crime.[127] A similar reticence is

125. Ibid.

126. *Talat Tunc v Turkey* 32432/96 (ECtHR 27/3/2007) 59, cited in *Saman v Turkey* 35292/05 (ECtHR 5/5/2011) 32, ruling a waiver of the right, 'once invoked, must not only be voluntary, but must also constitute a knowing and intelligent relinquishment of a right'; see also *Pishchalnikov v Russia* no. 7025/04 (ECtHR 24/9/2009).

127. Not altogether dissimilar to the approach of the Italian courts to admissibility of evidence comprising the *corpo del reato*: see section 6.3.1 below.

evident in another recent decision of the Court of Criminal Appeal, which although finding a breach of constitutional right of access to a lawyer to have occurred thereby rendering the detention unlawful, found that the unlawful detention was cured by what can only be described as the most minimal contact with a solicitor, and therefore a statement made by the appellant was found to have been correctly admitted. In *DPP v Ryan* the appellant appealed his conviction for murder.[128] The evidence in the case consisted of testimony from a witness in a witness protection programme, relating telephone conversations that had taken place between himself and the appellant, in which the appellant had intimated that he was going to 'get' the intended victim of the shooting (in fact a bystander had been shot) and there was evidence of these calls through telephone record data; as such, this latter was technically circumstantial evidence, while the evidence of the witness was to some extent dubious being evidence of a protected witness. The strongest evidence against the accused at trial was a statement in which he had admitted involvement in the crime. That statement had been made after the appellant had had a two-minute telephone conversation with the solicitor. While the detention had been unlawful prior to that, it was no longer considered to be unlawful from that point onwards, despite the very short time that the appellant had spent in conversation with his solicitor. The court found that there was no question that the Gardaí had cut short the phone call, so there was no deliberate refusal of reasonable access.

On the basis of these recent decisions, it would appear that in order to respect a person's constitutional right of access to a solicitor, all the Gardaí need do is to go through the motions of contacting a solicitor, but these are not required to be successful, and even where an unlawful detention arises through failure to respect the right of access, it would seem that an unlawful detention can be cured by very minimal contact with a solicitor. Whether this measures up to the effective access required by the ECtHR is questionable.

These decisions may be indicative of a malaise surrounding the strict exclusionary rule as espoused by *Kenny*, and a desire to move towards a discretionary approach generally, even where the breach of a constitutional right has occurred.[129] Charlton J recently made the most forthright criticism of the exclusionary rule in *DPP v Cash* where he stated:

> A rule which remorselessly excludes evidence obtained through an illegality occurring by a mistake does not commend itself to the proper ordering of society which is the purpose of the criminal law.[130]

128. [2011] IECCA 6.
129. This approach was also proposed in the Criminal Law (Admissibility of Evidence) Bill 2008 (never passed); see Seanad debate, 10 December 2008.
130. [2007] IEHC 108, 65–6.

An indication of such malaise may also be gleaned from the recent decision of the Court of Criminal Appeal in *DPP v Mallon*.[131] The case concerned evidence, a substantial quantity of drugs, obtained on foot of a warrant that had incorrectly stated the address of the appellant's premises which was searched. The address named on the warrant did not in fact exist. The question put to the Court of Criminal Appeal was whether every error on a warrant is enough to attract a strict exclusionary rule (in effect an absolute exclusionary rule). The court emphasised that if the 'remorseless logic' of *Kenny* was to be understood to require that every defect on a warrant should result in automatic exclusion of evidence, that would in effect mean that as a result of *Kenny* the law in Ireland is one that espouses an absolute exclusionary rule and that that was clearly not the intention of the judges in the *People (AG) v O'Brien*.[132] While accepting that *Kenny* has resulted in a large number of trials excluding evidence, the court was anxious to draw a limit in so far as possible by reiterating a distinction between defects on the warrant going to jurisdiction – one issued without proper authority – and defects which did not have this effect, a distinction which had been established by earlier cases dealing with the issue.[133]

The court focused on the nature of the defect on the warrant: was it a warrant that was issued under authority to do so? The warrant in *Kenny* had not been correctly authorised, since the peace commissioner had not himself been satisfied that there were reasonable grounds for issuing it; the warrant in this case was more akin to the warrant issued in *O'Brien* – one that contained an error describing the address that was to be searched. The court focused on the question of whether the warrant made sense: would the address as stated on the warrant be understood by the postman, for example, or a person giving someone directions to reach the address? Finding that it could be so understood, the court concluded that the error on the warrant was not sufficient to justify a dismissal of the charge.[134] It also made the following observation with regard to the exclusionary rule:

> So long as Irish law maintains an almost absolute exclusionary rule for evidence obtained as a result of an illegal and therefore unconstitutional search of a dwelling house, courts should be slow to invalidate warrants on the grounds of typographical, grammatical, or transcription errors, which are neither calculated to mislead, nor in truth do mislead, any reasonable reader of the words.[135]

131. [2011] IECCA 29.
132. Para. 5.
133. *People (DPP) v Balfe* [1998] 4 IR 50 (CCA) – errors did not necessarily invalidate the warrant; *People (DPP) v Edgeworth* [2001] 2 IR 131 (SC).
134. *Mallon* (note 131) 53.
135. Ibid., 54.

4.3.3 Confession evidence

Even though technically out of court statements, confessions and admissions are admissible evidence as an exception to the rule against hearsay.[136] A confession is an oral or written statement made by the accused that is adverse to their interest and made to a person in authority. An admission is a statement made to a person who is not a 'person in authority'. In order to be admissible as evidence, a confession may be oral or written, signed or unsigned. The old view was that a confession was 'the best evidence that can be produced'[137] since 'it is fairly presumed that no man would make such a confession against himself if the facts confessed were not true'.[138] It is now recognised that a person may indeed confess to facts that are not true, or that a confession may be the result of pressure from the experience of police custody or as a result of false hopes, so that the truth of the confession is put in question. To be admissible as evidence a confession must have been voluntary in that it must not have been obtained from the suspect 'either by fear of prejudice or hope of advantage exercised or held out by a person in authority',[139] nor may it be the result of oppressive questioning.[140]

The question of voluntariness must be decided on the basis of the effect of the threat or inducement on the person to whom it is made.[141] The court must evaluate whether the words used by the person in authority, viewed objectively, were capable of amounting to a threat or promise and whether the accused subjectively understood them as such. In addition, the threat or inducement must have caused the accused to confess.[142]

A confession may be ruled inadmissible at the discretion of the trial judge where it has been obtained in breach of the Judges Rules or the Custody Regulations.[143] If it has been found to have been taken as a result of a breach of the constitutional rights of the suspect and there is a causative link between the breach and the obtaining of the confession, the trial judge will have no discretion in the matter and must – and this is also the case with an involuntary confession – rule it inadmissible as evidence.

136. See hearsay rule, section 4.3.4 below.
137. *R v Baldry* (1852) 2 Den 430, 444.
138. *The King v Lambe* (1791) 2 Leach 552, 555.
139. *Ibrahim v R* [1914] AC 599, 609; as to the meaning of 'person in authority' see *Sullivan v Robinson* [1954] IR 161; *McCann* (note 83); *People (AG) v Murphy* [1947] IR 236; *People (DPP) v Paul Ward*, Special Criminal Court, 27 October 1998: a person in authority may by their silence adopt a threat/inducement made by one who is not a 'person in authority'.
140. For definition of oppressive questioning see: *People v Breathnach* (1981) 2 Frewen 43.
141. *People (DPP) v Hoey* [1988] ILRM 666; *McCann* (note 83).
142. *Pringle* (note 53); *Hoey* (note 141).
143. *Farrell* (note 66).

4.3.4 *Potentially unreliable evidence – hearsay evidence*

The adversarial trial proceeds on the basis that the only evidence that may be relied upon to reach a verdict is that which is given orally by the witness who has perceived the issue through their own senses and who is available to be tested on their testimony through cross-examination by the opposing side. Hearsay is considered potentially unreliable as it cannot be tested for its veracity.[144] If a witness gives evidence of what another person has told them, in order to check the accuracy of that account we would want to hear the original declarant, to find out whether what they said was correctly recounted by the witness, what the context was and to be in a position to test the overall reliability of the original declarant's perception of the matter. Equally with a document, it is not sufficient to simply accept the reporting of a fact or event in a document without hearing from the person who provided the information for that document, since the information might have been recorded incorrectly or may have been written in a particular context.

The classic definition of the common law rule against hearsay is that given by Cross as 'a statement other than one made by a person while giving oral evidence in the proceedings is inadmissible as evidence of any fact stated'.[145] The nub of this rule is that if the out-of-court statement is not given in evidence to prove the facts contained in the statement, it is not hearsay; but if the out-of-court statement is offered in evidence to prove the facts contained in the statement, it will be considered hearsay under the common law rule.[146]

In Ireland, the law follows the general common law rule for hearsay evidence, along with the numerous exceptions long recognised by the common law to provide for the admissibility of hearsay evidence.[147] Exceptions have also been established on a statutory footing so as to allow for the admissibility of certain documents,[148] and a most recent reform has radically altered the approach to the admissibility of documented statements made by a witness

144. Although hearsay may in some cases actually be reliable; see discussion in J Jackson, 'Hearsay: The Sacred Cow That Won't Be Slaughtered?' (1998) 2 *Int'l J. Evidence and Proof* 166.
145. R. Cross, *Cross on Evidence* (5th edn) (Butterworths 1979), cited in P. Roberts and A. Zuckerman, *Criminal Evidence* (Oxford University Press 2004) 581.
146. See *Cullen v Clarke* [1963] IR 368, 378, judgment of Kingsmill-Moore J.
147. Common law exceptions include: dying declarations; spontaneous statements considered to be part of the *res gestae.* Hearsay evidence has recently undergone considerable reform in England and Wales, see J. Spencer, *Hearsay Evidence in Criminal Proceedings* (Hart 2008). The Law Reform Commission were against extending the exceptions to the rule as was done by the English legislation, considering that such changes 'potentially render the rule against hearsay redundant', *Consultation Paper on Hearsay in Civil and Criminal Cases* LRC CP 60 (2010).
148. Criminal Evidence Act 1992, s. 5; Criminal Justice Act 2007, s. 57; Criminal Justice (Surveillance) Act 2009.

to the police in situations where the witness recants or gives inconsistent accounts at trial, or indeed refuses to give evidence at trial.[149]

It is the norm that evidence must be given by a witness orally in open court in the presence of the accused and that the witness is available for cross-examination. It is the inability of the defence to cross-examine the witness, and so test the reliability of their testimony, that is the principal rationale for excluding statements made out of court. If such a statement is tendered in evidence in the absence of the witness, and the evidence is in dispute, the jury has no ability to test the reliability of the witness who made it or of the veracity of the facts that they attest to.

The hearsay rule is bolstered by the constitutional right of an accused person to cross-examine prosecution witnesses that stems from the fair trial provisions.[150] The ECtHR has also emphasised the centrality of the availability of a witness for cross-examination to the provision of a fair trial, and have ruled that hearsay evidence which is 'decisive' to a conviction breaches the right protected under Article 6(3)(d) of a person 'to examine or have examined witnesses against him and to obtain the attendance and examination of witnesses on his behalf under the same conditions as witnesses against him'.[151]

In certain circumstances, evidence of witnesses may be received before the trial by means of deposition and the deposition may be admitted as evidence of the facts stated at the trial of the offence. This procedure allows the prosecution or defence to apply to the court of trial for an order requiring a person to appear before a judge of the District Court so that their evidence may be taken either by way of sworn deposition or through a live television link.[152] Provided the accused was present while the deposition was being taken and opportunity was given to cross-examine the witness, the deposition may be admitted in evidence at the trial of the accused if it is proved that the witness: is dead, is unable to attend to give evidence at the trial, is prevented from so attending or does not give evidence at the trial through fear or intimidation, unless the court is of opinion that to do so would not be in the interests of justice. Where the evidence is given through live television link under this procedure, the video recording shall be admissible as evidence at trial, again provided the accused was present and opportunity was given to cross-examine the witness.

(a) Recanted or inconsistent witness statements

A recent reform provides for the admission as evidence of statements made by a witness to the police if the witness, although available for cross-examination,

149. Section 16, Criminal Justice Act 2006.
150. Articles 38 and 40.
151. *Al-Khawaja and Tahery v United Kingdom* [GC] ECHR 2011.
152. Section 4F–G, Criminal Procedure Act 1967 (as amended by s. 9, Criminal Justice Act 1999).

refuses to give evidence, denies making the statement or gives evidence which is materially inconsistent with it. In order for it to be admitted it must be proved that the witness in fact made the statement and the court is satisfied that it was made voluntarily, is reliable and would be otherwise admissible. The court may at its discretion refuse to admit the statement having had regard to all the circumstances, including any risk that its admission would be unfair to the accused and that in the interests of justice it ought not to be admitted.[153] In deciding upon its reliability, the court must consider whether it was given on oath or affirmation or was video-recorded, and if not, whether there is other sufficient evidence in support of its reliability. In addition the court must consider the reasons for the witness's refusal to give evidence or for their inconsistent account or denial of the content of the statement.[154]

A key aspect of this provision is that the witness 'is available for cross-examination'. The provision would typically arise where the witness, having been called by the prosecution to give their testimony, which would be that based on the earlier statement that the witness gave to the police, either denies ever making the statement or maintains that they cannot remember any of the events to which the statement relates. The prosecution is thus put in the position that they cannot put the statement into evidence.

Under common law, where such a situation arose, the only available option for the prosecution was to apply to the judge to have the witness declared to be a 'hostile witness'. Where such an application was successful, the prosecution would then be permitted to question the witness on the contents of the statement, in effect through a cross-examination of their own witness, and in that manner the contents of the statement would be heard by the jury. However, the trial judge would be required to instruct the jury that they cannot use the statement as evidence of the truth of its contents, but simply use it as a basis for assessing the general credibility of the witness.[155] This common law position has not been abolished by the new legislation. The effect of the new provision is to allow the statement of the recanting witness to be read to the jury by the prosecution counsel and allows the jury to use the contents of the statement as proof of the facts referred to.

4.3.5 Potentially prejudicial evidence – evidence of bad character

It has been suggested 'the introduction of the accused's bad character into a criminal trial is an event which irreversibly changes the chemistry of the

153. Section 16, Criminal Justice Act 2006.
154. Section 16(3); interpreted by CCA in *DPP v Murphy* [IECCA] 13.
155. *The People (Attorney General) v Taylor* [1974] 1 IR 97, interpreting ss. 3, 4 and 5, Criminal Procedure Act 1865; *DPP v Hanley* [2010] IECCA 101, *Taylor* reaffirmed.

trial'.[156] Once a jury becomes aware of an accused's criminal past, there is a danger that they will follow the path of the 'forbidden reasoning' that if he has committed crimes in the past, it is more than likely that he has also committed the crime for which he is now being tried.

In Ireland bad character evidence is generally inadmissible, save for the limited situations provided under the Criminal Justice (Evidence) Act 1924. The Act provides firstly that an accused, while competent as a witness, is not compelled to give testimony. If the accused does elect to testify, he will be required just like any other witness to give his evidence under oath.[157] He may be cross-examined even if the questions asked might be incriminating with regard to the offence with which he is charged, but is nonetheless shielded from answering any questions that would reveal that he has been previously convicted or charged with any offence, or that he has previously committed any offence.

There are three exceptions to this rule: (a) the evidence is admissible because it constitutes what is often referred to as 'similar fact' evidence; (b) the accused has put his own (good) character in issue, or has impugned the character of the alleged victim of the offence or of the witnesses for the prosecution or of the alleged victim, where the latter is deceased or is so incapacitated as to be unable to give evidence;[158] (c) the accused has given evidence against a co-accused in the case. In these situations the accused loses his 'shield' and may be cross-examined as to his character, including any previous convictions he may have.

Similar fact evidence comes into play under s. 1(f)(i) of the 1924 Act which allows the proof that a person has committed or been convicted of another offence to be admissible to show that the accused is guilty of the offence for which he is being tried. The Balance in the Criminal Law Group considered this situation arises rarely in Ireland and recommended no change to the law.[159] It has been held that 'leave to adduce evidence of the bad character or prior misconduct of an accused should be given if the evidence has substantial explanatory value and the interests of justice require it to be admissible, even taking account of its potentially prejudicial effect'.[160]

The issue of admissibility of evidence of bad character will more often arise in situations where the accused has either put his own good character in issue or has impeached the character of prosecution witnesses. In approaching this issue the Irish courts, in contrast to their English counterparts, have taken an approach that facilitates the accused in putting forward his defence and

156. P. Murphy, 'Character Evidence: The Search for Logic and Policy Continues' (1998) 2 *Int'l J. Evidence and Proof* 71.
157. See sections 5.4.5(d) and 6.4.7 below for the contrasting position in France and Italy.
158. Inserted by Criminal Procedure Act 2010, s. 33.
159. Balance Report (note 1).
160. *DPP v McNeill* [2007] IECCA 95.

have allowed the accused to keep his shield intact despite imputations made against the character of a prosecution witness. This will quite often arise in relation to a denial that a statement was made to the police – the imputation being that the police are lying, since such denials are 'reasonably necessary' to enable him to establish his defence.[161] As will be seen later, this is in sharp contrast to the position in Italy where such imputations can in fact lead to a criminal charge of 'calumny'.

PART III

4.4 Receiving, presenting and challenging evidence

Once the decision to prosecute has been made by the DPP, the evidence is compiled and the book of evidence is served on the accused and his legal representatives. Following service of the book of evidence, the District Court sends the accused forward for trial, either to the local Circuit Court or, if the case relates to murder or rape, to the Central Criminal Court. In either case, the accused is tried before a jury. For certain specified offences the accused may be sent forward to the Special Criminal Court in which cases are tried by a panel of three judges sitting without a jury.[162] The book of evidence will also be forwarded to the trial court in advance of the trial and will be available to the trial judge. Once the accused is served with the book of evidence, he will be familiar with all the evidence that may be relied on by the prosecution in the case, and may use it to formulate a defence to the charge. As the law currently stands, there is no requirement for the accused to present a 'defence statement' so as to disclose to the prosecution how he intends to meet the prosecution case.[163]

161. *People (DPP) v McGrail* [1990] 2 IR 38; the law on the admissibility of bad character evidence has been reformed in England and Wales by the Criminal Justice Act 2003; see J. Spencer, *Evidence of Bad Character* (2nd edn) (Hart 2009).
162. The Special Criminal Court exists under Article 38.3 of the Constitution that allows for the establishment of special criminal courts for the trial of offences where the ordinary courts are deemed inadequate to secure the administration of justice; for a detailed discussion of the Special Criminal Court see D. Walsh, *Criminal Procedure* (note 70) Ch. 20; for analysis of the similar special court in Northern Ireland see J. Jackson and S. Doran, *Judge Without Jury: Diplock Trials in the Adversary System* (Clarendon Press 1995).
163. This procedure exists in England and Wales, Criminal Procedure and Investigations Act 1996; it has been suggested: 'When the defence must disclose its case prior to trial, criminal procedure moves further towards a truth-oriented model', in M. Redmayne, 'Process Gains and Process Values: the Criminal Procedure and Investigations Act 1996' (1997) 60 *MLR* 79, 85; the Balance in the Criminal Law Group in Ireland (note 1) were against any such change; notice of expert evidence to be adduced by the defence must be given (s. 34, Criminal Procedure Act 2010) and notice of alibi is required (s. 20, Criminal Justice Act 1984).

4.4.1 The presumption of innocence

In every criminal trial, the accused enjoys a presumption of innocence. The presumption of innocence is recognised under Irish law as a constitutionally protected right, arising from the Article 38 fair trial provisions.[164] The presumption of innocence is given further protection under the fair trial provisions (Article 6) of the ECHR.[165] As a result of the presumption of innocence the burden of proof rests on the prosecution throughout the trial and the accused is free to remain silent throughout the trial.

A distinction is drawn between the legal burden of proof and the evidential burden of proof. The legal burden of proof refers to the obligation of the prosecution to prove all the essential elements of the case. It arises in the criminal trial because of the presumption of innocence. The evidential burden of proof refers to the obligation to adduce a prima facie case – the party need not prove the existence of the fact conclusively but must produce some evidence that it exists. The evidential burden is on the accused in relation to defences so the accused must satisfy the trial judge that there is a prima facie case that defence exists on the facts.[166]

It has been suggested that the presumption of innocence principle embraces both a narrow evidentiary aspect encompassing the elements of the prosecution bearing the burden of proof and the concomitant right to silence of the accused, and also a wider meaning concerned with a reputational aspect.[167] This includes the idea that the State has a duty to recognise the accused as an innocent person prior to conviction and, related to this, 'that adjudicators ignore all pre-trial indications of guilt' and judge the accused solely on the evidence presented, free from any prejudice that may arise from the knowledge that the accused is of bad repute and considered by the State to require pre-trial custody.[168]

4.4.2 The trial setting

As a consequence of the wider aspect of the presumption of innocence just noted, the jury must not be made aware that an accused person is in custody

164. Article 38.1: 'No person shall be tried on any criminal charge save in due course of law'; examples of leading cases include *O'Leary v Attorney General* [1991] ILRM 454 (HC); [1995] 2 ILRM 259 (SC); *Rock v Ireland* [1998] 2 ILRM 35 (SC).
165. The European Convention on Human Rights Act 2003 incorporated the ECHR into Irish law; s. 4 requires judges must take 'judicial notice' of the Convention and decisions of the ECtHR.
166. For example, self-defence, provocation, duress; *O'Leary* (note 164), 460; *People (DPP) v Foley* [1995] 1 IR 267 (CCA).
167. Trechsel has described the presumption of innocence as including a 'reputation-related' aspect, *Human Rights in Criminal Proceedings* (Oxford University Press 2005) 178; see also J. Jackson and S. Summers, *The Internationalisation of Criminal Evidence: Beyond the Common Law and Civil Law Traditions* (Cambridge University Press 2012), 203; A. Ashworth, 'Four Threats to the Presumption of Innocence' (2006) 10 *Int'l J Evidence and Proof* 241.
168. Jackson and Summers (note 167) 202.

lest it may prejudice their verdict. The accused will always be brought into the courtroom before the jury panel assemble. The accused normally sits in the 'dock', which in the courtrooms I attended was at a distance of three benches away from the defence counsel, elevated and directly facing the judge.[169] Defence and prosecution counsel sit facing the judge, with their backs to the accused, and they are faced by their instructing solicitors who, since they have sight of the accused, also act as go-between to pass any 'on-the-spot' instructions from the accused to the defence counsel. The judge sits in an elevated position, while the jury sit in the jury box, at right angles to the judge and facing the witness box from which all witnesses (including the accused if he opts to do so) present their testimony.

Two trials will be highlighted in this part; one was a case I observed during an earlier research period and was the first case to be tried in Ireland under the provisions of the Criminal Justice (Drug Trafficking) Act 1996. Four co-accused were on trial for possession of a large quantity of cocaine that had been discovered on a boat that they had crewed from South America. This will be referred to as the drug-trafficking trial.[170] The other was a recent trial for the robbery of an employee of a betting shop (referred to as the robbery trial).[171] Taken together, these trials provide case studies to demonstrate the practical application of the rules of evidence already discussed.

4.4.3 The course of the trial

Trials commence with the assembly of jurors called to serve during the criminal sessions.[172] There follows the arraignment of the accused where the charge is read out by the court registrar, to which the accused is required to respond by pleading guilty or not guilty; if the former, no trial takes place and the accused will be sentenced by the judge, usually at a later hearing to allow time for probation and medical reports to be obtained. If the accused pleads not guilty, a trial proceeds and a jury is empanelled to try the case.[173] In the drug-trafficking case the captain of the boat pleaded guilty and his sentencing hearing was adjourned until the trial of his co-accused was completed.

169. The negative effect of the positioning of the accused in the dock has been noted by J. Miller, 'A Rights-based Argument Against The Dock' (2011) *Crim. LR* 216. In the robbery trial the accused was seated in the dock; in the drug-trafficking trial, in which five people were co-accused of importing a substantial amount of cocaine into Ireland, all the accused were seated in the benches behind the prosecution and defence counsel, separated from each other by unarmed police officers.
170. *DPP v Richards, Smolen, Da Silva Roy, Miller & Noel*, Cork Circuit Court 10–28 February 1997.
171. *DPP v O'Connor*, Cork Circuit Court 6–17 July 2011.
172. Prospective jurors are drawn from the electoral register: Juries Act 1976.
173. When the jury is being selected, prosecution and defence counsel may each challenge seven jurors without cause.

No details of the circumstances surrounding his guilty plea were given until the sentencing hearing. For ease of reference, the four co-accused in the case will be referred to as the captain's girlfriend, the cook, the navigator and the first mate.

Once the jury is empanelled the case which the prosecution intends to prove is presented to the jury by counsel for the prosecution, who must take care not to include any issue which is known will or is likely to give rise to an objection by the defence during the trial, and at the end of that presentation, the prosecution counsel immediately proceeds to present his evidence through examining each of the witnesses it relies on. Unlike the position in France and Italy, the defence presents no case to the jury at the outset of the trial. It is considered that since the burden of proof rests on the prosecution, the defence may simply cross examine any prosecution witnesses, but need only put forward their own witnesses, including the accused himself, if that is the course chosen; the court may remain in suspense right up to the closing address to the jury by the defence counsel as to the underlying reasons behind any questions asked in cross-examination.

(a) Examination of witnesses

Counsel for the prosecution examines the witnesses; leading questions may not be asked. In some instances, there may have been prior agreement between defence and prosecution counsel that a witness may be led, or indeed that certain witnesses need not be examined. In the robbery case, none of the police officers involved in the arrest of the accused were examined at trial, nor was the custody officer examined regarding the detention as no contentious matters arose. The witnesses proffered by the prosecution were the alleged victim of the robbery, another employee of the betting shop, the officers involved in gathering CCTV footage, two witnesses who had gathered and examined mobile phone logs, a DNA expert and two police officers involved in questioning the accused during his detention.

The normal course of a trial is that the victim of the offence is the first witness to be put forward by the prosecution, followed by any witnesses with information relating to the event, and it will be quite usual in a modern-day trial to rely to a greater or lesser extent on the testimony of witnesses relating to such evidence as CCTV footage, mobile phone-related evidence and technical forensic evidence based on items found at the scene and comparisons with forensic samples taken from the accused. All these types of evidence were relied on in the robbery trial. The CCTV footage and forensic data evidence require examination of the witnesses involved in obtaining the data in order to prevent it from constituting hearsay.

Any witnesses whose statements are contained in the book of evidence may be called by the prosecution, but the prosecution and defence may decide between themselves which witnesses are required – it would be unusual to have each and every witness listed in the book of evidence called to court to testify.[174] There is no culture of a trial judge himself calling witnesses, unlike, as will be seen later, the practice in France and Italy. There is, however, authority for the proposition that a trial judge may do so where the prosecution has decided not to call a witness listed in the book of evidence:

> If the prosecution appear to be exercising that discretion improperly, it is open to the judge of trial to interfere in his discretion in turn to invite the prosecution to call a particular witness, and, if they refuse, there is the ultimate sanction in the judge himself calling the witness.[175]

Nor is there a culture of the trial judge questioning witnesses. The trial judges I spoke to both accepted that their role is along the lines of an umpire:

> *J1*: It is fair to say that we are umpires but I would not say we are passive. It depends on the case. We can be difficult enough!
> *J2*: I would ask questions for clarification only. I can't jockey things along.

The robbery trial lasted for ten days, with the presentation of evidence to the jury through the examination of the prosecution witnesses followed in some but not all cases by cross-examination by the defence. A considerable amount of the trial time was spent on examining the principal evidence against the accused which consisted of CCTV footage allegedly depicting him entering the betting shop where the incident occurred, mobile phone records, forensic DNA evidence linking objects found near the scene with objects found in the accused's home, as well as DNA linking him with the banknotes taken during the robbery.

The victim of the offence was examined and cross-examined at length, and was the first witness to appear. In the ensuing days the evidence relating to the CCTV footage was presented, through examination first of the police officer who worked with that evidence in examining the footage and downloading it from the premises before the footage was shown to the jury. A full day was spent examining the witnesses who had obtained the data from mobile phone logs, with another day being devoted to technical evidence about mobile phone masts and the inferences that could be drawn from data found on these devices. Two full days were taken up with testimony relating to DNA evidence incriminating the accused.

The prosecution case in the drug-trafficking trial consisted of the evidence of coast guard and police officers relating to the discovery of the cocaine that had been concealed behind panels in the boat and to statements made by each of the co-accused during police custody. Since the drugs had been concealed,

174. This was related to me by counsel.
175. *People (DPP) v Lacy* [2005] IECCA 70, 16.

the prosecution had to prove that all the co-accused were aware of their presence on the boat.[176]

Witnesses who are called to give evidence are not normally kept out of earshot of other witnesses giving their evidence. In the robbery trial, the defence counsel made an application to exclude the witnesses from the courtroom until it was their turn to testify. Unless this application is made, all the witnesses may remain in the courtroom throughout the trial. The danger of allowing witnesses to hear the evidence of other witnesses is that they may then present their own testimony so as to try to keep it in line with the evidence of the other witnesses; there is a heightened danger of this happening when, for example, the witnesses are police officers called to give evidence relating to the detention and questioning of the accused while in custody. In my observations of criminal trials in the earlier period, in only one, the drug-trafficking trial, were the witnesses excluded.[177] In that case, the majority of witnesses were Garda officers, and the defence counsel was trying to ensure that there would be no collusion, since the main aspect of the defence case was that statements made in police custody had been obtained in breach of constitutional rights and of the Custody Regulations and in oppressive circumstances; nonetheless, I frequently observed the exiting witness have a quick conversation with the next witness before the latter entered the courtroom, relating to him what he had been asked and what he had replied.

In presenting their testimony, the witnesses are carefully controlled by counsel conducting the questioning so that they do not stray from the question; a subtle difference arises between the way police witnesses give their testimony and the way 'ordinary' witnesses do so. In the case of the former, I frequently observed that when answering the questions by counsel, the police officers would turn to face the judge when giving their response, and often preface their answer with 'Judge'; they also rely on their notebooks to a considerable extent. By contrast, the 'ordinary' witness will not usually have any document in front of them, and they generally respond as one would in the normal course of human behaviour by looking directly at the person who is asking the questions rather than at the judge. There may be a subliminal effect on the jury that the police witnesses are to be believed because they have clearly addressed their answer to the judge, along the lines of 'how could a police office look the judge in the eye and tell him bare faced lies?'

Testimony by witnesses is not given in the way one would normally recount an event but is given in a staccato manner, in short and to-the-point responses to the questions asked. It will be seen later how this is very different to the narrative manner of giving testimony in France and Italy. The effect of this is that the witness is prevented from giving any evidence other than what

176. For the essential ingredients to establish proof of possession see: *Minister for Posts and Telegraphs v Campbell* [1966] IR 69; *People (DPP) v Foley* [1995] 1 IR 267.

177. Trials observed during 1997–2001.

they have perceived by their own senses, they may not give any account of what someone else has told them, and because of the way the questioner controls the witness, no opportunity is given to them to stray beyond the parameters of the question. This prevents any evidence that can be categorised as hearsay evidence from going before the jury.

(b) The voir dire

It has been said that 'the nature of a criminal trial by jury is that once it starts, it continues right through until discharge of verdict. It has the unity and continuity of a play'.[178] The trial may indeed be said to unfold like the structure of a play, with the various scenes unfolding. However, it is often the case that some of the scenes will not always be played out in front of the jury, the decider of the facts of the case, or the audience to continue the metaphor of the play. They will not always come to know the complete story.

The focal point of the Irish criminal justice system is the trial itself; as such, there is no pre-trial stage where decisions about admissibility of evidence are made – these issues are raised during the trial itself.

It is the trial judge who decides whether evidence should be admitted or excluded, and this decision is made following an application by the party objecting to the evidence through a procedure known as *voir dire* or 'trial within a trial'. This procedure occurs during the currency of the trial, and the disputed evidence is generally tested through examination and cross-examination of the relevant witnesses. All applications to exclude the evidence are held in the absence of the jury, who are sent to the jury room until the hearing of the application is concluded. If the judge decides to exclude the evidence, the jury will never know of its existence. If there is no other evidence against the accused, the judge will direct the jury to find the accused not guilty. Should the trial judge decide the evidence is admissible the same evidence will again be tested through examination and cross-examination of the relevant witnesses, this time in the presence of the jury.

In the juryless trials before the Special Criminal Court, it is the presiding judges that hear any applications to exclude evidence through the same *voir dire* process. Where the evidence is ruled admissible, the course taken after the ruling is to recall the witnesses and ask whether they affirm the testimony they gave during the *voir dire* to be correct rather than proceeding to hear the testimony a second time.[179] Where evidence is ruled inadmissible, unlike the jury in the 'ordinary' courts, the triers of fact, who in the Special Criminal Court will be the same judges who ruled it inadmissible, will have full knowledge of the contents of the disputed evidence but are expected to banish it from their minds and may not rely on this evidence to reach their verdict.

178. Ó Dálaigh CJ in *People (AG) v McGlynn* [1967] IR 232, 239.
179. *People (DPP) v McGowan* [1979] IR 45.

Where the prosecution and defence agree, the *voir dire* procedure may simply consist of a consideration of the questions and answers made during Garda interviews being examined by the parties in the presence of the judge, and objected portions deleted where the parties agree, or if there is disagreement, following a decision on the point by the judge. This was the approach taken in the robbery trial: in effect it was very much a discussion and a sort of 'thinking out loud' between the counsel for each side, who both remained seated throughout, and the trial judge. In this way, counsel worked their way through the interview statements, the only intervention by the trial judge consisted in clarifying what parts they wished to be excluded so that he could excise them from his own copy of the statements.

It must be stressed that a *voir dire* relating to admissibility of evidence is always instigated by the parties' application and not by the judge; the judge has no role to decide whether a *voir dire* should be run other than in situations where he sees that a line of questioning is becoming problematic and needs to address counsel in the absence of the jury to clarify matters with them.

From observing criminal trials in Ireland, to continue the analogy of trial as a play, I would suggest that, for the jury, the intermissions are often lengthier than the acts. Applications to exclude illegally obtained evidence were a frequent feature of trials that I observed during the earlier period in the Irish courts. This was at a time when the use of electronic recording was rarely practised and applications were commonplace during trials to have the statements and memos of interviews taken while in Garda custody ruled inadmissible. On a number of occasions these applications were successful resulting in the collapse of cases. The jury would often be absent from the trial for lengthy periods, sometimes up to a week.

The drug-trafficking trial was dominated by a *voir dire.* This trial lasted for three weeks, most of which was taken up with examining the police officers who had interviewed the accused during their time in custody. During these applications, the jury was either sent to the jury room or sent home and was present for about a third of the entire trial.

The most incriminating evidence in the drug-trafficking case was the statement and memos of police interviews with the captain's girlfriend. The *voir dire* revealed that she had said in her interviews with police that the drugs had been dropped from a plane while the boat was at sea and that she and the first mate had helped the captain to conceal the drugs on board the boat; in later interviews, she to some extent incriminated the cook and the navigator, suggesting they must have known the drugs were on board, given their routine activities while on board.

The defence objection to the admission of these pieces of evidence was that they had been taken in breach of her constitutional rights and that any confessions contained in the statements were a result of oppressive circumstances. These included the fact that her two-year-old son, who she was still breastfeeding, was taken into care when she was arrested and that she did not fully understand that concept, believing that her son was to go to a babysitter provided by the Gardaí for a few hours, and she had no idea of the length of time she could be held in detention. She was a Venezuelan national with some knowledge of the English language but was not fluent; she was not assisted by an interpreter nor given consular assistance, and had no understanding of the concept of a 'solicitor'. She had not understood that she had a right to silence and believed it was 'not right not to answer police'. She was given access to a solicitor after she had signed a statement that contained the incriminating information. It was also revealed during the later sentencing hearing of the captain (who had admitted his involvement immediately when arrested, but stated he had smuggled the drugs in the face of duress in the form of threats to the safety of his girlfriend and her son) that he had said in his statement 'an aeroplane dropped the shit off while we were at sea'. These words were identical to those that appeared in one of the statements of the captain's girlfriend to the police.

The statements of the other co-accused were also objected to. Certain place names were contained in them that would not be known to people other than local residents, and it was contended that they were not the words of the co-accused but of the police. There were also breaches of the Judge's Rules. At the end of the *voir dire*, the trial judge ruled all the memos of interviews and statements of each of the co-accused inadmissible as evidence. The situation regarding applications to exclude statements made during police custody appears to have dramatically changed with the now regular use of electronic recording of interviews of suspects in police stations.

All practitioners that I spoke to said that what was once the norm is now a rarity, and suggested that applications relating to police questioning arise only from time to time in relation to old cases, for example where there has been retrial following an appeal. As one judge put it to me: 'The days of the heavy gang are gone!' Where applications are made to exclude police interview evidence, the trial judge on seeing the recording will often react by stating along the lines: 'What is wrong with that? I don't see anything unreasonable there', and then go on to rule that the evidence be admitted.[180]

At the close of the *voir dire* in the drug-trafficking case, the jury were directed by the trial judge to return a verdict of not guilty for the captain's girlfriend. She had been arrested in a house having come ashore, and consequently there was no evidence in the absence of her statements to connect her with the drugs found on board.

The trial then proceeded before the jury of the remaining co-accused. Two of the co-accused, the cook and the navigator, had boarded the vessel in Trinidad, after the drugs had been concealed on the boat. The first mate had been on board since the boat had first set sail from Venezuela. This information was revealed during the examination of the statements during the *voir dire* but was not revealed to the jury since all statements were ruled inadmissible.

180. The prosecution counsel in the robbery case recounted this to me.

All the jury had to go on therefore was that a boat with the crew members on board had been searched by customs officers and found to contain the cocaine. The charge against all the accused was possession so the proof could only be satisfied by showing that they knew the drugs were on board. The remaining prosecution evidence before the jury in the absence of the police custody statements was evidence of the search following the boarding of the vessel by customs officers and their accounts of the various reactions of the crew. Photographs of the boat were presented to the jury, in an effort to show that the place for concealing the drugs would have been obvious to them all.[181]

None of the exclusionary rules relating to unlawfully obtained evidence arose in the robbery trial. Nonetheless a number of applications were made to the trial judge in the absence of the jury. In many instances where a witness was about to be called, the defence or prosecution told the trial judge that there were some issues relating to the evidence the witness was set to give. Each time a possible difficulty with the evidence is foreseen, the jury must go to the jury room while the two sides, prosecution and defence present the issue to the judge, who will decide on how to proceed. The prosecution and defence may come to quick agreement between themselves. In the robbery case, for example, the defence objected to portions of interviews with the accused while in custody where the interviewing officers were showing the accused CCTV footage and making various comments such as 'we believe it is you' and asking for his response. The prosecution had no difficulty in agreeing with the defence counsel that such references in the memos should be excised since they were expressions of the Garda opinions and therefore matters which were not in their remit but within that of the jury.

Another instance related to a chain of evidence and a piece of missing evidence on which basis the defence argued that the trial should be stopped and the jury discharged; the evidence was not going to be relied on by the prosecution, but the defence argued it was necessary to their case and had sought its production that morning. The exhibits officer had retained it in his personal locker where all the evidence relating to the trial had been stored but he was unable to locate it.[182] The trial judge ruled that the defence argument had not made out that the accused would be at risk of an unfair trial and the trial proceeded. An issue also arose in relation to the presentation of CCTV footage to the jury as to which portions to show out of lengthy footage (only some short segments of the footage depicted the movements of the alleged perpetrator). This was very much an issue of simple editing and it

181. This could establish constructive knowledge so as to satisfy the requirement for proof of possession.

182. The manner of storing and accessing exhibits is very different from that in France and Italy where there is a system of official seals and a record is made where the seals are broken to access evidence.

seemed inefficient that such an exercise could not have been conducted prior to the commencement of the trial.

The issue of potentially prejudicial evidence arose after a week into the trial when the defence counsel applied for the jury to be discharged because there was a possibility that a jury member had seen the accused alighting from the prison transport van and entering the courthouse. Unless the exceptions to allow admission of bad character evidence come into play, the jury will never know if the person they are judging has led an exemplary life or has offended repeatedly. That is not to say that the trial judge will not be familiar with the previous behaviour of the accused, especially in the circuit courts given the fact that a judge may have tried the accused in the past. As the judge in the robbery trial put it to me in relation to the accused: 'It's not his first day out.'

Another trial judge suggested to me that where, as would often be the case, he is familiar with the criminal past of the accused, he would not be prejudiced by this fact in any applications made by the defence during the trial, nor during his charge to the jury; rather than being prejudiced, 'if anything, I would be particularly careful in the charge to the jury'. The application to discharge the jury is based on the prejudice that may arise in the minds of jurors where a jury has become aware that the accused is being held on remand, from which knowledge they may deduce that the accused is a criminal, at least in the minds of the authorities. The application in the robbery case was refused, but the issue took up most of an afternoon in the trial, during which time the jury had to remain in the jury room.

The emerging evidence during the trial is thus fairly constantly screened by the trial judge by means of the *voir dire* procedure, but only where requested by the parties. The juror's reaction in the robbery trial to being sent to their room changed from looks of bewilderment on the earlier occasions of being sent out, to near amusement as the frequency of instructions by the trial judge to go to their room increased. In some instances the jury were absent from the courtroom for lengthy periods in excess of two hours, and in one instance the defence counsel discovered he had been mistaken in thinking an issue arose and the jurors, some of whom had not even fully descended from their bench, were called to return to their seats immediately.[183]

(c) The defence case and the accused as witness

There is no obligation on the accused to testify at trial. Where the accused does give evidence, it is given under oath and presented from the witness box rather than from the dock. The accused will be examined by the defence counsel and cross-examined by the prosecution. In the drug-trafficking trial,

183. The Balance Group (note 1) 170–4 recommended legislation for admissibility issues to be determined prior to the swearing in of a jury as did the *Report of the Working Party on the Jurisdiction of the Courts: The Criminal Jurisdiction of the Courts*, May 2003 (PN 237 2003), 85.

both the cook and the navigator gave evidence, which was principally to deny all knowledge of the presence of the drugs on board the vessel; the first mate gave no evidence. Following the testimony of the two co-accused an application was made by each defence counsel that the case should be withdrawn from the jury and the jury be directed to return a not guilty verdict in relation to all the accused. The judge granted the application in relation to the cook and the navigator, but considered there was a sufficient case to go to the jury in relation to the first mate. The jury was accordingly directed by the trial judge to return a not guilty verdict in relation to them and to return the next day to hear closing speeches of counsel in relation to the first mate.

In the robbery trial, at the close of the prosecution case, the defence counsel informed the court that they would be going into evidence the following day, through the presentation of an expert witness (a DNA expert) who would be travelling from England, and would only then be in a position to know whether the accused himself wished to testify. The court was told the following morning that, following instructions from his client, the defence would not after all be calling that witness (this despite the fact that the witness had arrived from England!). Instead he informed the judge that the defendant wished to give evidence but before doing so it would be necessary to recall the alleged victim of the offence. Having acceded to this request, the judge adjourned the trial for the day to give time for that witness to be recalled.

That witness was cross-examined by the defence who put it to him that he had been the instigator, pointing to the fact that he had debts and therefore motive, and that what had occurred had been in fact a 'dummy robbery'. The witness vehemently denied the allegations, repetitively stating that he had never met the accused in his life and brought documents to the court proving that money which he had in his possession following the time of the robbery, and as he had stated during his original examination by the prosecution, came from an inheritance.

During the cross-examination of this witness, the accused made various facial expressions in an attempt to show that the witness was lying, and when exiting the courtroom the accused greeted him loudly enough for the jury to hear, using a nickname that would commonly be used for a person bearing the name of the witness.

The accused decided to testify. Before giving evidence, however, it was conceded by the prosecution (again in a discussion in the absence of the jury) that even though the defence counsel had clearly tried to impeach the character of the prosecution witness in alleging that the latter had staged the offence, the prosecution would not view it as allowing a drop to the shield under the Criminal Justice (Evidence) Act, but would follow the position set down in *McGrail* that it was an essential element to his defence.[184] The judge clarified with the prosecution counsel that in effect he agreed that the accused would

184. *McGrail* (note 161); see text to note 161 above; Criminal Justice (Evidence) Act 1924, s. 1(f)(ii).

not be cross-examined on any previous convictions, and accepting this, he told the defence counsel that notwithstanding the shield that the accused would continue therefore to enjoy:

> You can't resile from the types of questions which were put to [the prosecution witness]; you can't go off on a different canter now.

During examination by the defence counsel, the accused admitted that he had been involved and accepted that all the circumstantial evidence – the images of the person on CCTV footage, the money found in his house, the call logs and a discarded glove – accurately connected him with the event. However, he insisted that it was in fact the alleged victim who had masterminded the whole event, that the latter had approached him in the first place with the proposition to stage a robbery. Given that he was indicted with a sole count of robbery, he could not be found guilty of any other offence, and ran no risk that he could be found guilty of a handling or receiving offence, despite his admission in giving evidence that the cash found in his house was that taken from the betting shop.[185]

Having been presented with the book of evidence prior to the trial an accused person is fully aware of all the evidence against him and is thus put in a position to defend himself against the charge by seeing those pieces of evidence which may be challenged for lack of credibility of the witnesses, offering counter evidence such as alibi evidence or proffering an expert witness to counter the experts of the prosecution. Equally, however, an accused person may effectively construct a defence case by drawing on certain evidence in the book of evidence and putting a different 'spin' on it and this was clearly what was happening in the robbery case. The court was taken by surprise by the sudden turn around by the accused – days had been spent examining the CCTV footage, the witnesses on the call logs and the DNA evidence, but nonetheless he was suddenly admitting to all of it. In addition, despite the earlier application during the trial for a discharge of the jury on the grounds that the accused may have been seen emerging from the prison transport van, at one point in the examination of the accused, he openly volunteered the information that he was currently on remand and had been so for the past year!

At the end of the examination by the defence, the accused was cross-examined by the prosecution who pointed out to him that he was referring to the complainant throughout his testimony using a familiar nickname in an attempt to make it appear to the jury that he knew him well which was not the case at all, and over the course of 35 minutes the prosecution through vigorous cross-examination attempted to cast doubt on every aspect of the accused's version of events.

185. For a robbery to be proved there must be a theft; the defence case was that there was no theft, and indeed no robbery.

(d) Closing address by counsel

When the defence has closed its case, the next step in the trial is the closing addresses by both sides, beginning with the prosecution and followed by the defence. In both the robbery trial and the drug-trafficking trial, each side opened their address by explaining to the jury their role as the deciders of fact, what is required to establish proof of the offence, and the standard of proof that they must reach – proof beyond reasonable doubt, explaining this by way of analogy with major decisions a person might have to make in their own lives such as getting married or buying a house and the sort of doubts that they might encounter in deciding whether or not to go ahead. In the drug-trafficking trial, both the prosecution and defence side then focused on trying to convince the jury that the first mate must have known /could easily have not known the drugs were on board respectively.

On the prosecution side in the robbery trial, counsel pointed to the fact that, in light of all the admissions by the accused in his evidence that he was the person who was captured on CCTV and his admitted connection with all the other pieces of evidence, the case had boiled down to a 'classic case' of credibility. The jury were told that they were entitled to draw on evidence of both witnesses' demeanour in the witness box in reaching their conclusion, and also were reminded of the strong evidence in favour of the victim's credibility.

Counsel for the defence in turn focused on the credibility of the accused and aspects of the prosecution case that would support the contention that the accused's version that the alleged victim was in fact the prime mover could be correct.

(e) Judge's charge to the jury

Once the closing addresses of counsel to the jury are complete, it is then the turn of the trial judge, who up to now has remained relatively passive (except for his active decision-making role during applications in the absence of the jury), to play his role in instructing the jury before they retire to decide their verdict. In reaching a verdict, the jury are unaided by the judge in the jury room. As will be seen below, this is in sharp contrast to the position of juries in France and Italy where the judge in a jury trial will always decide in conjunction with the jurors.

The judge's address to the jury in the robbery trial began with an instruction to the jury on the law in relation to robbery and what they would have to find for the offence to be established. He instructed them on the standard of proof which they needed to reach and then summed up the relevant evidence and told the jury of the various exhibits in the case that would be made available to them, namely the CCTV footage, statements of the Garda interviews, the transcript of the 999 call by the alleged victim who reported the offence and the books of photographs. The statements of the witnesses as contained in the book of evidence are not normally made available;[186] it is the evidence that has been given at trial that is the only evidence that may be relied upon. In relation to the evidence of the Garda interviews, the edited versions were given to the jury.

In his summing up, the judge did not once refer to the book of evidence but relied exclusively on the notes he had taken during each witness's testimony. This exercise involved the judge reading through each answer that the witness had given, but in relying on his own notes, he sometimes appeared to have difficulty deciphering his own handwriting! The result was that the summing up seemed to be somewhat disjointed. In the circuit courts generally, the judges are not supplied with a typed transcript of the trial proceedings and so have to rely on their own notes. In the Central Criminal Court, judges are given a typed transcript and time to prepare their summing up, resulting in much more fluency and coherence.[187]

Where the accused has chosen not to testify, while the prosecution are prohibited from commenting on his failure to give evidence,[188] the judge may comment on the fact that the accused has not testified, 'provided that such comment was made fairly'.[189] In the drug-trafficking trial, as already noted, the first mate did not give evidence. The judge directed the jury by pointing out that he had denied any knowledge of the drugs to the customs officers and police when the boat was searched. Having told them that it is the right of an accused to decide whether or not to give evidence in his trial, he then went on to state:

> It is a matter for you to determine whether he was in up to his neck or whether he suspected it so well that he should have known; you have evidence of what this man said to customs officers. Did he know? If he didn't know, why did he not say it on oath before you? Counsel can't say this, but I can!

Once the jury retires, both sides may make any requisitions they see fit upon the judge's charge to the jury. In the robbery case, no requisitions were made. In the drug-trafficking case a requisition was made about the judge's comment on the fact that the accused had not testified, the defence counsel suggesting it had 'left the jury to draw one inference and one only'. The judge refused to recharge the jury holding that he was entitled to comment on the decision of the accused not to give evidence.

186. Unless the statement was admitted as evidence under s. 16, Criminal Justice Act 2006.
187. Interview with defence lawyer.
188. Criminal Justice (Evidence) Act 1924, s. 1(b): 'The failure of any person charged with an offence or of the wife or husband, as the case may be of the person charged, to give evidence shall not be made the subject of any comment by the prosecution.'
189. *DPP v Connolly* [2003] 2 IR 1 (CCA).

(f) Verdict

The jury must first try to reach a unanimous verdict, but after a period of time has elapsed, usually not before two hours, the jury will be instructed that they may at this stage return a majority verdict. In the robbery case, the jury deliberated for four hours, though included in this time may have been time spent reviewing the exhibits, so it is not possible to conclude that there may have been simply difficulties between jurors trying to agree. The jury in the robbery trial returned a verdict of guilty. In the drug-trafficking trial, after four hours deliberation it was one of not guilty.

In Ireland, the jury does not give any reasons for their verdict, so it is always an unknown as to how they reached their verdict or what evidence they relied upon or found credible.[190] It should be noted, however, that where a trial is conducted in the Special Criminal Court, it is the practice of the court to give reasons for its verdict; thus the judges may not *ostensibly* rely on any inadmissible evidence that they have been privy to during the course of the trial.[191]

It is a long-established principle that the jury must not be asked to reveal what occurred inside the jury room. Without intending to tantalise the reader, I was approached by the jury following the close of the drug-trafficking trial who told me (without being asked) of their very interesting reasons for acquitting the accused. Since it amounts to contempt of court to publish any information about the jury deliberations, even where not solicited, my findings therefore must remain secret!

At this stage, the work of the jury is over, and they play no part in the sentencing of the accused, which generally takes place at a separate hearing, unless the sentence is mandatory where the judge may immediately pass sentence. It is only at this point in the trial that the previous convictions, if any, are publicly revealed. In the robbery trial, it transpired during the sentencing hearing that took place the day after the jury had returned their verdict that the accused had in excess of twenty previous convictions, including convictions in relation to theft and robbery. The judge passed sentence of ten years' imprisonment.

In the drug-trafficking trial, the judge passed a sentence of 17 years on the captain who had pleaded guilty.[192] That sentencing hearing cast light on the

190. The implications for jury trial in light of the ECtHR decision in *Taxquet v Belgium* [GC] 926/05, ECHR 2010, have not been discussed in Ireland in any legislative or judicial context.
191. The practice of giving reasons for decisions is not legislated for. The Special Criminal Court is empowered by its Rules to 'have control of its own procedure in all respects': Offences Against The State Acts 1939–1998 (Special Criminal Court Rules) 2001, SI 536/2001; Offences Against the State Acts 1939–1972 (Special Criminal Court Rules) 1975, SI 234/1975. For discussion of reasoned verdicts in the Diplock court see Jackson and Doran (note 162) 24ff.
192. Later reduced to twelve years on appeal.

factual truth about the smuggling of the drugs on board the vessel. The evidence given revealed that after the plane drop the drugs had been concealed on the boat by the captain and 'another man'. It was clear that the drugs were taken on board out at sea at a time when the first mate was present and that he was the only other man on board.

Asked whether the trial system in Ireland is more concerned with fairness in the process than it is committed to a search for truth, the judges I interviewed responded:

> *J1*: Fairness is very important, an important part of our system; but I would hope we would be able to search for truth as well in the exercise of fairness.
> *J2*: Yes! The entire system is geared towards fair play to the defendant. At all costs!

The defence lawyer I spoke to had this to say:

> *D*: We would make out that we are searching for truth but in reality we are not. The jury I think do look for truth. No matter what you might say to them about disregarding evidence they may have heard which they should not have heard, they will take it on board anyway.

4.5 Conclusion

The distinctive features of the process of gathering and presentation of evidence in Ireland will now be summarised. This chapter has depicted an investigation practice and type of adversarial trial procedure that is typical of the common law traditional structure. The institutional design of the process is one that allocates complete control over the investigation to the police. In the investigative stage therefore the role of the police is paramount, and the initial case construction is formulated by them free from supervision by judges, other than the latter's role in issuing warrants and authorising extended detention, and without direction by prosecution officials. The police investigation is conducted secretly, in so far as any questioning of suspects is conducted in the absence of a lawyer, nor do the police have to provide either the suspect or the accused with information in their possession or provide lawyers with notes of interviews conducted with suspects. Nonetheless, this veil of secrecy is somewhat lifted by the now normal practice of electronic audio-visual recording since all that transpired during the secret interview may be exposed during the trial whenever it is required.

A prominent feature of investigation in Ireland is the limited availability of the suspect as a source of information during the investigative stage. The police may obtain evidence from the suspect only during the tight window of opportunity provided by the statutory detention periods. Once the suspect has been formally charged, even though the case may take a number of months before the book of evidence is completed, the police may no longer question him or confront him with witnesses or evidence gathered as the investigation proceeds, nor is there any place in the institutional culture for a pre-trial investigative phase by a prosecutor or judge in which the accused may be questioned following the formal charge.

Moreover, it has also been seen that there is no concept in the Irish system of a distinct body of prosecutors. The office of the DPP is one that is limited to deciding on whether to proceed with a prosecution, based on the information collected and sent to it by the police. It is for the DPP's office to compile the book of evidence based solely on the information that has been forwarded to it by the police, that is in turn based on the lines of inquiry that the police decided to pursue and which items of evidence to collect. The office of the DPP is not concerned with directing an investigation but only with directing the prosecution of the offence conducted on its behalf by the private practitioner prosecution counsel.

The discussion has shown that Ireland has a strict exclusionary stance towards unconstitutionally obtained evidence. The decisions of the appellate courts noted in this chapter nonetheless are indicative of a malaise surrounding the strict exclusionary rule and a desire to move towards a general discretionary approach, even where the breach of a constitutional right has occurred. It has also been seen that challenges to statements obtained during police custody have considerably lessened since the recording of interviews has become the norm. It is no longer easy for an accused to deny having made certain statements to the police or argue that statements have been inaccurately noted since the entire interview process is available for the trial judge to view. While it would seem to be the case that the greater transparency of the police questioning phase has had the effect of diminishing the frequency of challenges at trial to statements made to the police, the cases reviewed from the appellate courts show that challenges continue to be made to evidence obtained during the police custody period on the basis that it was obtained in breach of the right of access to a lawyer.

Clearly, Ireland has interpreted the ECtHR jurisprudence on access to a lawyer minimally. There is no provision for a lawyer being present during police interviews and while the law now requires that a suspect is given access to a solicitor before questioning begins, there is ambiguity as to whether questioning may nonetheless commence after the requisite waiting time has elapsed. Since the breach of the right of access is a breach of a constitutional right invoking the strict exclusionary rule, ambiguity around the precise scope of the right of access creates fertile ground for the exclusionary rule to flourish, despite the apparent malaise around its continued existence in its present rigorous format.

The trial process in Ireland has been shown to be one that strongly adheres to the classic adversarial type, leaving control over the selection and presentation of evidence in the hands of the parties in a trial presided over by an umpire-style judge, and placing the decision of guilt or innocence in the hands of the jury who come to their verdict unassisted by the judge. There are two parties only, the prosecution and the defence. A third party, a lawyer for the victim of the offence, does not feature in the Irish trial system. It is noteworthy that in establishing the juryless Special Criminal Court, no attempt was made to create a new procedure to accommodate the absence of a jury; trials are run as any normal adversarial trial before a jury would be run with the same adherence to exclusionary rules of evidence, albeit modified to the extent that the judges who exclude the evidence will nonetheless become privy to the information. Despite the 'adversarial deficit' suffered by the accused in these trials, they are not considered at odds with the classification of the Irish criminal trial as 'adversarial'.[193]

The trial is an oral process that adheres to a strict hearsay rule. The CCTV evidence and mobile phone data seen in the robbery trial – now commonplace informational sources in modern-day trials, would have amounted to hearsay evidence had they not been presented to the court by those persons directly involved in gathering the data. The hearsay rule is further bolstered by the manner of questioning witnesses and the control exercised over the witnesses by counsel when giving their testimony. The weakening of the hearsay rule in Ireland to allow prior inconsistent statements of witnesses to be used fully as evidence is a new provision that appears so far to be little used, so its effect on the Irish trial process cannot yet be appraised.

It has been seen that the point of time for decision-making about which evidence may be presented to the jury is during the trial itself through the *voir dire* procedure. While the judge here takes on an active role in that he is the person who ultimately decides what evidence the jury may hear, his role is still relatively passive in so far as he does not question the witnesses, nor seeks further evidence if unsatisfied with that which has emanated from the parties. Furthermore, the judge's role is purely reactive, since it is for the parties to decide if and when to challenge particular pieces of evidence.

The limited availability of the accused as an informational source that has been seen in the pre-trial stage is repeated in the trial. The accused in the trial is protected by the choice allowed to him to participate through testifying or not, though if he does elect to testify, he will be required just like any other witness to give his evidence under oath. The shield placed around his character further protects him. Nor is he called upon to present a defence case in answer to that put forward by the prosecution at the outset of the trial.

The effect of the exclusionary rules is to diminish the pool of information available to the jury. The drug-trafficking trial provided an example of how the factual truth surrounding an event is obscured, with concerns of fairness to the accused taking precedence. Had the jury heard all the evidence that was played out during the *voir dire*, they would have been aware that the first

193. For discussion of the 'adversarial deficit' in the context of the Diplock courts see Jackson and Doran (note 162).

mate was at least implicitly the person who had assisted in concealing the drugs in the vessel and perhaps would have reached a different verdict. Nonetheless the reasons for excluding that evidence were tied to a police custody environment that was shielded from public view in the absence of any electronic recording, a scenario that has since been rectified.

The apparent reticence of the appellate courts to rule inadmissible real evidence discovered through inaccurate search warrants may be indicative of a concern to elevate the importance of truth in the process to sit alongside concerns of fairness to the accused. However, any deeper invalidity in the warrant still results in real evidence being mandatorily excluded, giving the judge no discretion to try to balance fairness with establishing the truth of the matter. Fairness to the accused in the Irish process trumps truth.

5 Gathering, receiving and contesting evidence in France

5.1 Introduction

French criminal procedure is generally described as a mixed system, combining both inquisitorial and accusatorial elements.[1] The past decade has seen numerous reforms to the system, some in response to the condemnation of France by the European Court of Human Rights (ECtHR),[2] others in response to visible failings of the system, particularly during the pre-trial stage.[3] It has been suggested that some of the proposed reforms are of 'seismic' proportions, affecting the whole architecture of the criminal procedure in France.[4]

Since the case known as the *Outreau affaire*, the institution of the *juge d'instruction* (JI), a stalwart of criminal justice in France and one reflecting its closest link with inquisitorial procedure, has come under threat of extinction. That case in brief concerned the sending forward for trial by the JI of 17 persons accused of child abuse and paedophilia, of which four were finally found guilty; those who were innocent had spent up to three years in pre-trial detention. A committee was set up to inquire into the causes of the miscarriage of justice which focused its attention most specifically on the powers of the JI.[5] The solution of that committee (the Viout committee) was to develop a system

1. For example, F. Fourment, *Procédure Pénale* (Paradigme 2009) 10; C. Ambroise-Castérot, *La Procédure Pénale* (Gualino 2009) 44.
2. *Selmouni v France* [GC] no. 25803/94 ECHR 1999-V; *Tomasi v France*, 27/8/1992, Series A, no. 241-A; *Letellier v France*, 26/7/1991, Series A, no. 207; Article 5(1): *Faure v France*, no. 19421/04 (ECtHR 15/12/2009); *Funke v France*, 25/2/1993, Series A, no. 256-A; *Sartory v France*, no. 40589/07 (ECtHR 24/9/2009).
3. Reforming legislation includes: *loi* 2000-516 15/6/2000 renforçant la protection de la présomption d'innocence et les droits des victimes; *loi* 2007-291 5/3/2007 tendant à renforcer l'équilibre de la procédure pénale; the most recent reform is *loi* 2011-392 14/4/2011 relative à la garde à vue, allowing suspects the right to legal assistance in police custody including the presence of the lawyer during police questioning. Laws available at: <http://www.legifrance.gouv.fr>.
4. J. F. Renucci, 'Un séisme judiciaire' (2009) 9 *Recueil le Dalloz* 600.
5. Rapport du groupe de travail chargé de tirer les enseignements du traitement judiciaire de l'affaire dite 'd'Outreau', February 2005 (the Viout Report). Available at: <http://www.ladocumentationfrancaise.fr/rapports-publics>.

whereby pre-trial judicial investigations (*instruction*) would be conducted by collegial groupings of JI.

More recently, a committee was commissioned to explore ways of reforming criminal procedure in France that would respect, on the one hand, the public interest in repressing crime and on the other the fundamental rights of the individual. That committee, the *Comité de réflexion sur la justice pénale*, chaired by Philippe Léger, has recommended in its Report (the Léger Report) the abolition of the institution of the JI altogether, and instead placing the *procureur*, the public prosecutor, in charge of all criminal investigations.[6] This proposal, taken together with other recommendations in the Léger Report and the reforms to criminal procedure in France effected in the last decade have led some French commentators to conclude that French criminal procedure is moving more and more in an Anglo-American direction.[7]

The position of defence rights have also undergone considerable reform, both as a result of recent rulings from the *Conseil Constitutionnel*[8] and in response to the jurisprudence of the ECtHR.[9] There is no indication in any of the reform proposals of any change to the law of evidence in France – indeed it must be said that there is no distinct 'law of evidence' per se in French criminal procedure. The system follows the principle of 'free proof': offences may be established by all means of proof, which are evaluated by the court who may reach a verdict based on their *intime conviction*.[10]

This is not to say that no rules exist in relation to the gathering and presentation of evidence. As will be seen in this chapter, there are principles that must be respected in the gathering of evidence together with a nullity system for dealing with evidence gathered unlawfully. Furthermore, the recent reforms to the rights of defence may have created a new breeding ground for an exclusionary principle not altogether too dissimilar to the position in Ireland.

This chapter will provide an insight into the workings of French criminal procedure and describe the approach to evidence law in France under the two broad headings of gathering evidence in the pre-trial phase, and presentation and use of evidence at trial. An examination based solely on the legal provisions would give a limited insight; the law as practised presents a fuller picture and

6. The committee of reflection on criminal justice, chaired by Philippe Léger, Report September 2009 (the Léger Report). Available at: <http://www.ladocumentationfrancaise.fr/rapports-publics>.
7. Fourment (note 1) 10; Ambroise-Castérot (note 1) 293.
8. Questions of constitutionality of laws may be brought by the *Cour de cassation* (the Supreme Court) to the *Conseil Constitutionnel* (Constitutional Council) through a procedure known as *question prioritaire de constitutionnalité* (QPC) since *loi* organique 2009-1523 10/12/2009 relative à l'application de l'article 61.1 de la Constitution; see Article LO 630, *Code de Procédure Pénale* (CPP).
9. *Brusco v France*, no. 1466/07 (ECtHR 14/10/2010); reforms also resulted from recommendations by the Commission charged with examining the issue of increasing the rights of defence lawyers, the Delmas-Marty Commission (*Commission Justice Pénale et Droits de L'Homme*, 1991).
10. Ambroise-Castérot (note 1) 184.

provides a deeper understanding of the process. Therefore in addition to drawing on the relevant provisions of the French Code of criminal procedure and associated jurisprudence, cases I observed in the criminal courts in France will inform the discussion, together with interviews I conducted with practitioners.[11]

The first part will examine the roles and powers of those involved in the investigation of offences, to show the institutional arrangements for investigations and the powers available for the gathering of evidence in the pre-trial stage. The second part will examine the extent to which France may be said to include rules relating to illegally obtained evidence. The other two mainstays of common law evidence that have already been examined in the Irish context, the rule against hearsay and rules relating to character, will be discussed in the third part, which will describe how the evidence is presented at trial and the use to which evidence gathered in the pre-trial stage may be put at trial.

PART I

5.2 Gathering evidence in the pre-trial phase

5.2.1 Organisational structure of the pre-trial phase

Judges and prosecutors belong to a single judicial body, the *magistrature*. Within this body there is a division between the *magistrats du parquet*, the prosecutors, and the *magistrats du siège*, the judges.[12] This gives rise to a different hierarchical arrangement: the prosecutors are not fully independent, they are answerable to the Minister of Justice who has control over appointments and promotion of prosecutors and who may issue instructions in individual cases. The judges on the other hand enjoy complete independence from the executive. Within the *parquet*, there is a hierarchal structure whereby the *procureur de la République* (the public prosecutor) is answerable to the *procureur général* (prosecutor general). Prosecutors and judges are free to change roles during their career, thus a prosecutor may become a judge and vice versa,

11. I attended two trials in the *cour d'assises* in Toulouse and one trial in the *tribunal* in Angers in 2010. I interviewed two judges, a *juge d'instruction* who had previously been a prosecutor, and a president attached to the *cour d'appel*. I interviewed both these judges together in one of the judges' offices. These will be referred to as JI and J. I managed to speak briefly with the prosecutor during adjournments at one of the trials in the *cour d'assises*. I also interviewed a defence lawyer, referred to as Def. L1, and spoke to a defence lawyer at one of the trials in the *cour d'assises*, referred to as Def. L2; where my own questions feature in the interview sections I identify myself as Self. All interviews were conducted in French and tape recorded with prior permission from the practitioners, and all were conducted on an anonymous basis. All translations are my own unless otherwise stated.
12. Articles 64 and 65 of the Constitution set out the position of the *magistrature*.

having shared a common training structure, but they cannot maintain a position of prosecutor and judge at the same time.

Article 31 provides that 'the public prosecutor undertakes the public action and formally requests the law to be enforced'. Unlike Italy but similar to the Irish position, the prosecutor has a discretion whether to proceed with a case, but a decision to refuse to proceed may be appealed by the victim to the prosecutor general.[13] Unlike the Irish position where the DPP has no obligation to give reasons for not proceeding with a prosecution, in France where the public prosecutor decides not to proceed, he must inform the complainants and victims of the legal and factual reasons justifying his decision.[14]

The subordinate status of the prosecutor has been the subject of a recent ruling from the ECtHR which has held that the prosecutor is not a 'judicial authority' in the sense that the jurisprudence of the court has given to this concept, in that he lacks complete independence from the executive power.[15] As a result of this ruling, the Code of Criminal Procedure has required some modification: any decisions affecting fundamental rights now rest with the recently created figure of the *juge des libertés et de la détention* (judge of freedoms and detention (JLD)).[16] No changes to the status of the *procureur* as a judicial figure have been effected; however, the proposals to abolish the role of the JI have for the moment been put in abeyance.

Lawyers (*avocats*) follow a different training regime to that of the judges and prosecutors. They are fully independent from the *magistrature*, they belong to the Bar (*barreaux*) attached to their local *tribunal de grande instance* (courts with general jurisdiction) and are self-regulated by each Bar overseen by a national Bar Council. The position of the lawyer has been described as an 'outsider' who 'in general enjoys a lower status than magistrates'.[17]

The players involved in the pre-trial phase are the police, the public prosecutor, the JI and the JLD. The lawyer for the suspect has a role in the pre-trial phase, which up to recently was very limited at the initial stage where a suspect is held in police custody (*garde à vue*). Following that phase, his involvement depends on the type of investigation procedure employed: the

13. Article 40.1, CPP.
14. Article 40.2, CPP.
15. *Medvedyev v France*, 3394/03 (ECtHR 10/7/2008); *Moulin v France* 37104/06 (ECtHR 23/11/2010); see J. Hodgson, 'The French Prosecutor in Question' (2010) 67 *Wash. & Lee L. Rev.* 1361.
16. This judge is independent from the executive and the parties, with power to order release where detention is unjustified as required by *Medvedyev*.
17. J. Hodgson, *French Criminal Justice: A Comparative Account of the Investigation and Prosecution of Crime in France* (Hart 2005) 115; see also S. Field and A. West, 'Dialogue and the Inquisitorial Tradition: French Defence Lawyers in the Pre-trial Criminal Process' (2003) 14 (3) *Crim. L. Forum* 261; A. West, 'Reform of French Criminal Justice' (2000) 150 *NLJ* 1542, 1630 and 1667; Bedford also noted an outsider status of the defence lawyer in France in her observations at the Paris *Cour d'assises* in 1959: S. Bedford, *The Faces of Justice* (first published 1961, Faber & Faber 2011) 235.

ordinary procedure, *enquête preliminaire*, conducted by the public prosecutor, or the *instruction* procedure which is conducted by the JI.

In the case of the ordinary procedure, the police work under the direction of the prosecutor, who in turn must seek authorisation from the JLD to carry out some procedures affecting personal liberty. In the case of an *instruction* procedure, the police work under the direction of the JI. The role of the JLD was first created in 2000 for the purpose of authorising pre-trial detention (*détention provisoire*) but his functions were extended with each piece of reforming legislation in the following years to include authorising extensions of the *garde à vue*, authorising search and seizure in certain instances, and authorising telephone intercepts and surveillance.[18]

The police when involved in the investigation of crime[19] are known as the *police judiciare*, a body made up of officers from two main policing bodies, the *police nationale* and the *gendarmerie*, the former subordinate to the Ministry of the Interior, the latter to the Ministry of Defence. In their function of *police judiciare* they are answerable to the Ministry of the Interior. The *police judiciare* work under the authority and direction of the public prosecutor[20] and under the supervision of the *chambre d'instruction* (the investigating chamber) which may take disciplinary measures against individual officers. They are charged with detecting the commission of offences, gathering evidence and finding the culprits. They receive reports of offences, whether by way of simple complaint or denunciation: the former is made by a victim, whereby the victim reports the incident but does not express the intention to pursue a charge, as distinct from the victim actively constituting themselves as *partie civile* thereby becoming party to the proceedings. The denunciation is the reporting of an offence made by a third party who has not directly suffered from the commission of the offence.

5.2.2 *Enquête préliminaire* procedure; *instruction* procedure

The organisational structure of the pre-trial phase in France is determined by the nature of the offence. French law distinguishes between three broad categories of offence: *crimes* which are serious offences, *délits* which are less serious, and minor offences (*contraventions*).[21] The type of investigation employed depends on whether the offence is a *crime* or *délit*. In addition to the difference in the investigative arrangements for *crimes* and *délits*, there is

18. *Loi* 2006-64 23/1/2006 relative à la lutte contre le terrorisme et portant dispositions diverses relatives à la sécurité et aux contrôles frontaliers; *loi* 14/4/2011 (note 3).
19. As opposed to traffic duties etc.
20. Article 12, CPP.
21. *Contraventions* are dealt with by the police, who may process the case under direction of the prosecutor and bring it for summary hearing before the Tribunal de Police, these will not be discussed further.

a further difference in investigative powers where an offence, regardless of whether it is of the more serious or less serious category, can be classified as flagrant. This results in two types of investigation: *enquête de flagrance* and *enquête préliminaire* – the former requires clear evidence of commission of the offence, the latter may be opened based merely on suspicion of an offence having been committed.[22]

A flagrant offence arises where an offence is in the course of being committed, has shortly been committed or where shortly after the commission of the act there is a public denunciation: the offence has to be recent rather than committed in the past, or a person is found in possession of articles or appears to have traces of the act on his person.[23] Coercive powers of investigation granted to the police are greater where the offence is flagrant. Both *crimes* and *délits* may be flagrant. The duration of an investigation of a flagrant offence is limited to eight days, and time begins to run from the time of discovery of the flagrant offence, but the period can be extended by the public prosecutor for a further eight days where the 'investigations necessary for the discovery of the truth cannot be postponed'.[24] The significance of this is that the police continue to be facilitated in their use of coercive powers throughout the period.

Following the expiry of the time limit, the case proceeds either through the *enquête préliminaire* procedure or through the *instruction* procedure. In the case of *crimes* (flagrant and non-flagrant), the prosecutor is obliged to pass on the investigation to the JI whereas for *délits* the prosecutor retains full control of the investigation, whether it is flagrant or not, though he may involve the JI at his discretion.

5.2.3 Means of gathering evidence

The collection of evidence at the initial stage of an investigation will normally be the task of the police. On receiving a report of a flagrant offence, the police must immediately inform the public prosecutor and seize any evidence found at the crime scene.[25] The police are empowered to take non-intimate samples from anyone who they consider may provide information about the offence and may take fingerprints and photographs of persons suspected of committing the offence – it is an offence for a suspect to refuse to comply.[26]

22. It is proposed under the *Avant-Projet du Future Code de Procédure Pénal* to abolish the two different types of investigation and the *instruction*, replacing them with one single type, directed by the public prosecutor, to be known as *l'enquête judiciaire pénale*.
23. Article 53, CPP.
24. Ibid.
25. Article 54, CPP.
26. Article 55.1, CPP.

(a) Search and seizure powers

Police are empowered by the Code to carry out a search of a dwelling and to examine documents and electronic data prior to their seizure.[27] The search and seizure must be made in the presence of the person whose dwelling is being searched or a representative nominated by him, or in the presence of two witnesses nominated by the police officer.[28] Everything seized is immediately documented and placed under official seals. Failure to observe the formalities surrounding search and seizure is on pain of nullity.[29] The police are not empowered to search the homes or offices of lawyers, journalists or doctors; a judge or prosecutor must conduct such searches.[30] Where the police conduct a search and seizure, whether in relation to non-flagrant or flagrant offences, night-time searches are prohibited between the hours of 21:00 hours and 06:00 hours, under penalty of nullity;[31] however, authorisation may be sought by the prosecutor from the JLD to search during these hours.[32]

Search and seizure powers for non-flagrant offences are largely similar but with the additional requirement that the consent of the suspect is required before a search can be carried out, on pain of nullity. However, where the investigation relates to an offence for which the penalty is imprisonment of five years or more, the prosecutor may seek authorisation from the JLD to conduct a search without the suspect's consent.[33] In these cases, the search is carried out under the direction of the JLD.[34]

In both flagrant and non-flagrant offences the police may obtain evidence from any person, establishment or organisation likely to possess any relevant documents and this may only be refused on 'legitimate' grounds of professional secrecy.[35] This power may be exercised in the case of non-flagrant offences following authorisation by the public prosecutor.[36] Failure to respond to the request for information results in a fine of €3,750. In addition, the police may summon any person 'likely to give information in respect of the offence or of the articles and documents seized' and there is an obligation to appear regardless of whether the person is a mere witness or suspect, and the police may use force to compel attendance. Persons against whom there exists no plausible reasons to suspect they have committed an offence may

27. Article 56, CPP.
28. Article 57, CPP.
29. Article 59, CPP.
30. Articles 56.1, 56.2, 56.3, CPP.
31. Article 59, CPP.
32. Article 706.89, CPP.
33. Article 76, CPP.
34. The judge may attend to ensure that the law is observed.
35. Article 60.1, CPP.
36. Article 77.1.1, CPP.

be held only for as long as necessary for the purposes of questioning,[37] in any case no more than four hours.[38] Any statements made during the questioning are noted by the police in an official report and signed by the declarant; where the declarant refuses to sign, this is noted in the report.

This holding of persons for the purposes of obtaining information is a separate and distinct procedure from holding a person under police custody, the process of *garde à vue*. As such, persons so held may not avail themselves of any rights which accrue to those held under *garde à vue*. This raises an interesting issue with regard to their statements – they are not technically under arrest, but at the same time they are not free to leave.[39] As soon as there are any grounds for suspecting that they may be involved in the offence, they must be immediately given access to a lawyer and afforded all the rights of *garde à vue* that are enjoyed by suspects so held.[40]

(b) Surveillance

The police are not authorised to put in place telephone intercepts. These may only be authorised by the JLD or by the JI where a judicial investigation has been opened. Bugging devices are restricted to cases of organised crime. Evidence may be obtained through audio-visual devices which may be installed in private premises, dwellings and vehicles, only on the authorisation of the JI through a *commission rogatoire*;[41] where the device is to be installed in a private dwelling during night-time hours the JI must first seek authorisation from the JLD.[42]

(c) Obtaining evidence from the suspect in police custody (garde à vue)

In cases of both flagrant and non-flagrant offences, the public prosecutor must be informed at the beginning of the custody period, and a suspect may be held for an initial period of 24 hours, which may be increased by a further 24 hours by the public prosecutor by written authorisation.[43] Persons held in *garde à vue* under either regime are technically under arrest. They can be held only where plausible reasons exist that they have committed or attempted to commit an offence. Police custody is strictly regulated, although none of the provisions are stated to be 'on pain of nullity'.

37. Article 62, CPP (flagrant); Article 78 (non-flagrant).
38. Circular Crim-00-13 F1 4/12/2000.
39. Akin to the euphemism of 'helping the police with their inquiries'; in Ireland a person who is not *de facto* free to leave is technically under arrest and their statements could be inadmissible.
40. *Conseil constitutionnel*, Décision no. 2011–191/194/195/196/197 QPC 18/11/2011, 19.
41. The procedure by which the JI delegates acts.
42. Article 706.96, CPP.
43. Article 63 (flagrant offences); Article 77 (non-flagrant offences).

The person must be immediately informed of the nature of the offence that is being investigated.[44] They must be immediately informed of their right to have the person with whom they normally reside, a relative or their employer to be notified that they are in police custody, of their right to have an examination by a doctor[45] and of their right to consult a lawyer. They must also be informed of the provisions governing the length of police custody.[46] The fact of giving the above information must be included in the official report which is signed by the suspect, or a note is made of his refusal to sign.[47]

If the suspect does wish to avail himself of his rights – it is at the suspect's discretion – this does not suspend the investigation, and it has been held that an interrogation of a suspect may be conducted after a request has been made to see a doctor or to speak with a lawyer while awaiting their arrival at the police station.[48] The police officer must also note the length of the interrogations to which this person was subjected and that of the rest taken between these interrogations, the times at which he was allowed to eat and the date and time he was taken into custody and the reasons for doing so.[49] Unlike the position in Ireland, there are no maximum times set out in the code for the duration of questioning. The police conduct questioning of suspects but the arrival of the prosecutor, which is not obligatory, relieves the police officer of his powers.[50] The prosecutor may, however, order the judicial police officers to continue in their interrogations.[51]

(d) Right to silence

The law 'reinforcing the presumption of innocence' contained a provision that a suspect in police custody was to be immediately informed that he had the right to refuse to answer any question put to him.[52] This provision was replaced two years later by the provision that he should be immediately informed that 'he has the choice to make statements, to respond to questions or to remain silent'; the following year, the legislature abolished the provisions altogether.[53] As a result, the suspect (and the accused at trial[54]) had the right to remain silent arising from the presumption of innocence stated in the preliminary

44. Article 63.1; Circular Crim-00-13/F1 4/12/2000.
45. Article 63.3, CPP.
46. Contained in Article 63.
47. Article 63.1, CPP.
48. Crim-13/12/2006 05-87.606, *Bull. Crim.* 312; this would now be prohibited (note 3).
49. Article 64, CPP.
50. Hodgson found that the prosecutor more generally exercised powers of supervision by telephone, *French Criminal Justice* (note 17).
51. Article 68, CPP.
52. *Loi* 15/6/2000 (note 3).
53. *Loi* 2003-239 18/3/2003 pour la sécurité intérieure, Article 19.
54. See section 5.4.5(e) below.

article of the Code, though no specific mention is made in that article of the right to silence per se, but at no stage in the process was the suspect informed of his right. This position has been recently reformed, along with provisions that have radically reformed the rights of access to a lawyer while in police custody, to the effect that the suspect must be informed that he has the right to make statements, respond to questions or remain silent.

(e) Access to lawyer during police custody

Provision for access to a defence lawyer for suspects held in police custody under both flagrant and non-flagrant regimes is provided under Article 63.4. At the beginning of the custody period, the person may request to speak with a lawyer of his own choice, or where he cannot be reached, he may request a lawyer to be appointed to him by the president of the Bar. The latter is informed of such a request 'forthwith and by any means available'. Communications between lawyer and suspect are confidential. Little information is given to the lawyer beyond the type of offence under investigation and the time and date of its occurrence. The lawyer had no access to the investigative file prior to the reforms made to Article 63, CPP by legislation passed in 2011.[55]

The first meeting between lawyer and suspect continues to be limited to 30 minutes, but whereas prior to 2011 no further contact between suspect and lawyer could occur until the start of an extension of police custody for a further 24 hours, the suspect is now permitted to have his lawyer present during the police interviews, a radical change to criminal procedure in France. For certain offences involving commission by 'organised gangs', the first meeting with the lawyer may be delayed until 48 hours have elapsed. For offences of drug trafficking and terrorism, the first meeting may be delayed for 72 hours.[56]

These reforms to access have evolved from a number of different sources, primarily resulting from rulings of the *Conseil constitutionnel* and the interpretation of the jurisprudence of the ECtHR by the *Cour de cassation*. The Léger committee described the *garde à vue* as 'an indispensible tool for the manifestation of the truth';[57] the majority considered it necessary to strengthen the presence of the lawyer during the *garde à vue* so as to give him a real role, stressing that access in the first and twenty-fourth hour does not permit the lawyer to fully exercise his role. To protect the effectiveness of the *garde à vue* a number of members of the committee considered it necessary that the lawyer be present from the first hour and should be able to attend all interviews. However, the majority opposed this on the basis that it would interfere with the discovery of truth.

55. *Loi* 14/4/2011 (note 3).
56. Police detention for terrorism offences is six days (Article 706.29, CPP).
57. Léger (note 6) 18.

The majority were also against the idea of providing any access to the dossier during the *garde à vue* on the basis that the dossier is only being developed during that time. The majority proposed to maintain the first interview with the lawyer for a half hour; to permit a second interview after 12 hours at which stage the lawyer would have access to a report of the questioning undertaken so far; and possibly to permit the presence of the lawyer during questioning if the interview was extended by 24 hours. Nonetheless this concession should apply only to specific crimes and would not extend to terrorism, drug trafficking or organised crime; in those cases, access would be after 48 hours instead of 72 hours.[58]

(f) The 2011 reforms to garde à vue

In July 2010, an application was brought before the *Conseil constitutionnel* for a ruling on the constitutionality of the *garde à vue* provisions. The applicants argued that the provisions were unconstitutional on a number of grounds, including the fact that the lawyer has no access to the contents of the case file, that the lawyer is not present during questioning and that the person in custody is not informed of the right to remain silent. Furthermore, it was argued that the power of the police to detain a person in custody for questioning was contrary to the constitutional principle set out in Article 66 that the judicial authority is 'the guardian of the freedom of the individual',[59] in that it is the police who first decide to detain the suspect, that the public prosecutor is not an independent judicial authority and that he is only informed of the detention after the decision to detain has been made.

The *Conseil* noted that the number of cases tried in the *tribunal correctionnel* that had been preceded by the instruction procedure was minimal, and that the majority of cases reached that court either through the *enquête préliminaire* procedure or by the procedure of *comparution immédiate*.[60] As a result:

> Even in proceedings involving complex or particularly serious occurrences, a person is henceforth often tried on the sole basis of evidence obtained before the expiry of the period of remand in police custody, in particular on the basis of confessions made during this period of time. Remanding suspected offenders in police custody for questioning has thus often become the main phase of the putting together of the case for the prosecution on the basis of which the person remanded will be tried in court.[61]

58. Ibid., 19ff.
59. Article 66, Constitution.
60. A fast-track procedure for trial of *délits* whereby a suspect is brought to trial immediately (Articles 393–397, CPP).
61. *Conseil constitutionnel*, Décision no. 2010-14/22 QPC 30/7/2010, 16; see also B. McKillop, 'Readings and Hearings in French Criminal Justice: Five Cases in the *Tribunal Correctionnel*' (1998) 46 (4) *Am. J. Comp. L.* 757.

The *Conseil* dismissed the argument that detention in custody by police breached the Constitutional principle, stating that 'the Judicial Authority is composed of trial judges and prosecutors', and that in any event the extension of police custody beyond 48 hours could be effected only on the authorisation of a judge.[62] The *Conseil* went on to find that the provisions of the CPP which limited the right of access to a lawyer to a 30-minute consultation prior to interrogation, together with the fact that the provisions did not require a person in custody to be informed of their right to silence, were unconstitutional.[63]

The *Conseil* ruled that the effect of the declaration of unconstitutionality was to be deferred until July 2011 but then a series of decisions of the *Cour de cassation* resulted in the declaration being given immediate effect in May 2011. Those decisions held that the reliance on statements made by a suspect to police without the assistance of a lawyer rendered the statements invalid.[64] The *Cour de cassation* interpreted the jurisprudence of the ECtHR on the Article 6 fair trial guarantees to require that a person should have access to the assistance of a lawyer at the commencement of custody *and* that the lawyer must be present during interviews by the police.[65] The *Cour de cassation* has repeated in each case that this flows from the ECtHR decisions of *Salduz*, *Dayanan* and *Brusco*.[66]

As a result of the reforming legislation,[67] persons held in police custody in France now have the right to be assisted by a lawyer prior to and during interrogations by police.[68] Where a person has requested a lawyer, questioning must be delayed for a period of two hours. A person must also be informed that they have the right to make statements, to answer questions or to remain silent.[69] In cases where 'the needs of the investigation' require, the two-hour deferral of questioning may be dispensed with but must be supported by

62. *Conseil constitutionnel*, Décision no. 2010-14/22 QPC 30/7/2010, 26.
63. 'Articles 62, 63, 63-1 and 77 of the CCP, together with paragraphs 1 to 6 of Article 63-4 thereof are unconstitutional'.
64. Crim-31/5/2011, *Bull. Crim.* 10-88.809.
65. Ibid.: 'La personne gardée à vue doit bénéficier de l'assistance d'un avocat dans des conditions lui permettant d'organiser sa défense et de préparer avec lui ses interrogatoires, *auquel l'avocat doit pouvoir participer* … alors que toute privation de liberté, quelle que soit sa nature, suppose la notification du droit de se taire et de ne pas participer à sa propre incrimination' (emphasis added). ('The person in custody must have the assistance of a lawyer in such conditions as to allow him to organise his defence and to prepare for his interrogations, *in which the lawyer must be able to participate* … every deprivation of liberty, whatever its nature, presumes the notification of the right to silence and the right against self-incrimination.)
66. Ass. Plén 15/4/2011, *Bull. Crim.* 10-30.316, especially *Rapport de Mme Bardy* (citing *Brusco (n9)*; *Salduz v Turkey* [GC] no. 36391/02, ECHR 2008; *Dayanan v Turquie*, no. 7377/03 (ECtHR 13/10/2009); see also Crim-31/5/2011, *Bull. Crim.* 10 30.313.
67. *Loi* 14/4/2011 (note 3).
68. The right extends also to interviews with the prosecutor and for any confrontations with witnesses; exceptions are made, however, in the case of organised crime where access to the lawyer can be delayed for 48 hours or 72 hours in the case of drug trafficking.
69. Article 63, CPP, as reformed by *loi* 14/4/2011 (note 3).

written reasons from the prosecutor in response to a request from the police to conduct immediate interrogation.

The legislation gives a somewhat circumscribed role to the lawyer during the interrogation: the lawyer may not ask questions during the interview, but is limited to asking questions at the commencement of each interview; the police officers may not prevent any such questions unless they are such as to interfere with the proper course of the investigation. The police may also have the lawyer removed from the interview if they are considered to be interfering with the investigation, but must notify the local bar immediately so that another lawyer can be appointed. The lawyer may take notes during the interview and may submit written observations into the file, including reference to any questions that he was prevented from putting during the interrogation. The lawyer is given sight of the police custody record so as to be able to verify that the rights of the suspect were read to him, and to be appraised of any medical examinations that were conducted and of any statements made by the suspect. The lawyer may take notes but is not furnished with his own copy of this record.[70]

Following the enactment of the reforming legislation, a second application was taken to the *Conseil constitutionnel* arguing that the reformed Article 63 continued to be unconstitutional, on the basis that while it allowed the right to the assistance of a lawyer and to the presence of a lawyer during questioning, it was nonetheless deficient in providing effective protection. In particular, objection was made to the lack of any right for the lawyer to consult the case file during the questioning or during the face-to-face confrontation with witnesses or to obtain copies thereof; the possibility of commencing interviews before the lawyer's arrival, even if the lawyer has not had sufficient time to arrive at the police station; the time limit of thirty minutes for the meeting between the person in police custody and his lawyer; and the restriction of the lawyer's assistance solely to acts relating to interrogations or confrontation, to the exclusion of such assistance during the course of investigative acts such as searches. Objection was also made to the fact that the police officers could object to questions asked during the interviews by the lawyer and to the police power to remove the lawyer from the interview.

The *Conseil* rejected all these arguments and deemed the reformed provisions to be constitutional. It considered the provisions struck the right balance between the demands of the Code of Criminal Procedure that the police search for the evidence and the perpetrators of crimes on the one hand, and respect for individual rights on the other. The argument that the provisions breached the principle of balance of rights between the parties was in the *Conseil*'s view to be without foundation.[71]

70. Article 63.4.1, CPP, as reformed by *loi* 14/4/2011 (note 3).
71. *Conseil constitutionnel*, Décision 2011–191/194/195/196/197 QPC 18/11/2011, 28.

(g) Recording of garde à vue

Provision for the audio-visual recording of police interviews has been in force since 2008; as such it is a relatively young provision.[72] Its effect is limited in that firstly it applies only to police custody for the more serious offences (*crimes*), and secondly that its use may be avoided by the inclusion of a proviso in the law permitting interviews in the absence of recording, similar to the Irish legislation relating to electronic recording of interviews.[73] Furthermore, the recording provisions do not apply to certain crimes, principally crimes committed by an organised gang, drug-trafficking offences and terrorist offences. Since it is a new provision, and given the apparent resistance in Ireland when initially fully implementing the equivalent provisions, it was not too surprising to find similar reticence, as evidenced from the following discussion with the judges:

> *JI*: This has been in force only for a year; I don't think that it is working well.
> *J*: I agree, it does not work at all!
> *JI*: I have never been asked to listen to a recording.
> *J*: I have not come across it in any cases I have dealt with. It is supposed to be a further guarantee of fairness, from the point of view of gathering evidence, and to make police custody more transparent.
> *JI*: It is to guarantee fairness in the procedure; more so to ensure that the interrogation has been correctly transcribed, because there have been cases where it has been claimed that the police have not accurately transcribed what was said. It is mainly for that. As for being a check on police behaviour towards a suspect, well, if you want to hit someone that could take place outside of the recording – 'he fell down the stairs'! Mind you, perhaps he will be falling down the stairs less with the new system!

The defence lawyer was scathing of the provisions:

> *Def. L1*: The recording provisions are useless! For one thing, they are used only in investigations for *crimes*. But the police do not use these provisions! There are too many exceptions, ways of avoiding recording interviews. This is why lawyers' groups have constantly insisted that the lawyer should be present at the police interviews, and he should be present throughout. Then no one will be able to say 'I said that, I did not say that', no one will be able to say 'the police hit me'.

72. Article 64.1 was inserted into the Code in 2007, *loi* 5/3/2007 (note 3).
73. Article 64.1 provides an escape clause where technical resources are insufficient; reasons must be specified in a police report.

The Léger committee recommended extending the recording of interviews beyond *crimes* to cover all offences.[74]

(h) Investigation procedures following police custody

Following the expiry of the time limits for police custody, persons against whom evidence has been collected liable to give rise to a prosecution are either set free or referred to the public prosecutor, the *procureur*.[75] The case will then proceed either by way of investigation by the public prosecutor or by the police under supervision from the public prosecutor, through the preliminary inquiry procedure, the *enquête préliminaire*, or by way of the *instruction* procedure if it is in the category of *crime*, or where the public prosecutor has exercised his discretion to pass on a *délit* to the JI.

Regardless of which procedure is employed, and regardless of whether a suspect is at liberty or detained, in sharp contrast to the position in Ireland where a person may not be questioned after being formally charged by the district court, in France a suspect remains available as a source of information to the authorities and may be questioned at any time throughout the investigative stage and confronted with the evidence as the investigation develops.[76]

(i) Pre-trial detention

Whichever investigative procedure applies, the suspect may be detained while awaiting the decision to prosecute or to send forward for trial.[77] A person under judicial examination may be released on bail (*contrôle judiciaire*) by the JI (if the person has already been detained) or sent forward by the JI to the JLD to be held in pre-trial detention.[78]

The decision to detain a person before trial was made until 2000 by the JI. The law was changed in 2000 with the introduction of a new player: the JLD. Requests for pre-trial detention are normally made by the JI, but since 2004 the prosecutor may apply directly to the JLD in cases where the sentence is ten years or more.[79] A direct request by the prosecutor seeking pre-trial detention is circumscribed, however, by Article 144. That article permits the JI to seek pre-trial detention for any of the following reasons:

1. for the preservation of evidence, the protection of witnesses, victims and their families from pressure and for the prevention of conspiracy between persons under judicial examination and their accomplices;

74. Léger (note 6) 19.
75. Article 77, CPP.
76. Also in Italy.
77. Article 66 of the Constitution protects individual liberty from arbitrary detention.
78. The JI lost competence regarding pre-trial detention in 2000: *loi* 15/6/2000 (note 3).
79. *Loi* 9/3/2004 (note 32).

2. for the protection of the person under judicial examination, for ensuring his availability to judicial authorities and for preventing the continuance or repetition of the offence;
3. to put an end to exceptional public disorder caused by the seriousness of the offence, the circumstances in which it was committed or the gravity of the harm that it has caused.

The prosecutor may request the JLD to impose pre-trial detention only for the reasons listed under 2 and 3.

The hearing of the application to remand in custody must normally be made in open court and provide the opportunity for *un débat contradictoire*, usually translated as 'adversarial argument'.[80] A hearing *in camera* may be requested if the public hearing is likely to hinder the investigation, undermine the presumption of innocence of the accused or harm the interests of the accused or a third party.[81] Detention may be lengthy, with an outside limit of four years for certain serious offences.[82] In addition to these lengthy detention periods, a person may be refused communication with all persons except for their lawyer for a period of no greater than one month at the beginning of the pre-trial detention period. Given that the suspect may be questioned throughout the investigative period, pre-trial detention may therefore serve as a means of pressurising an accused into making a confession.

The Léger committee considered that pre-trial detention is used excessively and proposed that the exceptional nature of this measure be reinforced so as to promote a culture of liberty during the pre-trial stage. They also proposed a simplification of time limits and recommended that where a trial has not commenced by the end of these periods, the suspect should be released and placed under alternative security measures such as electronic tagging.[83]

(j) Enquête préliminaire *procedure*

The investigation supervised by the prosecutor continues until the decision by the prosecutor to send the suspect forward for trial. During this time the defence has little information to work with, having no right to read the police file. By contrast, if the case proceeds through the *instruction* procedure the involvement of the defence lawyer is more extensive. The suspect may be questioned by the public prosecutor or by the police and confronted with witnesses. During the course of the preliminary investigation the public prosecutor or, with his permission, a judicial police officer may order the taking of non-intimate bodily

80. I would argue that this is not an accurate translation.
81. Article 199, CPP.
82. Article 145.2, CPP: 'The normal period of detention should not exceed one year'; however, this may be extended.
83. Léger (note 6) 23; time limits ranged from six months to three years.

samples.[84] Where technical or scientific reports or examinations need to be carried out, the public prosecutor or a judicial police officer appointed by him may call upon any qualified person to undertake the acts in question. The results of these may be communicated to the person suspected of committing the offence as well as to the victims, on the instruction of the public prosecutor.[85]

The time limit for the preliminary inquiry is uncertain. Provision is made for the public prosecutor to fix time limits within which the inquiry must be carried out when he instructs the judicial police officers to proceed with the preliminary inquiry, and he may extend the time limit if requested by the investigators.[86] The time limit fixed by the public prosecutor, however, is not stated, but the article sets a time limit for the police when carrying out a preliminary inquiry on their own initiative, setting a limit of six months for the judicial police officers to give the prosecutor an account of its progress.[87] While there are limitation periods after which criminal actions are extinguished[88] these periods are of no assistance in establishing the time limits for investigations as the Code provides that the limitation periods date from the time of the last investigative act.[89] A circular issued in 2000 states that the limit of six months should be the norm for the time limit fixed by the public prosecutor, and should be the measure of any extensions to the investigation granted by the prosecutor.[90]

Any person held in police custody during the course of a preliminary inquiry or a flagrant offence investigation who, six months from the date of the end of police custody, has not been prosecuted, may inquire of the public prosecutor as to the outcome or likely outcome of the case.[91]

(k) Investigation procedure by the juge d'instruction

The concept of a judicial investigation, the *instruction* procedure, has been a feature of French criminal justice since the sixteenth century.[92] Its centrality in the procedure, described by a jurist in the early eighteenth century as the 'soul of the process',[93] nonetheless has become increasingly fragile. Following a recommendation from the Viout committee charged with examining 'the dysfunction of justice' following the Outreau scandal,[94] a new law aimed at

84. Article 55.1, CPP.
85. Article 77.1, CPP.
86. Article 75.1, CPP.
87. Article 95, CPP.
88. *Crimes* ten years (Article 7, CPP); *délits* three (Article 8, CPP).
89. Article 7, CPP.
90. Crim-00-13/F1 4/12/2000; Fourment (note 1) 78.
91. Article 77.2, CPP.
92. Created by Ordinance of 1539; the position of JI was created by Napoleonic Code in 1908.
93. Ambroise-Castérot (note 1) 228.
94. Viout (note 5).

creating a balance in criminal procedure provided for a modified system of *instruction* procedure whereby the JI, instead of acting alone, would be organised into a collegial grouping referred to as *pôle de l'instruction.*[95] The law was due to be incorporated into the Code in 2009 but it has since been deferred. It provides that in certain cases, due to the gravity or complexity of the case, the president of the court (*tribunal de grande instance*) may order that the case be dealt with through the collegial procedure. It is still uncertain whether these provisions will take effect.

There was also a further law published based on the Léger Report draft Code, which abolished the role of the JI altogether, a law which for the moment has effectively been shelved.[96] The Léger committee suggest that the JI is 'neither fully a judge nor fully an investigator' and, as such, he cannot act with complete impartiality.[97] Under the Léger committee proposals, all investigations would be conducted under the control and direction of the public prosecutor, who in turn would need to apply to the JLD for authorisation to carry out coercive acts affecting personal liberty. If the reforms proposing the abolition of the JI ever do materialise, the JLD will become known as the *juge de l'enquête et des libertés* (judge of investigation and freedom (JEL)).

The judges' views on these proposed reforms were as follows:

> *JI*: The reform project of Sarkozy is moving towards the Anglo-Saxon model – that is, prosecution against defence. We have the JI whose work is to seek out everything – the truth; it is a huge difference in practice. A lawyer will never go down a line of questioning which might go against his client, and the prosecutor is the same – he does not want to weaken his case; there are shady areas into which neither will go because it is not in their interest to go there. In principle, the JI, when he does his work properly, will go into all the shady areas, and the result, well it is quite different.
> *Self*: The Léger report suggests the JI is neither fully a judge nor fully an investigator and that he cannot act with complete impartiality. What are your views on this and of the proposed abolition of the JI?
> *J*: I would say he is both.
> *JI*: I think the idea of defining a judge according to his impartiality is really an Anglo-Saxon idea, but it is an idea that is really taking hold in France.
> *J*: The JI does not prosecute. He is totally independent; he has the same attitude to the hearing as the president to whom he sends on the file. For me, he remains neutral; I think the JI should remain in our system.
> *JI*: I agree that the JI is neutral, and he is especially neutral because he is independent; but at the same time he can be reproached for being both

95. *Loi* 5/3/2007 (note 3), Article 3.
96. Due to ECtHR in *Moulin* and *Medvedyev v France* (note 15) on status of prosecutor.
97. Léger (note 6) 6.

judge and investigator. Today there is a strong movement to abolish the JI, but one may ask whether we will have a fair procedure as a result. People will find themselves before the police and the prosecutor who are not independent; it will be the prosecutor who will carry out all the functions that are today undertaken by the JI, and as the prosecutor has the power to delegate his duties to the police, that will become the norm, in reality today, it is usually the police who perform all the investigative acts of the prosecutor.

Self: But the JI can also delegate to the police?

JI: Yes! But he is in control; he still supervises them more actively than the prosecutor.

Self: Would a JI usually attend a search?

JI: Yes, certainly!

Self: And reconstructions?

JI: Absolutely! Reconstructions are an excellent way of discovering the truth.

The primary aim of the *instruction* procedure is to determine whether the charges against the suspect are sufficient to send him forward for trial.[98] The JI may act only following a submission from the public prosecutor, which may be made against a named or unnamed person by a complaint with a petition to become a civil party.[99] The JI is seized *in rem* rather than *in personam*, in other words he is seized with the fact of a crime as set out in the reference from the public prosecutor or in the complaint made by the persons constituting themselves as *partie civile*. On that basis the JI is free to decide which persons should be subject to investigation.[100]

It is the duty of the JI to investigate the case impartially, *à charge et à décharge*, that is both for and against the person being investigated. There are two categories of 'suspects', the *mise en examen* and the *témoin assisté*. How a person is categorised depends on the level of suspicion existing: the *mise en examen* depends on the existence of 'serious and concordant' evidence making it probable that they have participated in the offence, whether directly or as an accomplice;[101] the *témoin assisté* is a witness who benefits from rights of defence – the evidence should point to the probability that they have participated in the offence but the evidence does not need to be 'serious and concordant'.[102]

The person may choose a lawyer or have one appointed on his behalf, and the lawyer must be given access to the file and have the opportunity to communicate with his client at least four days prior to the hearing. At the first

98. Hodgson (note 17) 215 found this was merely a formality.
99. Article 51, CPP; Article 85, CPP: procedure for civil party petitioning.
100. Fourment (note 1) 225.
101. Article 80.1, CPP.
102. Article 113.2, CPP.

hearing, which is to establish whether the person should be subjected to judicial examination (as either *mise en examen* or *témoin assisté*) or not, the person must be informed by the JI of the charges against him and their legal basis. The JI must inform the person that they may remain silent, make statements or be interrogated; if the person waives their right to a lawyer, they may either make a statement or remain silent but cannot be interrogated – the consent of the person to be interrogated must be obtained in the presence of the lawyer.

While the presence of a lawyer is not obligatory during the judicial investigation stage, the waiver of the right to a lawyer has a negative consequence: while the Code provides that the lawyer must be given access to the dossier prior to any interrogations or confrontations, it does not extend this to the person under investigation; this right does not accrue until they are sent forward for trial. The ECtHR has ruled that withholding the dossier from the person under judicial examination is not incompatible with Article 6.1 of the ECHR.[103] Any statements given by the person under investigation are unsworn, a position which dates back to 1798. This also holds true for the trial. This is a fundamental difference to the position in Ireland where the accused, if he elects to give evidence at trial, must do so under oath.[104] In effect it is implicitly recognised that the accused in France has 'a sort of right to lie'.[105]

Since 2007 all interrogations and confrontations that take place before the JI must be audio-visually recorded. The JI may decide, however, where there are a number of persons to be interrogated at the same time in separate proceedings or in the same proceedings that the interrogations will proceed in the absence of recording.[106] Recording may also be dispensed with due to technical impossibility, but this must be noted in the official record together with the nature of the technical impossibility. Where the JI makes the decision to place the person under judicial examination he must inform him of his right to ask for acts to be undertaken, and of his right to apply for any acts to be nullified during the course of the investigation.[107] In cases of emergency, the JI may interrogate the person or carry out confrontations in the absence of a lawyer: where a witness is in danger of death, where evidence is on the point of disappearing or in cases where the JI is present on the scene of the crime simultaneously with the prosecutor.[108]

Subsequent interrogations and confrontations of the person under investigation and of an assisted witness may only take place in the presence of a lawyer.

103. *Menet v France*, no. 39553/02 (ECtHR 14/6/2005).

104. In Italy the position is the same as in France in that the accused never gives evidence under oath; in Ireland the accused may still give unsworn statements from the dock, but these are of lesser evidential weight to sworn testimony.

105. Ambroise-Castérot (note 1) 263.

106. Article 116.1, CPP.

107. Article 116, CPP.

108. Article 117, CPP.

The prosecutor may attend and may put questions, as may the lawyer for the *partie civile* and that of the person under investigation, with the JI having overall control of the hearing.[109]

Where a judicial investigation is opened, the police work under the direction of the JI through the mechanism of a *commission rogatoire* whereby acts may be delegated to them by the JI. Any acts which are delegated through this mechanism must be precisely stated, so a general instruction to conduct an investigation without clearly stating the investigative acts which are required is not permitted. Furthermore, the JI may not delegate the interrogation or confrontation of a *mise en examen* to the police, though he may delegate the task to another JI.[110] If in the course of the investigation, the JI requires that a person be arrested and placed in *garde à vue*, the judicial police are permitted to conduct interrogations and confrontations of such persons and the *garde à vue* follows the same course as described above, except here the JI rather than the public prosecutor is in control and grants extensions etc.

During the investigation, the JI commissions an inquiry into the social circumstances and general character of the person under investigation. This is a far-reaching investigation carried out usually by a social worker or a police officer who may interview medical experts, for example psychologists, as well as persons close to the *mise en examen*. Reports of all these interviews, including reports relating to any previous convictions, will be included in the dossier sent forward to the trial judge where it will be examined during what is known as the *personalité* stage of the trial.[111]

Searches and seizures including searches of private dwellings carried out during the course of a judicial investigation operate in the same way as those conducted during a flagrant investigation.

Confrontations are a feature of French criminal justice that finds no counterpart in Ireland. The closest equivalent in Irish law would be the presentation by the police of a statement made by a co-accused to a suspect in custody, but while in Ireland the Judges' Rules prohibits the questioning of the accused about the statement,[112] the confronting of a suspect in custody or a person under judicial investigation with, not just the statements of others but the persons themselves, is a regular feature of criminal procedure in France.[113] It was explained to me by the JI in the following terms:

> *JI*: The JI puts questions to the witness and to the accused, or there may be a number of witnesses; they are present at the same time, and the lawyer for the accused also poses questions. The confrontation is a very

109. Article 120, CPP.
110. Article 152, CPP.
111. See section 5.4.5(b) below.
112. Rule viii, Judges' Rules.
113. Also a feature in Italy.

> important part of our system; it is in effect a hearing, a little court hearing which is held in private in the JI's office. It allows the *juge* to assess the credibility of the accused and each of the witnesses, and where it relates to *crimes*, it is recorded audio-visually.

In the police station during a *garde à vue* the confrontation would proceed in the same way, with the police in place of the JI putting the questions. The suspect could be confronted with a co-accused, the victim of the offence or witnesses, together or separately. The concept of reconstruction is also a feature of French criminal justice unknown to Irish law; it had been typically used by the JI during the investigation, but the *Cour de cassation* has ruled that it may equally be used by the police during an investigation into a flagrant offence.[114]

The *instruction* procedure is a written procedure: an official report is made of every act undertaken which then becomes the dossier that is passed on to the trial judge. The JI has the power to undertake 'all acts he considers useful for the manifestation of the truth'. Despite the broad sweep that this may suggest, the JI is equally bound as any other investigator to respect the principle of legality of proof and the principle of *loyauté* in obtaining proof.[115] The public prosecutor may ask the JI to undertake any acts he considers necessary 'to the manifestation of the truth', and may request to be present when these acts are carried out.[116] The parties (*mise en examen* and *partie civile*) or their lawyers may also request acts to be carried out 'that appear to them to be necessary', for example that certain witnesses be examined, a confrontation be held or for experts to conduct technical examinations. While this is clearly provided by the Code, expanded by the law in 2000 so as to ensure that French law respects the ECHR right to 'equality of arms'[117] it would appear that in practice it is not always adhered to. The defence lawyer put it thus:

> *Def. L1*: Balance, no! Today in France the balance is very uneven. Firstly, during all preliminary investigations, today it is usually the *parquet* that brings the action, and it is the practice that determines the balance – according to the texts everything is balanced! Even where an *instruction* is opened there is an imbalance. Why is there an imbalance? I will give you an example: according to the texts, the prosecutor and the defence may each ask for acts to be carried out, for example the prosecutor may ask that a witness be heard, for expert evidence to be obtained. Me too, the defence can also ask for witnesses to be heard; but what is noticeable

114. Crim. 26/2/2003, *Bull. Crim.* 56; Fourment (note 1) 84.
115. Section 5.3.1 below.
116. Article 82, CPP.
117. Article 6, ECHR.

is that if it is the prosecutor who is making the request, in 90 or 95% of cases the judge agrees to the request, but if it is the defence who asks he will agree maybe at most in 40% of cases. That is an imbalance!

Part II

5.3 Approach to evidence law in France

5.3.1 Principle of loyauté *with respect to gathering evidence – illegally obtained evidence*

The gathering and presentation of evidence is governed by the principle of legality of proof. This principle is reinforced by two further principles which have been established through the jurisprudence of the courts and general principles of law, although not specifically mentioned in the Code or the Constitution: the principle of *loyauté* in the search for evidence and the principle of *loyauté* in the examination of the evidence. Literally translated, the principle of *loyauté* means loyalty, in the sense that it is faithful to the law, so the gathering of evidence should 'respect the rights of the individual and the integrity of justice'.[118] In gathering evidence, the police, the public prosecutor and the JI must act 'without trickery, deception or provocation'.[119]

The police when searching for evidence are constrained by the principle, but it is accepted that the use of coercive methods, such as custody, are required in the investigation of crime. Nonetheless, police custody (*garde à vue*) is strictly regulated to prevent confessions being obtained through deprivation of sleep, food or violence (both physical and psychological). Furthermore, the actions of the police must be guided by the principle of proportionality.

As guardians of personal liberty,[120] judges, in seeking the truth, 'must do so without inspiring fear in the criminal by means of false threats or winning him over through false hopes'.[121] The principle of *loyauté* in the gathering of evidence applies to the judicial authorities. Up to recently it did not apply to the *partie civile*, but in a recent decision of the *Cour de cassation* it was held equally to apply both to the parties (defendant and *partie civile*) and to witnesses. Nonetheless:

> The fact that documents or recordings put forward as evidence by a party or witness have been gathered through disloyal procedures does not allow the JI to exclude them from the proceedings, since they only constitute means of proof that can be tested at trial through the *débat contradictoire*.[122]

118. Ambroise-Castérot (note 1) 172.
119. Ibid., 173.
120. Article 66, Constitution.
121. Ambroise-Castérot (note 1) 173.
122. Crim. 30/3/1999, *Bull. Crim.* 59; Ambroise-Castérot (note 1) 181.

Thus evidence that is obtained by the parties or witnesses through, for example, covert surveillance, recordings or telephone intercepts, which would be illegal if obtained by the police in the absence of authorisation, is considered unproblematic because of the possibility for testing the evidence through the *contradictoire* procedure. This is so even if it has been obtained through the commission of an offence: in relation to the offence of invasion of privacy whereby a wife had made a secret recording of her husband's confession of the murder of their son, the court held that 'a *partie civile* may give the JI recordings which she has made even though they could only have been obtained through the commission of an offence'.[123]

The safeguard of a *contradictoire* trial structure through which evidence may be challenged and debated has also been invoked in the context of illegal intercepts by the police: telephone intercepts by the police may only be undertaken upon the authorisation of a judge (JI or JLD), regardless of whether an offence is flagrant or not; however, a recent decision of the *Cour de cassation* ruled that a recording obtained without authorisation was admissible in the trial on the dual condition that it was subjected to a *débat contradictoire* and supported by other evidence.[124]

I asked the defence lawyer about the observance of the principle of *loyauté* in practice:

> *Def. L1*: In principle yes, but unfortunately there are cases where it is questionable that the principle of *loyauté* has been observed. For example, when a witness is asked to make a formal identification, the suspect is placed among five other people who resemble him, but often the witness will have already seen the suspect in the corridor, in handcuffs! Or the police use suggestive questioning and get the answers they want like that.
>
> There is not really a true respect for the principle in the gathering of evidence. On the other hand, there are legal formalities which give effect to the principle – the police cannot gather evidence through illegal interceptions or by committing a criminal offence; they cannot get proof through acts of violence. But that is the formal position. In reality, in practice … for example, take a search. For a search to be carried out it is supposed to be in the presence of the owner of the premises or in the presence of two witnesses. So you get cases where it is noted that the search was conducted in the presence of such and such a person, but then you have that person saying 'no, I was not there'. Normally the search should be annulled on that basis, but they are not annulled. So it is true that there is a principle of *loyauté*, a principle of fairness in gathering evidence, but it is also true that breaches of the principle are not always sanctioned by the nullity procedure. It is also true that there are means used for finding evidence, which

123. Invasion of privacy contrary to Article 226.1, CPP; Crim. 6/4/1993, *JCP* 1993 ll. 221–44.
124. Crim.13/10/2004, *Bull. Crim.* 243.

are not really, at least technically, disloyal, means that are not illegal. For example, 'if you don't tell me where your husband was ... the children will be put in care'. They use psychological pressure. But this does not exist officially.

5.3.2 Nullity system

Nullity is the sanction applied for breach of a prerequisite formality of a procedural act. Once an act is annulled, it is considered never to have existed. As one judge put it to me: 'it is thrown out; it is put in the rubbish bin'. Effectively, then, the approach is not altogether dissimilar to the common law approach of excluding evidence in the sense that the trier of fact may never know of the existence of a particular piece of information, but this will only be the case where the nullity issue has been raised during the investigation by the JI; in such cases it is removed from the file. However, in an investigation conducted by the prosecutor, the nullity will be raised during the trial itself and so the question becomes one of whether the evidence may be used to reach a verdict rather than a question of exclusion in the common law sense of the term; the evidence is fully revealed to the trier of fact so that a decision may be made about its use or non-use.

The nullity system is governed by Articles 170–174 and Article 802 of the Code, the former falling under the provisions governing judicial investigations, the latter under General Provisions. Article 171 provides:

> A nullity arises when the breach of a substantive formality provided for by a provision of the Code or by any other rule of criminal procedure has harmed the interests of the party concerned.

Article 802 provides:

> In the event of a violation of formalities prescribed by law under penalty of nullity or in the event of non-observance of substantive formalities, any court, including the *Cour de cassation*, which is seized of an application for annulment or which raises an irregularity of its own motion, may pronounce the nullity only where this has had the effect of damaging the interests of the party concerned.

The Code distinguishes between two types of nullity: textual nullity and virtual or substantive nullity. A textual nullity is defined as a breach of 'a formality that is prescribed by law under penalty of nullity'.[125] In other words, a textual nullity occurs where it is specifically stated in the Code that a breach of a

125. Article 802, CPP.

provision gives rise to a nullity.[126] No specific definition is given in the Code of a substantive or virtual nullity, therefore the act, where it is not specifically stated as giving rise to a nullity, must be examined to assess whether the character of the act is such that it should be annulled. Into this category would fall breaches of the guarantees during *garde à vue.* Article 171 also provides for nullities arising from breaches of law not specifically mentioned in the Code but covered 'by any other rule of criminal procedure'. Under this rubric the jurisprudence of the *Cour de cassation* has found nullity where there is a breach of the principle of *loyauté* in gathering evidence.[127]

There is also the potential to find a nullity where there has been a breach of a right guaranteed under the European Convention; however, it has been suggested that the *Cour de cassation* appears reluctant to sanction a breach of a Convention right by way of nullity.[128]

A prerequisite for applying the sanction of nullity that is clearly stated under both Articles 171 and 802 is that the act impugned must have had the effect of damaging the interests of the party concerned. There is a difference, however, between *nullités d'ordre public* and *nullités d'ordre privé.* The former, which relate to procedural aspects such as jurisdictional competence, do not require prejudice to the party to be established while the latter is the opposite. For a plea of nullity of private order to succeed the party applying for annulment of the procedural act must establish that it is prejudicial to their interests.

The position regarding the right to silence has been reformed since 2011, and it has been reiterated by the *Cour de cassation* that the suspect has a right to be told of his right to silence and of his right against self-incrimination. The court has held that reliance on incriminating confessions made by a suspect without having had access to a lawyer renders a conviction invalid, and in such cases have remitted the case back to the *Cour d'appel* for rehearing. In that rehearing the court would be unable to use the confessions as evidence, since they would have constituted a nullity. Effectively, then, the French nullity system does take an exclusionary approach to evidence in some situations.[129] This does not extend, however, to confessions that result from the psychological pressure of pre-trial detention:

> *JI*: A big failing of the nullity system in my view relates to pre-trial detention, and France has been repeatedly condemned by the European Court of Human Rights for its pre-trial detention regime, because a person could be in prison for two years, three years, and they may have committed no offence; the only consequence in such a case is that they

126. By way of example, Article 59 provides: 'The formalities mentioned in Articles 56, 56-1 and 57 (searches of dwellings) are prescribed on pain of nullity.'
127. Fourment (note 1) 53.
128. Ibid., 54.
129. Crim. 31/5/2011, *Bull. Crim.* 10-88.809.

may be paid compensation,[130] because the Supreme Court has consistently held that an excessive pre-trial detention never gives rise to a nullity. That is quite shocking. Sometimes a person is left in prison for many months simply to put pressure on them, and quite often a person is detained for that reason alone, to put them under pressure. That should give rise to a nullity but no; it results only in monetary compensation. The trial will go ahead and he may be found guilty regardless of the pressure that arose because of the pre-trial detention. (*J* agreed)

An application for annulment of a procedural act may be raised during the judicial investigation by the defence, the *partie civile*, the prosecutor, the JI or by an assisted witness, and the application is made to the *chambre d'instruction*.[131] Time limits apply. Where a case proceeds through the *instruction* procedure applications must be raised during the procedure before the case reaches trial – if not they are deemed to have been purged. The grounds for nullity of any procedure conducted before a suspects first interrogation by the JI or during that first interrogation must be raised within six months from being notified of being under judicial examination, unless the grounds for annulment were unknown at the time.[132] In cases that proceed via the *enquête préliminaire* process, the application may be raised at the trial itself.[133]

Part III

5.4 Receiving, presenting and challenging evidence

The different modes of investigation for *crimes* and *délits* have been noted. Trial of *crimes* and *délits* also differ, the former being tried in the *cour d'assises* presided over by three judges: a president and two assessors, and a jury of nine private citizens. The latter are tried in the *tribunal correctionelle* (the *tribunal*) presided over by a judge sitting alone or three judges depending on the seriousness of the case.

I attended two trials in the *cour d'assises* in Toulouse and one trial in the *tribunal correctionelle* in Angers (the *tribunal*). One of the trials in the *cour d'assises* was an appeal brought by the public prosecutor against an acquittal.[134] At his trial the accused had been acquitted of participation in an armed robbery in

130. Compensation is payable under Article 149, CPP.
131. Article 173, CPP; the *Chambre d'instruction* rules on appeals on acts of the JI, nullities and decisions of the JLD. It also supervises the activities of the judicial police with power of suspension.
132. Article 173, CPP.
133. Article 802, CPP.
134. Since 2002 the prosecutor may appeal against an acquittal. The appeal is a full rehearing of the case in which all the evidence is taken again.

which four co-accused had been convicted. The public prosecutor had struck out the charge of armed robbery and substituted a charge of complicity and belonging to an organised gang.

The other trial in the *cour d'assises* was a rape trial in which two women claimed to have been raped by two men, an Algerian father and his son, in two separate incidents. One of the women had alleged she had been held in the home of the accused against her will so the accused was also charged with this offence. Both accused had been held in pre-trial detention for three years, but the father had died while in detention leaving only the son to face trial. Rape trials would normally be held in camera as in Ireland, but the court acceded to a request by the two lawyers representing the women, each having been constituted as *partie civile*, to have the case heard in public.

The trial in the *tribunal* was a case against three co-accused charged with aggravated robbery. It was alleged that they had stolen two cars, then stolen property from a private dwelling, and in order to foil the efforts of two members of the *gendarmerie* who were in pursuit on motorbikes, had thrown a fire extinguisher from one of the cars which injured one *gendarme*. The two members of the *gendarmerie* appeared as *parties civiles* in the case.[135]

The trials in the *cour d'assises* each lasted two days, with the court sitting from 08:45–19:00 hours, with adjournments in each amounting to two hours in total.[136] The trial in the *tribunal* lasted six hours.[137] I will draw on the three cases to demonstrate the course of trials at the *cour d'assises* and the *tribunal*; for ease of reference they shall be referred to as 'the appeal case', 'the rape case' and 'the robbery case' respectively.

5.4.1 The trial setting

Cases are heard in the *cour d'assises* by the president of the court who sits in the middle of a raised bench structure flanked on each side by two assessors and a jury of nine for a trial or twelve for an appeal. In both trial and appeal cases, two extra jurors sit for the duration of the hearing as substitutes but they do not take part in the deliberations unless actually required to substitute an absent juror. The accused sits in a semi-enclosed area to the left of the

135. This would not be unusual.
136. By contrast, the murder trial in the *cour d'assises* documented by McKillop lasted one and a half days even though more witnesses were called (B. McKillop, 'Anatomy of a French Murder Case' (1997) 45 (3) *Am. J. Comp. L.* 527). A trial of a university law professor for the murder of his wife heard in Toulouse in 2009 lasted two weeks; he was acquitted, and following prosecutor's appeal, he was acquitted after a three-week trial. Trials therefore appear to last longer than McKillop found in his study. The *huissier* (court crier, tipstaff) told me that the duration depends on the number of witnesses, suggesting that witnesses are called to give their testimony in full rather than reliance being placed on their statements in the dossier, as happened in the case that McKillop documented.
137. Again considerably longer than McKillop (note 61).

president's bench just above floor level. In the rape case, being in custody, the accused was flanked by two armed prison guards and assisted by an interpreter who sat beside him. His lawyer sat in front of him at floor level. In the appeal case the accused, who was on bail,[138] sat behind his lawyer without prison guards.

Directly opposite the accused's position, to the right of the president's bench, the *partie civile* lawyer sits on the lower tier of a bench structure, the *greffier*[139] and the prosecutor sits on the upper tier at the same level as the president's bench. The *partie civile*, if present, sits in the body of the courtroom.[140] Witnesses when called to give their evidence stand at floor level directly in front of the president, their position marked by a simple writing stand. The seating arrangements in the *tribunal* are identical other than the presence of a jury.

5.4.2 Parties to proceedings

The victim and the *partie civile* are not synonymous concepts: the victim is the person who has suffered directly from the crime, but the victim may decide not to become a civil party and thus have no status in the trial (other than as a witness). The *partie civile* is the person who is joined to the proceedings[141] and is entitled to representation by a lawyer. The presence of the defence counsel is compulsory in the *cour d'assises*; an accused may not waive the right and defend himself. The position is different in the *tribunal* where the right to defence counsel may be waived.[142]

The prosecutor is not considered to be a 'party' to the proceedings. He is the person who 'undertakes the public action' and is nowhere referred to in the Code as a party.[143]

5.4.3 Jury selection

The jury pool assembled in the courtroom on the first morning of the appeal case. They had already been attending the court during the previous two weeks since the start of the *assises* sessions; jurors are selected from the pool and those not selected for the trial in hand are then sent home to appear again for

138. *Contrôle judiciaire*, Articles 137–138, CPP.
139. Court registrar.
140. The *partie civile* was not present in the appeal case.
141. Article 2, CPP: 'Civil action aimed at the reparation of the damage suffered because of a felony, a misdemeanour or a petty offence is open to all those who have personally suffered damage directly caused by the offence. The waiver of a civil action will not interrupt or suspend the exercise of the public prosecution.' In principle, the withdrawal of a complaint by a victim has no effect on the prosecution case; it may still proceed.
142. Article 317, CPP.
143. Article 31, CPP.

possible selection in the next trial on the list.[144] Being selected for one trial does not excuse the jurors for the remainder of the sessions, as would be the norm in Ireland, and of the twelve jurors who were selected by the president, by taking their names out of an urn, five had participated in the rape trial which had concluded the previous day. One juror was challenged by the prosecutor, none by the defence.[145] The jury then took the oath repeating it after a reading by the president: they must examine the charges against the accused 'with the most scrupulous attention' and decide the case impartially, according to the charges and the defence arguments.[146] An addition was made to the oath in 2000 that the jury must 'remember that the accused is presumed innocent and that he has the benefit of the doubt'.[147]

5.4.4 Witnesses

Witnesses present their identity documents to the *huissier* (court crier) following a roll call of witnesses by the president. They are then sent to the room reserved for witnesses, where they remain in the company of a member of the judicial police until called by the *huissier.* Witnesses are forbidden from discussing the case with others, and unlike the position in Ireland, are not privy to the testimony another witness has given.[148] The only witnesses who are permitted to remain in the courtroom during the trial are experts.

5.4.5 Course of the trial

(a) Reading of charges

Trials in the *cour d'assises* commence with the reading of the charge by the *greffier*, reading from a document that is supplied to all participants (other than witnesses) in the trial, including the jury.[149] In the *tribunal* this reading is done by the president. Thirteen pages of this document in the appeal case I attended related the facts of the case, being a summary of the commission of the offence, the discovery of three suspects through CCTV, road traffic cameras and mobile phone geographical locations, the discovery of certain items and fingerprints in the cars used in the incident and from searches carried out in the homes of the three suspects, a summary of the statements of these three suspects which had implicated two others, one of whom was the accused in this appeal, and a summary of the inquiry into the *personnalité* (social circumstances and

144. Jurors (aged over 23) are drawn from an annual list made from the electoral register: Articles 257, 262, 266–269, 289.
145. The defence may challenge five jurors and the prosecutor four, without cause.
146. Article 304, CPP.
147. *Loi* 15/6/2000 (note 3), Article 40.
148. Article 325, CPP.
149. I was supplied with this document for the appeal case in the *cour d'assises* by the *huissier.*

general character) of each of the five participants including their previous convictions.

The accused had three previous convictions. The summary of the police report revealed that the accused had admitted to the police officer that it had been his idea to steal the takings from a nightclub where he worked. He said that he had suggested the idea to his friend but they had both concluded that it would be difficult to do it on their own. His friend (who was convicted in the first trial and received a suspended sentence) had arranged for the accused to meet another man; they had agreed to carry out the theft along with two others, bringing the number to five in all. The three new recruits were all previous offenders with some serious offences on their records.

Between them they concocted an elaborate plan which involved kidnapping an employee of the club, using imitation firearms and forcing the employee to obtain the money from the owner of the club by pretending that the son of the employee was being held hostage and would be harmed should the owner try to contact the police or refuse to hand over the money. The accused gave the three men information about where the owner lived, having asked another employee for this information; he also gave the three men information about the general layout of the club, the routine for closing the club at night and the movement of the takings.

It was decided the robbery would take place, and the accused went along with the arrangements, but when the designated night arrived he phoned his best friend (who had not had any connection with the plan nor was charged) in a panic, asking him to phone one of the men to tell him that he had been taken to hospital and would therefore not be meeting them. The kidnap and robbery went ahead without the accused and the latter received none of the proceeds of the crime.

(b) Personnalité of accused

Following the reading of the charges, the taking of evidence begins, starting always in the *cour d'assises* with the evidence from the investigation into the background of the accused, referred to as the personnalité stage. This stage is not a discrete stage in trials in the *tribunal*; instead the social background and character evidence form part of the overall questioning of the accused by the president.

In the *cour d'assises*, the *personnalité* stage includes information about the general character of the accused including reference to any previous convictions or indeed encounters with the police that may not have resulted in either trial or conviction. The presentation and scope of this information is apparent from that given in the appeal case. The first witness to appear was a social worker who had carried out the inquiry relating to the accused's overall social background.[150] She spoke for 30 minutes without recourse to notes,

150. The rape trial commenced in the same way.

outlining his difficult childhood due to the absence in his life of a father figure, his school years, that he had been a good student, his need to succeed – overall painting the accused in a favourable light, other than the three convictions on his record for minor offences. No questions were asked by the president, the prosecutor or the lawyers for the parties following her testimony.

The second witness was a psychology expert who had examined the accused and related how he suffered from an inferiority complex and again stressed the absence of a father figure in his life; no questions were asked of this witness. The third witness was another expert, a psychoanalyst who had found no major problems in his examination of the accused; the only question that was asked of this witness was by the prosecutor who asked the expert how could he reconcile the crime with the accused's character, commenting that 'he would appear to be a "good boy"'; the expert responded that while the accused had no psychiatric problems, he had the tendency to be easily influenced and sought the approval of others.

Two other witnesses testified about the accused's character. One was a childhood friend who was a law student in Paris; no questions were asked of this witness except by the president who inquired at some length about his legal studies and his plans for his career in law! The other witness was the accused's aunt who had raised him due to his mother's inability to cope on her own, who spoke of the difficulty for the accused due to the absence of his father, her attempt to put the father in contact with her nephew but the refusal by the father to have any relationship with his son. She spoke of her shock when she had heard of the charge against her nephew, and of her belief that he had been implicated by others, who had greatly exaggerated any role her nephew may have played in the crime. The only questions asked of this witness were by the defence lawyer who asked for fuller details about her attempts to make contact with the accused's father and the effect of the latter's rejection on him. The statements of two absent witnesses were read out with the agreement of the prosecutor and the lawyers. Both related to an overall good character and a non-aggressive personality. A total of three and a half hours were devoted to the *personnalité* stage.

The function of the *personnalité* stage is to give the judge and jury an overall picture of the accused.[151] It is principally based on the information in the dossier compiled during the *instruction* under the supervision of the JI. In some instances the trial judge read statements from the dossier but for the most part the witnesses gave their evidence again at the trial. In compiling the file, the aim is not to search for evidence of guilt but rather 'to provide the judicial authority in an objective manner, without drawing conclusions about the case at issue, with an understanding of the accused's life, past and

151. S. Field, 'State, Citizen, and Character in French Criminal Process' (2006) 33 (4) *Journal of Law and Society* 522, 536.

present'.[152] As an observer from a common law tradition, the *personnalité* stage appears strange;[153] the trial appears to be somewhat back to front. The procedure suggests a sharp point of difference between the systems given the emphasis in the common law system of shielding triers of fact from the character, especially bad character, of the accused lest they become prejudiced in reaching their verdict. The Code provides that it cannot be used as evidence of guilt; however, that provision is addressed to the JI when compiling the *dossier de personnalité*. No similar limitation is addressed to the trial judge and jury.

Having explained to the judges the common law rules on character evidence, and the two-stage process of trial to ascertain guilt followed by a sentencing hearing in the absence of the jury, their response was the following:

> *JI*: That is a huge difference, a huge difference! It is possible for the judge (and jury) to use the evidence from the inquiry into the *personnalité* as evidence of guilt; it is not confined to the decision on sentence. Especially in the *cour d'assises* where the reasons for the decision are not given, so we have no way of knowing the factors which influenced the court in reaching a verdict of guilt.
>
> *J*: But also in the *tribunal correctionnelle*, where judgments are supposed to be reasoned; if you base your reasons for finding guilt on the previous convictions of the defendant, that is not forbidden.
>
> I was in Las Vegas to see how their procedure worked. I was very shocked to see that certain facts, which were known to the prosecutor, were not revealed to the jury. For example, there was a case concerning a fight between two rival criminal gangs. For most of the trial the jury were unaware that the victim belonged to a gang and the accused belonged to a rival gang. It was only when the defence lawyer made reference to the character of the victim that the true situation emerged. Then the jury knew. We were shocked, because it was decisive. The idea of a jury not knowing that that the person who was killed was part of a gang, and the person accused of the killing was part of a rival gang – we were really shocked. Everything should be put on the table, to discover the truth.
>
> *JI*: It's a big difference – we look for truth, you look more for fairness in the procedure; for you the truth is secondary, for us it is fundamental.

152. Article D 16, CPP provides: 'The purpose of the file is to provide the judicial authority in an objective manner, without drawing conclusions about the case at issue, with an understanding of the accused's life, past and present, it shall not have the aim of searching for evidence of guilt.'
153. Field has also found this (note 151) 524; see also McKillop (note 136); J. Hodgson, 'Conceptions of the Trial in Inquisitorial and Adversarial Procedure', in A. Duff, L. Farmer, S. Marshall and V. Tadros (eds), *The Trial on Trial Volume Two – Judgment and Calling to Account* (Hart 2006) 235.

By contrast, the defence lawyers had a different view:

> *Def. L1*: In France we, the lawyer groups, are asking that it should be the same as your system. In our system, where guilt and sentence are decided in the one procedure, the prosecutor might ask for a sentence of 30 years – that's a very long time. The accused has to say, 'well if by chance you find me guilty …'; you therefore have to discuss the punishment at the same time as trying to show the accused is not guilty, it's a bad system. The arguments about guilt or innocence, that should be a discussion solely relating to the evidence; in the discussion about punishment, yes it is OK to discuss previous convictions. In the single stage process, of course the jury will be influenced by an accused's previous behaviour: he did x before, he must be guilty! Of course they do that!

The other defence lawyer referred to the necessary strategy that a defence lawyer will need to adopt when defending a client with previous convictions:

> *Def. L2*: The fact that the accused has previous convictions naturally raises problems for the defence, because the court will take previous convictions into account. The jury may easily be influenced if a person has convictions – even if they are very minor the jury might still make a connection: he is already a criminal so he must be guilty. It is still important for the lawyer to discuss the previous convictions and the character of the accused in the closing address – the jury has already heard it in the trial, so the lawyer will need to show that the accused despite his previous behaviour is fundamentally a good person.

(c) Personnalité *of victim*

Evidence of the investigation into the social background and character (*personnalité*) of the victim may also be received by the court for the purpose of reaching a verdict.[154] This occurred in the rape trial in relation to both victims (both had constituted themselves *partie civile*). The expert witness who gave evidence in relation to one of the women was a psychologist who gave her testimony reading from notes. She related how the complainant had suffered ongoing psychiatric difficulty throughout her life and most of the evidence about her character related to psychological problems, difficulties in her marriage and feelings of persecution by her brother in law. The president asked no questions of this witness; the *partie civile* lawyer, the prosecutor and defence lawyer each had short clarificatory questions. The expert witness who had carried out the investigation on the *personnalité* of the second *partie civile* was a social worker. She gave evidence without recourse to notes,

154. Article 81.1, CPP.

describing her as vulnerable and having some addiction problems. No questions were asked of this witness.

(d) Interrogation of accused

One of the major differences between trials in Ireland and trials in France lies in the part played by the accused during the trial. In Ireland a trial might run its course without any testimony being given by the accused, or if he does decide to give evidence, it will be at the end of the prosecution's case. In France the situation is reversed: the accused is the first person to be questioned, and after each witness has given their evidence, he is often asked to comment on their testimony.[155] Unlike Ireland the accused never takes an oath.

The evidence against the accused in the appeal case for complicity and membership of an organised gang consisted of mobile phone traffic between the accused's phone and that of one of the accused who had been convicted in the first trial, statements made by the accused to the police and JI, statements of the four co-accused in the first trial to police and the JI (the four had all been convicted) implicating the accused as the primary mover in the whole operation, testimony from the police officer who had been in charge of the police investigation, and testimony from the police officer who had attended the scene of crime.

Having devoted the first morning of the trial to the *personnalité* of the accused, the afternoon commenced with the questioning of the accused by the president. He first questioned him about his previous offences, one for theft of a mobile phone. The accused said he did not know why he had done it; it was a spontaneous act that he accepted was foolish. Another was for being in possession of a knife; the accused explained he had been burgled and carried the knife because he was afraid. The president noted that he had not attended his trial for that offence and wanted an explanation for that; the accused said he had no money to go to the trial venue, that trial was in the north of France where the offence had occurred while he had been on holiday. He pressed him on why he had committed the offences in the past and concluded:

> *President*: While the impression from the evidence we have heard (from the *personnalité* stage) suggests you are a person of general good character, I think you have some underlying bad traits within you.

This despite the rule that the president is not supposed to show his opinion![156] He then moved on to question him about the facts of the case, asking him to

155. This has also been noted by R. Lerner, 'The Intersection of Two Systems: An American on Trial for an American Murder in the French *Cour d'assises*' (2001) (3) *U. Ill. L. Rev.* 791, 799.
156. Article 328, CPP: 'The president interrogates the accused and receives his statements. He has a duty not to show his opinions as to guilt.'

give his account and interrupting him at various junctures seeking clarification, at one point referring to a statement he had made to the police which differed to the account he was giving to the president. The response of the accused was:

> *Accused*: It was the police who made me say that, they were leading me, I said that because of the way they were questioning me.

Having spent two hours questioning the accused, the president then asked the lawyer for the *partie civile*, the prosecutor and the defence lawyer in that order if they had any questions for the accused. The *partie civile* lawyer questioned him about statements he had made to the JI; the prosecutor asked him about his attempted escape from police custody, and the defence lawyer brought this part of the trial to a close by asking him questions that had the effect of reiterating how the accused had withdrawn from the enterprise.

(e) Right to silence at trial

At no point during the questioning of the accused was he informed of his right to silence. The prosecutor in the appeal case explained it to me as follows:

> *Prosecutor*: The accused has a right to silence, yes, but there is a psychological pressure for him to speak at the trial. The president does not have to warn him about his right to silence, and when he asks him questions, well it would look bad if the accused said nothing; this is his opportunity to convince the court he is not guilty. How can you do that by saying nothing or refusing to answer? It would really go against him. He does not have to take the oath so he is free to lie; it is for us to try to find the truth between the lies.

These sentiments were displayed in an exchange between the president and one of the accused in the robbery case in the *tribunal*. The president was questioning the accused about stolen property that was found in one of the cars used in the incident; the accused had denied all charges of theft of property and of stealing the car:

> *President*: The stolen property was found in the car; the police caught you running away from that car! How can you say you had no part in the theft when the items were found in the car? We cannot just ignore that. That demands an explanation!
> (*The accused stood before the judge saying nothing in response.*)
> *President*: If you say nothing you are signing your own conviction!
> (*The accused still remained silent.*)
> *President*: Oh yes, of course, the accused has a right to remain silent! But if he does that in this court, if he remains passive, well … (*raising his arms in a motion of exasperation*).

The president persisted in asking for an explanation to no avail before eventually moving on.

(f) Hearing of witnesses

The next stage in a trial in the *cour d'assises* is devoted to hearing witnesses.

(I) POLICE WITNESSES

Two police officers gave evidence in the appeal case. The first police officer approached the witness stand clicking his heels and raising his hat to the president in a display of hierarchy.[157] He gave his evidence without notes, recounting the events of receiving the call from the *partie civile* and the findings from the scene of the crime. No questions were asked of this witness by anyone. The second police officer to give evidence was the director of the investigation, who approached the witness stand with the same clicking of heels and raising of hat as his colleague. He gave his evidence without interruption by the president of how the interrogations of the first three suspects during police custody had implicated the accused and recounted the interviews with the accused and his attempted escape from police custody.

The police officer had with him a file of the investigation but did not refer to it at any stage during questioning. It was clear from his account that he himself had not personally been involved in the interrogation of the accused during police custody. This point will be discussed further below in the context of hearsay evidence. The police officer was then asked four questions by the president, mainly relating to the attempted escape by the accused from custody, and the president then questioned the accused in relation to matters that the police officer had discussed in his testimony. The police officer was then dismissed with no questions coming from the lawyer for the civil party, the prosecutor or the defence lawyer.

(II) VICTIM AS WITNESS

The first afternoon in the rape trial began with evidence from one of the victims. As *partie civile*, she was not required to take the oath.[158] She was first questioned by the president about her recollection of the incident, giving her account in narrative form, occasionally interrupted and questioned by the president where her account differed from earlier statements she had made

157. The president at trial has no supervisory power over the police officer per se; however, he can raise nullities *ex officio*, which in turn may have disciplinary implications for a police officer. Furthermore, the judge in the *chambre d'instruction* who does have direct supervisory power over the judicial police is of the same rank as the trial judge.
158. Article 335, CPP.

to the JI. Following this the president asked the accused to comment on aspects of the evidence of the *partie civile*, and on what he had previously said to the JI and to the police where his responses differed from those statements contained in the *dossier*.

The *partie civile* remained at the stand during these exchanges and was in turn asked to comment on the accused's version. At the end of his questioning, the president asked the lawyer for the *partie civile*, the prosecutor and the defence lawyer in that order if they wished to ask any questions, but none of them had any.

The *partie civile* was then recalled to the stand. The president asked her about an earlier statement she had made which appeared to contradict the evidence given by her counsellor; the defence lawyer then questioned her about the account she had given earlier to the president and in relation to statements she had made to the JI which contradicted those made to the president; the *partie civile* lawyer was asked if he had any questions; he had none. The prosecutor then questioned the accused at length about the inconsistencies between his account and that of the *partie civile*, during which time the *partie civile* remained at the stand. This was followed by further questioning of the *partie civile* by the defence lawyer. Neither the prosecutor nor the defence lawyer were interrupted or hindered by the president.

Following this the second *partie civile* was called to the stand; she gave her account in narrative form, the president intermittently asking her questions. She maintained she had been the accused's girlfriend but had ended the (very short-lived) relationship and had been then held against her will and raped by the father and the accused at the same time. (This incident was on a separate occasion to the alleged rape of the first *partie civile* who was her friend.)

The accused on being questioned by the president denied he knew her and that there had been any relationship. A direct confrontation then ensued between the *partie civile* and the accused:

> *President* (*to accused*): You don't seem to have much luck with women.
> *Accused*: I was not her boyfriend; I don't have anything to do with prostitutes.
> *Partie civile* (*shouting at accused*): I am not a prostitute! Look me in the eye and say you were not my boyfriend!
> (*The accused instead looked towards the president.*)
> *Lawyer for partie civile*: Look her in the eye. Answer her question!
> *Accused* (*facing partie civile*): I don't know you, I have nothing to do with market girls like you!

The accused and *partie civile* continued in this vein for a further three minutes, all the time uninterrupted by the president. This type of direct uninterrupted confrontation between the parties, either by themselves or through their lawyers, appears to be a normal feature of criminal trials in France. I observed a similar exchange between the parties' lawyers in the *tribunal* where they were positively shouting at each other in an exchange lasting over five minutes. The defence lawyer then questioned the *partie civile* at some length, focusing on the different accounts she had given to the JI and that which she had given to the president earlier, also pointing to the physical impossibility of being raped at the same time by the two men, especially considering the age and weakness of the father.[159]

(III) OTHER WITNESSES

In the appeal case, the four co-accused who had been convicted in the accused's first trial were called as witnesses. Of the four co-accused, three were still serving their sentence and were brought from the prison to give their evidence, each one arriving separately in handcuffs which were removed before they gave their evidence, each accompanied by two armed prison officers who sat in the body of the court as each prisoner gave their testimony. The witness who had received a suspended sentence remained in the witness room along with the other witnesses until called to give his testimony. Three further witnesses were called: two had worked with the accused at the nightclub and had unwittingly given the accused information about the routine for removing the takings after closing time and the address of the nightclub owner's home; the other was the friend of the accused who had made the phone call to the co-accused to tell them the appellant was ill and would not be meeting them. All the witnesses were questioned by the president, no questions were put to them by the lawyer for the *partie civile* or the prosecutor; only the defence lawyer put questions to the accused's friend to draw attention to the accused's attempts to extricate himself from the enterprise. All witnesses gave their testimony under oath.

In the rape trial only one witness gave testimony (besides the victims and those giving evidence regarding *personnalité*). Her evidence was essentially identity evidence. This witness who had been living in an adjacent building gave evidence on oath of having seen a 'blond fat woman' through the window of the apartment shouting for help and that she was being held by a man who the witness also claimed to have seen. The *partie civile* who had alleged that she had been held against her will in addition to her allegation of rape was dark haired and thin. The witness testified that neither the accused nor the *partie civile* were previously known to her. She was very certain that neither the *partie civile* nor the accused were the people she had seen. No questions were put to this witness following her questioning by the president.

159. Neither *partie civile* were asked to describe in any detail the specific act of the rape, which would be a requirement in an Irish court.

(IV) WITNESSES IN THE *TRIBUNAL*

In the *tribunal*, a number of witnesses had made statements to the police during the investigation. No witnesses, however, were called to give evidence at the trial; instead the president read their statements from the dossier. This is possible on the basis of the provision in the Code relative to hearings in the tribunal which provides that, 'except where the law otherwise provides, offences may be proved by any mode of evidence and the judge decides according to his innermost conviction'. Although the second paragraph of the same article provides that 'the judge may only base his decision on evidence which was submitted in the course of the hearing and contradictorily discussed before him',[160] it would appear that such contradictory discussion does not require the actual presence of witnesses for questioning provided that their statements which are read by the president from the dossier may be challenged by the parties opposing them.

Challenging a statement, however, is quite different from cross-examining the maker of the statement as would happen in a trial in Ireland. For example, in the robbery case one witness had made a statement to the police identifying one of the accused; she had identified him as having 'stocky build with large arms', which indeed matched the description of the accused; however, she had failed to mention the very obvious tattoos which covered both arms entirely.[161] The defence lawyer pointed to this omission in challenging the statement of identification evidence, but the president dismissed it as inconsequential: 'She may have just forgotten – the rest of her statement describes the defendant perfectly.'

(g) Hearsay evidence and prior inconsistent statements

The use of statements as just described in the *tribunal* without their maker being present in court marks a major difference between the rules of evidence in France and Ireland. Under Irish law these would normally amount to hearsay and therefore be inadmissible evidence.[162] Hearsay is not prohibited in trials in France; this holds equally for trials in the *cour d'assises* and in the *tribunal*. Article 429 provides:

> Any official record or report has probative value only if it is formally regular and if its drafter acted in the performance of his duties and reported what he personally saw, heard or found on a subject matter within his jurisdiction. Every official record of an interrogation or a hearing must contain the questions that were answered therein.

160. Article 427, CPP
161. From my position of about ten feet away I could clearly see these tattoos.
162. Section 4.34 above.

The judges explained the use of out of court statements to me as follows:

> *JI*: Yes they can be used as evidence. Proof is completely free in France. It is the judge who decides whether the statements, or other proofs, appear to him to be of interest or not.
> *J*: The only thing that is limited is where an anonymous statement is given to the police, statements made by police informers; they would not have the same authority as a statement by a police officer – if the officer says 'I saw that', that is an absolute proof, if the police say 'X told me that', that has less value, but at the same time, it can be used. Everything is used as evidence, even the anonymous statement. We have no such thing as the Anglo-Saxon rule relating to hearsay.

The reliance on statements from the dossier rather than hearing the witnesses first hand does not offend against any rule of hearsay; it does not breach the principle of *contradictoire* which encompasses the idea that evidence at trial stage should be received through oral testimony rather than documented statements, a principle of orality, because once there has been some opportunity to challenge the statement at the pre-trial stage, *un débat contradictoire* has been effected. The defence lawyer was clearly frustrated by the lack of adherence to the principle of orality in practice:

> *Def. Ll*: Yes it exists; it is sacred! In the Code! But as for the practice, not so much! Why? Because the president has the dossier! What does the principle of orality mean? It means that the witness comes to court, and the witness gives his evidence to the court. But in practice this is how it works:
>
> > The president says to the witness: 'You said in your statement to the police that this man, the accused, came into the bank with a gun, and then you formally identified him.'
> > Witness: 'Well, that was two years ago. Today, well I am not sure.'
> > President: 'What do you mean you are not sure? In your statement you said you were sure that this was the man you saw come to the bank.'
> > Witness: 'Oh, did I say that?'
> > President: 'That was just after the time of the crime, you were sure then.'
> > Witness: 'I remember I said it looked quite like him, I never said I was sure it was him. Perhaps the police did not write down everything that I said.'
> > The President then produces the statement contained in the dossier: 'Sir, is that not your signature?' The witness agrees.
> > President: 'And above your signature, it says "after having read", so therefore you must have read it before you signed, and you said then that you were sure, so that is accurate. I will take that statement as the evidence.'

> That is not a trial according to the principle of orality! That is trial by the dossier (*slamming his hand on the table to emphasise his point*). If an American or English judge saw that, they would think they were at the cinema! If you want real orality then you do not use the dossier. And if the witness says he told the police that he was not sure, that is what the jury should hear. He should be able to give his testimony.

McKillop found in his study of a trial in the *cour d'assises* that:

> The dossier … formed the basis of the hearing … the hearing thus became essentially a public review and confirmation of the contents of the dossier, and hence of the conclusions that were reached in the investigation.[163]

I put McKillop's findings to the judges who responded as follows:

> *J*: Absolutely, that is indisputable. In the tribunal correctional it is 100%, but in *cour d'assise* it is much less so, because the witnesses have to come back to give their testimony orally. But you have to remember that our dossier has been compiled by a judge who is investigating for and against the accused, a judge who is independent, impartial, so in principle the dossier is fair. In the correctional court, however, it is the police who have complied the dossier. When it works properly, when the dossier has been compiled by people who are doing their work properly, then it is a guarantee for those who come before the courts, much more so than the American system.
> *JI*: It is a dossier that, since all the reforms that have taken place in France, is compiled more and more in a manner that is *contradictoire.* During the investigation, the role of the lawyer has become much more important than twenty years ago, and it is fairly usual that during the investigation the defence lawyer poses questions and asks for investigative acts to be undertaken, so the dossier which reaches the trial is also that of the defence. That is important to remember.

Taking account of the oral nature of the procedure (at least in theory), only the president has access to the dossier. He may give documents from the dossier to the assessors and jury during the course of the trial at his discretion. While agreeing that the 'cardinal principle of orality' should be retained, the Léger committee was unanimous that the jury and assessors should be enabled to reach their decision under the best possible conditions and should therefore have access to all the content of the dossier at the end of the trial. The defence lawyer took the opposite view:

> *Def. L1*: I do not agree with this proposal, not at all. It is completely contrary to the principle of orality. The jury must decide on what they

163. McKillop (note 136) 564–5.

have seen for themselves, what they have heard themselves, *during the trial.* Not on the contents of the dossier.

In the appeal case as already mentioned, the accused had disputed a statement he had made to the police, yet the police officer was not called as a witness to be questioned about the circumstances surrounding the taking of the statement. I raised this point with one defence lawyer:

> *Self*: Is it usual practice to call a police officer to give evidence about statements made by the accused to the police that the accused refutes?
> *Def. L1*: You can ask that the police officer be called as a witness. Normally they will not be called but where they are, this is how it plays out: the accused says he did not say 'he was sure', he said 'perhaps'. So the officer is called and this is generally what happens:
>
> > President: 'Well sir, you are a police officer with 20 years service. I see that you have excellent credentials. Could it have happened that you would have distorted a statement?'
> > Police officer: 'What Mr President! No, that is impossible! I would never do that, we have nothing to achieve in doing such a thing.'
> > President: 'This man says he said "perhaps", and you, you have written that he said, "I am sure".
> > Police officer: 'I give you my word, and I have taken the oath, this man said he was sure. If he had said "perhaps" then that is what I would have written down.'
>
> So what can you do? The judge will usually believe the police officer!

(h) Requisitions, submissions and burden of proof

When the taking of evidence is complete, the next stage of the trial is the submissions by the lawyers for the parties and the requisitions by the public prosecutor. Article 9 of the Declaration of the Rights of Man declares that everyone is presumed innocent until proven guilty.[164] It is accepted in French law that the presumption of innocence as propounded by the Declaration, together with the preliminary article of the Code ('every person suspected or prosecuted is presumed innocent until his guilt is established'), comprises also the concept that the burden of proof lies with the public prosecutor and that the accused is not required to prove his innocence.[165]

164. Thereby given constitutional status.
165. Ambroise-Castérot (note 1) 155.

The *partie civile* bears no burden of proving the case against the accused. The lawyer for the *partie civile* is always the first to make a submission, followed by the requisitions of the prosecutor and finally by the submissions of the defence lawyer. In the appeal case the lawyers and the prosecutor each spoke for one hour. The lawyer for the *partie civile* began her address by discussing what must feed into the court's *intime conviction*: their view of the facts, their emotions and the law (clearly the latter was intended for the jurors rather than the judges). She went on to explain what was required for participation in an offence, and gave definitions of the offence of complicity, setting out the actions of the accused to demonstrate how they fitted with the requirements of the offence. She explained the aggravating circumstances of the offence – the use of the imitation weapons, linking this to the effects of the crime on the victims. To emphasise her point she passed a photograph to the judge's bench of the imitation firearm to demonstrate the fearful affect the weapon would have had upon the victims, despite the fact that it was an imitation firearm.

The *partie civile* does not make any request for monetary compensation at this stage before the verdict is passed, but is seeking a decision of guilt. The address by the *partie civile* lawyer was a setting out and summing up of the prosecution case, just as a prosecuting counsel would do in Ireland. Despite the principle that the burden of proof is on the public prosecutor, it would seem that he is greatly assisted in discharging this burden by the closing address of the *partie civile.*

The prosecutor's requisition was largely similar to that of the lawyer for the *partie civile,* beginning with a further definition of complicity spelling it out in plain terms with everyday examples, recapping the facts in the case and pointing to how the accused's actions easily fitted with the definition. He focused on the continued commission of the offence despite the accused's last minute decision not to go through with the actual participation. He closed his address by asking the court to return a guilty verdict and to impose a sentence of seven years' imprisonment.

My impression was that the accused is faced with three adversaries: the president, the prosecutor and the *partie civile.* I raised this with the accused's lawyer who responded as follows:

> *Def. L2*: There is no balance between the parties. I think much of the problem arises from the fact that the judges and prosecutor all belong to the *magistrature* – this gives rise to a sort of schizophrenia: for example, the president of the court may once have been a prosecutor; he retains the investigative mentality while he is acting as president.
>
> A further imbalance exists because in reality the accused is faced with three parties, the president, the prosecutor *and* the *partie civile.* The burden of proof is supposed to be on the prosecution, but really in practice this is not the case; it is the judge who does all the work to reach a guilty verdict.

The other defence lawyer echoed his views:

> *Def. L1*: You are perfectly right; the accused is faced with three accusers, certainly it appears that way, even if in fact, in the texts, there is only one – the prosecutor.

Following the requisitions of the prosecutor, the defence lawyer then made his closing address, playing to the common sense of the court:

> If you change your mind, if you have two choices, one bad and one good, your mind is poisoned by the bad choice, but in the end you take the good choice. Should you be convicted for something that in the end you did not do?

and playing to their emotions:

> Every time I meet his aunt, so worried about this young man, in tears …

He then referred to the previous convictions focusing on this aspect of the accused's life for about twenty minutes of his address, emphasising his relative youth, his steady employment and his desire to settle with his girlfriend who had stood by him and start a family, and then pleaded with the court for a verdict of not guilty.

In the rape case the submissions of the defence lawyer were of a different nature, placing great emphasis on the fact that the burden of proof rested with the prosecution and that the only evidence in the case was the statements of the two women, which were constantly changing and inconsistent, both those given during the trial and those made during he investigation. There was no DNA evidence as both women had not made their complaint immediately following the incident, but had waited for over six months.

I spoke to the defence lawyer in the appeal case about his submissions and the absence of any mention of the burden of proof:

> *Def. L2*: I will sometimes discuss the burden of proof, but in this case it was a bit difficult – there was proof that the accused was technically guilty, so I would not want to emphasise the burden of proof – it was a question of trying to draw the jury away from the technicalities of the definition, suggesting for example that he had committed no offence because he did not in the end get any share of the stolen money; really it was appealing for mitigation of sentence, trying to avoid a custodial sentence.

Following the submissions and requisitions, the Code requires the accused to be given the opportunity to have the last word. In the appeal case the accused apologised for his actions and for the pain it had caused to his aunt, he accepted he had been out of his depth once the three co-accused had become involved but insisted he had withdrawn, and pleaded to the court to allow him to continue in his employment and fulfil his hopes to start a family with his girlfriend. In the rape case the accused stated that while he may have been a thief in the past, he would never commit acts of violence against a woman.

In the appeal case some of the jurors took notes; all appeared to listen attentively.[166] One of the assessors, however, was clearly asleep during one of the witness's testimony and for the most part of the closing speech of the defence! In the rape case none of the jurors took notes. In neither case did the assessors or jurors ask any questions of the accused or witnesses as they are permitted to do with leave of the president.[167]

(i) President's instruction to jury

The final stage of the trial is the president's instruction to the jury before the latter retire to deliberate together with the president and the two assessors. The president first reads out the questions that the court and jury must answer, the facts and any aggravating circumstance which must be proved, followed by the definition of *intime conviction* and what is required to reach their verdict as provided by Article 353:

> The law does not ask the judges to account for the means by which they convinced themselves; it does not charge them with any rule from which they shall specifically derive the fullness and adequacy of evidence. It requires them to question themselves in silence and reflection and to seek in the sincerity of their conscience what impression has been made on their reason by the evidence brought against the accused and the arguments of his defence. The law asks them but this single question, which encloses the full scope of their duties: are you inwardly convinced?

The president then declares the hearing closed and the court retires to consider the verdict.

5.5 Verdict

Following two hours of deliberation in the rape case and two and a half in the appeal case the president, assessors and jury returned to the courtroom. The president read out the answers to the questions the court had to answer and declared the verdict. In the rape case the accused was found guilty and received

166. Article 340, CPP permits the judges, jurors and prosecutors to take notes during statements of witnesses or of the accused provided it does not interrupt the hearing; the article is silent regarding note-taking by the defence or *partie civile* lawyers.
167. Article 311, CPP.

a sentence of 12 years. A guilty verdict was also returned in the appeal case; the accused received a sentence of five years, to be served through control by electronic tagging instead of imprisonment.[168] (It is at this point in the trial that the lawyer for the *partie civile* makes requisitions for civil damages, which is decided by the judge and the two assessors in the absence of the jury. In each case this process took under five minutes.)

5.5.1 Reasons for decision

The *cour d'assises* is not required to give reasons for their verdict; indeed the oath taken by the jury at the outset of the trial obliges them to 'preserve the secrecy of deliberations, even after the end of your service'.[169] The position is different in the *tribunal* where reasons for the verdict must be given. The Léger committee recommended that the practice of the *tribunal* be extended to the *cour d'assises*, on the basis that, 'as a matter of principle, the requirement of giving reasons is a guarantee against arbitrary decisions'.[170] They considered that a decision is more acceptable to the parties if they understand the reasons, and that it is illogical not to require reasons to be given for the most serious offences. The committee pointed out that since 1791 it was deemed that through the intermediary of the jury the people passed judgment, and the jury was thus sovereign and infallible. That in turn justified the absence of appeal from their verdicts and the absence of a requirement to give reasons. This conception of the jury was in their view removed once appeal against decisions in the *cour d'assises* was introduced.[171]

In supporting their recommendation, the committee highlighted two decisions of the ECtHR: *Papon v France* had ruled that the requirement for giving reasons must also accommodate the particular nature of the procedure, notably that before the *cour d'assises* where the jury are not required to give reasons.[172] On the basis of that ruling the committee suggested that the principle of reasoned verdicts is not an absolute principle, but considered that the more recent decision of *Taxquet v Belgium* may have changed that position.[173] In that case Belgium was condemned for not giving reasons, the court holding that the trial court should mention the main reasons for reaching a guilty verdict. The Léger committee was of the view that as a result of that ruling, France could be found to be in breach of Article 6 of the ECHR.[174] In light of this

168. Each *partie civile* was awarded €15,000 in the rape case; €12,000 was awarded in the appeal case. This is paid by a State fund in cases where the defendant has no means to pay.
169. Article 304, CPP.
170. Léger (note 6) 37.
171. Ibid., 38.
172. *Papon v France*, no. 54210/00, ECHR 2002-VII.
173. *Taxquet v Belgium* [GC] no. 926/05, ECHR 2010.
174. Ibid., 90: 'For the requirements of a fair trial to be satisfied, the accused, and indeed the public, must be able to understand the verdict that has been given; this is a vital safeguard

the committee considered that reasoned verdicts are 'not only desirable but also inevitable'.[175]

The committee noted the practical difficulties that would arise if reasons for verdicts were introduced: the Code requires that the court deliberates without interruption and returns its verdict immediately after the deliberations. It would therefore be difficult to elaborate on reasons in such a limited time. Two solutions were proposed: a summary of reasons would first be given at the time of giving the verdict; these would be elaborated in a subsequent report drawn up by the president and the two assessors. Alternatively, reasons could be given by way of written responses to specific questions relating to the evidence given at the trial. A number of committee members were opposed to reasoned verdicts, believing that it would signal the end of the popular jury, that it would strongly reinforce the influence of the professional judges, and that the principle of *intime conviction* is incompatible with a system of reasoned verdicts.

Although reasons for decisions must be given in the *tribunal*, in the robbery case the president simply declared that he found the evidence supported a verdict of guilty, following his deliberations with the two assessors. (They took under an hour to reach their verdict, and imposed sentences of three, five and seven years on the three accused.) Such a practice was confirmed by the judges that I interviewed, both of whom were in disagreement with the Léger committee recommendations:

> *J*: Yes – in principle the judge in the *tribunal* is supposed to give reasons for his decision – in practice, the reasons would be of a very summary nature; unfortunately in most decisions the judge will simply say that the result of the case is that the person is guilty. That is not enough but unfortunately this is what happens. As for the proposal that reasons should be given in the *cour d'assises*, that would be a big problem; it would be very difficult; I don't see how it could be done – how can it coexist with the principle of *intime conviction*?
>
> *JI*: It would be impossible; what would happen for example where there were different opinions amongst the jurors? Or amongst the judges? Would you also have to give the reasons for the opposing verdict?
>
> *J*: I can't see how it would work if the reasons of the jury would have to be given; it could surely only be the president who would have to give reasons, but the reasons of all twelve? In any case I find that the reasons for guilt are often fictitious. You might have two witnesses, one who you find more credible than the other. So why do you find one more credible than the other? You just do! Can you really say that finding one witness

against arbitrariness.' Ibid., 92: 'Article 6 requires an assessment of whether sufficient safeguards were in place to avoid any risk of arbitrariness and to enable the accused to understand the reasons for his conviction.'

175. Léger (note 6) 38.

more credible than the other is a reasoned decision? I don't think so. In a system of total freedom of proof, it comes down to 'am I satisfied/am I not satisfied'. In a system of legal proof, where you have half proofs, three-quarter proofs, you can simply point to each, and you can give reasons simply by adding them together, that is a truer reasoning.

5.6 Role of president of the court at trial

One of the most striking features of a French criminal trial to an observer from the common law tradition is the role the president of the court plays during the proceedings. The questioning of defendant and witnesses is predominantly conducted by the president; questioning conducted by the prosecutor and the parties is minimal by comparison. Furthermore, like his Italian counterpart, the president may order the collection of more evidence where he feels the evidence is lacking.[176] This did not arise in the cases I observed, and in the view of the judges I interviewed it is an infrequent occurrence. One of the recommendations of the Viout committee was that this power should be exercised more frequently.[177] While the Léger committee focused mainly on the investigation stage of the process, they addressed the role of the president at trial at some length:

> When an accused denies a fact, it naturally is the role of the judge to question him on the evidence gathered against him during the investigation; this double function, prejudicial as it is during the instruction, is equally so during the trial phase. It inevitably leads to the president siding with the accuser. The practice of the *greffier* in the *cour d'assises* and the president in the *tribunal* reading out the case against the accused at the start of the trial contributes to a blurring of roles and could be considered to undermine the principle of *contradictoire.*

The majority believed it necessary to reinforce the neutrality of the judge but without at the same time emulating the procedures of Anglo-American jurisdictions. They proposed that the judge should have a role more akin to that of an arbitrator. To this end he would no longer conduct the questioning but would instead oversee the proper conduct of the proceedings. They proposed a trial along adversarial lines whereby the charges would be read out by the prosecutor; the accused would then be questioned first by the prosecutor, followed by the *partie civile* and finally by the defence lawyer. During this 'cross-examination' the president would preside over the fairness of the proceedings. Nonetheless the president would still retain the power to pose questions himself. Victims, witnesses and experts would be questioned in the

176. See section 6.4.8 below.
177. Viout (note 5) 59.

same way. No change was suggested to the ordering of questioning – the trial would still commence with the defendant being questioned first. In addition, the president would still be empowered to seek additional information and 'to ask the parties to produce anything which he considers necessary to discover the truth'.[178]

There had been a previous attempt at such a reform which was later repealed when found to be unsuccessful; the Léger committee therefore considered that to effect such a reform again would require training of all parties before coming into force.[179] The committee was conscious that it could lead to longer trials so suggested that the reform should therefore incorporate a procedure of guilty pleas. A proposition to have a less formal and more flexible procedure in the *cour d'assise* by reducing the number of jurors was rejected by the committee.

The views of the judges on the Léger committee proposal that the president take a lesser role were as follows:

> *J*: I think this is a good reform proposal, and in any case I think it is unavoidable. I think that the role of the president hinders the role of others; it is he, or appears to be him, that is making the accusation at the start of the trial. I don't agree with that; I would prefer the prosecutor to start the trial, to present the charges. We have two very different types of president – one type is a 'classic' president, and the other type is the president who takes more of a background role. Those who take a background role, their verdicts are much more unpredictable, and in general much harsher. The classic president is a person who begins before the trial to decide, 'this should get 12 years', and he does everything he can to reach a verdict of guilt, with a punishment of 12 years, and he usually does reach that verdict.
>
> *JI*: The French system, when it does not function well, and it is quite often that it does not function well – in our system an accused would be under the impression that he is first faced with the JI, and in fact there are many JIs who investigate really only against the accused, then the accused is faced with the prosecutor who is against him, and then he has the president who is also against him! And of course they are also faced with the *partie civile* who is very, very strong. When justice in France does not work well it is terrible, terrible! When it works it is good! But I think it works badly more than it works well.

5.7 Conclusion

The analysis of investigation and trial in France reveals a number of striking differences from the procedures that pertain in Ireland. The investigation

178. Léger (note 6) 32.
179. *Loi* 93-2 4/1/1993 portant réforme de la procédure pénale, Articles 83–98 and 100–101.

procedure has been seen to be one that allocates wide coercive powers to the police including arrest and search and seizure without prior authorisation. At the same time, police overzealousness is restrained through hierarchical control by the judicial authority, in so far as the *chambre d'instruction* may take disciplinary measures against police officers, and by the direct supervision of investigations by the public prosecutor or the JI depending on the type of case involved.

While it is apparent that the vast majority of investigations are supervised by the public prosecutor, who as has been seen is not fully independent, it has been suggested by commentators, by the judges I interviewed and implicitly by the *Conseil constitutionnelle* that prosecutorial supervision is at a remove and often *ex post* so that in reality it is the police investigation that forms the basis of the trial. By contrast, where investigations are conducted by the JI, the police work under the direction of the JI and appear to be more closely supervised. Crucially, the JI may not delegate the interrogation to the police. As described by the judges I spoke to, the role of the JI is very much hands on and in practice he is more impartial than the prosecutor. Nonetheless those who would see the role modified or abolished have called his impartiality into question.

A distinct contrast to the position in Ireland is the continuous availability of the suspect throughout the investigation stage as a source of information. The suspect may be questioned at any time and confronted with the evidence as the investigation develops; moreover, some of the procedures available as investigative tools such as reconstructions and confrontations are completely unknown in the Irish common law pre-trial process.

A further contrast to the position in Ireland is the manner in which France has reformed its laws relating to access to a lawyer by suspects in police custody. It has been seen that France has interpreted the ECtHR jurisprudence to mean that presence of a lawyer during interrogatons is required rather than simply requiring access to consultations with the lawyer outside the interview room, as Ireland has understood the position. Nonetheless, the presence as has been seen is circumscribed in that the lawyer is not permitted an active role during the interrogation, and like in Ireland, has no right to consult the case file. The involvement of the defence lawyer continues to be limited during investigations by the prosecutor due to the unavailability of the case file, whereas under the *instruction* procedure the involvement of the defence lawyer and access to the file is much more extensive.

While it has been suggested by commentators that the rules of evidence are more exacting in common law systems, the French system does include a considerable amount of rules to exclude evidence through the nullity procedure and the concomitant demands of the principle of *loyauté*. It has been seen that failure to observe the formalities surrounding search and seizure is on pain of nullity and evidence found is in consequence inadmissible. It has also been seen that statements made by a suspect to police without the assistance of a lawyer results in the invalidity of those statements. Since the application for annulment must be made during the *instruction* phase, this has the effect of depriving the trial court, at least in the *cour d'assises*, of any knowledge of evidence that has been ruled inadmissible, just as a jury would be similarly deprived by dint of the *voir dire* procedure in the Irish context. Effectively, then, the French system may be said to take an exclusionary approach to evidence in certain situations even if it is conceded that breaches of the principle of *loyauté* are not always sanctioned by the nullity procedure.

What is noteworthy, however, is the faith that the *Cour de cassation* has placed in the fact that the criminal process is grounded on the principle of a *procédure contradictoire*: the fact that the system provides for the possibility to challenge the evidence (both during the investigation and during the trial) is seen as a safeguard. As such it is not necessary to exclude illegal evidence, at least where that evidence may be classified as real evidence; all that is required is that such evidence is open to challenge by the party adversely affected.

One rule of common law evidence that is distinctly absent from French procedure is that relating to character evidence. One of the most striking aspects of the French trial is the *personnalité* stage. Whereas Irish trial procedure shields the triers of fact from any knowledge of the accused's past transgressions, the French trial provides a detailed account of all aspects of the accused's life, both good deeds and bad. This is explained by the singular institutional structure of the French trial, in which the collaborative body of judges and jurors in a unified trial context decides both the verdict and sentence. Any prejudice that this may create in the minds of the triers of fact is not considered problematic.

As to whether it can be said that French trials are adversarial comparable with the common law model, I would suggest they are more in the nature of distant cousins. Now and again vague family similarities appear, for example where the prosecution and defence side examine and cross-examine a witness after the president has completed his questioning, but for the most part, it is difficult to see the resemblance. The questioning of witnesses by the prosecution and defence is nowhere near as probing, nor is the witness controlled in what they say but permitted instead to give a narrative account; hearsay is freely admitted and the contents from the pre-trial dossier are relied on throughout the trial. Some evidence that would be subject to vigorous probing through cross-examination in Ireland, for example the identity evidence of the witness in the rape case and that in the robbery case, was hardly tested; indeed, the latter would not have been admissible in Ireland due to its hearsay character but it was accepted as reliable by the judge in the *tribunal* after the most minimal challenge by the defence lawyer. Cross-examination of police officers by defence lawyers, the stock-in-trade of defence lawyers in trials in Ireland, was also a rarity.

A very distinct difference between the common law adversarial trial process and the French trial is the role the trial judge plays in questioning witnesses, and for the most part prosecution defence and *partie civile* lawyers seemed content to allow the trial to be dominated by him. A further distinctive feature is the part played by the accused during the trial. In France the accused is very much in the foreground throughout trial, and though not required to take an oath, is asked by the trial judge to comment on the witnesses' testimony as it emerges during the trial. Furthermore, he is allowed to confront the witness directly as was seen in the rape trial, in a manner that would most likely be immediately called to a halt by a trial judge in Ireland.

A further point of difference between trials in France and Ireland arises regarding the burden of proof. While in theory resting on the prosecution, in reality the prosecution appears to be assisted in the discharge of that burden by the active role played by the *partie civile* lawyer. The fact that there is a separate hearing to assess the damages to be awarded to the *partie civile* underscores the point that their lawyers' function during the trial is like that of the prosecutor, to establish that the accused is guilty.

The prosecutor is also assisted in discharging the burden of proof by the active trial judge whose line of questions may be favourable to the prosecution case; moreover, the trial judge has a residual power to seek further evidence where he sees fit. Indeed it may be said that despite the presumption of innocence rhetoric, the accused in being frequently asked to comment on the emerging prosecution evidence is in some sense being sought to disprove the prosecution case. The constant recourse to the accused throughout the trial would appear to render illusory any theoretical right to silence that an accused in France is supposed to enjoy.

The trial process in France strongly adheres to a structure that is *contradictoire*, requiring that evidence be given opportunity to be tested through *un débat contradictoire*, a principle that equally applies at the pre-trial stage. However while this term may be loosely translated as 'adversarial argument', the trial in France does not by dint of that alone translate into a fully-fledged adversarial trial. While in some instances it could to a limited degree be likened to the adversarial practice of cross-examination, the 'contradictory debate' occurs not just between witnesses and the prosecution or defence sides, but between whoever has the floor so to speak; it can arise as between the judge and witnesses, the judge and the accused, and even between the accused and the victim in the manner outlined above.

Moreover, the entire structure of the trial does not resemble that of the archetypical adversarial trial: it is difficult to conceive of the process as a clash between two opposing sides, prosecution and defence, who decide what evidence to present given the very active role of the trial judge both in his questioning of the witnesses and the accused and his power to seek evidence. That, taken together with the unitary structure of the trial and the collaborative decision-making arrangement of judges and jurors relating to verdict and sentence militate against giving the French trial a label of 'adversarial'.

Finally, this chapter has demonstrated that the discovery of truth is central to the French trial culture. While the principle of *loyauté* would suggest that fairness of procedure is a vital consideration, the importance of truth discovery would appear to be equally so. Reference to discovery of truth arises frequently in the Code; it was raised by the Léger committee on a number of occasions in their report and arose in various different contexts during my interviews with the judges. As far as illegally obtained real evidence goes, as opposed to illegally obtained statements, the inclination of the *Cour de cassation* would appear to be to admit the evidence so that it may be tested through the *contradictoire* procedure, rather than exclude it and thereby lose a source of factual truth.

6 Gathering, receiving and contesting evidence in Italy

6.1 Introduction

Italy adopted a new Code of criminal procedure in 1989 through which it attempted to adopt, as noted by commentators, an adversarial trial model.[1] It has been suggested that Italian criminal procedure has thus 'moved in the direction of England, the United States and the common law'.[2] A central objective of the Italian reform was to separate the investigative phase from the trial phase, on the premise that the act of investigation of a crime creates a bias on the part of the investigator. In separating the two stages, the Code aimed to ensure that the judge trying the case would come to the trial largely ignorant of what had transpired during the investigation and would be therefore in an impartial position to adjudicate upon the case.

It has been suggested that the new Code, by circumscribing the roles of those involved in the investigative stages and imposing a boundary between pre-trial investigation and trial, has given rise to 'an actual law of evidence', claimed to be 'first among all continental codes'.[3] If it is indeed the case that Italy has moved closer to the common law adversarial trial method, is it also the case that Italy has adopted a law of evidence similar to that practised in common law jurisdictions, with rules regarding admissibility of evidence as would traditionally be associated with those jurisdictions?

The reform in Italy has not given rise to a separate and distinct 'law of evidence' as such; it remains entwined with the law of criminal procedure. In order to get an understanding of the Italian law of evidence, the provisions relating to gathering, use and presentation of evidence need to be identified from the Code. The law of evidence at the same time cannot be understood

1. The interchangeable use by commentators of the terms adversarial and accusatorial has already been noted in section 3.3.1 above.
2. M. Delmas-Marty and J. Spencer (eds), *European Criminal Procedures* (first published 2002, Cambridge University Press 2005) 25; see also E. Grande, 'Italian Criminal Justice: Borrowing and Resistance' (2000) 48 (2) *Am. J. Comp. L.* 227 who refers to the Italian reform as an 'adversarial mode modelled upon practices in the United States'.
3. E. Amodio, 'The Accusatorial System Lost and Regained: Reforming Criminal Procedure in Italy' (2004) 52 *Am. J. Comp. L.* 489, 491.

outside of its procedural context and so the trial structure in which it operates needs to be examined. Is the 'adversarial trial' as practised in Italy one and the same with that which is practised in the Anglo-American world? Even if it can be said that the reform in Italy has embraced an adversarial trial method, it has superimposed it upon an institutional structure that by and large has remained unchanged. Italy therefore provides an example of how a law of evidence operates when it is removed from the traditional institutional context of the common law trial. Italy also provides a useful example to highlight the difficulties that may be encountered when a new criminal justice system is imposed upon a legal culture, which by its nature perhaps is impervious to legislative change.

This chapter will explore how evidence laws function in Italy, looking at the procedures for the gathering of evidence in the pre-trial phase and the subsequent presentation and use of evidence at trial. The first part will examine the roles and powers of those involved in the investigation of offences, thereby showing the institutional arrangement as well as the means available to gather evidence: inspections, searches, interceptions and taking of statements. The second part will examine the extent to which Italy has adopted those rules of evidence that are the traditional bastions of common law evidence: rules relating to illegally obtained evidence, the rule against hearsay and evidence of bad character.

Part III will discuss how the evidence is presented at trial, and the use to which evidence gathered in the pre-trial stage may be put at trial. It will examine how Italy has attempted to adapt to adversarial means of presentation of evidence through examination and cross-examination of witnesses by the parties, while at the same time allowing the trial judge an active role in the process.

The discussion throughout will be informed by an examination of the relevant provisions of the Code of Criminal Procedure (*Codice de Procedura Penale* (CPP)) together with the relevant case law of the Italian courts. The practical application of the Code will be appraised based on insights gleaned from interviews I conducted with judges, prosecutors and defence lawyers, together with reflections based on hearings that I attended in the Italian criminal courts.[4]

4. I attended two trials in the *corte di assise*, one in Bologna and one in Modena, but since trials in Italy do not sit as a continuous hearing as they do in Ireland and France, it was possible to observe only segments of these trials. I also attended appeal hearings in the *corte di appello* in Turin (this hears appeals from verdicts given at first instance by the *tribunale*). I interviewed three judges, a trial judge (*giudice di dibattimento*) who previously had been a prosecutor, who will be referred to as JT; a prosecutor (P) also participated in this interview. The other two judges were a GIP (*giudice del indagini preliminare*) and a GUP (*giudice dell'udienza preliminare*) who will be referred to as JB1 and JB2; I also interviewed a defence lawyer (referred to as D); where my own questions feature in the interview sections I identify myself as Self. All interviews were conducted in Italian and tape recorded with prior permission from the practitioners. Interviews were conducted on an anonymous basis. All translations are my own unless otherwise stated.

PART I

6.2 Gathering evidence in the pre-trial phase

6.2.1 Organisational structure of the pre-trial phase

The principal players in the criminal investigation are the police, the public prosecutor, the defence lawyer and judges. The police, when exercising their function of investigation of crime, are known as the judicial police.[5] The police are directly at the disposal of the judicial authority, the latter being comprised of judges and public prosecutors, similar to the position in France.[6] When investigating offences the police operate under the control and guidance of the public prosecutor, although the prosecutor does not have disciplinary power over the police.[7] The police are charged with securing 'the sources of evidence, collecting everything necessary for the reconstruction of facts and identifying the culprit'.[8] They carry out all acts delegated by the public prosecutor; nonetheless they are empowered to act on their own initiative in many instances, but wherever this occurs they must inform the public prosecutor promptly.[9]

Once the public prosecutor is informed of police initiatives, he directs the investigation and makes decisions on the sufficiency of evidence to sustain a prosecution.[10] Once notified of a crime, the prosecutor has six months to complete the investigation, but an extension may be granted up to 18 months. Any evidence obtained after the expiry of the time limit cannot be used at trial. While in theory the prosecutor is the controlling force in the investigation, it has been suggested that in practice it is only in serious cases that the prosecutor exercises real control, and that in the majority of cases it is the police who set the agenda for investigation, requesting the prosecutor to issue any orders they need to proceed.[11]

While, at least in theory, the prosecutor is in charge of the investigation, he does not have an entirely free reign. Two judges are also involved in criminal

5. The judicial police (*polizia giudiziaria*) are drawn from the two main policing bodies in Italy, the *Polizia del Stato* and the *Carabinieri*.
6. Article 109, Constitution.
7. But may inform the General Appeal Prosecutor of police activities causing concern, who may instigate disciplinary action; see M. Caianiello and G. Illuminati, draft contribution to 'Rethinking European Criminal Justice', a project under the auspices of the Max Planck Institute 2009 (draft supplied to me by the authors).
8. Article 55, *Codice de Procedura Penale* (CPP).
9. Article 348, CPP.
10. Under the new Code the prosecutor in supervising the investigation has taken over the role previously vested in an investigating judge, the *giudice istruttore*, who functioned in a similar way to the French *juge d'instruction*.
11. Caianiello and Illuminati (note 7).

investigations. The *giudice del indagini preliminare* (GIP) has the role of overseeing the preliminary investigation and making decisions on any measures that restrict the liberty of the accused. An order for detention may be issued only by the GIP and interception of communication must be authorised by the GIP. The GIP also presides over the *incidente probatorio* – a procedure conducted during the pre-trial stage for the purpose of gathering evidence that may disappear or deteriorate before trial. At the close of the preliminary investigation the case moves into the remit of another judge, the *giudice dell'udienza preliminare* (GUP), who makes the decision whether to send the case forward for trial.

6.2.2 Means of evidence-gathering during investigation

As in any criminal justice system, the police are usually first to come across the commission of a crime, though the Code provides that the public prosecutor may obtain information of a crime through his own initiative or through information from public officials or private parties.[12] A person may enter the criminal justice system through a summons procedure or through arrest. Prior to that, they may have been under investigation through surveillance, used extensively in Italy, so a certain amount of information may already be in the hands of the police and the public prosecutor by the time a person first appears before them.

The Code requires the prosecutor to conduct all acts necessary to initiate criminal proceedings. In practice this will include ordering searches to be conducted of persons and places, seizure of any evidence discovered, ordering surveillance and the placing of intercept devices, and questioning suspects and witnesses. The Code also requires the public prosecutor to ascertain facts favourable to the person under investigation. This has been interpreted as requiring the prosecution to gather evidence in favour of the suspect simply for the limited purpose of deciding whether or not to prosecute.[13] It has been described as a 'ghost provision, in the sense that it formally exists but it is not respected in substance. It is very unusual for the prosecutor to search specifically for evidence of innocence'.[14]

The Code places strict control around using evidence gathered by the police in the form of statements. This is a sharp break with the practices under the Fascist regime. Under the Criminal Code the police were extensively involved in amassing the evidence and using it fully as the basis for conviction.[15] The police and prosecution authorities were placed above the

12. Article 333, CPP.
13. Grande (note 2) 235.
14. Caianiello and Illuminati (note 7).
15. *Codice Penale* 1930, referred to as the Rocco Code, after the Minister for Justice of the period; this Code remains in force but has been amended since end of the Second World War.

law, having wide powers to detain citizens rumoured to be engaged in any activity contrary to the national interest, and any persons so accused had no right to be heard before a court – their fate was entirely in the hands of the police who enjoyed immunity from prosecution for criminal acts committed in the course of their duty, an immunity described by Plowscow as 'one of the pillars of the Fascist dictatorship'.[16] This immunity has been removed since the end of the Fascist era through provisions amending the Criminal Code that create offences of abuse of authority[17] and prohibitions on illegal arrests,[18] arbitrary searches and inspections,[19] and illegal installation of intercept devices in abuse of powers.[20] The reformed Code of Criminal Procedure prohibits the discovery of proof through the use of methods or techniques likely to undermine a person's freedom of self-determination or which alter a person's ability to remember or evaluate facts.[21]

6.2.3 Search and seizure

In Italy, a person's dwelling is inviolable under the Italian Constitution except in cases provided by law, and similar constitutional protection extends to privacy of correspondence and other forms of communication.[22] The Code makes provision for inspections and searches and seizure to be carried out on the order of the public prosecutor who must give reasons as to why they are considered necessary. Inspections of persons and places may be ordered when it is necessary to ascertain traces and material effects of a crime.[23] The inspection must be carried out respecting personal dignity and as far as possible, the modesty of the person under inspection. A doctor may also carry out the personal inspection.[24] Where an inspection involves obtaining DNA samples, the police may obtain hair and saliva samples without consent of the suspect but they are not permitted to take intimate bodily samples.

Where there is a reasonable belief that items are concealed on the person, a personal search may be ordered; if there is reason to believe that items are hidden in premises, including a private residence, a search of the premises may be ordered.[25]

16. M. Plowscow, 'Purging Italian Criminal Justice of Fascism' (1945) 45 (2) *Columbia LR* 240, 246.
17. Article 608, *Codice Penale* (CP).
18. Article 606, CP.
19. Article 609, CP.
20. Article 617 *bis*, CP.
21. Article 188, CPP.
22. Articles 14 and 15, Constitution.
23. Article 244, CPP.
24. Article 245, CPP.
25. Article 247, CPP.

A search is a means of finding proof, and presupposes proper grounds for belief exist that evidence will be found on the person or in the place.[26] The legitimacy of the procedure is not linked to a mere suspicion but must be based on a probability of discovering the items, not simply on discovering the existence of any crime. It must not therefore be an arbitrary search but must be connected to a particular pre-existing hypothesis where there are specific and concrete elements suggesting the commission of an offence.[27] Personal searches must be carried out in a way that respects personal dignity and the person to be searched must be given a copy of the search order.[28] Searches of dwellings must be carried out in daytime except in urgent cases.[29] Searches and inspections of lawyers' offices are permitted only where the lawyers themselves are accused.[30]

The police are under a duty to seize any items of evidence discovered during the search.[31] They are also obliged to seize anything found which is linked indirectly to criminal behaviour – anything can be pertinent to the crime provided it is tangibly linked.[32]

6.2.4 Intercept evidence

While there is constitutional protection of privacy of communications, Italy relies on surveillance and intercept evidence very extensively, both for serious offences and those of average seriousness.[33] Telephone and other forms of telecommunication intercepts are permitted for a broad range of offences and can be used as evidence, except where they have been obtained beyond the scope permitted by law.[34] The public prosecutor must seek authorisation to install an intercept from the GIP who may grant the request where there are 'serious indications' of a crime and the intercept is absolutely necessary to further the investigation. The public prosecutor may order the intercept device to be placed without prior authorisation in cases of urgency but this action must be brought before the GIP within 24 hours to be validated.

If the GIP, who in turn must decide within 24 hours of receiving notice from the public prosecutor, finds reason not to validate the placing of the intercept, then the intercept must be withdrawn and any results yielded from

26. The Italian term, *corpo del reato*, usually translated as the body of evidence, means those things by which or through which the crime was committed, as well as the products and profits of the crime, and anything connected to the crime (Article 253.2, CPP).
27. Cass. pen. 10/9/1997, no. 84.
28. Article 249, CPP.
29. Searches must be in principle carried out between 07:00 and 20:00 hours.
30. Article 103, CPP.
31. Article 253, CPP.
32. Cass. pen. 9/6/1998, no. 1671; Cass. pen. 25/5/2000, no. 4587.
33. Caianiello and Illuminati (note 7).
34. Article 266, CPP.

it in the interim may not be used as evidence.[35] The police may intercept correspondence but must send the intercepted items intact to the public prosecutor unless it is a case of urgency in which case the police may obtain authority from the public prosecutor to open them.[36] The contents of the intercepted communications (telecommunication and correspondence) must be documented in full or in summary form, and the full transcripts of the intercepts are placed in the trial judge dossier.[37]

6.2.5 Obtaining evidence from the suspect

(a) Summons procedure

The public prosecutor may obtain information from any person who may have useful information for an investigation.[38] Depending on the information they divulge, such persons may themselves become suspects in the crime. The public prosecutor may issue a summons to a person under investigation to appear before him. The summons must contain the type of investigative act for which he is being summoned, and if it is for questioning, the summons must contain a summary of the facts that have resulted from the investigation so far and may also contain sources of proof.[39]

(b) Arrest and detention

Police are under obligation to make an arrest for crimes *in flagranza*[40] and for a number of specified offences,[41] and have a discretionary power of arrest for non-fatal offences for which the penalty is over three years and fatal offences where the penalty is not less than five years.[42] An arrest (*fermo*) may be ordered by the public prosecutor where a crime is suspected, although not *in flagranza*, the suspect poses a flight risk, and the offence involves firearms or explosives, or terrorism.[43] Immediately following an arrest the police must notify the public prosecutor and the arrested person must be brought before the prosecutor no

35. Article 267, CPP.
36. Article 353, CPP.
37. Article 268.7, CPP; see section 6.2.5(h) below.
38. Article 362, CPP.
39. Article 375, CPP.
40. Article 382, CPP; private citizens may make an arrest for crimes *in flagranza* but must deliver the person to the police immediately: Article 383, CPP.
41. Article 380, CPP; *inter alia* crimes against public safety, sexual offences, organised crime and drug offences.
42. Article 381, CPP; police also have discretionary arrest powers for crimes including corruption, threats to public officials and domestic violence.
43. Article 384, CPP. This type of arrest is known as *fermo*. The police may make this type of arrest before obtaining the order in urgent situations.

later than 24 hours following arrest.[44] The prosecutor must apply for an arrest validation hearing within 48 hours from the time of arrest, and the hearing must be held within 48 hours of the application.

The validation hearing is held by the GIP in the presence of the defence lawyer and the arrested person, and the public prosecutor.[45] If the GIP is satisfied that the arrest procedures have been correctly followed, he may validate the arrest and proceed to make an order for detention of the suspect on the request of the public prosecutor.[46] 'Preventive detention' is permitted in circumstances where the suspect poses a flight risk, where there is a risk of interference with evidence or to prevent the commission of further offences.[47] It should only be applied where it is proportionate to the risks posed and other measures, for example house arrest, are inadequate. Since the Constitution protects personal liberty as an inviolable right,[48] a person's freedom may be restricted by detention only where there are 'serious indications of guilt'.[49] In making this assessment, the GIP may not rely on anonymous statements, for example those of police informants who are not examined as witnesses at the hearing, or on illegally obtained intercepts. If statements of co-accused are to be relied upon, they must be corroborated by other elements.[50] 'Serious indications of guilt' have been held to be different from that which would found a conviction; it is sufficient if there is a 'probability' of the suspect's responsibility.[51]

(c) Access to lawyer

The police must inform the arrested person of their right to appoint a defence lawyer and once nominated inform the lawyer.[52] Where the suspect does not appoint a lawyer the police must appoint one on the suspect's behalf.[53] In Italy, unlike the position in Ireland and France, the appointment of a lawyer is obligatory. It is not possible to waive the right to a lawyer at any stage in the proceedings. Access to a lawyer is provided not simply in situations of arrest. In cases of searches of the dwelling, notice of the right to be assisted by a lawyer must be given, although such assistance may be granted only where a lawyer would be immediately available; however, even where a lawyer

44. Article 386, CPP.
45. Article 391, CPP.
46. Article 291, CPP.
47. Article 274, CPP; *misure cautelari* literally translated means 'precautionary detention'; Italian academics I spoke to agreed that it could equally be translated 'preventive detention'; since this term is more easily understood in the English context it is the term I use here.
48. Article 13.
49. Article 274, CPP.
50. Article 273, CPP.
51. Cass. pen. 16/4/2003, no. 18103.
52. Article 369 *bis*, CPP.
53. Article 386, CPP.

would be available in a short time, the search does not need to be delayed until the lawyer arrives.[54] In practice, it is very rare for a lawyer to attend a search, unless it is a complicated case where the items of evidence sought consist mainly of documents or computer data, for example in cases of financial fraud.[55] Before a personal search is conducted, the person to be searched must be notified of the right to assistance by a lawyer if they can be promptly available.[56]

There may be an agreement between the lawyer and the client that the lawyer will not attend at certain procedural acts, for example during a search, but in any proceedings the suspect/accused does not have a right to represent themselves. It has been held in a number of cases that the failure to inform the arrestee of the right to nominate a lawyer or to notify the defence lawyer of the arrest does not invalidate the arrest.[57] Nor do the police have an obligation to locate a nominated lawyer beyond acting upon the information furnished to them by the arrested person; they may simply appoint a lawyer from the general pool of duty lawyers.[58]

An arrested person may consult with a lawyer immediately upon arrest, but this may be delayed by the public prosecutor from the time of arrest up to the time of appearance before the GIP at the arrest validation hearing.[59] Since the prosecutor must apply for this validation hearing within 48 hours from the time of arrest, and the hearing must be held within 48 hours of that application, an arrested person may therefore find themselves without access to a lawyer prior to their first appearance before a judge for 96 hours.[60] The rationale of this provision, as suggested by Caianiello, 'is to avoid the suspect "arranging" with his/her counsel a "credible" version of the facts to be given to the prosecutor'.[61] More broadly, it has also been connected with the concern that in Mafia-related arrests the lawyer could voluntarily or through duress provide information to *Mafiosi* thereby endangering the safety of prosecutors and judges.

A suspect held in preventative detention has the right to consult a lawyer from the start of the detention. Once an order of detention is made, it will often be the case that a person is detained right up to the final disposal of the case, which refers to the time when all appeals have been heard rather than the time

54. Article 250, CPP.
55. Information supplied by defence lawyers interviewed.
56. Article 249, CPP.
57. Cass. pen. 8/10/ 2007, no. 36941; Cass. pen. 11/11/2003, no. 43063; by contrast with Ireland, see section 4.3.2 above.
58. Article 97, CPP; Cass. pen 7/4/1993, no. 16256.
59. Article 104.4, CPP.
60. Article 390, CPP.
61. M. Caianiello, 'Italy', in E. Cape, Z. Namoradze, R. Smith and T. Spronken, *Effective Criminal Defence in Europe* (Intersentia 2010) 393.

of decision in the trial at first instance.[62] Detention may therefore be lengthy: the Code places an outer limit for detention, setting the longest at six years for crimes for which the penalty is life imprisonment or imprisonment exceeding 20 years.[63]

During the preliminary investigation of the offence, similar to the position in France the suspect continues to be used as a source of information and can be questioned throughout as the need arises, for example where it is deemed necessary to confront him with other witnesses or with other information gathered throughout the investigation stage. In the course of preliminary investigations on request of the public prosecutor, the GIP may delay the right to consult with a lawyer for no more than five days where there are specific and exceptional reasons.[64]

(d) Statements

Statements may be obtained through questioning by the police or prosecutor, or by means of spontaneous statements made in the immediate aftermath of the offence. The police, however, are quite restricted in their powers of questioning and a distinction is drawn between questioning by the police and questioning by the prosecutor.

In the initial stage of the investigation, the police may question the suspect, provided they are not under arrest. The questioning process at this stage is known as *sommario informazione* and encompasses obtaining information concerning identity, ascertaining the facts and probing the suspect's responsibility in the offence. Such police questioning may not take place in the absence of a lawyer and this process of *sommario informazione* is understood to be a separate and distinct process to the formal *interrogatorio* by the prosecutor.[65] Any information gathered through police questioning in the absence of the lawyer cannot be documented or used later at trial.[66] A less restrictive approach is taken to spontaneous statements. These may be taken without the presence of a lawyer even if the person is arrested *in flagranza* and such spontaneous statements may be relied upon for the purpose of furthering the investigation.[67]

It has been held by the Supreme Court that spontaneous statements made by a suspect immediately after the act, even if the judicial police have solicited those statements, are not equivalent to 'questioning' in the technical sense.

62. Following the trial at first instance, the *tribunali* (Article 6, CPP) or the *corte di assise* (Article 5, CPP), an accused has a right of appeal to the *corte di appello* or *corte di assise di appello* respectively (Articles 593–605) and onwards to the *corte di cassazione* (Articles 606–628, CPP).
63. Article 303, CPP.
64. Article 104.3, CPP.
65. Article 350, CPP.
66. Article 350.6, CPP.
67. Cass. pen. 13/1/2009, no. 1150.

It follows that, in taking such statements, it is unnecessary to ask the suspect to nominate a lawyer or to deliver the warning that the suspect has the right not to reply.[68] While the Supreme Court referred to spontaneous statements in the context of the immediate aftermath of the act, the Code does not limit the taking of spontaneous statements to any particular timeline; they can be received at any time.[69] It has been suggested that this provision provides the police with a means to sidestep the safeguard available to suspects of access to a lawyer, and that 'spontaneous statements' may not always be as 'spontaneous' as they would appear.[70]

While the public prosecutor may delegate a number of tasks to the police in order to complete the investigation, this does not extend to formal questioning (*interrogatorio*). Questioning in this instance must be conducted by the prosecutor in all cases where the person under investigation is detained (whether through arrest or by preventative detention).[71] He must give timely notice of the interrogation to the defence lawyer.[72] He must inform the arrested person of the reasons for the interrogation, the facts which point to his involvement in the offence and, if it will not prejudice the investigation, the sources of information.[73] While the defence lawyer has the right to attend the suspect's questioning by the prosecutor, and to intervene in so far as making his 'requests, observations and objections' known to the prosecutor, in cases of urgency the prosecutor may proceed to question the suspect in the lawyer's absence.[74] The presence of the lawyer during questioning by the prosecutor is therefore not absolutely mandatory; however, failure to give notice to the lawyer that the interrogation is to be conducted will render the interrogation invalid.[75]

Where the person remains at liberty, the questioning may be delegated to the police but may not be undertaken without a lawyer being present. Every interrogation of a person in detention must be fully documented by tape or audio-visually, and if not then it may not be used as evidence.[76] An interrogation of a person who remains at liberty that is not so recorded will render any statements made being inadmissible as evidence against the person who made the statement, but it may be used against those who have been implicated by the statement.[77]

68. Cass. pen. 12/12/2008, no. 46040.
69. Article 350.7, CPP. The judicial police may take spontaneous statements from the person under investigation, but these may not be used at trial other than pursuant to Article 503.3, CPP (i.e. to contest statements of other witnesses in the trial).
70. See Caianiello, 'Italy', in Cape *et al.* (note 61) 394.
71. Article 370, CPP.
72. Article 364, CPP.
73. Article 388, CPP.
74. Articles 364.7, 364.4, 364.5, CPP.
75. Caianiello (note 61) 392.
76. Article 141 *bis*, CPP.
77. Cass. pen. 13/2/2008, no. 6743.

(e) Right to silence

Before any interrogation begins, the person must be warned that their statements may be used against them and other than providing information concerning their identity, they have the right to remain silent; questioning will nonetheless continue even where they do remain silent. They must also be warned that where they make statements regarding the responsibility of others, they will assume the quality of witness in relation to those statements.[78] It has been suggested that although there is a general rule that the judge cannot infer proof of an accused's guilt from their silence, a provision which is generally observed at trial, it is often infringed in the pre-trial phases, especially in relation to imposing an order of detention pending trial:

> In practice the judges often place the defendant in custody pending the proceedings when they remain silent during the interrogations, or if there is a denial of responsibility. Of course, in the written justification for the decision, it is not explicitly asserted that the defendant has to have their freedom limited because of the fact that they did not confess their guilt; however, every time the restriction of liberty issued by the judge is justified on the basis of a 'lack of awareness by the defendant of their conduct,' or something similar, it is reasonable to consider that such words hint at the fact that the suspect did not confess.[79]

The prospect of lengthy pre-trial detention may therefore have the effect of putting pressure upon suspects to waive their right to silence in the hope of remaining at liberty pending trial.

(f) Evidence gathering by defence

The defence lawyer may carry out an investigation on behalf of the suspect that may include conducting scientific tests, subpoenaing witnesses where necessary, and using private investigators to seek out information. When questioned by the defence lawyer, witnesses have the right to remain silent, but if they choose to answer, they are obliged to tell the truth. The lawyer may choose to record (in writing or on tape) the information gathered from a witness.[80] If a witness remains silent, the lawyer can request the prosecutor to question them and if that is done – the prosecutor is not bound to do so – the lawyer has the right to participate and to put questions first. The defence lawyer does not have any duty to disclose the results of their investigation to the prosecutor but may instead transmit the records to the GIP directly, both during the investigation and at the preliminary hearing.

78. Article 64, CPP.
79. Caianiello and Illuminati (note 7).
80. Article 391 *ter*, CPP.

(g) Evidence-gathering through the incidente probatorio

The *incidente probatorio* is a hearing for gathering evidence for use at the trial that may be held during the preliminary investigation stage and could to some extent be likened to the procedure of taking depositions by a judge in the pre-trial stage of a trial in Ireland.[81] The rationale of the *incidente probatorio* is to guard against the passage of time between investigation and trial prejudicing proof-taking at trial.[82] Either party, defence or prosecution, may ask the GIP for a hearing to be held where there is a risk that evidence may be unavailable at the trial stage. The hearing is held by the GIP in camera in the presence of the prosecutor and the defence lawyer, and the person under investigation has the right to attend where a witness is to be examined.

The parties may ask that testimony be taken:

1. from a person where there are reasons to hold that that person will not be available to be examined at trial because of illness or other serious impediment;
2. where there are concrete indications that the person may be susceptible to violence, threats or bribery so as not to testify or to give false testimony;
3. for a person under investigation to be examined in relation to facts concerning the responsibility of other parties where the circumstances set out in (1) and (2) exist;
4. for the examination of a person accused in a related proceedings where the circumstances set out in (1) and (2) exist;
5. for a confrontation between persons who in another *incidente probatorio* or before the public prosecutor have made contradictory statements where circumstances as set out in (1) or (2) exist;[83]
6. to hear an expert or conduct a judicial experiment, if the proof refers to a person or an object which would be subject to inevitable change;
7. for an identification to be conducted where reasons of urgency indicate that it will not be possible to conduct such identification at trial.[84]

The structure of the hearing follows that of a trial in that it allows examination and cross-examination of witnesses by each party and the judge may also ask questions of the witnesses.

(h) Assembly of evidence at the preliminary hearing

At the close of the preliminary investigation, the public prosecutor requests that the case be sent forward for indictment.[85] At this point the prosecutor

81. Provisions contained in Articles 392–404, CPP.
82. L. Cuomo and F. Scioli, *L'Incidente Probatorio* (Giappichelli 2007) 85.
83. Article 211, CPP; see section 6.4.5 below.
84. See also Article 213, CPP re identification evidence.
85. Article 407, CPP.

submits the investigative file containing all the documents and reports collected during the investigation to the court registry.[86] The case is then passed along to the judge for the preliminary hearing, the *giudice dell'udienza preliminare* (GUP). The person under investigation at this stage is referred to as the accused.[87]

The preliminary hearing, presided over by the GUP, is held in camera in the presence of the parties.[88] In the hearing the public prosecutor gives a summary of the preliminary investigations and the justifications for sending the case forward for trial, working from the investigation file. The defence, also working from the investigation file, and the file developed from defence investigation if such has been carried out, argues against sending the case forward for trial. During the preliminary hearing the accused may make spontaneous statements or may ask to be examined (*interrogatorio*) by the judge.[89] If the accused opts to make a spontaneous statement, he cannot be asked any questions in relation to it but he must be warned beforehand that his statements may be used against him and that he has the right to remain silent. Where the accused asks to be examined, he may be asked to indicate anything that may be useful to his defence and where he refuses to respond to questions this must be noted in the report[90] and he may be cross-examined.[91] The judge (GUP) may ask the parties for any additional evidence he considers necessary.[92]

While in theory the preliminary hearing should provide the opportunity for scrutiny of the preliminary investigations and prevent unfounded cases from progressing further, it has been suggested that the procedure is simply a formality:

> The judge applies an extremely lenient standard to the prosecutor's case: a weak case is not a basis for dismissal, rather a judge may dismiss the case only if he concludes that no crime actually took place, that the events do not constitute a crime or that the defendant clearly did not commit the crime.[93]

If the judge decides that the case should go forward for trial, the file for the trial judge is assembled in the presence of the prosecutor and defence. Based on the premise that 'the act of investigating a crime itself creates a bias on the

86. Article 416, CPP.
87. *Imputato*; Article 60, CPP.
88. Article 420, CPP.
89. The accused may consent to the preliminary hearing being conducted in his absence, though a lawyer must represent him: Article 420 *quinquies*, CPP.
90. Article 65, CPP which applies to all interrogations of the suspect/ accused.
91. Article 421, CPP.
92. Article 421 *bis*, CPP.
93. W. Pizzi and L. Marafioti, 'The New Italian Code of Criminal Procedure: The Difficulties of Building an Adversarial Trial System on a Civil Law Foundation' (1992) 17 (1) *Yale J. Int'l L.* 1, 12.

part of the investigator' the Code creates a clear-cut separation between the criminal investigation and the trial.[94] This is achieved through the 'double dossier' system whereby the prosecutor's file and that of the trial judge remain separate, but some of the prosecutor's file contents are transferred into the trial judge's file at the close of the preliminary hearing.

The trial judge may reach a verdict based only on the contents of the trial file. The trial file will reach the trial judge with a certain amount of information, which qualifies as 'usable' evidence for the verdict. This can include the reports of 'non-repeatable acts' (such as searches) made by the police, the prosecutor and the defence; reports of evidence taken during the *incidente probatorio*; the *corpo del reato* (that is physical evidence of the crime and things pertinent to same) and, where both sides agree, documented acts contained in the public prosecutor's file as well as documents relating to the defence investigation.[95]

Ensuring the separation between investigation and trial, the judges who presided over the preliminary investigation and the preliminary hearing may not act as trial judge.[96] In theory at least the trial judge comes to adjudicate upon the case with a reasonably virgin mind. However, there is one situation where the trial judge may come to be familiar with the entire prosecution file, and that is where a person who has been placed in detention pending the trial seeks a review of the detention order. The detention may be reviewed throughout the process, and such reviews will be dealt with by whichever judge is involved at that moment in time, so if the detention is sought to be reviewed during the trial, then it will be the trial judge's remit. Whichever judge is reviewing the detention may avail himself of the material contained in the public prosecutor's file which was used for the original application of the measure.[97] This to some extent thwarts the aim of the Code that the trial judge be shielded from the investigation so as to remain impartial: while a decision of guilt can not be formally based upon information seen in the prosecutor's file, there is no guarantee that the trial judge will not be influenced nonetheless.

PART II

6.3 Rules of evidence

In the Italian Code of Criminal Procedure concepts familiar to the common law of evidence may be found such as the burden of proof, the standard of proof, the presumption of innocence and rules on various types of evidence: unlawfully obtained evidence, hearsay, opinion evidence, circumstantial evidence

94. M. Panzavolta, 'Reforms and Counter-reforms in the Italian Struggle for an Accusatorial System' (2004–5) 30 (3) *NCJ Int'l L. & Com. Reg.* 577, 585.
95. Article 431, CPP.
96. Article 34, CPP.
97. Article 299, CPP; Cass. pen. 27/10/1993, no. 3115.

and privilege.[98] That said, there is no discrete discipline of evidence law; rather, it forms part of criminal procedure as a whole. The Code contains a section devoted to evidence (*prova*), which is broken into three sections: general provisions, means of proof and means of gathering proof.[99] One must look to other parts of the Code to get the full picture regarding testimony, procedural rights and rules for exclusion, or more correctly 'non-usability' of evidence.

Overall the system of evidence law does not exclude evidence in the common law sense so that the trier of fact is precluded from ever knowing of its existence; rather, the issue is whether the information put before the triers of fact may be used to reach a verdict. This part will examine the approach taken in Italy to the three categories of evidence already examined in the Irish and French systems – unlawfully obtained evidence, hearsay evidence and character evidence – basing the discussion on the Code provisions and associated case law, and interviews I conducted with practitioners.

6.3.1 Unlawfully obtained evidence – nullity system

The system of admissibility of evidence involves consideration of separate Code provisions, those contained in the part concerning procedural acts which relate to the system of annulling acts undertaken in contravention of provisions of the Code, and those falling under the section devoted to proof, within which there is a further distinction to be considered relating to 'means of proof' and 'means of finding proof'. The nullity system is contained in the section of the Code entitled 'Acts' (*Atti*), which regulates the undertaking of procedural acts.[100] It encompasses the procedures for documentation of acts, notification to the parties where their participation is required, regulations for acts undertaken by the judge the most important of which is the obligation to give written reasons for decisions and orders, time limits, correction of errors and the procedure for annulling procedural acts.

The non-observance of provisions in undertaking procedural acts gives rise to annulment of those acts in cases prescribed by law.[101] Provisions relating to the capacity of judges, the taking of criminal action by the public prosecutor, and the guarantees of legal assistance and representation of the accused must always be observed on pain of nullity, in other words they are absolute nullities.[102] These nullities may be raised by the parties or by the judge *ex officio* at any time during the proceedings, whether at the preliminary hearing or at trial. Nullities relating to acts undertaken during the preliminary investigations or during an *incidente probatorio* hearing and those relating to the preliminary

98. Professional secrecy: Article 200, CPP.
99. Book 3, CPP.
100. Book 2, CPP.
101. Article 177, CPP.
102. Article 178, CPP.

hearing (*udienza preliminare*) must be raised prior to the delivery of the decision of the presiding judge (the GUP).[103] Nullities are cured if the interested party has expressly waived the objection or has accepted the effects of the act.[104] There is, however, a distinction between nullities of a general nature and absolute nullities. General nullities may be cured, whereas those of an absolute nature listed above, and any others defined as absolute by specific provisions of law, may not be cured.[105]

The effects of the declaration of nullity are set out in Article 185, CPP:

1. The nullity of an act invalidates subsequent acts arising from the act declared as null.
2. The judge declaring the nullity of an act orders its renewal, where necessary and feasible, awarding costs against the party whose fraudulent intent or gross negligence has given rise to the nullity.
3. The declaration of nullity entails the return of the proceedings to the state and level at which the annulled act has been performed, unless otherwise established.
4. The provision of paragraph 3 does not apply to nullity relating to evidence.

While the effect of the statement of nullity under Article 185 renders all consecutive acts which depend on the annulled act invalid,[106] at first glance this might suggest that any evidence obtained in consequence of a breach of procedure would be unavailable for use at trial. There is a difference, however, between the approach taken to material evidence (*corpo del reato*) and items connected with the crime on the one hand, and the approach to statements, both of witnesses and the accused, on the other. In relation to the former, it has been consistently held by the Supreme Court that there is a distinction between the act of searching and the act of seizure.[107] Seizure of an item of evidence connected with the crime by the police or prosecutor is considered to be an obligatory act, and it has been held that in terms of an illegal search and seizure, the invalidity of the search is not transferred to the seizure:

> A statement of nullity in this instance determines neither the non-usability of the objects found for the purpose of evidence, nor the nullity of the seizure of evidence, within the meaning of Article 185. Such nullity is in fact excluded because Article 185.4 explicitly excludes evidence from the system of the consequential nature of the nullity.[108]

103. Article 181, CPP.
104. Article 183, CPP.
105. Article 179, CPP.
106. Cass. pen. 19/6/2007, no. 23887.
107. Cass. pen. 9/7/1993, no. 6861; R. Van Cleave, 'Italy', in C. Bradley, *Criminal Procedure: A Worldwide Study* (2nd edn) (Carolina Academic Press 2007) 303, 312ff.
108. Cass. pen. 27/12/1995, no. 2793.

The nullity system must be read in conjunction with Article 191 which refers to illegitimately acquired evidence.[109] That provides:

1. Evidence acquired in breach of statutory prohibitions may not be used.
2. Its non-usability[110] may be identified, even *ex ufficio*, in any stage and at any level of the proceedings.

The Supreme Court has held that the prohibition on use of evidence generally provided by Article 191 'refers to evidence acquired in breach of statutory prohibitions, not to evidence whose acquisition is permitted but which has not been obtained in accordance with the prescribed formalities, in which case the discipline of procedural nullity must be applied.'[111] This follows an earlier ruling of the court holding that:

> Non-compliance with the formalities prescribed by law for the legitimate acquisition of evidence in a trial is not in itself sufficient to render the evidence unusable, due to the effects of the provision of Article 191. Whereas the latter provision provides non-usability of evidence to be a sanction of a general nature, applicable to evidence acquired in breach of prohibitions relating to evidence, it has not in fact thereby eliminated the instrument of nullity, in that the categories of nullity and non-usability of evidence, albeit operating in the area of unlawful evidence, are separate and autonomous since they are associated with different presuppositions: the first category consistently pertains only to the failure to observe certain formalities for the acquisition of evidence – a flaw that does not place the procedure of acquisition completely outside the normative framework but merely relates to the failure to comply with certain of its specific prerequisites; the second category, on the other hand, presupposes the existence of evidence that is 'prohibited' due to its intrinsic, objective illegitimacy, or due to the procedure of acquisition, whose manifest illegitimacy undoubtedly places it outside the procedural system.[112]

The distinction between 'means of proof' and 'means of finding proof' has been explained in a number of cases. The notion of means of proof and means of finding proof are distinctly different. This is reflected in the fact that all the means of proof, be they related to persons or things such as testimony,

109. Book 3, CPP.
110. The term used is *inutilizzabilità* in relation to evidence that may not be used for the decision, rather than the more familiar common law word of inadmissibility of evidence. In Italy there is a distinction between inadmissibility (*inammissibilità*) and non-usability (*inutilizzabilità*); the meaning of admissibility/inadmissibility as opposed to usability/non-usability is discussed in section 6.43 below.
111. Cass. pen. 31/10/2008, no. 40973.
112. Cass. pen. 16/5/1996, no. 5021.

examination of the parties, confrontations, identifications, judicial experiments, experts and documents, are contained in Title II of Book 3, CPP and means of finding proof, referring to inspections, searches, seizures and intercepts, 'find their specific and autonomous discipline in Title III'.[113] In interpreting Article 247, which sets out the law in relation to conducting searches, the court has explained:

> If the search has been carried out without authorisation and other than in the 'cases' and by the 'methods' laid down by law, as prescribed by Article 13 of the Constitution, this amounts to a means of searching for evidence that is incompatible with the safeguarding of the citizen's freedom, as expressed in the recognition of the inviolability of his home. As a result, since a means of search cannot be categorised as unusable but only the evidence itself, the search is null and a seizure effected on that basis cannot be used as evidence; however, that is subject to the provisions of Article 253. The effect of that Article is that the seizure of material evidence and items pertinent to the crime is obligatory, and therefore that obligation renders the manner in which that act is arrived at altogether irrelevant.[114]

One of the judges explained the position to me as follows:

> *JB1*: We are a Latin people, and the Latin people often draw many distinctions; you – the Anglo-Saxon people – are a bit more clear-cut – a situation is black or white; we tend to see different shades: white, bright white, black, darker black, various shades of colour to mean that between black and white, there are many situations which call for a different order of response.
>
> As a private citizen, if I obtain items of proof from you, I don't have a power to undertake a search of you, or your property – here you have a patent breach of the Constitution. Where there is such a violation of the Constitution then the item of evidence cannot be considered. On the other hand the Constitution says the police can search, therefore if the police can carry out a search, and the laws establish the procedures for searches, and these procedures are breached, then the law says: 'the police who have this power have not exercised it in accordance with law'; in such cases the law responds by prosecution, or disciplinary measures; but if they have gathered evidence of a crime that a judge evaluates to be proof of the crime, then that proof is legitimately taken at trial. Therefore where there is a violation of a law that permits the act to be done, the discourse changes, and the proof may be taken into account.

113. Cass. pen. 9/7/1993, no. 6861.
114. Cass. pen. 16/5/1996, no. 5021.

In effect, therefore, unless something is seized in the absence of *any* legal authority in breach of constitutional rights, it may be used as evidence. Where it is a case of seizing evidence where the police have the authority but are in breach of the procedure, the breach would not result in the fruits of the seizure being excluded. The Supreme Court has held: 'Even where items are seized during an unlawful search, they must nonetheless be considered to have been obtained in accordance with the power and duty of the police as provided by Article 354.2' (referring to the obligation on police to secure items in cases where there is a danger of deterioration, loss or change before the public prosecutor can intervene).[115] The approach is therefore to respond by a disciplinary sanction on the offending officer but, in sharp contrast to the situation in Ireland, to allow the fruits of their breach to be used as evidence.

The idea of excluding an item of material evidence if it had been obtained in breach of procedure seemed anathema to those I interviewed. I described an Irish case to them in which a computer containing images of child pornography was held to be inadmissible as evidence since it had been seized on the basis of an expired warrant – though only by a day – causing the case to result in a directed verdict of not guilty.[116] This was met with expressions of dismay. While conceding that evidence obtained by force or other means by a person with absolutely no authority to do so would not be admissible, no Italian court would refuse to admit material evidence obtained by a body authorised to do so, albeit in breach of procedure. One of the judges put it to me thus:

> *JB2*: In our system we do have a system of rules in the acquisition of proof that must be respected; however, not every breach of the rules determines a nullity of an act and of a fact. The acquisition of the *corpo del reato* is an act of the police, but it is an act that ends up in the trial. There are rules that regulate the acquisition. Only the cases expressly provided by the law, where the law is not respected, could I declare a nullity, and nullity means that the act is null, and therefore cannot be evaluated by the judge in reaching a judgment. But in Italy, not all bad conduct, including that provided for in the Code, results in the act being invalid; this is what the Constitutional Court has found, so where there is an illegal search, we say the search was incorrectly carried out but the admission of the resulting body of evidence is correct nonetheless. For you this might appear strange!

The nullity system and the provisions of Article 191 are more concerned with the obligation to check for the commission of a breach of procedure of a disciplinary or even criminal nature than with correcting the shortcomings of

115. Cass. pen. 18/2/2004, no. 6842.
116. *DPP v Curtin* 26/4/2004, Tralee Circuit Ct.

the investigation by excluding the evidence from trial. A defence lawyer explained to me thus:

> *D*: The jurisprudence does not see a link between search and seizure. If the police do find something illegally, they commit a disciplinary offence; the sole purpose of nullities is disciplinary. There is a law of evidence in Italy, definitely, but its purpose is not really concerned with excluding evidence. The law of evidence covers all proofs and not just material proofs. The jurisprudence in respect of material proof is not concerned really with exclusion; it is more used in the sense that you could be calling for the restitution of goods; or you could argue that the seized items are unconnected with the crime and thus they should be excluded.

The police have power to do warrantless searches on their own initiative, for example for drugs or arms, but the police use these powers to find other things. In this case you could challenge the admission of the evidence on the basis that the power of warrantless search is for item x, but item y is found instead; you could try to argue that it should be excluded, but the jurisprudence is not concerned with excluding evidence obtained in consequence of an illegal act. The law of evidence in Italy as an exclusionary mechanism is very limited.

I asked the judge and prosecutor how often evidence is 'unusable'.

> *P*: Not often, maybe never. The prosecutor's investigation may only last six months (normally). If the evidence is obtained after the six months it is unusable, but if the prosecutor asks in the trial to examine a witness, the problem is over and you can listen directly to that witness in front of the judge. I think the problem of evidence being admitted or not is not a great problem in Italy. This is because the police do not normally question the arrested person; it happened in the past, with the Rocco Code; it happened often that the police would question a suspect and then put the statement in the file for the judge, and then you would have to argue why the statement should not be admitted and the trial went on like that. It was a problem. Now it is almost an irrelevant issue today. Now the police cannot say to the judge what the accused said to them, this is a very important rule. Very important!
> (*Judge interjects*)
> *JT*: And if the police say 'but the accused told me …' you have to stop them: 'you cannot say that'; the police cannot even say anything where an accused made a confession to them, they cannot say anything about what the accused told them; if they try and I do not stop them, the defence will object anyway!
> *Self*: So anything that is said to the police is worthless?
> *JT*: No, it is not worthless. The prosecutor may have used it to develop his own questioning. But normally we try not to ask the police what a witness has said to them – we have adopted a sort of hearsay rule.

While the material evidence gathered in breach of procedure will not result in the evidence being unusable, the position is much stricter when statements have been made to the police in the absence of a lawyer. A recent high-profile trial in Italy of an American student charged with the murder of her housemate provides an example of a case where statements made to the police without a lawyer being present were ruled to be unusable for the verdict.[117] This was the finding of both the trial at first instance in which the accused was found guilty of murder and the subsequent appeal court decision that overturned her conviction.

While the 'spontaneous statements' that she made to the police were unusable because of the oppressive circumstances in which they had been taken together with the fact that they were made in the absence of a lawyer, the written memorandum of the statement was nonetheless admissible for the purposes of assessing her liability for a separate charge of 'calumny'.[118] That charge arose as a result of a false accusation of her employer that she made to the police in her 'spontaneous statement', stating that he was the perpetrator of the crime. The memorandum of the statement formed the *corpo del reato* (material evidence) for the offence of calumny and was therefore fully usable for trying that offence.

Since the calumny charge and the murder charge were tried simultaneously, this resulted in a situation where the adjudicators had detailed statements available for use for one purpose but not for another. No account was taken of any possible prejudice that the statements could create in the minds of the adjudicators. Provided the reasoned decision of the trial court, in relation to the offence for which they do not constitute the *corpo del reato*, makes no reference to them, it is presumed that they have not been relied upon in assessing guilt.

6.3.2 Hearsay evidence

As originally adopted, the Code included a strong exclusionary approach to out-of-court statements, essentially creating a species of hearsay rule which prevented the use of out-of-court statements as substantive evidence in the trial. As a result, police officers were not permitted to testify about statements gathered during the police investigation. This exclusionary effect was clawed back by the Constitutional Court in the early years of operating the new Code, unhappy with the idea that valuable evidence could be withheld from the arbitrator of fact.[119] Grande has argued that the approach of the Constitutional

117. *Knox and Sollecito* 8/2008, *Corte di assise di Perugia* 5/12/2009.
118. Literally translated, slander; *calunnia* is a criminal offence provided by Article 368, CP.
119. These decisions were: Cass. pen. 31/1/1992, no. 24; Cass. pen. 3/6/1992, no. 254; Cass. pen. 3/6/1992, no. 255; see: Grande (note 2) 238; W. Pizzi and M. Montagna, 'The Battle to Establish an Adversarial Trial System in Italy' (2004) 25 (2) *Mich. J. Int'l L.* 429, 449; Panzavolta (note 94) 596; Amodio (note 3) 493; G. Illuminati, 'The Frustrated Turn to

Court was a clear demonstration of a resistance to the adversarial principles, and exemplifies the difficulties of transplanting an adversarial system onto the inquisitorial structure because of the discomfort that that can pose for the treatment of 'truth' in the process.[120]

Pizzi and Montagna have argued that the early decisions of the Constitutional Court, in placing 'a strong emphasis on the primacy of the search for truth at trial', viewed the procedural protections of the Code as 'unfair hindrances' to fighting crime.[121] He suggests, however, that the decisions should be seen not so much as an indication of resistance to the new system but more in the broader context of the difficulties posed to the justice system by the Mafia, in a year in which two judges had been assassinated.[122]

In the aftermath of these judgments the Code underwent a number of reforms until the position was finally stabilised by an amendment to the Constitution that has become known as the 'due process reform'.[123] It provides the accused with *inter alia* the right to confront and cross-examine witnesses and provides a constitutional basis for a hearsay prohibition. Reflecting this, the Code now provides that the accused cannot be convicted on the basis of out-of-court statements where the maker of the statement has not been subjected to cross-examination.[124] Exceptions are provided in cases where the accused consents to their use, where the maker of the statement is unavailable (for example due to death or infirmity)[125] or where the witness is unlawfully prevented from testifying.[126] In these cases the statement may be fully relied upon as evidence.[127] The reform also restored the original prohibition, rejected by the earlier Constitutional Court decision, on the police testifying to statements gathered during the police investigation.[128] Witness statements recounting information based on anonymous sources may not be used as evidence.[129]

Out-of-court statements of a witness who fails to attend the trial may not be used to prove guilt,[130] nor may statements made by a witness where the

Adversarial Procedure in Italy (Italian Criminal Procedure Code of 1988)' (2005) 4 *Wash. U. Glob. Stud. L. Rev.* 567, 574.

120. Grande (note 2) 251.
121. Pizzi and Montagna (note 119) 457.
122. Ibid., 454.
123. Article 111.
124. Article 195, CPP.
125. Article 195.3, CPP.
126. Article 500.4, CPP.
127. Cass. pen. 15/10/2008, no. 38894, holding there must be evidence to show the witness has been threatened such as to compromise the trial testimony.
128. Article 195.4, CPP: judicial police officials and officers may not testify on the content of the statements of witnesses acquired during questioning of persons who can provide useful information for the investigation, statements of oral accusations or statements obtained during questioning of persons under investigation and spontaneous statements made by the latter.
129. Article 194.7, CPP.
130. Article 526.1 *bis*, CPP.

witness refuses to be examined or cross-examined, except where this is shown to be as a result of threats made to the witness.[131] Here, the Italian Code has closely followed the common law approach by allowing hearsay statements to be used, not as proof of content of the statement but as evidence going towards credibility. The prior statement may thus be used to challenge inconsistent testimony given by the witness at trial,[132] whether the inconsistency is a result of a different account being given at trial or where the witness simply does not remember the incidents referred to in their previous statement.[133] However, if there is evidence to show that a witness has been subject to threats so as to prevent him testifying to the previous statement, then the prior statement may be used in full. Hearsay statements may also be used in full if neither party has requested that the original declarant be called to give evidence.[134]

Italy's approach to hearsay rule as far as out-of-court statements are concerned is now equally, or possibly even more, exclusionary than that of Ireland since the recent reform in the latter jurisdiction. Italy takes a similar approach to the common law doctrine of hostile witness, in so far as a prior statement may be used for credibility purposes alone; however, where a witness recants or offers a different account, the position is similar to Ireland in that the statement may be used in full. Nonetheless, arguably a higher threshold must be crossed in Italy since the Supreme Court has held there must be evidence to show the witness has been threatened, whereas in Ireland, in deciding whether to allow the statement to be considered as evidence, the court must simply consider the reasons for the witness's refusal to give evidence or for their inconsistent account or denial at trial.[135]

6.3.3 Statements of the accused

Article 62 prohibits statements made by the accused in the course of proceedings to be used as evidence. The ban on using statements of the accused refers only to those made to the police or prosecutor, because the Supreme Court in applying this article has consistently focused on the phrase 'in the course of proceedings' so as to allow the admission of statements in which the suspect has incriminated himself to other persons. In a number of cases the court has held that statements made to a cellmate may be used as evidence since they cannot be said to have been made 'in the course of proceedings' nor made to a person with authority to take statements.[136] The Court has also confined the application of the provision to statements made by a suspect or

131. Article 500.3, CPP.
132. Article 500.1, CPP.
133. Cass. pen. 16/2/2006, no. 6221; Cass. pen. 9/12/2008, no. 45496.
134. Cass. pen. 6/10/2008, no. 38076.
135. See note 127 above; see section 4.3.4 above.
136. Cass. pen. 24/7/1997, no. 2005; Cass. pen. 5/2/2008, no. 5636.

an accused and not to spontaneous statements made by a person before they had obtained that status.[137] Moreover, it extends only to formal statements as opposed to simply utterances of a person during an act that is outside of proceedings.[138] Prior statements of an accused made to the prosecutor may be substantively used as evidence if he fails to appear or refuses to be examined at trial.[139]

Spontaneous statements made by a suspect to the police may not be used in the trial other than in challenging trial testimony.[140] They may be used at the trial in an indirect fashion, however, since the court has held that in addition to it being permissible for the police to use statements made by the suspect immediately after the act in the absence of his lawyer for the purpose of furthering the investigation, it is legitimate to receive the testimony of the police officer of the outcome of such further inquiries as well as the elements gathered as a result of the information received from the suspect.[141]

6.3.4 Documentary evidence

While the common law rule against hearsay embraces documented statements broad enough to include even the designation of country of origin of goods, for example 'produce of Morocco',[142] the Italian version of a hearsay rule is limited to the out-of-court statements described above. Documentary evidence[143] may therefore be used at trial as evidence except for documents relating to public opinion in relation to the trial or relating to the morality of the parties, witnesses or experts in general.[144] Documents constituting material evidence of the crime must be acquired regardless of who has drafted them or who holds them.[145] Anonymous statements cannot be used as evidence unless they constitute material evidence or originate from the accused.[146] Documents constituting communication between the lawyer/client may not be seized unless the judge has well founded reasons to believe that they constitute material evidence.[147]

Intercepted statements in which a person incriminates himself of committing crimes may be used as evidence provided they have been obtained

137. Cass. pen. 3/7/1998, no. 7844.
138. Cass. pen. 12/3/1997, no. 2389.
139. Article 513.1, CPP.
140. Article 350.7, CPP.
141. Cass. pen. 3/11/2008, no. 41040.
142. The allusion here is to the decision of the Privy Council *Patel v Comptroller of Customs* [1965] AC 356 in which such a 'statement' was found to constitute hearsay.
143. Documents include 'representation of facts through writing, photograph, phonograph or through any other means': Article 234, CPP.
144. Article 234, CPP.
145. Article 235, CPP.
146. Article 240, CPP.
147. Article 103.6, CPP.

through authorised intercepts.[148] Results of intercepts cannot be used if they have been illegally executed.[149] Nor can they be used as evidence where they relate to privileged communications, unless the persons covered by the privilege made depositions on the same facts or otherwise divulged them.[150] Intercepts of lawyers' telephones or other means of communication are prohibited where the lawyers are exercising activity related to defence matters, but the prohibition does not extend to conversations that embrace crimes themselves, so where a lawyer had warned his client of a police initiative, giving him advice on how to avoid capture, thus committing the crime of aiding and abetting, the intercept was valid and admissible as evidence.[151]

6.3.5 Character evidence

In considering whether character evidence is available to a decider of fact in Italy, a further difference in institutional structure between archetypal common law trial and trials in Italy must be considered: trials in Italy, similar to the system in France, run as a singular structure in which the determination of guilt and determination of sentence are decided as part of the one procedure. Guilt and sentence are determined on the basis of the evidence contained in the trial dossier at the close of the trial. This will include records of any previous convictions an accused may have which are inserted into the trial dossier when the case goes forward for hearing following the preliminary hearing. Where there is a jury, the jury have access to the full dossier, and they determine the issue of guilt and sentence along with the judge.

A judge, or a mixed panel of judges and jury, cannot use the fact of a previous conviction as a basis for their decision of guilt; the information on previous convictions is supposed to be used only for consideration of sentence. Nonetheless, having access to the full trial dossier runs the risk that the deciders of fact might use the bad character information to travel down the path of 'the forbidden reasoning' to conclude that because the defendant has offended in the past, it follows that he has offended on this occasion. At the same time, however, the fact that the Italian deciders of fact must justify their decision by written reasons means that they have to at least formally rely on other reasons besides the defendant's bad character. Even where subconsciously they have taken it into account, bad character evidence cannot be the sole reason for their decision, since there would still have to be sufficient evidence to give rise to a finding of guilt.

148. Cass. pen. 29/3/2007, no. 12874.
149. Article 271, CPP.
150. Article 271.2, CPP.
151. Article 103.5, CPP; Cass. pen. 17/9/2003, no. 35656.

I asked one of the judges whether the knowledge of an accused's previous convictions had any influence on judges' verdicts:

> *JB1*: No! Absolutely not! We can never be influenced by the accused's previous behaviour. We have a system that never allows us to say: since he has committed crimes in the past, he has also committed this one. No! Absolutely not! That is not part of our system. It only has a bearing on the sentence that is given – but only after you have decided he is guilty.

PART III

6.4 Receiving, presenting and challenging evidence

This part will examine how Italian evidence law works through the course of the trial, and considers how a species of the adversarial trial concept has been adapted to the Italian setting. To give a better insight into how the trial process works, I will draw on interviews I conducted with practitioners and my observations of segments of two trials that I attended at two separate *corte di assise*.

6.4.1 The trial setting

The trial is presided over by a single judge in the *tribunale* for offences punishable by less than ten years, or three judges where punishment is over ten years. For more serious offences, trials proceed in the *corte di assise*[152] before three judges (the president of the court and two more junior judges) and six 'popular judges' (*giudici popolari*) – ordinary citizens.[153] The Constitutional 'due process reform' guarantees the right to trial before an impartial judge and provides that the trial shall proceed in accordance with the principle of *contraddittorio*,[154] guaranteeing a position of equality between the parties. In Italy, the presumption of innocence is constitutionally protected[155] and while there is no specific provision in the Code that directly states it, it is widely accepted that the burden of proof rests on the prosecution.[156]

152. The *corte di assise* has jurisdiction to hear cases for which the penalty is life or not less than a maximum of 24 years (Article 5, CPP).
153. The provisions for the selection of jurors in the *corte di assise* and the *corte di assise di appello* are contained in Law 287 10/4/1951, 26 *Gazz. Uff.* No. 102, 7 May 1951, *Riordinamento dei giudizi di assise*. All jurors who pass verdict must have been in attendance throughout the trial.
154. Translated (in official translations of ECtHR cases) as 'adversarial proceedings' or 'adversarial argument' in identical manner to the translation of *contradictoire*; see discussion in section 3.3.6 above on the issues raised by this 'uncomfortable translation'.
155. The words 'presumed innocent' are not used; Article 27 of the Constitution provides 'the accused is not considered to be guilty until the sentence is final'.
156. See section 6.4.8.

By way of choreography of the trial, in the *corte di assise* the lay assessors sit on the same level as the President of the court and the two judges. The prosecutor, who used to sit on the same bench as the judges, reflecting the fact that the prosecutor and judges belong to the same hierarchical level of *magistratura*, now sits on the same level as the defence opposite to the adjudicating body.[157] While the new Code does not effect any change to the hierarchal relationship between judges and prosecutors, the positioning of the prosecutor seated on the same level as the defence and in front of the judge is more in keeping with the way in which an adversarial trial would play out in a common law courtroom, where the prosecution and defence are clearly parties fighting out the contest before an impartial judge. To this extent, one can get the sense in an Italian courtroom that one is attending an adversarial, common law style trial.

The *parte civile* may also be present and represented by a lawyer at the trial.[158] It is often argued in the context of the issue of separate legal representation for victims in Ireland and England that a third lawyer would be unable to fit in comfortably within the two-sided adversarial structure of prosecution and defence, that they would somehow upset the balance. In Italy, although adopting the adversarial type format of prosecution and defence, the role for the *parte civile* lawyer was retained.

The role of the 'jury' is different to its common law counterpart. They reach their verdict in conjunction with the judges and also decide on the sentence, which like the French system is part of the single trial process. One judge described it to me thus:

> *JB1*: Your system delegates all responsibility to a jury – for us that would be unthinkable! For us the law has by necessity technical aspects that the popular judges would not be able to understand. This is one of the main differences in mentality between our Romano-Germanic system and the common law Anglo-Saxon. Where there is a jury, they see the entire trial file. They are in a position of equality with the judge; they participate in the trial as equals with the judges.

6.4.2 The course of the trial

Despite a provision in the Code that trials should be completed in one day or if necessary may be adjourned until the following day, in reality that provision is completely ignored.[159] Trials are sporadic. A case will proceed with a certain

157. Article 146, CPP (*norme di attuazione*).
158. A victim may only take an active part in the trial by seeking the civil remedy of damages. In such cases the victim becomes *parte civile* (a civil party) and is allowed to participate in the trial, introduce evidence and examine and cross-examine witnesses.
159. Article 477, CPP.

number of witnesses listed to give their testimony and will then be adjourned to another date, often a few months later, when another set of witnesses will testify, and the trial continues in this manner until all the testimony has been heard. A trial can take anything up to two years to complete, depending on the number of witnesses to be called.[160] One judge was clearly frustrated by this aspect of the process:

> *JT*: The difficulty for us is we have too much work, we have trials also for minor crimes, for the minor crimes we have to apply all the guarantees, I have to run a trial for a minor crime just as I have to for a serious crime like murder.
>
> For us, when we begin a trial, we have too many trials and the procedure is too complex, even for the minor offences; even though the Code says a trial must continue once it has begun, in reality – I may start a trial today and hear some witnesses, but tomorrow I may have a different case to hear, so I must find some time free in my diary to hold another hearing for the first trial, this may even be a few months later, and so on until all the witnesses have been heard.

I asked the judge to outline the average timeline of the pre-trial to end of trial process:

> *JT*: The preliminary investigation can take anywhere between six months and up to two years; normally it is one year for preliminary investigation for serious crimes; I would say one year for the preliminary investigation, one year for first grade, and always they go to the appeal court.[161]
> *Self*: How many hearings would be held during the trial stage?
> *JT*: That depends on the number of witnesses; a judge would usually have four or five hearings to hear the witnesses, then to hear the arguments of the prosecutor and defence lawyer, and the *parte civile*; then you need time for considering the verdict; you can never run a case in the same week; I might often have to wait for three months before I can find a time to fit in a second hearing and then another three months for the next one and so on; it is not my fault. I don't have enough time to manage all my trials; if a person is in pre-trial detention normally there is some priority given to those cases, but many people are in pre-trial detention so that is a problem also. Often, however, those people will choose

160. According to practitioners. The trial at first instance of Knox and Sollecito (see text accompanying note 117 above) lasted a full year, commencing on 4/12/2008 and concluding on 5/12/2009. In all there were 20 separate hearings during the trial.

161. There is a right to appeal from decisions of the *corte di assise* (open to both prosecution and defence) to the *corte di assise di appello*. This will be a full rehearing before a judge, two assessors (judges also) and six jurors (*giudici popolari*).

> the shortened procedure.[162] We are not very happy, because it is very difficult to run the amount of trials that we now need to, the problem is the overloading. We should simplify the procedure for petty crime, and for serious crimes keep the guarantees.

Where the trial takes place in front of a jury the position is no different to trials presided over by judges alone. The jury are thus expected to pick up where they left off a few weeks or months beforehand. This must cause difficulty for jurors trying to keep the whole 'story' in mind, and it was not surprising to see a number of them appearing somewhat bored and detached from the proceedings at the hearings I attended.

I attended hearings in two trials in the *corte di assise.* One trial related to a homicide charged against two co-defendants. Each was charged with unlawfully carrying a knife in a public place, causing the death of the deceased by repeated stabbing and doing acts to prevent his rescue by other people by assaulting one of them. Both accused were Tunisians; the parents and sister of the deceased were constituted as civil parties (*parti civili*) who were represented in court by a single lawyer, but neither *parte civile* were personally present. Each accused was individually represented by a defence lawyer. This trial was held in Modena.

The other trial, held in Bologna, was a case against six accused (five Tunisians and one Moroccan) charged with membership of, promoting and financing an organisation formed to carry out terrorist activity.[163] The actual activity for which they had been arrested was fraud: an allegation of staging a car crash in order to claim insurance money. It was alleged that the proceeds of their crime went towards financing an al-Qaeda cell in Bologna of which they were alleged to be members. The prosecution case was supported by evidence derived from Internet activity 'promoting holy war and jihad', intercepted emails and telephone calls allegedly using coded language. Five of the accused were present; one was absent 'at large' and so was tried *in absentia.* One lawyer was representing five of the accused including the absentee, and one accused had a separate lawyer.

In the homicide trial that I attended, the incident had occurred in April 2008; one accused who had been injured had been arrested in hospital on the evening of the attack and had been in detention since that time; the co-accused had been arrested some months later having fled to Belgium; the investigation had been concluded by the prosecutor in January 2009, the case was returned for trial by the GUP in April 2009 and the first trial hearing was held in June 2009. The hearing I attended in November 2009 was the sixth hearing that had been held and lasted for one day at the end

162. *Giudizio abbreviato* (Articles 438–443, CPP) is a fast-track trial mechanism that may be applied for by the accused at the preliminary hearing if the prosecutor consents.
163. Contrary to Article 270 *bis* 1, 2 and 3, CP.

of which it was adjourned. The trial was finally concluded in December 2009. Altogether there were 52 witnesses who gave oral testimony. In all, the trial took seven months from the first trial hearing to the consideration and delivery of the verdict – a total of nine separate hearings, each lasting a full day, normally starting at 09:30 and concluding at 19:00 in the evening with two short coffee breaks and a one-hour lunch break. The terrorist trial also lasted seven months. The original incident had occurred in August 2006; all the accused bar one had been arrested in August 2008, and had remained in detention since that date. I attended the first trial hearing in November 2009 which lasted a morning; the case was then adjourned for three months and the trial was finally concluded in June 2010.[164]

In the terrorist trial, the five accused were led into the courtroom in shackles and put in the *gabbia*, a four-sided metal cage, where their shackles were removed but they were locked in for the duration of the hearing and answered any questions from that position. In the homicide trial, the defendants were seated in an enclosed area, a more modern structure with glass screening instead of iron bars. When one of the defendants gave evidence, he was called out of the glass partition area and seated in a chair closer to his lawyer, but a prison officer stood two steps away from him holding a firearm, lowered but 'at the ready'. On this basis, it would be clear to a jury that an accused is in custody – the presumption of innocence as a reputational protection begins to look fictitious!

Witnesses do not sit in the courtroom during the proceedings but are called in when it is their turn to testify. They are prohibited from communication with the parties, or with other witnesses, and they should not see or hear or be otherwise informed of what transpires during the hearing.[165]

6.4.3 Presentation of evidence

The trial commences with a reading of the charges by the auxiliary judge.[166] These are contained in a document, the *decreto che dispone il giudizio*, drawn up by the office of the GUP, and a copy is supplied to all the members of the bench, including to the lay jurors.[167] In the case of the terrorist trial, this document contained a list of the accused (*imputati*), giving their names, nationality (five Tunisian and one Moroccan), address in Italy and their current residence – prison! There followed five pages of description of the

164. Since I was unable to attend all hearings, I followed up the cases through media reports to augment documents made available to me by the presidents in both trials, which revealed, *inter alia*, the number of earlier hearings. The appeal was concluded in May 2011.
165. Article 149, CPP.
166. Article 492, CPP.
167. The president of the court gave me a copy of this 'return for trial' document.

case against the six accused, listing the charges, and a summary of the evidence which supported the allegations, detailing that there was evidence of Internet activity promoting holy war and jihad, intercepted emails and telephone calls using coded language.

The trial then proceeds with a statement by the prosecutor of the facts that he intends to prove and a request to the judge to admit his supporting evidence. In sharp contrast to a common law adversarial trial, a statement by the defence lawyer of the facts that he intends to prove, and a similar request to admit his supporting evidence immediately follows the prosecutor's opening statement.[168] The judge then makes a ruling on the admissibility of the evidence proposed by the parties.[169] This admissibility ruling, however, is not akin to that which occurs in an Irish trial during the *voir dire*, though the judge is not precluded from hearing objections to evidence during the course of the trial.[170] There are no lengthy legal submissions arguing for or against its admissibility. The admissibility question is really to settle what information the judge is prepared to hear in the trial, but it does not settle whether it may be finally judged 'usable' in the evaluation of the evidence. The practice was explained it to me as follows:

> *JT*: In the Italian trial, at the beginning of the trial, it is the judge who admits the proposed evidence, at the very beginning, on the day of the trial opening. You open the trial, and then the prosecutor presents the evidence that he wants to be admitted in trial, and the defence may also do the same. In other words, it is a summary of the evidence you want to use during the trial, and the judge decides whether to admit it or not, at the very beginning.
> *P*: Usually it is admitted; because we don't ask for evidence to be admitted which could not be admitted (if illegal for example); we know the rules.

Nonetheless, the judge may at any point in the trial order the 'unusability' of illegally obtained evidence,[171] that which is deemed to be a nullity[172] and evidence deemed to be superfluous or irrelevant.[173] This order may be made following an objection raised by the parties or by the judge himself *ex officio.* Nonetheless, even if the information is judged to be unusable, it will still have reached the minds of all who must reach a verdict on the case, the judges and

168. Article 190, CPP; Article 493, CPP.
169. Article 495, CPP.
170. Article 495.4, CPP.
171. Meaning evidence obtained contrary to law as provided by Article 191, CPP. Objection to such evidence may be raised at any stage of the proceedings; even if it was found to be unusable as evidence by the GUP during the preliminary hearing, it can be revisited at the trial.
172. Article 179; Article 181, CPP.
173. Article 493, CPP.

the jury; there is no similar shielding from such information as is the case in Ireland under the *voir dire* procedure.

The manner in which a trial opens makes it difficult, from the perspective of an observer from a common law tradition, to accept the idea that the burden of proof in Italy rests on the prosecution. In the common law system a defendant is entitled to put the prosecution to proof, and to decide at the close of the presentation of the prosecution's case whether or not to give evidence on behalf of the defence.[174] In the terrorist trial, the 'case construction' offered by the prosecution in the opening address was that the defendants had perpetrated the fraud to raise funds for al-Qaeda, and were in communication with other persons resident in Italy of the Muslim faith to promote jihad. The defence lawyer countered this at the end of the prosecutor's opening address with her theory, to the effect that the accused collected money for other Muslims living in the city in a charitable enterprise aimed at assisting Muslims who found it impossible to find work in the city because of prejudice.

What effect does this have on the burden of proof? Even if it is conceded that it does not remove the onus from the prosecution to prove its case, can it be said that the defence is in some way assisting the prosecution? Under the common law variant, the defence is effectively saying 'you made the accusation, therefore prove it, and I need not assist you in any way'. This is reinforced in the common law by the right enjoyed by the accused to remain silent, both at the pre-trial stage and during the trial. Where the defence present their case at the very outset of the trial, as is the Italian method, there is at least a sense that the defence is aiming to disprove the prosecution case. In the common law adversarial trial the defence can literally sit back and present absolutely no evidence, simply relying on the weakness of the prosecution case, in the hope that by probing the prosecution case through cross-examination of the prosecution witnesses, it can generate enough doubt so that the case will not pass the requisite standard of proof beyond reasonable doubt.

6.4.4 Witnesses

Once the trial judge has ruled on the evidence to be admitted, the questioning of prosecution witnesses then commences. In the terrorist trial, most of the questioning was conducted by the prosecutor, followed by further questioning by the president of the court. The defence lawyer cross-examined only one of the six witnesses presented, much of which was interrupted by the president of the court whenever the lawyer asked a question which in the president's opinion the witness had already answered sufficiently. After each witness was questioned, the statement contained in the prosecution file was then passed to the judge to be included in the trial dossier.

174. But see defence statement in England, s. 6A, Criminal Procedure and Investigations Act 1996.

Everyone has the capacity to testify, but the judge may, in evaluating their statements, take account of their physical and mental abilities to give testimony.[175] Witnesses are obliged to respond truthfully but cannot be obliged to testify to facts that might incriminate them.[176] They are examined on the facts that constitute 'objects of proof'[177] but are not permitted to testify to the character of the accused, or to give evidence of their opinion.[178]

6.4.5 Examining and cross-examining witnesses

Under the former Code the task of examining witnesses belonged to the trial judge. Under the new Code, the party calling the witness is the person who examines the witness followed by cross-examination by the other party and re-examination. The party calling the witness may not pose leading questions.[179]

The president of the court is charged with ensuring that the examination of a witness is conducted in a respectful manner. The witness may be permitted by the judge to consult documents to refresh their memory. During the examination of a witness the president may intervene to ensure the relevance of the questions, the genuineness of the responses, the fairness of the examination and the propriety of challenges, ordering where challenge occurs the exhibit of the section of the statement used for contesting the testimony.[180] While the Code sets out an examination and cross-examination process by the parties similar to that found in common law jurisdictions, in practice it is played out quite differently in that witnesses answer questions in a long-winded manner, giving a narrative of events rather than the closely controlled answers which would be the norm in a common law style examination. The possibility for hearsay evidence being part of their testimony is thereby increased. One trial judge explained to me the purpose of cross-examination as follows:

> *JT*: To make the witness weep! The defence tries to break the prosecution witness and the prosecutor tries to break the defence witness, and I try to understand which is the truth. The judge has the task to ensure that all the questions asked are relevant, which is very important. The prosecutor may ask the judge to intervene if he feels the defence lawyer is asking questions that are not relevant, but also the judge may ask 'why are you asking these questions' without a request from the prosecutor.

175. Article 196, CPP.
176. Article 198, CPP.
177. Article 194, CPP; Article 187, CPP, defines 'objects of proof' as facts that refer to the charge, criminal liability and determination of sentence and security measures.
178. Cass. pen. 7/10/2008, no. 38221.
179. Article 499.2, CPP.
180. Article 499.6, CPP.

I recounted to them how a judge had continually stopped the defence lawyer asking questions in a cross-examination I had observed during a hearing in the court when she considered the witness had already sufficiently answered the question.

> *JT*: You cannot allow the questions if the witness has already answered the question before. He could not ask the same question disguised in a different way, it is up to the judge to stop him.

In addition to cross-examination, the Code affords another 'means of proof': the possibility of conducting a *confronto*. This provides a device for scrutiny of witnesses' testimony where the witnesses have already testified in the course of proceedings but there is a contradiction between them with regard to important facts or circumstances given by each witness.[181] A prerequisite is that they have each already testified or have undergone questioning (*interrogatorio*) in a pre-trial hearing or during the trial itself.[182] Both witnesses are brought face to face in the court and each is questioned about the disputed fact by the judge and about the testimony given by the other witness on the point. The *confronto* is not a mandatory procedure[183] and is 'in substance a continuation of an examination or interrogation which has already taken place'.[184] In the homicide trial, technical evidence relating to the wounds inflicted had been given at the earlier hearings as well as evidence of intercepted calls and evidence from the surviving members of the group. At the hearing I attended, evidence was given by a technical expert (technical consultant) on behalf of the defence, who was questioned by the defence lawyer. That evidence was in conflict with the evidence given at an earlier hearing by the prosecution expert (technical consultant).

Because there was a conflict between the experts, a *confronto* was held, at the instigation of the president of the court, between both expert witnesses, neither of whom would have been privy to the other's testimony or reports.[185] The expert who had just been examined was seated in a chair facing a chair where the opposing expert sat. The latter gave his evidence of what he had found, evidence he had already given at an earlier hearing in the trial. He gave a summary of the findings in relation to the disputed technical evidence, giving his account in narrative form, occasionally interrupted by the prosecutor to clarify an issue or occasionally by the judge, again for clarification purposes. The expert for the defence was then given an opportunity to contradict what

181. Article 211, CPP (contained in Book 3, CPP, in the section 'means of proof').
182. For a *confronto* during a pre-trial hearing see Article 392(e); Cuomo and Scioli, *L'incidente probatorio* (note 82) 30.
183. Cass. pen. 17/6/2002 (ud.16/5/2002).
184. Cass. pen. 26/6/1997, no. 6282.
185. A *confronto* may be instigated by the judges or by the parties on application to the judge.

the prosecution expert had said and each became enmeshed in an argument, really just holding their respective positions for a short time, and were throughout questioned by each of the lawyers. The judge took a position more of observation than of intervention, and at the end had a brief discussion with the two lay assessors who sat beside him on the bench. He then stated he would seek a court-appointed expert to appear at a later hearing.

While cross-examination has been described as 'the greatest legal engine ever invented for the discovery of the truth',[186] the *confronto* adds a further carriage. Recalling that witnesses in an Italian trial do not hear what other witnesses have said, when confronted with an alternative view of the fact in dispute, face to face with the person giving the contradictory testimony, a witness might be more inclined to entertain doubts about their original version under the questioning and watchful eye of the judge, unless they are very certain of their position. However, the *confronto* is a device that is used quite rarely during the trial; it is mostly employed where the witnesses who are giving contradictory testimony are the parties' experts (technical consultants).[187]

6.4.6 Questioning by the trial judge

Any impression of being present at an adversarial common law style trial is soon weakened once the judge invokes the power to intervene in the examination of witnesses. Judges appeared to interrupt the questioning quite considerably in both examination and cross-examination of witnesses, often taking over the questioning themselves on particular points after they had been initially raised by either party. One defence lawyer told me that judges tend to intervene 'hugely', pointing out that in many instances the judge wants to get through the trial as quickly as possible, so great is their workload and ever present backlog of cases.[188] They want to be able to get sufficient evidence to reach a decision without wasting time with questions that they do not need answered in order to reach their decision.

Nor does the invocation of the power to intervene in questioning depend on the age of the judge, that is to say on whether they have been accustomed to the practice under the old Code where they were in control of the proceedings and hence find the transition to the new Code difficult. It depends on the individual judge, even where they have had no operational experience under the former system.[189]

186. J. H. Wigmore, *Treatise on the Anglo-American System of Evidence in Trials at Common Law including the Statutes and Judicial Decisions of All Jurisdictions of the United States and Canada*, Vol. 3 (Little, Brown 1923) Book 1, Chapter xliv, para. 1367.

187. Interview with judge JT; *confronto* may be also used during the pre-trial stage, which would be frequent as between the accused and witnesses.

188. Similar frequent intervention by the trial judge was found by Freccero, 'An Introduction to the New Italian Criminal Procedure' (1993–4) 21 (3) *Am. J. Crim. L.* 345.

189. Interview with defence lawyer.

6.4.7 Evidence from the accused

As in Ireland, it is open to the accused to decide whether or not to give evidence; however, if he chooses to do so, unlike the position in Ireland but similar to that in France, no oath is taken by the accused. In the homicide trial, the accused opted to give evidence. During this part of the hearing, the defence lawyer remained seated and the president of the court reminded the accused that he had a right to silence and did not have to say anything; the accused responded that he wanted to tell what happened and the president then asked him to give his account. The account given by the accused was that the event related to a prior drug deal with a group of men, one of whom was the deceased and all Albanian nationals, and that the group were demanding payment for drugs the accused had been given to sell on their behalf. He recounted how he had hidden the money but it had later 'disappeared', so he had no payment to give to the group; fearing for trouble he had gone to a prearranged meeting with the group armed with a knife – he also spoke of phone calls that one of the Albanians had made to him to arrange this meeting.

The prosecutor interrupted the accused saying his account was inconsistent with an earlier statement he had made to the prosecutor but the judge stopped the prosecutor:

> *J*: I want his version and not just that which the prosecution want me to hear. I want to hear from him first and then you can go through any inconsistencies.
> (*Then, turning to accused, in a benevolent tone he said:*)
> Now, tell us all about what happened.

The accused then gave a full uninterrupted account setting out how he had been introduced to the deceased by a drugs contact and how he had managed to lose all the takings from the drugs run. The account by the accused was in the nature of a conversation between the judge and the accused, with the judge not questioning him as such but interrupting only where he was trying to be clear about what the accused had said to clarify that he had understood him correctly. The prosecutor tried to intervene twice more, but the judge curtly responded on both occasions:

> *J*: No! The accused is giving me an account of his version, and then you will be able to cross-examine, line by line if you wish, but for now …

He then invited the accused to resume.

Two police officers who had been in charge of the investigation were seated beside the prosecutor. Throughout the time that the accused was giving his account, wherever there was an inconsistency with what had been stated in the interrogations during the investigation, one of these officers very visibly by her demeanour – shaking her head in disagreement – would indicate all these inconsistencies to the prosecutor by pointing them out and then marking with a highlighter on the statement, or searching for another report from the high stack of box files which contained all the pre-trial investigation records. Such behaviour, combined with the physical presence of the earlier file in the courtroom by dint of the prominent box files, may have the subliminal effect of bringing the police investigation into play and to some extent indicates that the role of the pre-trial documented investigation continues to make its presence felt despite the commitment to adversarial oral trial.

When the accused had finished giving his account he was asked some specific questions by the judge about the phone calls the accused had received from the deceased. At that point the judge told the prosecutor that he could now cross-examine the accused. The prosecutor responded that he would prefer to wait until the co-accused in the case had given his account before going into cross-examination. The hearing was then adjourned to a date one month later.

6.4.8 Power of trial judge to seek further evidence

Another feature of the Italian system that sits uneasily with the common law understanding of the burden of proof is the power given to the judge to seek further evidence at the close of the presentation of evidence by the parties.[190] Article 507 provides that at the end of the presentation of evidence, the judge may, if it is absolutely necessary, order that further evidence be taken, including in relation to the evidence already contained in the trial dossier. The Supreme Court, later endorsed by the Constitutional Court, has interpreted Article 507 to mean that the judge could introduce evidence at any point even where the parties had tendered no evidence or before the presentation of evidence requested by the parties, despite the apparent wording of the provision that the judge could introduce evidence *after* both parties had completed their presentation of evidence.[191]

Instead, it has been interpreted to indicate that the judge can call for more evidence, not just at the close of the parties' presentation of evidence, but even before the time for presentation of evidence in the trial has transpired.[192] The Constitutional Court has held that just because the Code places the primary burden on the parties to call witnesses and proffer evidence, this does

190. Such powers are not unknown to common law, but it has been found in trials presided over by a single judge sitting without a jury under the Diplock regime in Northern Ireland that, despite the availability of this power, intervention by the judge was more often in the form of questions to clarify points: J. Jackson and S. Doran, *Judge Without Jury: Diplock Trials in the Adversary System* (Clarendon 1995) 179–84.
191. Cass. pen. 21/11/1992, no. 11227.
192. Cass. pen. 23/11/2000, no. 12081.

not preclude the trial judge from introducing other evidence 'if it is necessary for a just decision in the case'.[193]

The type of additional evidence that may be sought by the judge is not set out in the Code. It could be a request to hear additional witnesses on a particular issue, but the more common type of additional evidence sought by the judge is expert evidence. Article 225 provides for the nomination of experts by the parties, referred to as 'technical consultants'; however, the judge may nominate his own expert:[194]

> *JB1*: Where there are experts for both sides the judge is faced with the conclusions of the different experts; he may nominate his own expert to verify if one or the other is correct – it depends a lot on the type of expert evidence at issue. The judge's expert must give reasons why he favours one or the other. But often the judge will say, 'this expert is right as opposed to that expert' – because the judge is the expert of the experts!

Another type of additional evidence that may be called for by the trial judge is a 'judicial experiment' that may be used to determine if a fact could have occurred in a particular way. This may be achieved through 'a re-enactment of the fact as it is claimed to have occurred to establish whether it was possible for it to occur in the manner alleged'.[195] The judge may nominate an expert to carry out the re-enactment.[196]

The power of ordering new evidence to be taken can be exercised by the trial judge when there has been no previous collection of the specific evidence or where the parties could have asked for such evidence to be received but did not ask for it. At the same time, the judge cannot look for more evidence simply to support his own autonomous theory about the case.[197] The power of the judge to seek more evidence has been described as a supplementary power to guard against negligence and inertia on the part of the parties,[198] but while the Code had clearly envisaged the provision as auxiliary to the parties' powers, it has been noted that it has become 'widespread and autonomous'.[199]

Pizzi and Montagna suggest that the Constitutional Court may have felt pressure to give the trial judge broader power to call witnesses than would be the case in common law trials because under the civil law tradition the trial judge has always felt responsible for the accuracy of trial verdicts and 'with a strong civil law heritage, it is harder for judges in Italy to adopt a more limited

193. Pizzi and Montagna (note 119) 448.
194. Article 221, CPP.
195. Article 218, CPP.
196. Article 219, CPP.
197. Cass. pen. 18/12/2006, no. 41281.
198. Cass. pen. 9/8/2001, no. 31085.
199. Panzavolta (note 94) 601.

role'.[200] Thus if the trial judge felt the prosecutor had been negligent in not calling a witness, or that evidence that might support the defence had not been presented, the trial judge would feel compelled to seek it, because 'the trial judge in Italy has always been viewed as having a paternalistic obligation to protect the defendant'.[201] One judge suggested it is in part as a result of the career paths open to prosecutors:

> *JT*: I was a prosecutor at the beginning of my career for four years; after I was a judge of the preliminary hearing – a GUP for 14 years. Now I am a trial judge since four years ago. We can change career, but before it was very easy to change from prosecutor to judge, and now they are trying to completely separate the careers, but not yet. There are some difficulties now already though, as if you change career you also have to change districts – a person from Turin, for example, would need to move to Milan or Genoa. They are afraid that the judge and public prosecutor are too close, and that's not true, especially in a big court; I don't know all the prosecutors here because there are so many of them, there are at least 60 I think here. They [the government] don't trust us!
>
> As I have been a prosecutor before being a judge, for me it is an enhancement to have been both, because I know how to interrogate an accused or a witness since I have a lot of experience of doing that as a prosecutor. And as a judge, I know what proof I need to make out a case, so if there is some gap in the inquiry I can find it, and with my powers I can make the public prosecutor bring more evidence. For me that is very important. Of course it may be abused also. There are judges and prosecutors who might abuse their collegial position, but that view I think is exaggerated.

There was unanimous agreement among practitioners I interviewed that the Code places the burden of proof on the public prosecutor. This in their view is not in conflict with the power given to the judge under Article 507. This is difficult for an observer with the common law understanding of the burden of proof to come to terms with. On that understanding, if there are weaknesses in the prosecution case, the jury must come to their verdict only on the evidence that has been presented to them, they cannot look for more. If there are gaps in the prosecution case, which may arise because the prosecution failed to present a piece of evidence or where their evidence was ruled inadmissible, this may prove favourable to the defence since the jury may not be able to reach a decision beyond reasonable doubt due to the weakness in the prosecution case. Furthermore, under the common law system, after all the evidence has been presented by the prosecutor the defence may submit that

200. Pizzi and Montagna (note 119) 448.
201. Ibid., 449.

the prosecutor has not made out a case on which a jury could reasonably make a finding of guilt and ask the trial judge to direct the jury to return a verdict of not guilty. One judge explained it to me thus:

> *JB2*: Yes, the prosecutor bears the burden of proof, but we do not say that the burden of proof is entirely resting on the prosecutor. It is possible to have some intervention by the judge – in terms of the judge asking for more evidence. There are those who hold the view that if the prosecutor has failed to bring the evidence that should be the end of it. The Code foresees the role of the judge in calling for more evidence as one of assistance, as auxiliary in the event that the prosecutor has failed to bring forward evidence. It is true that this provision has been interpreted very broadly. Usually the intervention should be because the case is incomplete, for example the public prosecutor has failed to bring forward some evidence; intervention by the judge may also be for the benefit of the defence; the judge will not leave the case entirely in the hands of the parties. Naturally there are cases where the judge takes all the proof – questioning the witnesses etc. That is not strictly speaking their role.

The fact that the judge can call for more evidence has given rise to the belief by some Italian commentators that the judge has removed the burden of proof from the prosecution:

> The broad interpretation of what was designed to be an exceptional power can in theory be attributed to the need to search for the truth. In reality, however, it has the effect of counter-balancing weaknesses in the prosecution case and reversing the onus on it to prove its case.[202]

It has been suggested that:

> When the judge introduces evidence he is transformed into a researcher and loses his impartiality and, moreover, the provision collides with the presumption of innocence and the related rule of placing the burden of proof on the prosecution … If the evidence is lacking to the extent that the judge cannot make a decision, he should acquit the accused – the prosecution has simply failed to meet its burden. When a judge instead searches for evidence, it demonstrates his belief that the defendant is guilty.[203]

202. L. Marafioti, 'Italian Criminal Procedure: A System Caught Between Two Traditions', in J. Jackson, M. Langer and P. Tillers (eds), *Crime, Procedure and Evidence in a Comparative and International Context: Essays in Honour of Prof. Mirjan Damaška* (Hart 2008) 93.
203. Panzavolta (note 94) 605.

However, this does not take account of the fact that the judge can seek further evidence from both parties, prosecution *and* defence. Does the judge seeking more proof thereby loose his impartiality? If a referee in a game asks the linesman for his perspective of an alleged foul or seeks a video replay, he is seeking more evidence that the foul indeed occurred and was committed by a player of one or other team, but he still continues to be the referee and will decide, on the basis of the further evidence, whether to award the penalty to the one side or the other. But since he could award the penalty to either side, depending on the further evidence supplied, can he thereby be said to have lost his impartiality? Is it not the case that he is simply trying to ensure that his decision will be based on the most accurate picture of the event?

The same could be said of the Italian judge. If seeking further proof does not result in a loss of the impartiality of the judge, does that puncture the argument that he has removed the burden of proof from the prosecution? It certainly introduces a different dynamic to the burden of proof: in some sense it would appear to become more of a shared burden of contributing evidence to enable an accurate verdict to be obtained between the prosecution, the defence and the judge alike. This may be explained by the desire of the judge to obtain as much accuracy as possible since the judge is involved in producing the verdict, and the reluctance to break with traditional legal culture. Grande suggests that:

> Italian judges … feel personal responsibility for aiming at an accurate and just result; therefore they want authority over the fact-finding process … their sense of responsibility is at the same time enhanced and justified by the duty to give written reasons for their findings. Accordingly, not accustomed to a passive role, Italian judges broadly interpreted Article 507 in order to recapture their traditional role in the fact-finding process.[204]

One judge responded to this proposition as follows:

> *JB2*: The idea of a completely passive judge would be foreign to an Italian. We used to have an inquisitorial system with the figure of the judge being very dominant; now we have a system whereby the judge, according to the Constitution, is subject to the law, and therefore puts him in a position of dependence on the law; he must apply the law, and therefore he is not in a position of total indifference to the acts in the trial.

Another judge described it thus:

> *JB1*: Yes. The prosecution must prove the case. That is without a doubt. It is not for the judge to prove the case. However, the judge may require

204. Grande (note 2) 251.

> other proof to be brought into the trial to reach a decision, even if the prosecution or the defence have not asked that the proof be taken – the judge has the power to seek further proof, autonomously. The judge has the power to intervene. The system in Italy is perhaps a little different from the Anglo-Saxon system; the judge, to understand the issue, to verify it, to ascertain the facts, may say 'I also need this proof, that you [the parties] have not brought me'. Therefore we would describe the function of the judge as this: the judge in Italy is not the conductor of the orchestra, he also plays the music a little himself; that is a fact of our system, he must be a bit active.

Regardless of how much of the music he plays, this does not take away from the fact that in official discourse at least, the burden of proving the accusation rests on the prosecution. Even if additional evidence has been produced at the behest of the judge, it is the case put forward by the prosecution that must be proved to a standard of beyond all reasonable doubt.[205] The burden is not on the defence to disprove. Even so, the judge's power to call for more evidence where he feels the evidence presented by the prosecutor is lacking means that the Italian decider of fact may have more evidence on which to base their decision than their Irish counterparts. The Irish fact-finder must decide whether the prosecution has discharged his burden of proving the accusation on the basis of evidence presented to them. If there is insufficient evidence to dispel all reasonable doubt, they cannot ask for more and will have to resolve any doubts arising because of a shortfall in the evidence in favour of the accused.

Grande has described the burden of proof in Italy as being something more akin to an idea of shared burdens, contrasting the approaches of the Italian system to the common law system by drawing an analogy with 'rumba' dancing on the one hand as opposed to 'tango' dancing on the other. The adversarial system can be associated with the idea of a 'tango justice'; the non-adversary one with that of a 'rumba justice'. 'Tango' can be performed by two dancers and only by those two, acting together in the venture of establishing the adversarial truth. 'Rumba', on the contrary, is performed by a variable number of dancers occasionally alone and occasionally in groups … a genuinely communal performance in the collective search of an objective truth. [206]

The judges had mixed ideas about the nature of the criminal trial in Italy:

> *JB2*: In Italy we see our system as accusatorial, and not adversarial. By adversarial I mean a process that puts everything in the hands of the

205. Article 533, CPP: *al di la di ogni ragionevole dubbiò.*
206. E. Grande, 'Dances of Criminal Justice: Thoughts on Systemic Differences and the Search for the Truth', in Jackson *et al.* (note 202) 145, 155.

parties, like the Anglo-Saxon method; but our system is different from that because we allow the judge to intervene. We do not see the trial as a contest between two sides, the idea of contest is more Anglo-Saxon; we speak of a *confronto*, and in this confrontation, the judge is an arbiter, who can intervene to see if something is correct, or he can seek further information or clarification. Therefore he is an active figure who nonetheless can vie between the parties. It is not easy for a judge to know the confines of what he may do; there is a grey area around the idea of a judge calling proof. While the Code provides that he must seek the proof where it is 'absolutely necessary', what does that mean? It is a torment for the judge!

JB1: Yes the trial is a contest between the two parties, but the trial judge may also decide things regardless of what the parties have done. We have the possibility to intervene. The judge is on the side of both parties.

6.4.9 Use of evidence from the prosecutor's file through the 'readings' system

Information contained in the prosecution's file may side step the principle of orally presented testimony by means of the system of 'readings' and thereby becomes evidence that may be relied upon to reach a verdict. The Code provides that the judge, on the request of a party, may order that the acts done by the police, prosecutor or in the preliminary hearing be read where, due to unforeseeable facts, they are impossible to repeat.[207] In this way, the evidence from the prosecutor's file is transferred to the judge's file thereby becoming fully usable as evidence for the decision.[208] Statements made by the defendant during the preliminary inquiries, at the preliminary hearing or during an *incidente probatorio* may be 'read', i.e. transferred to the trial judge file, where the accused refuses to submit to examination at trial.[209] Since spontaneous statements made to the police cannot be used except to contest testimony given at trial, they cannot form part of the readings.[210]

6.5 Evaluation of evidence and judgment

Once all the evidence in the case has been heard, and each piece of evidence has moved from the prosecutor's file, the defence file and through the 'readings' to the trial file, the trial reaches its final stage. Following closing speeches by the prosecution, defence and the *parte civile*, the judge and assessors retire to consider their judgment on the basis of all that is contained in the trial file.

207. Article 512, CPP.
208. Article 515, CPP.
209. Article 513, CPP.
210. Cass. pen. 11/3/2004, no. 11526.

One of the judges explained the approach to the evaluation of evidence as follows:

> *JB2*: Certain proof has different ways of being approached to other means of proof; for example, a statement made by a co-accused is not the same as a statement made by another witness; however, one can still use it in reaching judgment. It must be evaluated in a way that looks to both the subject matter of what the declarant has said and whether there are other elements in the trial that confirms what he has said. This is a rule about judging but it refers, not to the acquisition of proof nor the means of proof, but the next part, the pronouncement of the verdict – this proof can be used by the judge for reaching a verdict but only in the way permitted by the law.

While the Italian system contains the principle of *libero convincimento del giudice* – free evaluation of evidence – this should be understood in contradistinction to the old idea of legal proof where a certain quantity of evidence was required before a decision of guilt could be reached. Despite the free evaluation principle, the judge is nonetheless constrained by underlying corroboration requirements in the Code.[211] The Supreme Court has held:

> In evaluating the evidence the judge must take into consideration each single fact and all of them together, not in a fragmented and non-contextual manner.[212]

In sharp contrast to the system in Ireland and France, the judge must give written reasons for the judgment and the criteria adopted in reaching the decision.[213] A typical reasoned judgment will commence with a statement of the facts, the charges against the accused, the closing request of the prosecution seeking a particular sentence to be imposed, the requests of the civil parties for the damages sought, and the request of the defence lawyer (either seeking acquittal or, if appropriate, a lenient sentence). This document may be extremely lengthy and is effectively a résumé of the evidence given at the trial, with the emphasis on the evidence given by the witnesses that the court finds persuasive.[214]

211. Article 192.2, CPP
212. Cass. pen. 5/9/1996, no. 8314.
213. Article 192, CPP.
214. An example of reasoned decision is Knox; the reasoned decision runs to 427 pages, see (in Italian): <http://www.injusticeinperugia.org/Massei_Report.pdf>. The convictions were overturned on appeal one year later, by which time both accused had been imprisoned for nearly four years. The conviction was reinstated by *Corte d'assise d'appello di Firenze* on 30/1/2014.

The judgment of guilt or innocence will be pronounced as soon as the adjudicating panel of judges and assessors have reached their decision and the sentence will be there and then pronounced. The reasoned document must be produced normally within 15 days of the sentence being pronounced, but in cases of complexity or those involving numerous charges, an outer limit of 90 days is permitted.[215] One of the judges was to some extent sceptical about the value of reasoned judgments commented:

> *JB2*: The police and the accused are not on the same level. If the witness is a member of the police – it is not written down in the Code, but in practice he is considered more trustworthy than another witness who is not a member of the police; I am not saying that this is right, I am saying that in fact, the reasoning of the judge will often be: this is a police officer; it is his duty to find out what happened. Why should he lie to me? Therefore, the judge's way of reasoning makes a police witness more credible than other witnesses. This is very dangerous, because the police may have made errors; a good judge should be able to spot any signs that might point to something amiss about the statement.
>
> Where statements made during the investigation are only available for deciding the credibility of a witness it is true that the judge will learn of the facts contained in the statement, but he cannot base his reasons for decision upon these facts. But it would be the same even if the judge had not seen any statements but read reports in the media pertaining to the case; he must forget all that, as in he must not write it down in his reasoned judgment! But it is, in fact, never a problem what the judge believes personally. Provided he does not write it, there is nothing to stop a judge from following his own belief, because he simply must make his reasoned decision logical and coherent; more often than not, a judge's reasons for decisions are 'I preferred this evidence', 'I preferred this witness account', etc. There are some critics who say that the moment a judge has looked at the file he has reached a decision and spends the rest of the trial trying to justify it!

6.5.1 Search for truth

As noted above, commentators have highlighted the difficulties posed by the attempt to embed 'adversarial principles' into the Italian system.[216] The early decisions of the Constitutional Court limiting the interpretation of the reforms have been explained as indicative of a malaise towards the adversarial principles because the latter were considered to interfere with the importance of discovering the truth at trial. The centrality of truth in the process has also

215. Article 544, CPP.
216. See sections 6.3.1 and 6.3.2 above.

been considered one of the reasons for the active role that the judge plays in the trial, both in questioning witnesses and the accused and in seeking further evidence. I asked the judges whether, since the 'due process' reforms have become established, the Italian trial process is now more concerned with the idea of a fair trial than with the search for the truth:

> *JB2*: I do not think these are two concepts in conflict with each other; the truth that is sought in the trial is the truth of what happened, and that truth must be sought fairly. Through fairness, loyalty to the process, loyalty to the proper conduct of the case, we can arrive at a truth, which is the truth of the trial. If, to arrive at a truth you twist the rules, you will arrive at a truth, but it is no longer the truth of the process, which brings you into a debate about which truth you are seeking, the historical truth, the truth of the trial? I can say that our system is seeking the truth, but in a fair manner.
>
> *JB1*: We have a process that looks for the truth in a fair manner. Both aspects are needed. Because a trial that is only 'fair' can be a bit artificial, I mean, too much of a game where the rules are the most important thing. However, it cannot provide the truth about the facts. We need to temper fairness with truth.
>
> I need to understand the truth, and the truth does not reveal itself only through compliance with the law. I must be able to evaluate the evidence even if it has not been obtained legitimately, so unless it has been obtained violently in the example I gave earlier, I must evaluate it.
>
> *JT*: The trial in Italy is based on procedural fairness I think, not on a search for truth. We have trials now for something that may have happened eight years ago. The witness does not remember what happened eight years ago, so if I can't use the report of what he said eight years ago, and the witness when giving evidence orally at trial, as he is obliged to do, doesn't remember anything, well, you can lose a lot of evidence, and obviously truth, because of that.

6.6 Conclusion

The foregoing discussion of the procedures for gathering and presentation of evidence in Italy reveals a criminal process that, at least from my perspective as an observer from the common law, could not be said to fall squarely within the type of investigation and trial process that would be typical of a common law adversarial model.

A prominent feature of the investigation stage in Italy is the degree to which the powers of the police have been reined in by the new Code in relation to questioning suspects, the subsequent limited use at trial that may be made of that information and the concomitant increased power given to the prosecutor. Given the fact that the latter is a member of the 'judicial authority', the majority of coercive activities may be carried out at his behest. In addition, the fact of being a judicial figure gives rise to the assumption that his investigation will be conducted impartially, although, as has been suggested by commentators, theory does not necessarily translate into reality.

While the prosecutor is a powerful figure in the pre-trial stage, some degree of oversight is allocated to the pre-trial judges, the GIP and the GUP, although the value of this oversight, at least in relation to the decision-making function of the latter in sending forward the case for trial, has been criticised by commentators.

In terms of defence rights, suspects in Italy are given a broad right of access to a lawyer at all stages of the process, and unlike the position in Ireland and France, the right to counsel cannot be waived. As a general rule, a lawyer must always be present during the questioning of suspects, whether by police or prosecutor, and in addition a suspect is to some extent informed of the information in the hands of the authorities before being questioned by the prosecutor.

Similar to the position in France and unlike that in Ireland, a suspect is available as a source of information throughout the preliminary investigation and may be confronted with the evidence against him and asked to respond to it. While suspects and accused enjoy a right to silence, its value is somewhat illusory in that such silence will be noted where it has been exercised during the preliminary hearing, and as far as using statements of the accused, while there is a general prohibition on using as evidence statements made 'in the course of proceedings', prior statements of an accused made to the prosecutor may be substantively used as evidence if the accused fails to appear or refuses to be examined at trial. It would appear therefore that it would generally be in the accused's interest to give an account at trial since that account must be the one used as evidence in keeping with the principle of orality and not the prior statement to the prosecutor. However, that renders any right to silence of the accused at trial largely illusory. In addition since the report of the preliminary hearing is inserted into the trial file and may therefore be used as evidence, the exercise of a right to silence at that stage of proceedings, if such has occurred, will also be apparent to the trial court thereby increasing the danger that adverse inferences may be drawn.

It has been seen that while Italy has included a species of a law of evidence in the new Code, it is by and large not committed to the idea of excluding evidence, at least from a common law understanding of such practice. Italy's approach to the issue is to judge whether information may be used for reaching a verdict, a decision that is taken after the information has been presented, so there is no similar notion to the Irish practice of excluding evidence with the result that it never reaches the trier of fact. This may be explained on the basis that the trial structure in Italy is not bifurcated like the Irish trial: trial and sentence are adjudicated by a single panel in a single proceeding. To a limited extent, courts in Italy will 'exclude' certain types of information gathered during the preliminary investigation, including invalid intercept evidence, statements made in the absence of a lawyer and interrogations of a person in detention that have not been electronically recorded.

Nonetheless, since objections to this evidence are made before the entire adjudicating panel of judges and jurors, the information reaches their minds, even if they cannot use it in their decision. In relation to evidence discovered on foot of a search where the search has been unlawful, the Italian courts approach the matter by responding to the unlawful activity of the police through use of civil or criminal sanction, but nonetheless accept the fruits of the unlawful search as evidence that may be used to reach a verdict.

Italy's approach to a hearsay rule against out-of-court statements is now equally, or possibly more, exclusionary than that in Ireland since the recent reform in the latter jurisdiction. Italy takes a similar approach to the common law doctrine of hostile witness, in so far as a prior statement may be used for credibility purposes alone; however, where a witness recants or offers a different account, the position is similar to Ireland in that the statement may be used in full. Nevertheless, although adopting a species of hearsay rule, Italian evidence law allows for certain documents to be usable as evidence without the necessity of witnesses to be examined orally. In this regard, it has not totally abandoned its previous written procedure practice. The movement of evidence from the prosecutor's file to the trial file through the readings system also provides a means of avoiding the principle of orally presented testimony.

As far as evidence of character is concerned, it has been seen that documents relating to the previous convictions of the accused are available at the outset to the trial court including the jury; however, it has also been highlighted that any such information may not be used other than in considering sentence. The trial court will also be in no doubt as to the status of the accused as a detainee simply by the positioning of the accused in the courtroom and by reason of the clear reference in the sending forward for trial document that the accused is a 'guest of the nation'. However, unlike the jurisdictions of Ireland and France, the evidence relied on by the trial court is, at least in theory, revealed through the mandatory publication of the reasons for the decision. As such, evidence of bad character may never be substantively used as evidence against the accused, but the requirement of reasoned decisions does not necessarily diminish any prejudice that may arise in the minds of the judges and jurors as a result of access to such information.

6.6.1 Adversarial trial?

The analysis of the Italian criminal trial has reflected, from my perspective as an observer of criminal trials in a common law adversarial jurisdiction, on the degree to which the Italian trial may be considered to be likewise adversarial. It has been shown that, similar to the system in France, the criminal trial runs as a singular structure (notwithstanding the sporadic nature of the hearings) in which the determination of guilt and determination of sentence are decided as part of the one procedure. Again similar to France, it has been seen that the role of the 'jury' is different to its common law counterpart in that the verdict is reached by the judges and jurors together, who also decide on the sentence and have access to the full trial dossier.

To a limited degree there is some resemblance to the Irish style adversarial trial, for example the idea that witnesses may be examined and cross-examined by the prosecution and defence sides. However, the very active role played by the trial judge, the manner in which witnesses present their testimony in narrative form and the practice of the defence side giving their alternative 'theory' at the outset of the trial all militate against a finding that the Italian trial could be described as 'adversarial' within the meaning given to that term by the common law tradition. Firstly, there are not just two sides to a case; there may also be a third party, the *parte civile.* At the terrorist trial no *parte civile* was constituted; in the homicide trial, the *parte civile* lawyer was present but the part played by this lawyer in the trial appeared to me to be quite subdued and much less visible than her counterparts in France. Although always given the opportunity to put questions to the witnesses, she rarely took up the invitation to do so.[217] The manner of examination and cross-examination of witnesses by the parties allowing scope to witnesses to narrate their version of events and the practice of the *confronto* also serve to weaken any sense of being present at an adversarial trial.

The trial becomes less and less familiar as a common law model the more the trial judge intervenes by questioning witnesses himself. Crucially, the idea of an adversarial trial disappears out of view when the power of the judge to seek further evidence is considered, a power that is not limited to the trial judge but also extends to the judge in the preliminary hearing (the GUP). While commentators suggest that seeking further evidence by the judge affects his impartiality, I have suggested that since the judge may do so to benefit both prosecution and defence sides, this may not necessarily be the case. The idea of the burden of proof resting on the prosecution nonetheless becomes skewed, and Grande's idea of a common 'rumba' enterprise in searching for truth becomes quite apparent.

Nonetheless, even if it cannot be said that the trial is 'adversarial', there is apparent throughout the Italian criminal process the idea of proceedings that are *contradittorio.* The suspect is given the opportunity throughout the process, through the *incidente probatorio* procedure, the *confronto* (whether held during the preliminary investigation or at trial) and during the trial itself, to contradict the witnesses and evidence against him.

It has been suggested by commentators that truth-seeking is the paramount concern of the Italian criminal process. While two of the judges viewed the Italian process as equally concerned with truth and fairness, the third judge took the opposite view; nonetheless, her views appeared more related to

217. Though it must be said that I did not have the opportunity to observe a final stage of a trial to hear closing speeches; it may be that the lawyer takes on a similarly persuasive role towards the jury akin to that which I observed in trials in France.

the idea that truth is lost due to the delays inherent in a system that insists on all accused persons being tried in a procedural context where the evidence may be tested, rather than to any ideas of truth being lost due to evidence being excluded. As far as the latter is concerned, the approach of the Italian courts to admitting evidence even where found in breach of procedure appears to point to truth-seeking as being paramount.

In addition, the fact that the system has not taken a comparable path to the common law method of exclusion, a method that conceals inadmissible evidence from the triers of fact, but rather has opted for a system that *reveals* all the information so that it may be examined by the triers of fact to see whether they may *use* it, may also be explained in terms of the priority given to truth-seeking in the process. Even if they may not ultimately use the information to justify their verdict, they are at least aware of the full picture unlike their Irish counterparts who must reach a verdict without knowing the entire story, a position that would appear anathema to the Italian legal culture. The involvement of judges in questioning witnesses, appointing their own expert witnesses and seeking more evidence where required also points to truth-seeking as, if not the overriding interest, one that is just as central to the process as fairness.

7 Prospects for realising a mutual admissibility system in light of the differences revealed

7.1 Introduction

This book set out to explore through the case studies of Ireland, France and Italy whether the EU systems originating from the two broad legal traditions are too diverse and irreconcilable to achieve the EU aspiration for a mutual admissibility of evidence principle. This chapter aims to draw together the comparative strands examined through each of the case studies so as to assess the prospects for realising that aspiration. Following a brief résumé of the theoretical approaches drawn upon in this work, the first part of this chapter will review such differences as have been revealed relating to evidence-gathering at the investigative stage, to the rights afforded to suspects at that stage, to the rules of evidence and to the trial structure pertaining to the three jurisdictions. The second part will then attempt to synthesise the differences so as to obtain a better insight into the question of whether the differences posed by two distinct procedural arrangements relating to inadmissibility of evidence present the greatest obstacle to the attainment of a mutual admissibility principle.

PART I

7.2 Differences

7.2.1 Theoretical considerations

Various theoretical approaches were advanced in Chapter 2 for the comparative analysis of the criminal procedural systems. The historical approach attempted to highlight how practices became embedded over the centuries resulting in the establishment of two predominant legal cultures and how, despite undergoing degrees of cross-fertilisation and degrees of convergence, differences persisted, most notably in the area of the approach to proof, with one system moving towards strict evidentiary rules while the other eschewed any rigid system of proof.

The inquisitorial/accusatorial dichotomy, despite the terminological confusion surrounding the latter, remains useful to highlight the way in which the investigation stage of the procedure became such a decisive part of the French criminal process, with the trial functioning as more a formal validation of the pre-trial findings, while the common law system adhered to the accusatorial system where the emphasis lay on the oral public trial as the principal procedural event. These tendencies are still noticeable today in that the investigation stage of the procedure in France continues to be viewed as a vital part of the process that exerts a strong influence on the subsequent trial, while the Irish system continues to use the trial as the centrepiece of the process. Italy falls somewhere in between.

Damaška's hierarchical and coordinate models were outlined because of their value in identifying how the former are more suited to policy implementation than the latter, given that the mutual admissibility principle is clearly a policy-driven proposal. Most reliance was placed throughout this work on the adversarial/non-adversarial theoretical models as the tool for analysis, with the addition of what I argued to be more reflective of continental practice, the model of *procédure contradictoire.*

7.2.2 Differences in pre-trial investigation procedure

The pre-trial investigation has been seen to be quite distinct in each of the three jurisdictions. Ireland assigns complete control of the investigation to the police who operate without any direction from superiors; while the police need judicial authorisation to undertake certain coercive activities, it is the police who make the decision to conduct that activity in the first place, and once authorised, conduct that activity unsupervised and in the absence of independent witnesses.

By contrast, while suspects in France may also find themselves subject to coercive activity by the police, for which the police in many instances do not need prior authorisation and may undertake on their own initiative, the police are nonetheless subject to strict hierarchical control. Errant activity by a police officer may be sanctioned by the court through the imposition of disciplinary measures, which in turn will have an impact not only on the individual officer's career but also on the credibility of any evidence such officer produces to a judge in future cases. In sharp contrast to Ireland, the police investigation in France is conducted under the supervision of those higher up the hierarchical ladder, the prosecutor in the majority of cases and the *juge d'instruction* in the minority. Nonetheless, it has been seen that the supervision by the prosecutor tends to be one that for the most part delegates the investigative activity to the police, so that in reality suspects in France in the majority of cases will be predominantly questioned by the police just as they would be in Ireland.

However, where the investigation is supervised by the *juge d'instruction,* any likenesses with an Irish police investigation quickly dissolve. The police are more directly supervised; the task of questioning the suspect may not be delegated but must be carried out by the *juge* himself. The investigation phase in Italy is in turn distinct. Again sharp contrasts appear and it falls somewhere in between the position in Ireland and France. What is noteworthy in the Italian reform of their criminal procedure system is the apparent uneasy trust in the police; the police are restricted in their powers and this is especially true in relation to questioning. The prosecutor is more active in the whole investigation process and may not delegate formal questioning to the police; this must be conducted by the prosecutor in person.

While Italy may be contrasted to France in that it has abolished the idea of an investigating judge and passed on that role instead to the prosecutor, it has not abandoned the involvement of judges in the preliminary investigation phase. In one sense the judges in the pre-trial investigation are to a limited extent akin to their Irish counterpart of the District Court judge, in so far as they have the same role of authorising certain activities, making decisions about detention and bail, and making the decision to send forward for trial. However, they exercise a more extensive role than their Irish counterparts, in that they provide oversight of the investigation and play an active role in collecting evidence through the *incidente probatorio* procedure. There is nonetheless some similarity between the latter and the Irish procedure that permits the taking of evidence by deposition by a District Court judge.

Perhaps the most striking difference between the pre-trial phases of the three jurisdictions is the position of the suspect during the investigation. It has been seen that in Ireland the suspect is available as a source of information only during the short period of police custody, whereas in both France and Italy, the suspect may be questioned throughout the entire investigation phase. The availability of the suspect throughout the pre-trial investigation has a direct implication for the whole issue of receiving, presentation and challenge of evidence in the process. This point will be revisited below.

7.2.3 Differences in right of access to a lawyer afforded to suspects

As to access to a lawyer across the three jurisdictions, again differences are apparent. Ireland allows access before police questioning, but does not allow the presence of a lawyer in the interview room; France now provides access before police questioning *and* permits the lawyer to be present during the interview while Italy does not permit questioning in the absence of a lawyer, both in relation to that carried out by the police and the formal questioning by the prosecutor (*interrogatorio*). Nonetheless, the role of the lawyer during interrogation in France is constrained in that he cannot intervene during the interrogation and, similar to Ireland, has no right to consult the case file. The intervention of the lawyer in Italy is more extensive during interrogation in so far as he may make his objections known to the prosecutor, and unlike both France and Ireland, a suspect will be given some of the information in the hands of the authorities before being questioned by the prosecutor. Regardless of whether questioning of suspects is conducted solely by the police, by a prosecutor or by a *juge d'instruction*, the three jurisdictions now share in common the requirement that the questioning must be electronically recorded.

7.2.4 Differences in approach to rules of evidence

Although it is true that France and Italy have no separate and distinct 'law of evidence' in the common law sense, there is no doubt that French and Italian criminal procedure law contains evidence rules. Thus there are specific rules in both these jurisdictions relating to the collection of evidence, for example that searches of dwellings be effected in the presence of witnesses and generally in daytime hours, and rules relating to the questioning of suspects, together with broad guiding principles aimed at respecting the rights of individuals and the overall integrity of justice.

The major point of distinction between the common law system of evidence law and the continental system is that the former largely operates as an exclusionary mechanism that generally deprives the fact-finder from knowledge of facts deemed to be inadmissible, while the focus of the evidentiary systems of France and Italy for the most part tends to be directed at the use that may be made of particular pieces of evidence.

A slight degree of movement towards a common law exclusionary type stance is revealed from the case study of France: there are some, albeit rare instances where evidence is not revealed to the fact-finders in France, for example statements of suspects made in the absence of a lawyer in cases preceded by the *instruction* procedure. Since in those cases the statements are removed from the file they do not reach the presiding judges and jury at the trial so, just as in Ireland, the fact-finders are in the dark about the existence of that evidence.

Italy in principle follows some type of exclusionary notion in that it prohibits the use as evidence of statements made to the police in the absence of a lawyer. In general those statements may not be heard, and they do not move from the prosecutor's file to the judge's file and so cannot be seen by the fact-finders. However, the continental idea of evidence law being more related to 'rules of decision' rather than rules of exclusion in the common law sense was very evident in the Knox case.[1] There the adjudicators were fully aware of her statements made to the police because, while they were on the one hand 'unusable' to reach a verdict on the murder count, they were nonetheless fully usable for the separate calumny charge that was tried in the same proceedings.

Any need to shield the fact-finders from the potentially incriminating evidence contained in her statements is theoretically made unnecessary by the requirement that reasons for the decision be publicly stated, a sharp point of difference between Italy on the one hand and France and Ireland on the other.

1. See section 6.3.1.

However, a similarity does arise between this practice in Italy and the practice in the Irish Special Criminal Court of the court giving reasons for its verdict, and it proceeds from a similar basis that the reasoned judgment will provide a safeguard against judges relying on any inadmissible evidence that they have been privy to as a ground for their decision.

While there would appear to be a consensus across the three jurisdictions that statements made by a suspect in the absence of access to legal advice may not be used to found a conviction, the reaction of Member States to the blanket rule of inadmissibility proposed by the Commission for statements obtained in breach of their proposed right of access to a lawyer serves to highlight the resistance to an exclusionary method as practised by the common law (where the evidence is withheld from the fact-finder) by the continental States, who prefer the approach of making the evidence visible and leaving it to the judge to decide the value to be given to the statement.

The approach to using unlawfully obtained 'real' evidence by the three jurisdictions shows a very notable difference as between Ireland on the one hand compared with France and Italy on the other; it has been seen that Ireland's strict exclusionary stance towards unconstitutionally obtained evidence results in cogent evidence being completely hidden from the fact-finder, whereas in France and Italy such an approach is anathema to the legal culture.

While there are some signs of a desire by Ireland to soften the mandatory exclusionary rule in so far as the decisions seem to indicate a desire to allow the evidence to be admitted on a discretionary basis, nonetheless, even if a discretionary approach were to be adopted, it would still result, in cases where the discretion is used to exclude the evidence, in the fact-finders being kept completely unaware of its existence. That is still a very considerable distance from the approach in Italy and France where the idea is that 'everything should be on the table'. In these jurisdictions, even if it is ultimately decided that the evidence may not be relied on for use in the verdict, the evidence will at least have been presented to the fact-finders so they know of its existence.

7.2.5 Differences in evidence procedure within trial structure

The different approaches of the three jurisdictions to character evidence and hearsay evidence are best reviewed in the overall context of the trial phase for it is here that stark differences emerge. The structure of the trial in Ireland has been seen to be fundamentally different from that in France and Italy. The trial in Ireland is one that adheres to the classic adversarial model of a bifurcated procedure. The deciders of fact in the Irish trial are the jury who must reach their verdict alone, without assistance by the judge beyond the directions given to them by the judge before they retire to consider their verdict (with the exception of the Special Criminal Court). The structure of the trial process is one that allocates one procedure to determine guilt or innocence, followed by a separate hearing without the involvement of the jury where the judge alone determines the sentence.

The trial in France is by contrast a unitary structure in both respects. The verdict is a collaborative one taken by the judges and jury together, and the trial structure is also unitary in which the object of the trial is to determine the issues of guilt and sentence in a single proceeding, with both issues being decided by a single panel of judges and jury retiring together. The same is true of Italy, where the unitary trial structure was retained by the reforming Code.

Largely as a result of this bifurcated unitary contrast, one rule of common law evidence is markedly absent from French and Italian trial procedure, that relating to character evidence. In Ireland as a rule the bad character of the accused is fully concealed from the jury. By contrast, the character of the accused in France is central to the proceedings, displayed in detail to the triers of fact and a factor that may be considered in reaching a verdict. In Italy, the position falls somewhere midway between these positions: there is no similar highlighting of the background of the accused as occurs during the *personnalité* phase of the French trial but the fact-finders will always be aware of any convictions that the accused has accrued.

The prohibition of character evidence in Ireland is rationalised on the basis of the danger of prejudicing the fact-finders. The availability of character evidence is rationalised in France by the unitary structure of trials where both guilt and sentence are decided by the collaborative panel in a singular proceeding and by the desire to judge 'the whole man'. Italy permits its inclusion on the basis of its similarly unified trial structure since it is necessary to justify the sentencing aspect of the decision; however, it comes closer to Ireland in so far as bad character may not be used as a basis for conviction. It therefore recognises that such evidence is potentially prejudicial, but at the same time does not appear to be troubled by possible prejudice informing the verdict at an unspoken level.

There is also a notable difference between the systems in their approach to permitting the presentation of the accused in the courtroom as one appearing to be of bad character. This highlights another difference connected to the approach to character evidence in these jurisdictions: character evidence in the common law variant is linked with the presumption of innocence; the prejudice that arises where the bad character of the accused is revealed is precisely the assumption that he is guilty, therefore the presumption of innocence principle is directly challenged if the principle is considered in the wider sense of including a reputational aspect. The French and Italian systems show no difficulty in presenting the accused in the courtroom as a person that is in custody; the practice of presenting the accused in the courtroom in a patently custodial character, suggesting as it does that he is a dangerous person who needs to be constrained, by contrast could be challenged in Ireland as an attack on the presumption of innocence, on the basis that the fact-finders may be prejudiced in their verdict. Despite the presumption of innocence rhetoric underlying the systems of France and Italy, this practice in their courts renders the presumption illusory.

While the fundamental principle of the presumption of innocence is shared by the three jurisdictions, and equally understood to comprise the interrelated threads that the accused enjoys a right to silence and that the burden of proof rests on the prosecution, from my common law perspective the first thread appears to be almost non-existent in French and Italian trials, while the second is difficult to reconcile with the common law understanding of the concept.

In relation to the right to silence, what is striking, particularly so in France, is the prominent role played by the accused during the trial. It has been seen that there is a constant exchange between, most often, the judge and the accused, and the accused may also intervene to confront the witness directly during their testimony. The accused in Ireland is by contrast almost invisible; the accused is never asked to comment on the testimony given by a witness, as is the norm in France. Moreover where he wishes to contradict what the witness is saying this is done by way of hurriedly scribbled notes from the accused that are passed down to the solicitor who in turn passes them on to the barrister. The accused in France is expected to speak. So too in Italy, and although in each of these jurisdictions the accused enjoys a right of silence at trial, it is generally not in their best interest to avail themselves of that right. It has been seen in the case study of Italy that where an accused chooses to exercise a right to silence at trial, any prior statements he made to the prosecutor will be used to fill the gap.

While all the systems adhere to the principle that burden of proof rests with the accuser, from a common law perspective this is understood to mean that the accused does not have to assist the prosecutor in any way in discharging that burden. On that basis the defence does not present a case in answer to that put forward by the prosecution at the outset of the trial, and the accused may choose to testify or not once the presentation of the prosecution case is completed. By contrast, in Italy the defence case is presented at the outset, and that gives rise to an impression at least that the defence is trying to disprove the prosecution case.

In both France and Italy, while it is ultimately the prosecution's case that must be proved, it has been seen from the case studies of France and Italy that the prosecutor is at least assisted in discharging the burden of proof by others in the process. The inclusion in these jurisdictions of a third party to the proceedings, the *partie civile*, who has a strong interest in the prosecution succeeding in proving guilt, means that the prosecution has a strong ally; since the *partie civile* lawyer presents a closing address to the jury, the prosecution case is thus repeated to the triers of fact, effectively increasing its impact.

The residual power of the judge in both these jurisdictions to seek further evidence also strains the common law idea of the burden of proof, as does the constant recourse to the accused throughout the trial in France; the practice of seeking comment from the accused on the prosecution case as it emerges during the trial gives an impression at least that the accused is being asked to actively disprove the prosecution case.

The prosecutor is also assisted in discharging the burden of proof in France and Italy by the active role of the trial judge in questioning the witnesses and the accused. Here a very stark difference arises between trials in Ireland and those of France and Italy. It has been seen that in Ireland the trial judge takes a relatively passive role at the trial stage; his role is reactive, limited to deciding what evidence may be heard if an application is made to him by the parties, and deciding the sentence where the jury returns a guilty verdict. He has no role in questioning witnesses. By contrast, the judge in France and Italy dominates the trial. This may assist the prosecution in discharging the burden of proof where the judge's line of questioning is favourable to the prosecution case. Nonetheless, the rhetoric persists in these systems that the judge is an impartial adjudicator.

As far as hearsay evidence goes, Italy appears to have moved more in the direction of the common law position in that it has adopted some form of hearsay rule, but only insofar as certain statements are concerned; it continues to rely on other documents that would be classified as hearsay in the Irish context. France has no aversion to hearsay, provided that the maker of a statement has at some point been made available for challenge and other documentary evidence is freely admissible as in Italy. In both France and Italy, regardless of any hearsay rules, the trial practice of permitting witnesses to give their testimony in narrative form allows the opportunity for hearsay evidence to come before the fact-finders. This highlights a difference of approach to hearsay between these jurisdictions and that of Ireland where in addition to the, albeit reformed, rule against hearsay, the witness is tightly controlled by counsel to prevent any hearsay entering the trial by the back door.

PART II

7.3 Synthesis

7.3.1 Adversarial and contradictoire *types of procedure*

Any sense that the systems have converged to a point where they all share in common adversarial features, because of the ECtHR requirement that evidence be presented with a view to 'adversarial argument', I would argue, starts from a false premise that adversarial and *contradictoire* are one and the same concept. I would argue trials in Ireland, France and Italy share in common only that which is fundamentally required by the ECHR, which is that the evidence must be made available for challenge.

The only meaningful resemblance of French and Italian trials with the classic adversarial trial lies in the fact that the systems of France and Italy provide a role for the parties in their trial structures to examine and cross-examine witnesses.

Even this resemblance is obscured by the practice seen in the case studies of France and Italy, whereby the judge conducts the bulk of the questioning and the parties play second fiddle. Where they do take up their role, it has been seen that they do not probe in any way as vigorously as would be the stock-in-trade of practitioners in the Irish courtroom.

The starkest contrast between the systems in Ireland and those of France and Italy lies in their adherence to differing underlying procedural types. Ireland's trial is classically adversarial with its features of control of the selection and presentation of evidence by two parties, prosecution and defence, the examination and cross-examination of witnesses by the parties, and the exclusion of evidence from the sight of the fact-finders where it has been ruled inadmissible in their absence by the trial judge who otherwise does not intervene in the receiving of evidence process.

The trials in France and Italy have been seen through the case studies to follow a procedural format that is more properly described as *contradictoire*, a procedural method that is distinctly different to an adversarial procedural method. Crucially the *contradictoire* procedure involves an approach to receiving evidence that distinguishes it from the adversarial method: it requires the evidence to be presented to the fact-finder in order that it may be contradicted in front of the fact-finder; it is therefore anathema to exclude it from the fact-finder because if it is concealed no contradictory debate may be held. Although in common with their Irish counterparts, the French and Italian fact-finders may ultimately be prohibited from using the evidence to reach a verdict, they are in a very different position from their Irish counterparts, who do not use it because they simply do not realise that it even exists. The principle of *contradictoire* is considered a safeguard against dubious evidence because it allows dubious evidence to be challenged. The adversarial procedure is considered a safeguard because it is the mechanism by which dubious evidence may be withheld.

At the heart of this contrasting approach to inadmissible evidence is a fundamental opposition between the legal culture of France and Italy, on the one hand, and that of Ireland on the other: in the former the aim of the criminal process is primarily to discover the truth and appropriately sanction the offender if he is proved to have truly committed the act; in the latter, trials are also a truth-seeking exercise but a lesser priority may be given to finding the truth where the value of fairness is seen to be jeopardised. That is not to say that France and Italy discount the value of fairness in the process; both may be accommodated because they consider the value of truth-seeking and the value of fairness to be inextricably linked to each other.

There is another vital difference between processes that adhere to the principle of *contradictoire* as opposed to processes that adhere to the adversarial procedure, a difference that relates to the point of the availability of the suspect during the pre-trial. The pre-trial phase is conducted in both France and Italy also in accordance with the principle of *contradictoire/ contradittorio.* The suspect is continually confronted with the evidence and witnesses against him and given the opportunity to contradict the information being put to him. The pre-trial and trial stages are in this sense a continuous process of testing the evidence. The Irish system does not use the pre-trial stage in this way. The suspect in Ireland is not confronted with the evidence as it develops and is indeed kept in the dark about the evidence against him until served with the book of evidence. There is no forum for adversarial argument before the trial. In this regard, therefore, the pre-trial process in Ireland cannot be described as 'adversarial'. If anything, it leans more towards an inquisitorial direction in so far as the secrecy of the investigation is concerned. The adversarial system in Ireland in reality refers only to the trial phase; the *contradictoire* procedure in France and Italy refers to both stages.

7.3.2 Prospects for a principle of mutual admissibility of evidence

What are the implications arising from this discussion for an EU-wide principle of mutual admissibility of evidence? It should first be noted that the new EU institutional framework (from unanimity to majority) appears to have shortened the time span for proposals to evolve into adopted legislation. The Stockholm Roadmap measures already adopted are clear indicators of this, most notably the Directives on access to a lawyer and access to information, adopted after circa two-year negotiation periods as compared to the lengthy periods of negotiations over proposals in the past. This acceleration is in no small measure a result of the new opt-in procedure provided by the Lisbon Treaty. However, the possibility for opt-in under the new institutional framework itself militates against a principle of mutual admissibility of evidence across *all* Member States. It is still an unknown as to whether Ireland and the UK will eventually decide to opt in to the Directive on access to a lawyer and the proposed EPPO Regulation, and, in the case of Ireland, to the proposed EIO.

In terms of the Roadmap measures, most notably the right of access to a lawyer, while all EU systems appear to converge in recognising that a suspect should have access to legal advice during police custody, the detail of allowing the lawyer to be present in interviews with police together with the role a lawyer should play during police interviews poses difficulties for jurisdictions that do not provide for this already. These difficulties are in part connected to issues of resources, but in some jurisdictions, the difficulties relate to matters of principle. For example, it was seen that Belgium, while not being opposed to permitting the lawyer to be present during questioning, considered that active participation by the lawyer upset the fundamentals of their system; in Scotland access to a lawyer during questioning has been opposed on principled grounds that it will inevitably lead to the diminution of other safeguards, including the right against self-incrimination.[2]

2. P. Ferguson, 'Repercussions of the Cadder Case' (2011) 10 *Crim. LR* 743.

As to the issue of admissibility of statements taken in breach of a right of access to a lawyer, all Member States appear to accept that such statements ought not be used, but a difference going to the fundamentals of the systems relates to whether the information should be entirely excluded from the fact-finders, or whether it should first be examined by the fact-finders in order that a decision may then be taken on the value to be given to it.

In an Irish setting, where the trial judge rules the statement to be inadmissible, the evaluation of the statement would be that of the trial judge alone during a *voir dire*, so the fact-finders would never come to be aware of it. Despite the radical changes that have arisen in the evidence law of England and Wales, the practice of screening evidence through a *voir dire* procedure has not been abandoned so here, too, evidence that is ruled inadmissible continues to be held back from the fact-finders.

In the continental setting, while the procedure is geared towards examining material and then deciding whether or not it may be used, there is an indication from the French and Italian practices that statements made in the absence of legal advice are not always revealed to the fact-finders, so the differences here between the systems may be narrowing in this respect. Achieving a mutual admissibility agreement on this type of evidence therefore might be a not unrealistic proposition. However, the institutional differences of the investigation phase also pose problems; for example, given that the Italian system requires interrogations to be conducted by the public prosecutor and not by the police, that gives rise to difficulty if Italian authorities are presented with interrogation statements from Ireland, where there is no such similar office of public prosecutor.

When it comes to the gathering of real evidence through search and seizure, the differences between jurisdictions could be resolved through using the EIO mechanism of requesting particular formalities to be observed, for example those relating to searches being conducted in daytime hours and that witnesses attend. Since searches are not conducted in the presence of witnesses in Ireland, Ireland would need to establish some mechanism to appoint such witnesses, arguably not an insurmountable difficulty; existing offices such as the Peace Commissioner could provide a possible solution.

However, where the evidence has been unlawfully obtained, there is a gulf of difference between the jurisdictions. As I have already pointed out in Chapter 2, the instruments tackle only two aspects of a mutual admissibility regime, the gathering of evidence and the rights that must be respected of persons affected in that regard. Even the Commission's attempt in the legal advice Proposal to devise a blanket inadmissibility rule only went so far as to say that the illegally obtained evidence should not be used. It said nothing about how that evidence might be received. The complexities involved in the issue of admissibility itself have so far not been tackled head on.

A principal obstacle that may prevent the achievement of a meaningful mutual admissibility regime stems from the makeup in the EU of legal systems originating from the two broad traditions of inquisitorial and accusatorial.

These originating traditions have moulded the environment for the presentation, receiving and challenge of evidence, in that those of the former tradition have taken the route of proceedings that are *contradictoire* while those of the latter have followed the adversarial path.

In devising any Proposal relating directly to mutual admissibility of evidence, the following impasse will have to be overcome. The principle of free proof and the quest for substantial truth makes it anathema to the cultural tradition of continental Member States to accept a principle of mutual admissibility that would embrace any exclusionary mechanism such as is typical of the common law tradition; the idea that the trier of fact should not be aware of all relevant evidence is disturbing to the continental legal tradition. Equally it is largely anathema to the common law tradition to present to the fact-finder that evidence which it wants to have excluded from the fact-finder; the exclusionary mechanism deliberately operates to keep the fact-finder unaware of the evidence, even if it is relevant. Any Proposal would thus have to attempt to reconcile these two positions.

A mutual admissibility principle cannot hope to be achieved until the questions of reception, presentation and challenges to evidence are tackled and included in the overall design for a mutual admissibility system; a design that addresses only the evidence collection and the rights of persons affected by the collection is an incomplete blueprint, lacking a vital brushstroke. However, while the cornerstone of judicial cooperation, the mutual recognition principle, proceeds from the basis of tolerance of diversity of legal systems, the diverging methods of receiving, presenting and challenging evidence at the trial stage may prove to be too fundamental to the integrity of the criminal procedures of the two broad traditions, procedural traditions to which they each remain faithful, to permit them to be embraced by a principle of mutual admissibility.

Bibliography

Alegre, S. and Leaf, M., 'Mutual Recognition in European Judicial Cooperation: A Step Too Far Too Soon? Case Study – The European Arrest Warrant' (2004) 10 (2) *European Law Journal* 200.

Allen, R. and Alexakis, G., 'Utility and Truth in the Scholarship of Mirjan Damaška', in J. Jackson, M. Langer and P. Tillers (eds), *Crime, Procedure and Evidence in a Comparative and International Context: Essays in Honour of Prof. Mirjan Damaška* (Hart 2008).

Ambroise-Castérot, C., *La Procédure Pénale* (Gualino 2009).

Amodio, E., 'The Accusatorial System Lost and Regained: Reforming Criminal Procedure in Italy' (2004) 52 *Am. J. Comp. L.* 489.

Arnull, A., Barnard, C., Dougan, M. and Spaventa, E. (eds), *A Constitutional Order of States? Essays in EU Law in Honour of Alan Dashwood* (Hart 2011).

Ashworth, A., 'Four Threats to the Presumption of Innocence' (2006) 10 *Int'l J. Evidence and Proof* 241.

Beattie, J., 'Scales of Justice: Defence Counsel and the English Criminal Trial in the Eighteenth and Nineteenth Centuries' (1991) 9 (2) *Law & Hist. Rev.* 221.

Bedford, S., *The Faces of Justice* (first published 1961, Faber & Faber 2011).

Bell, J., 'English Law and French Law – Not So Different?' (1995) 48 (2) *CLP* 63.

Blackstone, *Commentaries* (first published Clarendon Press 1765–9, Hein 1992).

Bradley, C., *Criminal Procedure: A Worldwide Study* (2nd edn) (Carolina Academic Press 2007).

Brants, C., 'Procedural Safeguards in the European Union: Too Little, Too Late?', in J. Vervaele (ed.), *European Evidence Warrant: Transnational Judicial Inquiries in the EU* (Intersentia 2005).

Caianiello, M., 'Italy', in E. Cape, Z. Namoradze, R. Smith and T. Spronken (eds), *Effective Criminal Defence in Europe* (Intersentia 2010).

Caianiello, M. and Illuminati, G., draft contribution to 'Rethinking European Criminal Justice', a project under the auspices of the Max Planck Institute 2009.

Cape, E., Hodgson, J., Prakken, T. and Spronken, T., *Suspects in Europe – Procedural Rights at the Investigative Stage of the Criminal Process in the European Union* (Intersentia 2007).

Cape, E., Namoradze, Z., Smith, R. and Spronken, T., *Effective Criminal Defence in Europe* (Intersentia 2010).

Chase, O., 'Legal Processes and National Culture' (1997) 5 *Cardozo J. Int'l & Comp. L.* 1.

Corso, P., *Codice di Procedura Penale e Processo Penale Minorile: Commentati con la Giurisprudenza* (Casa Editrice La Tribuna 2009).

Cross, R., *Cross on Evidence* (5th edn) (Butterworths 1979).
Cuomo, L. and Scioli, F., *L'Incidente Probatorio* (Giappichelli 2007).
Damaška, M., 'Evidentiary Barriers to Conviction and Two Models of Criminal Procedure: A Comparative Study' (1973) 121 *U. Pa. L. Rev.* 506.
Damaška, M., 'Structures of Authority and Comparative Criminal Procedure' (1974–5) 84 *Yale LJ* 480.
Damaška, M., 'Truth in Adjudication' (1998) 49 *Hastings LJ* 289.
Damaška, M., *Evidence Law Adrift* (Yale University Press 1997).
Damaška, M., *Faces of Justice and State Authority: A Comparative Approach to the Legal Process* (Yale University Press 1986).
Delmas-Marty, M., 'Reflections on the "Hybridisation" of Criminal Procedure', in J. Jackson, M. Langer and P. Tillers (eds), *Crime, Procedure and Evidence in a Comparative and International Context: Essays in Honour of Prof. Mirjan Damaška* (Hart 2008).
Delmas-Marty, M. and Spencer, J. (eds), *European Criminal Procedures* (first published 2002, Cambridge University Press 2005).
Delmas-Marty, M. and Vervaele, J. (eds), *The Implementation of the Corpus Juris in the Member States*, Vol. IV (Intersentia 2001).
Demleitner, N., 'More Than "Just" Evidence' (1999) 47 (3) *Am. J. Comp. L.* 515.
Dervieux, V., 'The French System', in M. Delmas-Marty and J. Spencer (eds), *European Criminal Procedures* (first published 2002, Cambridge University Press 2005).
Duff, A., Farmer, L., Marshall, S. and Tadros, V. (eds), *The Trial on Trial Volume One: Truth and Due Process* (Hart 2004).
Duff, A., Farmer, L., Marshall, S. and Tadros, V. (eds), *The Trial on Trial Volume Two: Judgment and Calling to Account* (Hart 2006).
Duff, A., Farmer, L., Marshall, S. and Tadros, V. (eds), *The Trial on Trial Volume Three: Towards a Normative Theory of the Criminal Trial* (Hart 2007).
Esmein, A., *A History of Continental Criminal Procedure with Special Reference to France* (Little, Brown 1913).
Evans, W., 'Of the Law of Evidence', in Pothier, *Treatise on Obligations*, Appendix No. XVI, Vol. 2 (Robert Small 1826).
Ferguson, P., 'Repercussions of the Cadder Case' (2011) 10 *Crim. LR* 743.
Fichera, M., *The Implementation of the European Arrest Warrant in the European Union: Law, Policy and Practice* (Intersentia 2011).
Field, S., 'State, Citizen, and Character in French Criminal Process' (2006) 33 (4) *Journal of Law and Society* 522.
Field, S. and West, A., 'A Tale of Two Reforms: French Defence Rights and Police Powers in Transition' (1995) 6 *Crim. L. Forum* 473.
Field, S. and West, A., 'Dialogue and the Inquisitorial Tradition: French Defence Lawyers in the Pre-trial Criminal Process' (2003) 14 (3) *Crim. L. Forum* 261.
Field, S., 'Fair Trials and Procedural Tradition in Europe' (2009) 29 (2) *OJLS* 365.
Fletcher, M., Lööf, R. and Gilmore, B., *EU Criminal Law and Justice* (Edward Elgar 2008).
Fourment, F., *Procédure Pénale* (Paradigme 2009).
Fraher, R., 'Conviction According to Conscience: The Medieval Jurists' Debate Concerning Judicial Discretion and the Law of Proof' (1989) 7 (1) *Law & Hist. Rev.* 23.
Frankel, M., 'The Search for Truth: An Umpireal View' (1975) 123 *U. Pa. L. Rev.* 1031.
Frase, R., 'Comparative Criminal Justice as a Guide to American Law Reform: How Do the French Do It, How Can We Find Out, and Why Should We Care?' (1990) 78 (3) *Cal. L. Rev.* 539.

Frase, R., 'Sentencing and Comparative Law Theory,' in J. Jackson, M. Langer and P. Tillers (eds), *Crime, Procedure and Evidence in a Comparative and International Context: Essays in Honour of Prof. Mirjan Damaška* (Hart 2008).

Freccero, S., 'An Introduction to the New Italian Criminal Procedure' (1993–4) 21 (3) *Am. J. Crim. L.* 345.

Friedman, L., 'Anchors and Flotsam: Is Evidence Law "Adrift"?' (1998) 107 (6) *Yale LJ* 1921.

Friedman, L., 'Law, Lawyers, and Popular Culture' (1988–9) 98 (8) *Yale LJ* 1579.

Gallanis, T., 'The Rise of Modern Evidence Law' (19989) 84 (3) *Iowa L. Rev.* 499.

Garraud, F., 'History of the Continental System of Evidence', in A. Esmein, *A History of Continental Criminal Procedure with Special Reference to France* (Little, Brown 1913).

Goldstein, A. and Marcus, M., 'Comment on Continental Criminal Procedure' (1978) 87 (8) *Yale LJ* 1570.

Goldstein, A. and Marcus, M., 'The Myth of Judicial Supervision in Three "Inquisitorial" Systems: France, Italy and Germany' (1977) 87 (2) *Yale LJ* 240.

Goldstein, A., 'Reflection on Two Models: Inquisitorial Themes in American Criminal Procedure' (1973–4) 26 (5) *Stan. L. Rev.* 1009.

Grande, E., 'Dances of Criminal Justice: Thoughts on Systemic Differences and the Search for Truth', in J. Jackson, M. Langer and P. Tillers (eds), *Crime, Procedure and Evidence in a Comparative and International Context Essays in Honour of Prof. Mirjan Damaška* (Hart 2008).

Grande, E., 'Italian Criminal Justice: Borrowing and Resistance' (2000) 48 (2) *Am. J. Comp. L.* 227.

Griffiths, J., 'Ideology in Criminal Procedure or a Third Model of the Criminal Process' (1969–70) 79 (3) *Yale LJ* 359.

Groot, R., 'The Jury of Presentment before 1215'(1982) 26 (1) *Am. J. Legal Hist.* 1.

Hamilton, J., 'Mutual Assistance in Criminal Matters in Ireland and the Proposed European Evidence Warrant' (2005) *ERA Forum*: Special Issue on European Evidence Warrant, 53.

Hildebrandt, M., 'European Criminal Law and European Identity' (2007) 1 *Criminal Law and Philos.* 57.

Hinarejos, A., Spencer, J. and Peers, S., *Opting out of EU Criminal Law: What Is Actually Involved?*, CELS Working Paper, New Series, No. 1; online at: <http://www.cels.law.cam.ac.uk/publications/working_papers.php>.

Ho, L., *A Philosophy of Evidence Law* (Oxford University Press 2008).

Hodgson, J., 'Conceptions of the Trial in Inquisitorial and Adversarial Procedure', in A. Duff, L. Farmer, S. Marshall and V. Tadros (eds), *The Trial on Trial Volume Two: Judgment and Calling to Account* (Hart 2006).

Hodgson, J., 'Constructing the Pre-trial Role of the Defence in French Criminal Procedure: An Adversarial Outsider in an Inquisitorial Process?' (2002) 6 (1) *Int'l J. Evidence & Proof* 1.

Hodgson, J., 'Safeguarding Suspects' Rights in Europe: A Comparative Perspective' (2011) 14 *New Criminal Law Review* 612.

Hodgson, J., 'Suspects, Defendants and Victims in the French Criminal Process: The Context of Recent Reforms' (2002) 51 *Int'l & Comp. L. Q.* 781.

Hodgson, J., 'The French Prosecutor in Question' (2010) 67 *Wash. & Lee L. Rev.* 1361.

Hodgson, J., 'The Future of Adversarial Criminal Justice in 21st Century Britain' (2010) 35 *NCJ Int'l L. & Com. Reg.* 319.

Hodgson, J., *French Criminal Justice: A Comparative Account of the Investigation and Prosecution of Crime in France* (Hart 2005).

Hofstede, G., *Culture's Consequences: Comparing Values, Behaviors, Institutions and Organizations Across Nations* (2nd edn) (Sage 2001).

Illuminati, G., 'The Accusatorial Process from the Italian Point of View' (2010) 35 *NCJ Int'l L. & Com. Reg.* 297.

Illuminati, G., 'The Frustrated Turn to Adversarial Procedure in Italy (Italian Criminal Procedure Code of 1988)' (2005) 4 *Wash. U. Glob. Stud. L. Rev.* 567.

Jackson, J., 'Adrift but Still Clinging to the Wreckage' (1997–8) 49 (2) *Hastings LJ* 377.

Jackson, J., 'Hearsay: The Sacred Cow that Won't Be Slaughtered?' (1998) 2 *Int'l J. Evidence and Proof* 166.

Jackson, J., 'Playing the Culture Card in Resisting Cross-Jurisdictional Transplants: A Comment on Legal Processes and National Culture' (1997) 5 *Cardozo J. Int'l & Comp. L.* 51.

Jackson, J., 'Taking Comparative Evidence Seriously', in P. Roberts and M. Redmayne (eds), *Innovations in Evidence and Proof: Integrating Theory, Research and Teaching* (Hart 2007).

Jackson, J., 'The Effect of Human Rights on Criminal Evidentiary Processes: Towards Convergence, Divergence or Realignment?' (2005) 68 (5) *MLR* 737.

Jackson, J., 'The Effect of Legal Culture and Proof in Decisions to Prosecute' (2004) 3 *Law, Probability and Risk* 109.

Jackson, J. and Doran, S., *Judge Without Jury: Diplock Trials in the Adversary System* (Clarendon 1995).

Jackson, J. and Kovalev, N., 'Lay Adjudication and Human Rights in Europe' (2006) 13 *Columbia J. European Law* 83.

Jackson, J. and Summers, S., *The Internationalisation of Criminal Evidence: Beyond the Common Law and Civil Law Traditions* (Cambridge University Press 2012).

Jackson, J., Langer, M. and Tilers, P. (eds) *Crime, Procedure and Evidence in a Comparative and International Context: Essays in Honour of Prof. Mirjan Damaška* (Hart 2008).

Kerr, M., 'Angevin Reform of the Appeal of Felony' (1995) 13 (2) *Law & Hist. Rev.* 351.

King, M., 'Security, Scale, Form and Function: The Search for Truth and the Exclusion of Evidence in Adversarial and Inquisitorial Justice Systems' (2001–2) 12 *Int'l Legal Persp.* 185.

Kirkpatrick, L., 'Evidence Law in the Next Millennium' (1997–8) 49 (2) *Hastings LJ* 363.

Klip, A., *European Criminal Law An Integrative Approach* (Intersentia 2009).

Landsman, S., 'From Gilbert to Bentham: The Reconceptualization of Evidence Theory' (1989–90) 36 *Wayne L. Rev.* 1149.

Landsman, S., 'The Rise of the Contentious Spirit: Adversary Procedure in Eighteenth Century England' (1989–90) 75 (3) *Cornell L. Rev.* 497.

Langbein, J., 'Mixed Court and Jury Court: Could the Continental Alternative Fill the American Need?' (1981) (1) *Am. B. Found. Res. J.* 195.

Langbein, J., 'The Criminal Trial Before Lawyers' (1977–8) 45 (2) *U. Chi. L. Rev.* 263.

Langbein, J., 'The Historical Foundations of the Law of Evidence: A View from the Ryder Sources' (1996) 96 (5) *Columbia L. Rev.* 1168.

Langbein, J., 'The Historical Origins of the Privilege Against Self-Incrimination at Common Law' (1993–4) 92 (5) *Michigan L. Rev.* 1047.

Langbein, J., *The Origins of Adversary Criminal Trial* (Oxford University Press 2003).

Langbein, J., *Torture and the Law of Proof: Europe and England in the Ancien Régime* (first published 1977, University of Chicago Press 2006).

Langbein, J. and Weinreb, L., 'Continental Criminal Procedure: "Myth" and Reality' (1978) 87 (8) *Yale LJ* 1549.

Laursen, F., *Denmark and the Ratification of the Lisbon Treaty: How a Referendum Was Avoided*, Conference Paper 4th annual EUCE conference, Dalhousie University, 6–8 June (2010).

Law Society Gazette, 'No Garda Questioning Without Solicitors Present in future?', March (2013) 10.

Legrand, P., 'European Legal Systems are Not Converging' (1996) 45 (1) *Int'l & Comp. L. Q.* 52.

Lena, J. and Mattei, U., *Introduction to Italian Law* (Kluwer 2002).

Lerner, R., 'The Intersection of Two Systems: An American on Trial for an American Murder in the French *Cour D'Assises*' (2001) (3) *U. Ill. L. Rev.* 791.

Ligeti, K. (ed.), *Toward a Prosecutor for the European Union: A Comparative Analysis*, Vol. 1 (Hart 2012).

Luban, D., O'Sullivan, J. and Stewart, D., *International and Transnational Criminal Law* (Aspen 2010).

McKillop, B., 'Anatomy of a French Murder Case' (1997) 45 (3) *Am. J. Comp. L.* 527.

McKillop, B., 'Readings and Hearings in French Criminal Justice: Five Cases in the *Tribunal Correctionnel*' (1998) 46 (4) *Am. J. Comp. L.* 757.

Macnair, M., 'Vicinage and the Antecedents of the Jury' (1999) 17(3) *Law & Hist. Rev.* 537.

Maitland, F., Montague, F. and Colby, J. (eds), *A Sketch of English Legal History* (Lawbook Exchange 1915).

Marafioti, L., 'Italian Criminal Procedure: A System Caught Between Two Traditions', in J. Jackson, M. Langer and P. Tillers (eds), *Crime, Procedure and Evidence in a Comparative and International Context Essays in Honour of Prof. Mirjan Damaška* (Hart 2008).

Markesinis, B. (ed.), *The Gradual Convergence: Foreign Ideas, Foreign Influences and English Law on the Eve of the 21st Century* (Clarendon Press 1994).

Merryman, J., *The Civil Law Tradition: An Introduction to the Legal Systems of Western Europe and Latin America* (3rd edn) (Stanford University Press 2007).

Miller, J., 'A Rights-based Argument Against the Dock' (2011) *Crim. LR* 216.

Mitsilegas, V., *EU Criminal Law* (Hart 2009).

Montana, R., 'Adversarialism in Italy: Using the Concept of Legal Culture to Understand Resistance to Legal Modifications and Its Consequences' (2012) 20 *European Journal of Crime, Criminal Law and Criminal Justice* 99.

Morgan, C., *The Draft Directive on the Right to Information in Criminal Proceedings*, paper given at ERA Conference 'Guaranteeing Procedural Safeguards in the EU – A First Step Taken', Trier, 18–19 November (2010).

Morrison, C., 'Some Features of the Roman and the English Law of Evidence' (1958–9) 33 (3) *Tul. L. Rev.* 577.

Munday, R., 'Jury Trial, Continental Style' (1993) 13 *Legal Studies* 204.

Munday, R., 'What Do the French Think of Their Jury' (1995) 15 *Legal Studies* 65.

Murphy, P., 'Character Evidence: The Search for Logic and Policy Continues' (1998) 2 *Int'l J. Evidence & Proof* 71.

Nelken, D. (ed.), *Contrasting Criminal Justice: Getting from Here to There* (Ashgate 2000).

Nelles, U., *Steps Towards Harmonisation – Steps Towards Friction*, Paper 3rd annual conference of European Society of Criminology, Helsinki (2004).

Nijboer, J. F., 'Common Law Tradition in Evidence Scholarship Observed from a Continental Perspective' (1993) 41 (2) *Am. J. Comp. L.* 299.

Packer, H., 'Two Models of the Criminal Process' (1964–5) 113 (1) *U. Pa. L. Rev.* 1.

Padoa-Schioppa, A., 'A Sketch of Legal History', in J. Lena and U. Mattei (eds), *Introduction to Italian Law* (Kluwer 2002).

Panzavolta, M., 'Reforms and Counter-reforms in the Italian Struggle for an Accusatorial System' (2004–5) 30 (3) *NCJ Int'l L. & Com. Reg.* 577.

Peers, S., 'In a World of Their Own? Justice and Home Affairs Opt-Outs and the Treaty of Lisbon' (2007–8) 10 *Cambridge Yearbook of European Legal Studies* 383.

Peers, S., 'The Proposed European Investigation Order', Statewatch Analysis, November (2010); online at: <http://www.statewatch.org/>.

Perrodet, A., 'The Italian System', in M. Delmas-Marty and J. Spencer (eds) *European Criminal Procedures* (first published 2002, Cambridge University Press 2005).

Pizzi, W. and Marafioti, L., 'The New Italian Code of Criminal Procedure: The Difficulties of Building an Adversarial Trial System on a Civil Law Foundation' (1992) 17 (1) *Yale J. Int'l L.* 1.

Pizzi, W. and Montagna, M., 'The Battle to Establish an Adversarial Trial System in Italy' (2003–4) 25 (2) *Mich. J. Int'l L.* 429.

Plowscow, M., 'Purging Italian Criminal Justice of Fascism' (1945) 45 (2) *Columbia LR* 240.

Pollock, F. and Maitland, F., *The History of English Law before the Time of Edward I* (Cambridge University Press 1895).

Proffatt, J., *A Treatise on Trial by Jury including Questions of Law and Fact* (Whitney 1877).

Quintard-Morenas, F., 'The Presumption of Innocence in the French and Anglo-American Legal Traditions' (2010) 58 (1) *Am. J. Comp. L.* 107.

Reamey, G., 'Innovation or Renovation in Criminal Procedure: Is the World Moving Towards a New Model of Adjudicating?' (2010) 27 (3) *Ariz. J. Int'l & Comp. L.* 693.

Redmayne, M., 'Process Gains and Process Values: the Criminal Procedure and Investigations Act 1996' (1997) 60 *Modern Law Review* 79.

Renucci, J., 'Un séisme judiciaire' (2009) 9 *Recueil le Dalloz* 600.

Roberts, P., 'Faces of Justice Adrift?', in J. Jackson, M. Langer and P. Tillers (eds), *Crime, Procedure and Evidence in a Comparative and International Context: Essays in Honour of Prof. Mirjan Damaška* (Hart 2008).

Roberts, P., 'On Method: The Ascent of Comparative Criminal Justice' (2002) 22 (3) *OJLS* 539 (review article of D. Nelken (ed.), *Contrasting Criminal Justice: Getting from Here to There* (Ashgate 2000)).

Roberts, P. and Hunter, J. (eds), *Criminal Evidence and Human Rights: Reimagining Common Law Procedural Traditions* (Hart 2012).

Roberts, P. and Redmayne, M. (eds), *Innovations in Evidence and Proof: Integrating Theory, Research and Teaching* (Hart 2007).

Roberts, P. and Zuckerman, A., *Criminal Evidence* (Oxford University Press 2004).

Ryan, A., 'Arrest and Detention: A Review of the Law' (2000) 10 *ICLJ* 2.

Ryan, A., 'Avoiding the Hard Question: DPP v Buck and the Constitutional Right of Access to Legal Advice' (2003) 25 *DULJ* 257.

Ryan, A., 'The Criminal Justice (Drug Trafficking) Act 1996: Decline and Fall of the Right to Silence?' 1997 7(1) *ICLJ* 22.

Ryan, A., 'The European Evidence Warrant: The Emergence of a European Law of Evidence?' (2006) 16(4) *ICLJ* 8.

Ryan, E. and Magee, P., *The Irish Criminal Process* (Mercier Press 1983).

Sayers, D., *The European Investigation Order: Travelling Without a 'Roadmap'* (CEPS Liberty and Security in Europe, June 2011).

Scarre, C., *The Penguin Historical Atlas of Ancient Rome* (Penguin 1995).

Shapiro, B., 'To a Moral Certainty: Theories of Knowledge and Anglo-American Juries 1600–1850' (1986–7) 38 (1) *Hastings LJ* 155.

Sklansky, D., 'Anti-Inquisitorialism' (2008–9) 122 (6) *Harv. L. Rev.* 1634.

Spencer, J., 'Evidence', in M. Delmas-Marty and J. Spencer (eds), *European Criminal Procedures* (first published 2002, Cambridge University Press 2005).

Spencer, J., 'The Green Paper on Obtaining Evidence from One Member State to Another and Securing Its Admissibility: The Reaction of One British Lawyer' (2010); available at: <http://www.eucriminallaw.com/publications/>.

Spencer, J., *Evidence of Bad Character* (2nd edn) (Hart 2009).

Spencer, J., *Hearsay Evidence in Criminal Proceedings* (Hart 2008).

Spronken, T., *An EU-Wide Letter of Rights: Towards Best Practice* (Intersentia 2010).

Spronken, T. and Vermeulen, G., *EU Procedural Rights in Criminal Proceedings* (Intersentia 2009).

Stephen, J., *A History of the Criminal Law of England*, Vol. 1 (Macmillan 1883).

Strachan-Davidson, J., *Problems of the Roman Criminal Law*, Vols 1 and 2 (Rothman 1991).

Summers, R., 'Formal Legal Truth and Substantive Truth in Judicial Fact-Finding – Their Justified Divergence in Some Particular Cases' (1999) 18 *Law and Philosophy* 497.

Summers, S., *Fair Trials: The European Criminal Procedural Tradition and the European Court of Human Rights* (Hart 2007).

Thayer, J. B., *A Preliminary Treatise on Evidence at the Common Law* (Little, Brown 1898).

Trechsel, S., *Human Rights in Criminal Proceedings* (Oxford University Press 2005).

Twining, W., *Rethinking Evidence* (2nd edn) (Cambridge University Press 2006).

Twining, W., *Theories of Evidence: Bentham and Wigmore* (Stanford University Press 1985).

Urbom, W., 'Toward Better Treatment of Jurors by Judges' (1982) 61 (3) *Nebraska L. Rev.* 409.

Van Cleave, R., 'Italy', in C. Bradley (ed.), *Criminal Procedure: A Worldwide Study* (2nd edn) (Carolina Academic Press 2007).

Van Kessel, G., 'European Perspectives on the Accused as a Source of Testimonial Evidence' (1997–8) 100 (4) *W. Va. L. Rev.* 799.

Vermeulen, G., *Free Gathering and Movement of Evidence in Criminal Matters in the EU* (Maklu 2012).

Vervaele, J. (ed.), *European Evidence Warrant: Transnational Judicial Inquiries in the EU* (Intersentia 2005).

Vogler, R., *A World View of Criminal Justice* (Ashgate 2005).

Walsh, D., *Criminal Procedure* (Thomson Round Hall 2002).

Weber, M., 'Objectivity in Social Science', in H. Finch and E. Shils (trans and eds), *The Methodology of the Social Sciences* (Free Press 1949).

Weigend, T., 'Is the Criminal Process about Truth? A German Perspective' (2003) 26 (1) *Harv. J. L. & Pub. Pol'y* 157.

Weigend, T., 'Should We Search for Truth, and Who Should Do It?' (2010–11) 36 (2) *NCJ Int'l L. & Com. Reg.* 389.

West, A., 'Reform of French Criminal Justice' (2000) 150 *NLJ* 1542, 1630 and 1667 (three-part article).

Wigmore, J. H., *Treatise on the Anglo-American System of Evidence in Trials at Common Law including the Statutes and Judicial Decisions of All Jurisdictions of the United States and Canada*, Vol. 3 (Little, Brown 1923).

Wills, A., *Crime and Punishment in Revolutionary Paris* (Greenwood Press 1981).

Index

accusatorial 1, 10, 12, 48–50, 65–70, 76, 80, 81, 133, 187, 229, 238, 248
admissibility of evidence 3, 4, 11, 12–16, 20, 21–3, 25–7, 29, 34, 40, 43, 44, 46–8, 78, 82, 86, 88, 94, 96–8, 105, 106, 109, 112, 113, 119, 120, 123, 187, 202, 204, 218, 238, 239, 242, 247–9
adversarial 2, 4, 7, 8, 10, 29, 48, 60, 68, 69, 72, 77, 78, 79, 83, 109, 118, 129, 130, 131, 148, 181, 184, 185, 187, 209, 213, 214, 218, 219, 222, 224, 232, 233, 235, 236, 242, 245, 246, 247, 249, 275; and non-adversarial 9, 12, 50, 70, 71, 76, 80, 229, 239
Ambroise-Casterot, C. 68, 69, 78, 133, 134, 149, 152, 155, 175
Amodio, E. 69, 187, 208
approximation 16, 19, 20, 35
arrest 37–9, 54, 84, 85, 87, 88, 91, 92, 120, 140, 153, 183, 190, 191, 193–6

book of evidence 84, 101, 113, 116, 117, 125, 127, 130, 247
burden of proof 65, 114, 116, 175, 176, 177, 185, 201, 213, 219, 224, 226, 227, 228, 229, 236, 244, 245

Caianiello, M. 198, 190, 192, 195, 197, 198
calumny 113, 208, 241
Cape, E. 21, 38
causative link 99–102, 108
character evidence 6, 13, 73, 82, 97, 111–13, 123, 135, 153, 200, 164–7, 184, 212, 235, 242, 243
circumstantial evidence 58, 106, 125, 201
confrontation 9, 55, 58, 61, 144, 145, 152–154, 170, 183, 199, 205
Confronto 221, 222, 230, 236
Contradictoire 4, 12, 21, 29, 48, 50, 68, 77–9, 81, 148, 155, 156, 173, 174, 181, 184–6, 213, 239, 245–7, 249
convergence 2, 4, 9, 10, 12, 18, 19, 65, 79, 238
coordinate model 50, 74,75, 80, 239
Corpus Juris 11, 21, 22, 78
Cour d'assise 63, 64, 159, 160–3, 165, 169, 172, 174, 179–82, 184
Corte di assise 213–16
cross-examination 29, 51, 57, 60, 68, 79, 109–11, 116, 117, 119, 124, 125, 181, 184, 185, 188, 199, 209, 220–2, 224, 236, 246
culture 4–7, 11, 12, 49, 55, 88, 117, 130, 148, 185, 188, 228, 237, 238, 242, 246
custody regulations 87–9, 95, 96, 98, 100, 104, 105, 108, 118

Damaška, M. 8, 50, 66, 68, 69, 71–5, 77, 78, 80, 81, 239
Delmas-Marty, M. 11, 21, 66, 78, 134, 187
differences, between common law and continental systems 2, 3, 4, 5, 6, 7, 9, 12, 13, 20, 23, 39, 43, 47, 48, 50, 70, 72, 74, 76, 152, 165, 167, 172, 182, 184, 185, 212, 214, 238–43, 245, 246, 248
Director of Public Prosecutions (DPP) 84, 85, 113, 130, 136
divergence, of common law and continental systems 3, 4, 49, 53, 64, 65, 80
diversity, of legal systems 2, 3, 18, 47, 48, 249
documentary evidence 57, 109, 155, 195, 196, 201, 205, 211, 224

Doran, S. 65, 72, 113, 128, 131, 224
dossier 66, 143, 152, 153, 154, 160, 164, 165, 170, 172, 173, 174, 184, 193, 201, 212, 219, 224, 236

ECHR (European Convention on Human Rights) 2, 15, 20, 21, 22, 33, 34, 35, 36, 37, 42, 43, 47, 77, 78, 79, 82, 84, 90, 154, 245
electronic recording of interviews 87, 88, 95, 96, 120, 121, 129, 132, 146, 234, 241
equality of arms 38, 78, 154
Esmein, A. 1, 51, 53, 57, 58, 61, 62, 63
European Arrest Warrant (EAW) 43, 44
European Evidence Warrant (EEW) 12, 15, 24–8, 31, 33
European Investigation Order (EIO) 12, 15, 24, 25–32, 47, 247, 248
European Public Prosecutor (EPPO) 27, 48, 247
evidentiary rules 1, 73, 74, 238
exclusionary rule 3, 7, 12, 13, 41, 48, 78, 82, 97–100, 106, 130–1, 134, 158, 184, 207, 208, 210, 241, 242
experts, evidence by 17, 58, 113, 125, 153, 154, 162, 164, 166, 181, 199, 205, 211, 221, 222, 225, 237
extraordinary procedure 53, 54, 62

fair trial 7, 32, 33, 35, 36, 37, 41, 77, 79, 81, 82, 83, 84, 110, 114, 129, 144, 151, 165, 179, 233, 246
Field, S. 6, 10, 76, 136, 164, 165
Fourment, F. 68, 69, 133, 134, 149, 151, 154, 158
French Revolution 61, 66

Garde à vue 136, 137, 140, 142, 143, 146, 153–5, 158
Garraud, F. 57, 59
Giudice del indagini preliminare (GIP) 190, 192, 194, 195, 196, 198, 199, 234
Giudice dell'udienza preliminare (GUP) 190, 200, 203, 216, 217, 218, 234, 236
Goldstein, A. 5, 65, 66, 67, 70
Grande, E. 9, 69, 187, 190, 208, 209, 228, 229, 236

harmonisation 10, 18, 19, 42
hearsay 13, 29, 30, 47, 56, 58–60, 73, 82, 97, 109, 110, 116, 119, 131, 172, 173, 184, 188, 201, 207–11, 220, 235, 245
hierarchical model 50, 74–5, 80, 239
Hodgson, J. 6, 34, 70, 136, 141, 151, 165

Illuminati, G. 68, 69, 189, 190, 192, 198, 208
inadmissibility 3, 4, 16, 20, 34, 40, 48, 204, 238, 242, 248
incidente probatorio 190, 199, 201, 202, 230, 236, 240
inferences from silence 93–5, 234
inquisitorial 1, 2, 9, 10, 21, 45, 48, 50, 53, 54, 57, 61, 65–70, 76–8, 80, 98, 133, 209, 228, 238, 247, 248
intime conviction 134, 176, 178, 180

Jackson, J. 2, 5, 10, 63, 65, 72, 74, 76, 77, 109, 113, 114, 128, 131, 224
Judges Rules 95, 96, 108, 153
Juge d'instruction (JI) 133, 137, 138, 140, 147, 149, 150–5, 156, 159, 164, 165, 170, 182, 183, 189, 239, 241; proposals for abolition of 134, 136, 150
Juge de l'enquête et des libertés (JEL) 150
Juge des liberté et de la détention (JLD) 136, 137, 139, 140, 147, 148, 150, 156, 159
jury 5, 6, 22, 51, 52, 53, 55, 56, 57, 61, 62, 63, 64, 65, 71, 72, 73, 74, 77, 97, 110–15, 118–24, 126, 128, 131, 159, 160–2, 165, 166, 174, 178, 179, 212, 214, 216, 217, 219, 226, 235, 241–4

Landsman, S. 1, 59, 60
Langbein, J. 1, 5, 8, 55, 56, 57, 59, 60, 66, 67, 70
legal proofs, system of 54, 57–9, 61, 62, 181
Léger Committee 134, 142, 147, 148, 150, 174, 179, 180, 181, 182, 186
Loyauté, principle of 154, 155–6, 158, 183, 184, 185

McKillop, B. 7, 11, 143, 160, 165, 174
Montagna, M. 69, 208, 209, 225, 226
moral proofs, system of 57, 62, 64
mutual recognition 2, 15, 16, 18–20, 24, 31, 32, 35, 47, 249
mutual trust 18, 20, 32–3, 35

nullity 134, 139, 140, 156, 157–9, 169, 183, 184, 202–6, 218

oath 52, 53, 54, 57, 59, 61, 87, 111, 112, 123, 127, 131, 152, 162, 167, 168, 169, 171, 175, 179, 185, 223
opt in to post-Lisbon instruments by Ireland and UK 30, 31 39
orality, principle of 57, 60, 62, 109, 131, 173, 174, 230, 234, 235

ordeal, proof by 52, 53
ordinary procedure 53, 54

Partie civile : in France 151, 153, 154, 155, 156, 160, 161, 166, 169, 170, 171, 176, 179, 181, 182, 184, 185; in Italy 214, 215, 216, 230, 236
personnalité 162, 163–6, 167, 184, 243
police investigation 5, 6, 84, 88, 129, 130, 137, 138, 139, 140, 141, 145, 155, 167, 169, 172, 174, 183, 189, 190, 192, 196, 208, 209, 211, 224, 233, 239, 240, 247
preliminary examination, in England 55, 56; in France 63–4
preliminary investigation: in France 65, 141, 148–9, 154, 240; in Italy 68, 190, 196, 199, 200, 201, 202, 215, 234, 236, 240
presumption of innocence 35, 51, 56, 66, 67, 68, 114, 141, 175, 185, 201, 213, 217, 227, 243–4
pre-trial detention 133, 137, 147, 148, 158, 159, 160, 190, 198, 215, 216
public hearing/trial 29, 51, 53, 57, 61, 63, 65, 68, 69, 77, 78, 81, 148, 239
Public Prosecutor: in France 63, 69, 134–40, 143, 147–50, 151, 153–5, 159, 161, 175, 176, 183; in Italy, 189–97, 199–201, 211, 216, 226, 227, 248

reasonable doubt 71, 126, 219, 226, 229
right to information 35, 36–9, 142, 148, 247
right to lawyer 16, 21, 34, 38, 39–46, 47, 48, 60–2, 64, 65, 86, 87, 90, 92, 94, 100, 102, 105, 106, 129, 130, 133, 140, 142–6, 148, 151, 152, 153, 158, 161, 174, 183, 194–6, 197, 199, 200, 208, 214, 234, 240, 242, 247, 248
right to silence 33, 38, 93, 94, 114, 121, 141, 142, 144, 158, 168, 185, 198, 223, 234, 244
right to translation 33, 35, 36, 38

search and seizure 85, 86, 97, 98, 99, 100, 107, 129, 132, 183, 190, 191, 203, 205, 206, 207, 248
secrecy of proceedings 54, 55, 61, 63, 65, 66, 68
sovereignty in criminal justice matters 18, 47
Special Criminal Court 113, 119, 128, 131, 242

terrorism 10, 142, 143, 146, 193
torture 53, 54, 55, 56, 58, 59, 62, 66
trial judge: active participation by 9, 51, 55, 57, 64, 68, 69, 71, 126, 131, 185, 229, 230, 233, 236, 245; intervention by 71, 120, 222, 224, 227; passive role of 51, 60, 64, 71, 74, 117, 126, 131, 228, 245
Tribunal Correctionnel 64, 143, 159, 160, 161, 162, 163, 165, 168, 171, 172, 174, 179, 180, 184
truth: commitment to in process 4, 7, 27, 72, 113, 129, 131, 132, 142, 150, 151, 154, 155, 165, 168, 182, 185–6, 198, 209, 220, 227, 232, 233, 236, 237, 246, 249; consensus theory of 8–9; correspondence theory of 8–9; interpretative 9; ontological 9; procedural 9; -impairing tendency 61

usability of evidence 201, 202, 203, 204, 205, 207, 208, 218, 230, 235, 241

verdict, reasons for 71, 73, 128, 165, 179–80, 231–2, 241, 242
Voir dire 97, 119–21, 123, 131, 184, 218, 219, 248

witnesses, absent 29, 30, 164
written procedure 51, 55, 57, 60, 63, 64, 66, 68, 154, 235

For Product Safety Concerns and Information please contact our EU representative GPSR@taylorandfrancis.com Taylor & Francis Verlag GmbH, Kaufingerstraße 24, 80331 München, Germany

Batch number: 10725973

Printed by Printforce, the Netherlands